A·N·N·U·A·L E·

Management

Eleventh Edition

03/04

EDITOR

Fred H. Maidment

Western Connecticut State University

Dr. Fred Maidment is associate professor of management at Western Connecticut State University in Danbury, Connecticut. He received his bachelor's degree from New York University and his master's degree from the Bernard M. Baruch College of the City University of New York. In 1983 Dr. Maidment received his doctorate from the University of South Carolina. He resides in Connecticut with his wife.

McGraw-Hill/Dushkin

530 Old Whitfield Street, Guilford, Connecticut 06437

Visit us on the Internet

http://www.dushkin.com

Credits

1. **The War on Terror**
   Unit photo—United Nations photo by John Isaac.
2. **Managers, Performance, and the Environment**
   Unit photo—© 2003 by PhotoDisc, Inc.
3. **Planning**
   Unit photo—© 2003 by PhotoDisc, Inc.
4. **Organizing**
   Unit photo—© 2003 by PhotoDisc, Inc.
5. **Directing**
   Unit photo—TRW Inc. photo.
6. **Controlling**
   Unit photo—© 2003 by PhotoDisc, Inc.
7. **Staffing and Human Resources**
   Unit photo—Courtesy of Digital Stock.
8. **Perspectives and Trends**
   Unit photo—Courtesy of Robin Gallagher.

Copyright

Cataloging in Publication Data
Main entry under title: Annual Editions: Management. 2003/2004.
1. Management—Periodicals. I. Maidment, Fred, *comp.* II. Title: Management.
ISBN 0–07–254838–X 658'.05 ISSN 1092–4876

Eleventh Edition

Cover image © 2003 PhotoDisc, Inc.
Printed in the United States of America 1234567890BAHBAH543 Printed on Recycled Paper

Editors/Advisory Board

Members of the Advisory Board are instrumental in the final selection of articles for each edition of ANNUAL EDITIONS. Their review of articles for content, level, currentness, and appropriateness provides critical direction to the editor and staff. We think that you will find their careful consideration well reflected in this volume.

Staff

EDITORIAL STAFF

Ian A. Nielsen, Publisher
Roberta Monaco, Senior Developmental Editor
Dorothy Fink, Associate Developmental Editor
Iain Martin, Associate Developmental Editor
Addie Raucci, Senior Administrative Editor
Robin Zarnetske, Permissions Editor
Marie Lazauskas, Permissions Assistant
Diane Barker, Proofreader
Lisa Holmes-Doebrick, Senior Program Coordinator

TECHNOLOGY STAFF

Richard Tietjen, Senior Publishing Technologist
Jonathan Stowe, Executive Director of eContent
Marcuss Oslander, Sponsoring Editor of eContent
Christopher Santos, Senior eContent Developer
Janice Ward, Software Support Analyst
Angela Mule, eContent Developer
Michael McConnell, eContent Developer
Ciro Parente, Editorial Assistant
Joe Offredi, Technology Developmental Editor

PRODUCTION STAFF

Brenda S. Filley, Director of Production
Charles Vitelli, Designer
Mike Campell, Production Coordinator
Laura Levine, Graphics
Tom Goddard, Graphics
Eldis Lima, Graphics
Nancy Norton, Graphics
Juliana Arbo, Typesetting Supervisor
Karen Roberts, Typesetter
Jocelyn Proto, Typesetter
Cynthia Powers, Typesetter
Cathy Kuziel, Typesetter
Larry Killian, Copier Coordinator

To the Reader

In publishing ANNUAL EDITIONS we recognize the enormous role played by the magazines, newspapers, and journals of the public press in providing current, first-rate educational information in a broad spectrum of interest areas. Many of these articles are appropriate for students, researchers, and professionals seeking accurate, current material to help bridge the gap between principles and theories and the real world. These articles, however, become more useful for study when those of lasting value are carefully collected, organized, indexed, and reproduced in a low-cost format, which provides easy and permanent access when the material is needed. That is the role played by ANNUAL EDITIONS.

On September 11, 2001, the world changed. It could be said that one era ended and another began on that date. Washington, D.C., and New York City were brutally attacked by terrorists who killed about 3,000 people plus those who died in an airplane crash in Pennsylvania. Organizations, led by the government of the United States, are responding to the need to defeat the terrorists. But in order for the United States to achieve victory in this new kind of war, American organizations, including corporations, will have to utilize and manage their resources effectively. This means that managers in both the civilian and military sectors of the country will have to perform their tasks in an efficient and effective manner. Directing the nation's resources against these terrorists will be the primary focus of this country's government for the foreseeable future. Victory can only be achieved through constant vigilance and attention to detail, and it will be managers who will have the primary responsibility for those functions.

Since managers are the people charged with getting things done in today's society—a society that has been molded by the success of the management profession—the many new challenges that the world faces will be met, at least in part, by managers.

Some of the challenges will include dealing with the new environment that resulted from the September 11 attacks. These attacks ushered in a new era for Western democracies, as well as for the businesses and corporations that have flourished in the capitalist environment provided by these democracies. There are going to be changes both in the United States and abroad, and managers are going to play an important role in those changes.

Managers must respond to a changing environment by keeping informed on the developments in the field. The articles that have been chosen for *Annual Editions: Management 03/04* represent a cross section of the current writings on the subject, along with a few selected classics. This collection addresses the various components of management, with emphasis on the functions of planning, organizing, directing, controlling, and staffing. Readings have been chosen from a wide variety of publications, including *The Harvard Business Review, Business Week, Business Horizons,* and *Fortune.*

This publication contains a number of features that are designed to make it useful for people interested in management. These features include a *table of contents* with *abstracts* that summarize each article, highlighting key ideas in bold italics, and a *topic guide* for locating articles on a specific subject. Also, there are selected *World Wide Web* sites that can be used to further explore the topics.

This volume is organized into eight units, each dealing with specific interrelated topics in management. Each unit begins with an overview that provides the necessary background information that allows the reader to place the selections in the context of the book. Important topics are emphasized, and *key points to consider* address major themes. Also, at the end of units 2–8, there are short cases and exercises that are designed to illustrate and expand on the general topic of the unit easily and effectively.

This is the eleventh edition of *Annual Editions: Management,* and we hope that it will be one of a long line of books addressing the evolution of management. This collection, we believe, provides the reader with the most complete and current selection of readings available on the subject. We would like to know what you think. Please take a few minutes to complete and return the postage-paid *article rating form* at the back of the volume. Any book can be improved and we need your help to improve *Annual Editions: Management.*

Fred Maidment
Editor

Contents

UNIT 1
The War on Terror

Two offerings discuss the nation and world management issues that face government and business as the U.S. government wages its "war against terror."

UNIT 2
Managers, Performance, and the Environment

The six articles in this section examine some of the dynamics of management in today's business environment.

The concepts in bold italics are developed in the article. For further expansion, please refer to the Topic Guide and the Index.

UNIT 3
Planning

Five unit articles discuss the elements of decision making, strategic analysis, and strategic management.

The concepts in bold italics are developed in the article. For further expansion, please refer to the Topic Guide and the Index.

UNIT 4
Organizing

In this section, four selections examine the impact of organization on the job of managing. Topics discussed include elements of organization, job design, and what is needed to fundamentally change a business.

UNIT 5
Directing

The five selections in this section examine how the elements of leadership, performance, and communication contribute to the art of directing a business organization.

The concepts in bold italics are developed in the article. For further expansion, please refer to the Topic Guide and the Index.

UNIT 6
Controlling

Four articles in this section consider what makes up effective control of the business organization.

The concepts in bold italics are developed in the article. For further expansion, please refer to the Topic Guide and the Index.

UNIT 7
Staffing and Human Resources

This section's four selections examine the elements necessarily considered when a workforce is developed.

UNIT 8
Perspectives and Trends

These nine articles examine business challenges. Topics include multinational enterprise, corporate culture, and ethics.

The concepts in bold italics are developed in the article. For further expansion, please refer to the Topic Guide and the Index.

The concepts in bold italics are developed in the article. For further expansion, please refer to the Topic Guide and the Index.

Topic Guide

This topic guide suggests how the selections in this book relate to the subjects covered in your course. You may want to use the topics listed on these pages to search the Web more easily.

On the following pages a number of Web sites have been gathered specifically for this book. They are arranged to reflect the units of this *Annual Edition.* You can link to these sites by going to the DUSHKIN ONLINE support site at *http://www.dushkin.com/online/.*

ALL THE ARTICLES THAT RELATE TO EACH TOPIC ARE LISTED BELOW THE BOLD-FACED TERM.

Multinational corporations

Not-for-profit organizations

Organized labor

Performance

Productivity

Social responsibility

Strategy

Technology

TQM

War on terror

Workforce development

World Wide Web Sites

The following World Wide Web sites have been carefully researched and selected to support the articles found in this reader. The easiest way to access these selected sites is to go to our DUSHKIN ONLINE support site at *http://www.dushkin.com/online/*.

AE: Management 03/04

The following sites were available at the time of publication. Visit our Web site—we update DUSHKIN ONLINE regularly to reflect any changes.

General Sources

HBS Educators & Research

http://www.hbs.edu/educators.html

Surf through the many valuable links attached to this Educators & Research News site and preview upcoming issues of the *Harvard Business Review.*

The New York Times

http://www.nytimes.com

Browsing through the extensive archives of the *New York Times* will provide you with a vast array of articles and information related to management issues.

STAT-USA

http://www.stat-usa.gov/stat-usa.html

This site, a service of the U.S. Department of Commerce, contains daily economic news, frequently requested statistical releases, information on export and international trade, domestic economic news, statistical series, and databases. Also try *http://www.fedstats.gov* for statistics produced by over 70 U.S. federal government agencies.

The Wall Street Journal

http://interactive.wsj.com

This is an Internet edition of the *Wall Street Journal,* a newspaper that is used by managers the world over to put their business environments in context.

Workforce Online

http://www.workforceonline.com

This site, sponsored by *Workforce* magazine, discusses trends and resources, legal information, and fluctuating pay methods data, and also offers a research center.

UNIT 1: The War on Terror

Terrorism Research Center

http://www.terrorism.com

The Terrorism Research Center features original research, counterterrorism documents, a comprehensive list of Web links, and monthly profiles of terrorist and counterterrorist groups.

UNIT 2: Managers, Performance, and the Environment

Design for Competitive Advantage

http://www.dfca.org/toc.html

Read the many articles, consider the various points of view, and click on the links suggested in this site to explore important business-related theories and issues such as cost management and living systems theory and design.

Krislyn's Favorite Advertising & Marketing Sites

http://www.krislyn.com/sites/adv.htm

This extensive list of Web sites includes information on marketing research, marketing on the Internet, demographic sources, organizations, and associations. The site also features current books on business management and marketing.

Sheffield University Management School

http://www.shef.ac.uk/uni/academic/I-M/mgt/research/research.html

The Current Research page of this British school will lead you to information on real-world management issues. Links include the economics, finance, and management of technological change, labor economics, and industrial relations.

Two Scenarios for 21st Century Organizations

http://ccs.mit.edu/21c/21CWP001.html

The MIT Scenario Working Group here presents "Shifting Networks of Small Firms" and "All-Encompassing 'Virtual Countries'" that will be of interest to any company involved in organizing and structuring to meet the demands of the new business environment.

UNIT 3: Planning

American Civil Liberties Union (ACLU)

http://www.aclu.org/issues/worker/campaign.html

The ACLU provides this page on workplace rights in its "Campaign for Fairness in the Workplace". Briefing papers on workplace issues cover such privacy issues as lifestyle discrimination, drug testing, and electronic monitoring.

Benchmarking Network

http://www.well.com/user/benchmar/tbnhome.html

This Web site is an international resource guide to benchmarking as a method of corporate planning.

GBN Scenario Planning

http://www.gbn.org/public/gbnstory/scenarios/

Scenario planning is a fundamental tool for thinking strategically about the future. This site, which contains many scenarios, helps organizations to understand the external environment in relation to their own business ideas and competence.

Innovation in the Workplace

http://www.managementfirst.com/articles/workplace.htm

This page aims to provide insight into what the future holds for employers and employees. It points you to books and other resources about such topics as teleworking.

UNIT 4: Organizing

From Foosball to Flextime: Dotcommers Are Growing Up

http://www.fastcompany.com/invent/invent_feature/act_childcare.html

This article by Cecilia Rothenberger explains how dot.com companies are maturing and providing flextime, on-site day care, and other benefits that "grown-up" companies have provided for years.

Sympatico: Careers
http://www.ntl.sympatico.ca/Contents/Careers/

This Canadian media site provides an electronic network with a "GripeVine" for complaining about work and finding solutions to everyday career problems.

U.S. Department of Labor (DOL)
http://www.dol.gov

Browsing through this DOL site will lead you to a vast array of labor-related data and discussions of issues affecting managers, such as the minimum wage. It presents statutory and regulatory information, and more.

Work and Organizational Psychology, Stockholm University
http://www.psychology.su.se/units/ao/ao.html

Explore topics related to job design and other management organizational concerns through this site presented by Stockholm University's Department of Psychology, Division of Work and Organizational Psychology.

UNIT 5: Directing

ADR (Alternative Dispute Resolution): General
http://www.opm.gov/er/adrguide/

Essays on the subject of alternative dispute resolution can be found at this page, which includes an ADR glossary, a definition, techniques and evaluations, issues and problems facing judges, evaluation of ADR procedures, and much more information important to the area of conflict management.

Equity Compensation, Employee Ownership & Stock Options
http://www.fed.org

The Foundation for Enterprise Development is a nonprofit organization that suggests strategies to those who are making critical decisions to improve their companies' bottom lines. This site includes interactive resources and case studies.

NewsPage
http://www.individual.com

This site provides daily briefings and in-depth stories of interest to managers. These links relate to such major fields as computing and media, finance, and health care insurance.

UNIT 6: Controlling

Bill Lindsay's Home Page
http://www.nku.edu/~lindsay/

Professor William M. Lindsay's home page points to a variety of interesting Internet sources to aid in the study and application of Total Quality Management principles.

Computer and Network Security
http://www.vtcif.telstra.com.au/info/security.html

Telstra provides this index for those interested in technology/ security issues. It provides links to Web sources, including commercial, educational, and government materials.

Internal Auditing World Wide Web
http://www.bitwise.net/iawww/

Valuable news, resources, events, and associations related to business auditing topics are provided here.

Office of Financial Management
http://www.doi.gov/

This site of the Office of Financial Management, in the U.S. Department of the Interior, describes its financial policy and procedures, financial reporting, management control program, accounting policy and systems, and auditing follow-up.

The Potential Downside of the National Information Infrastructure
http://www.annenberg.nwu.edu/pubs/downside/

Annenberg Senior Fellow Stephen Bates discusses the National Information Infrastructure (NII). View this page for discussions of NII, including issues regarding privacy rights in the workplace.

Total Quality Leadership (TQL) vs. Management by Results
http://deming.eng.clemson.edu/pub/den/files/tql.txt

Brian L. Joiner and Peter R. Scholtes describe the reasons why the TQL system of management should replace management by results for most companies, whether small or large. It addresses such concerns as to how TQL can improve customer service and return on investment, lead to higher productivity and more jobs, and affect utilization of information technology.

Workplace Violence
http://www.osha-slc.gov/SLTC/workplaceviolence/

The Occupational Safety & Health Administration (OSHA) maintains this site, which provides information and resources on workplace violence. OSHA has developed guidelines and recommendations to reduce worker exposures to this hazard.

UNIT 7: Staffing and Human Resources

Electronic Frontier Foundation "Privacy" Archive
http://www.eff.org

This civil liberties site organization provides links to articles, FAQs, and databases having to do with protection of privacy and free expression in the workplace. Drug testing and electronic communications privacy are explored.

School of Labor and Industrial Relations Hot Links
http://www.lir.msu.edu/hotlinks

This page links to government statistics, newspapers, libraries, and international intergovernmental organizations.

U.S. Equal Employment Opportunity Commission
http://www.eeoc.gov

Consult this site for small business information, facts about employment discrimination, and enforcement and litigation.

UNIT 8: Perspectives and Trends

Institute for International Economics
http://www.iie.com

The site of this nonpartisan research institution, devoted to the study of international economics, contains views, reviews, working papers, publications, and press releases.

Small Business Management
http://management.tqn.com/msubs.htm

Information on how to start and effectively manage a small business is available on this site.

World Trade Organization (WTO) Web Site
http://www.wto.org/index.htm

At the home page of the WTO, click on About the WTO, Site Map, Search, and Links to Related Organizations.

We highly recommend that you review our Web site for expanded information and our other product lines. We are continually updating and adding links to our Web site in order to offer you the most usable and useful information that will support and expand the value of your Annual Editions. You can reach us at: *http://www.dushkin.com/annualeditions/*.

UNIT 1

The War on Terror

Unit Selections

1. **Address by George W. Bush, President of the United States**, *Vital Speeches of the Day*
2. **Hearts, Minds, and the War Against Terror**, Joshua Muravchik

Key Points to Consider

- How do you think the war on terror has changed the way managers conduct their businesses?
- Where do you think the largest and most important battlefield will be in the war on terror? Defend your answer.

DUSHKIN ONLINE **Links: www.dushkin.com/online/**
These sites are annotated in the World Wide Web pages.

Terrorism Research Center
http://www.terrorism.com

On September 11, 2001, the world changed. For people in business and industry it meant that a new era had arrived. Over the years, people involved in the production of goods and services had gone through many trials and hardships. Two world wars, the Great Depression, the cold war, as well as other events have proven the mettle of the American worker and American industry. Now the workers and managers in the United States and the Western world face a new challenge. It is a challenge that seeks to alter and change the very basis of American and Western society. It challenges the very assumptions upon which modern industrial society is based. The ideas of John Locke and Jean-Jacques Rousseau are being challenged by the ideology of Osama bin Laden and the Islamic extremists.

Bin Laden would turn back the clock to a darker and more terrible time, a time when women and children were held as property by their husbands, a time when anyone who did not believe in the same god as the governing body was an infidel, and a time when nations and peoples were ruled not by the rule of law and the consent of the governed, but by messengers who transmitted their version of the word of *god*.

The task of business and industry is to assist in the defeat of this ideology that would abolish the progress and success that the Western democracies have accomplished over the past 500 years, an ideology that would return Western society to an era when people thought the Earth was flat because the religious leaders of the day said it was. Finding the best method to defeat these terrorists is now the task of this country and this government. President George W. Bush called the nation to this task in his address to the Congress and the nation soon after the attacks on the World Trade Center and the Pentagon, and the people have responded.

President Bush has clearly stated that the task before the nation is both difficult and long. This war will be fought on many fronts, not the least of which will be for "Hearts, minds and the war against terror." While the United States will undoubtedly win many battles on the military front, the real waging of this war will not be on battlefields but in people's minds and hearts.

Americans must pull together and cooperate, avoiding war profiteering and disunity in the face of the enemy while at the same time maintaining the traditions of freedom and liberty so artfully espoused by John Locke and Jean Jacques Rousseau. The very heart of Western civilization is at stake in this war. The bedrock assumptions that have made the industrialized countries so successful are being challenged by a voice and dogma rooted in the darkest past of the human experience. It is a philosophy that has already been discredited by Islam itself, and one that would surely bring an end to the era of enlightenment we now enjoy, and a beginning of a dark age we cannot allow.

Article 1

Address by GEORGE W. BUSH, President of the United States Delivered to a Joint Session of Congress and the American People, Washington, D. C., September 20, 2001

Mr. Speaker, Mr. President pro tempore, Members of Congress, and fellow Americans: In the normal course of events, presidents come to this chamber to report on the state of the Union. Tonight, no such report is needed. It has already been delivered by the American people.

We have seen it in the courage of passengers, who rushed terrorists to save others on the ground—passengers like an exceptional man named Todd Beamer. Please help me to welcome his wife, Lisa Beamer, here tonight.

We have seen the state of our Union in the endurance of rescuers, working past exhaustion. We have seen the unfurling of flags, the lighting of candles, the giving of blood, the saying of prayers—in English, Hebrew, and Arabic. We have seen the decency of a loving and giving people, who have made the grief of strangers their own.

My fellow citizens, for the last nine days, the entire world has seen for itself the state of our Union—and it is strong.

Tonight we are a country awakened to danger and called to defend freedom. Our grief has turned to anger, and anger to resolution. Whether we bring our enemies to justice, or bring justice to our enemies, justice will be done.

I thank the Congress for its leadership at such an important time. All of America was touched on the evening of the tragedy to see Republicans and Democrats, joined together on the steps of this Capitol, singing "God Bless America." And you did more than sing, you acted, by delivering forty billion dollars to rebuild our communities and meet the needs of our military.

Speaker Hastert and Minority Leader Gephardt—Majority Leader Daschle and Senator Loti—I thank you for your friendship and your leadership and your service to our country.

And on behalf of the American people, I thank the world for its outpouring of support. America will never forget the sounds of our National Anthem playing at Buckingham Palace, and on the streets of Paris, and at Berlin's Brandenburg Gate. We will not forget South Korean children gathering to pray outside our embassy in Seoul, or the prayers of sympathy offered at a mosque in Cairo. We will not forget moments of silence and days of mourning in Australia and Africa and Latin America.

Nor will we forget the citizens of eighty other nations who died with our own. Dozens of Pakistanis. More than 130 Israelis. More than 250 citizens of India. Men and women from El Salvador, Iran, Mexico, and Japan. And hundreds of British citizens. America has no truer friend than Great Britain. Once again, we are joined together in a great cause. The British Prime Minister has crossed an ocean to show his unity of purpose with America, and tonight we welcome Tony Blair.

On September the eleventh, enemies of freedom committed an act of war against our country. Americans have known wars—but for the past 136 years, they have been wars on foreign soil, except for one Sunday in 1941. Americans have known the casualties of war—but not at the center of a great city on a peaceful morning. Americans have known surprise attacks—but never before on thousands of civilians. All of this was brought upon us in a single day—and night fell on a different world, a world where freedom itself is under attack.

Americans have many questions tonight. Americans are asking:

Who attacked our country?

The evidence we have gathered all points to a collection of loosely affiliated terrorist organizations known as al-Qaida. They are the same murderers indicted for bombing American embassies in Tanzania and Kenya, and responsible for the bombing of the U. S. S. Cole.

Al-Qaida is to terror what the mafia is to crime. But its goal is not making money; its goal is remaking the world—and imposing its radical beliefs on people everywhere.

The terrorists practice a fringe form of Islamic extremism that has been rejected by Muslim scholars and the vast majority of Muslim clerics—a fringe movement that perverts the peaceful teachings of Islam. The terrorists' directive commands them to kill Christians and Jews, to kill all Americans, and make no distinctions among military and civilians, including women and children.

This group and its leader—a person named Usama bin Ladin—are linked to many other organizations in different countries, including the Egyptian Islamic Jihad and the Islamic Movement of Uzbekistan.

There are thousands of these terrorists in more than sixty countries. They are recruited from their own nations and neighborhoods, and brought to camps in places like Afghanistan where they are trained in the tactics of terror. They are sent back to their homes or sent to hide in countries around the world to plot evil and destruction.

The leadership of al-Qaida has great influence in Afghanistan, and supports the Taliban regime in controlling most of that country.

In Afghanistan, we see al-Qaida's vision for the world.

Afghanistan's people have been brutalized—many are starving and many have fled. Women are not allowed to attend school. You can be jailed for owning a television. Religion can be practiced only as their leaders dictate. A man can be jailed in Afghanistan if his beard is not long enough.

The United States respects the people of Afghanistan—after all, we are currently its largest source of humanitarian aid—but we condemn the Taliban regime. It is not only repressing its own people, it is threatening people everywhere by sponsoring and sheltering and supplying terrorists. By aiding and abetting murder, the Taliban regime is committing murder. And tonight, the United States of America makes the following demands on the Taliban:

Deliver to United States authorities all the leaders of al-Qaida who hide in your land.

Release all foreign nationals—including American citizens—you have unjustly imprisoned, and protect foreign journalists, diplomats, and aid workers in your country.

Close immediately and permanently every terrorist training camp in Afghanistan and hand over every terrorist, and every person in their support structure, to appropriate authorities.

Give the United States full access to terrorist training camps, so we can make sure they are no longer operating.

These demands are not open to negotiation or discussion. The Taliban must act and act immediately. They will hand over the terrorists, or they will share in their fate.

I also want to speak tonight directly to Muslims throughout the world: We respect your faith. It is practiced freely by many millions of Americans, and by millions more in countries that America counts as friends. Its teachings are good and peaceful, and those who commit evil in the name of Allah blaspheme the name of Allah. The terrorists are traitors to their own faith, trying, in effect, to hijack Islam itself. The enemy of America is not our many Muslim friends; it is not our many Arab friends. Our enemy is a radical network of terrorists, and every government that supports them.

Our war on terror begins with al-Qaida, but it does not end there. It will not end until every terrorist group of global reach has been found, stopped, and defeated.

Americans are asking: Why do they hate us?

They hate what we see right here in this chamber—a democratically elected government. Their leaders are self-appointed. They hate our freedom—our freedom of religion, our freedom of speech, our freedom to vote and assemble and disagree with each other.

They want to overthrow existing governments in many Muslim countries, such as Egypt, Saudi Arabia, and Jordan. They want to drive Israel out of the Middle East. They want to drive Christians and Jews out of vast regions of Asia and Africa.

These terrorists kill not merely to end lives, but to disrupt and end a way of life. With every atrocity, they hope that America grows fearful, retreating from the world and forsaking our friends. They stand against us, because we stand in their way.

We are not deceived by their pretenses to piety. We have seen their kind before. They are the heirs of all the murderous ideologies of the twentieth century. By sacrificing human life to serve their radical visions—by abandoning every value except the will to power—they follow in the path of fascism, and Nazism, and totalitarianism. And they will follow that path all the way, to where it ends: in history's unmarked grave of discarded lies.

Americans are asking: How will we fight and win this war?

We will direct every resource at our command—every means of diplomacy, every tool of intelligence, every instrument of law enforcement, every financial influence, and every necessary weapon of war—to the disruption and defeat of the global terror network.

This war will not be like the war against Iraq a decade ago, with its decisive liberation of territory and its swift conclusion. It will not look like the air war above Kosovo two years ago, where no ground troops were used and not a single American was lost in combat.

Our response involves far more than instant retaliation and isolated strikes. Americans should not expect one battle, but a lengthy campaign, unlike any other we have seen. It may include dramatic strikes, visible on television, and covert operations, secret even in success. We will starve terrorists of funding, turn them one against another, drive them from place to place, until there is no refuge or rest. And we will pursue nations that provide aid or safe haven to terrorism. Every nation, in every region, now has a decision to make. Either you are with us, or you are with the terrorists. From this day forward, any nation that continues to harbor or support terrorism will be regarded by the United States as a hostile regime.

Our nation has been put on notice: We are not immune from attack. We will take defensive measures against terrorism to protect Americans.

Today, dozens of federal departments and agencies, as well as state and local governments, have responsibilities affecting homeland security. These efforts must be coordinated at the highest level. So tonight I announce the creation of a Cabinet-level position reporting directly to me—the Office of Homeland Security.

These measures are essential. But the only way to defeat terrorism as a threat to our way of life is to stop it, eliminate it, and destroy it where it grows.

Many will be involved in this effort, from FBI agents to intelligence operatives to the reservists we have called to active duty. All deserve our thanks, and all have our prayers. And tonight, a few miles from the damaged Pentagon, I have a message for our military: Be ready. I have called the armed forces to alert, and there is a reason. The hour is coming when America will act, and you will make us proud.

This is not, however, just America's fight. And what is at stake is not just America's freedom. This is the world's fight. This is civilization's fight. This is the fight of all who believe in progress and pluralism, tolerance and freedom.

We ask every nation to join us. We will ask, and we will need, the help of police forces, intelligence services, and banking systems around the world. The United States is grateful that many nations and many international organizations have already responded—with sympathy and with support. Nations from Latin America, to Asia, to Africa, to Europe, to the Islamic world. Perhaps the NATO Charter reflects best the attitude of the world: an attack on one is an attack on all.

The civilized world is rallying to America's side. They understand that if this terror goes unpunished, their own cities, their own citizens may be next. Terror, unanswered, can not only bring down buildings, it can threaten the stability of legitimate governments. And we will not allow it.

Americans are asking: What is expected of us?

I ask you to live your lives and hug your children. I know many citizens have fears tonight, and I ask you to be calm and resolute, even in the face of a continuing threat.

I ask you to uphold the values of America, and remember why so many have come here. We are in a fight for our principles, and our first responsibility is to live by them. No one should be singled out for unfair treatment or unkind words because of their ethnic background or religious faith.

I ask you to continue to support the victims of this tragedy with your contributions. Those who want to give can go to a central source of information, libertyunites.org, to find the names of groups providing direct help in New York, Pennsylvania and Virginia.

The thousands of FBI agents who are now at work in this investigation may need your cooperation, and I ask you to give it.

I ask for your patience, with the delays and inconveniences that may accompany tighter security—and for your patience in what will be a long struggle.

I ask your continued participation and confidence in the American economy. Terrorists attacked a symbol of American prosperity. They did not touch its source. America is successful because of the hard work, and creativity, and enterprise of our people. These were the true strengths of our economy before September eleventh, and they are our strengths today.

Finally, please continue praying for the victims of terror and their families, for those in uniform, and for our great country. Prayer has comforted us in sorrow, and will help strengthen us for the journey ahead.

Tonight I thank my fellow Americans for what you have already done and for what you will do. And ladies and gentlemen of the Congress, I thank you, their representatives, for what you have already done, and for what we will do together.

Tonight, we face new and sudden national challenges. We will come together to improve air safety, to dramatically expand the number of air marshals on domestic flights, and take new measures to prevent hijacking. We will come together to promote stability and keep our airlines flying with direct assistance during this emergency.

We will come together to give law enforcement the additional tools it needs to track down terror here at home. We will come together to strengthen our intelligence capabilities to know the plans of terrorists before they act, and find them before they strike.

We will come together to take active steps that strengthen America's economy, and put our people back to work.

Tonight we welcome here two leaders who embody the extraordinary spirit of all New Yorkers: Governor George Pataki, and Mayor Rudy Giuliani. As a symbol of America's resolve, my administration will work with the Congress, and these two leaders, to show the world that we will rebuild New York City.

After all that has just passed—all the lives taken, and all the possibilities and hopes that died with them—it is natural to wonder if America's future is one of fear. Some speak of an age of terror. I know there are struggles ahead, and dangers to face. But this country will define our times, not be defined by them. As long as the United States of America is determined and strong, this will not be an age of terror; this will be an age of liberty, here and across the world.

Great harm has been done to us. We have suffered great loss. And in our grief and anger we have found our mission and our moment. Freedom and fear are at war. The advance of human freedom—the great achievement of our time, and the great hope of every time—now depends on us. Our nation—this generation—will lift a dark threat of violence from our people and our future. We will rally the world to this cause, by our efforts and by our courage. We will not tire, we will not falter, and we not fail.

It is my hope that in the months and years ahead, life will return almost to normal. We'll go back to our lives and routines, and that is good. Even grief recedes with time and grace. But our resolve must not pass. Each of us will remember what happened that day, and to whom it happened. We will remember the moment the news came—where we were and what we were doing. Some will remember an image of fire, or a story of rescue. Some will carry memories of a face and a voice gone forever.

And I will carry this. It is the police shield of a man named George Howard, who died at the World Trade Center trying to save others. It was given to me by his mom, Arlene, as a proud memorial to her son. This is my reminder of lives that ended, and a task that does not end.

I will not forget this wound to our country, or those who inflicted it. I will not yield—I will not rest—I will not relent in waging this struggle for the freedom and security of the American people.

The course of this conflict is not known, yet its outcome is certain. Freedom and fear justice and cruelty, have always been at war, and we know that God is not neutral between them.

Fellow citizens, we will meet violence with patient justice—assured of the rightness of our cause, and confident of the victories to come. In all that lies before us, may God grant us wisdom, and may He watch over the United States of America. Thank you.

From *Vital Speeches of the Day*, October 1, 2001, pp. 760-763.

Hearts, Minds, and the War Against Terror

Joshua Muravchik

THE SCOOP appeared in the *New York Times* in February: as part of "a new effort to influence public sentiment and policy makers in both friendly and unfriendly countries," it revealed, the Pentagon was "developing plans to provide news items, *possibly even false ones*, to foreign media organizations" (emphasis added).

According to the *Times*, what had prompted the creation of this so-called Office of Strategic Influence (OSI) was the worry of "many administration officials" that "the United States was losing support in the Islamic world after American warplanes began bombing Afghanistan." And what had prompted the leak of the story? It seems that a number of people inside the Pentagon, whether for reasons of principle or for reasons of turf, were concerned that the new office, by combining the tasks of public relations with those of covert operations, would thereby taint the former. "It goes from the blackest of black programs to the whitest of white," an anonymous official was quoted, thus fueling the impression that the office would be peddling lies.

In fact, the U.S. has rarely done anything like this in its history. (The term "black operations" in this context properly refers to the practice of hiding the role of the government as the source of a given story rather than to the practice of spreading disinformation.) Nevertheless, the *Times* weighed in the very next day with an editorial denouncing the new office, which it called "Orwellian," while the columnist Maureen Dowd contributed her own broadside against what she dubbed the Office of Strategic Mendacity. In no time, scores of other newspapers around the country had registered their indignation, causing Defense Secretary Donald Rumsfeld to protest that "the Pentagon is not issuing disinformation to the foreign press or any other press."

But the die had been cast. Within a week of the first *Times* story, Rumsfeld announced he had closed the office down.

THIS ABORTED mission was not the only effort by the Bush administration to wage a battle for hearts and minds as part of its larger war against terrorism. The State Department had already brought in Charlotte Beers, formerly the head of the giant advertising agency Ogilvy & Mather, as undersecretary for "public diplomacy." According to Beers, her aim was to do for the United States what she had done for IBM in the 1990's—namely, to "rebrand" it. But her new job, she confessed, would be even tougher than her old one—indeed, "the most sophisticated brand assignment I have ever had." "It is almost," she added, "as though we have to redefine what America is."

If the goal sounded ambitious, she could at least count on the full backing of her formidable patron, the Secretary of State. For Colin Powell himself, it turns out, had been keen on the Madison Avenue approach to public diplomacy even before September 11, much preferring it to the more traditional and overly intellectual methods of the now-defunct United States Information Agency (USIA). In congressional testimony soon after taking office, Powell had declared: "I'm going to be bringing people into the public-diplomacy function of the department who are going to change from just selling us in the old USIA way to really branding foreign policy, branding the department, marketing the department, marketing American values to the world."

In the wake of September 11, and in line with the new spirit, Beers was reported to be considering "TV and radio spots in which sports stars and celebrities [would] talk up the U.S." Her office's major product was a shiny and colorful 25-page pamphlet, *The Network of Terrorism*, distributed in 36 languages and featuring vivid photographs of the September 11 destruction, harsh commentary on al Qaeda and the Taliban, and denunciations of terrorism by such world leaders as Kofi Annan, Tony Blair, and Jiang Zemin. By far the most prominent quotations, spread throughout the pamphlet in huge type, were by Muslims—three Arab sheiks, one Indonesian cleric, and the Council on American-Islamic Relations (CAIR)—repudiating the September 11 attacks and the taking of innocent life.

As the war began, the White House also created another agency, the Coalition Information Center (CIC), with offices in Washington, London, and Pakistan. Its purpose was (and remains) to publicize our side's war aims and to provide instantaneous rebuttal of enemy claims about civilian casualties or battlefield successes. Widening its writ, the CIC also gave impetus to the "Afghan women's initiative," which pressed for a role for women in post—Taliban power structures, thereby underscoring the humanly liberating aspect of a victory in Afghanistan.

More important than the work of any of these agencies, the hallmark of America's outreach efforts was the activity of George W. Bush himself. Three days after September 11, the President led an ecumenical service at the National Cathedral at which a spokesman for America's Muslims helped officiate. A few days later, the President visited the Islamic Center, a Washington mosque, where he proclaimed that "Islam is peace" and went on to castigate Americans who had made threatening gestures toward Muslims in the days since September 11. "Women who cover their head in this country must feel comfortable going outside," he declared. "Moms who wear cover must not be intimidated in America."

Bush's embrace extended beyond American Muslims to Muslims around the globe. In his address to Congress nine days after the attack, he enunciated several themes to which he has returned repeatedly in the months since:

> I also want to speak tonight directly to Muslims throughout the world. We respect your faith. It's practiced freely by many millions of Americans, and by millions more in countries that America counts as friends. Its teachings are good and peaceful, and those who commit evil in the name of Allah blaspheme the name of Allah. The terrorists are traitors to their own faith, trying, in effect, to hijack Islam itself. The enemy of America is not our many Muslim friends; it is not our many Arab friends.

To demonstrate his earnestness in this matter, the President invited a group of American Muslim spokesmen to breakfast at the White House in order "to discuss... what our country is going to do to make sure that everybody who is an American is respected." In November, he also invited the ambassadors of the member states of the Organization of the Islamic Conference (OIC) to pray and break the daylong Ramadan fast at the White House, expressing his esteem for Muslim "believers [who] built a culture of learning and literature and science" and with whom "we share the same hope for a future of peace." Secretary of State Powell held a similar dinner at the State Department, and U.S. ambassadors around the world were instructed to do likewise.

TO REINFORCE Bush's message of openness to the faith whose teachings the September 11 terrorists had invoked in attacking us, Charlotte Beers's office printed up thousands of posters in a series called "Mosques of America," for distribution around the world. She herself declared that "We... have to be as good at listening as we are at proposing our point of view," so that our interlocutors will "understand... that they don't need to kill us to get our attention."

But if we had been better listeners, we might have been disconcerted by what we heard. Thus, the very same Islamic spokesmen whom the administration was celebrating for their anti-terrorist sentiments turned out to have, at best, mixed records on the issue. The first of the three sheiks featured in the State Department's pamphlet was Yussef al-Qaradawi of Qatar, who had praised suicide bombings—especially those directed against innocent Israeli civilians—as "martyrdom operations"; according to a columnist in the London Arabic newspaper *Al Hayat*, Qaradawi also endorsed a fatwa issued by another sheik supporting the killing of Americans. The pamphlet's second sheik, Mohammed Sayyed al-Tantawi of Egypt, had indeed criticized attacks on women and children, but subsequently qualified his position by stating that "whoever blows himself up among aggressors... who violate the dignity of our brothers in Palestine... is a martyr." The third sheik, Abdul Rahman al-Sudais of Mecca, although more outspoken than either of the other two in decrying violence, nonetheless was ambiguous when it came to the bottom line, appealing to Muslims "not to mix up the concepts of real terrorism and legitimate jihad."

The records of the American Muslims to whom the administration turned were no less clouded. CAIR, cited in large print in the State Department's publication and one of the hosts of the President's visit to the Islamic Center, is headed by Nihad Awad, who announced in the wake of the 1993 Oslo accords that he was shifting his support from the PLO to Hamas. Some of the guests at the White House breakfast for Islamic spokesmen likewise boasted histories of support for Hamas or Hizbullah, two groups that had done and continue to do much to earn their places on the United States list of terrorist organizations. And so forth.

IF THE only Muslim spokesmen we could find to second our message were themselves highly compromised, additional and devastating evidence was soon to emerge of how faintly that message was getting through. In March, the Gallup organization released the results of polling in nine predominantly Muslim countries. In only two of them did the proportion of respondents with a "very favorable" opinion of the United States exceed a tenth of the population: Lebanon, where the number was 18 percent, and Kuwait, where it was 11. But these pro-American respondents were themselves offset by the 30 percent of Lebanese and 23 percent of Kuwaitis who recorded their opinion of us as very *un*favorable. In Saudi Arabia, meanwhile, a mere 7 percent said they held a very favorable view of us, with seven times that number, or 49 percent, at the opposite end of the spectrum; in Pakistan, Gallup had to report an asterisk under "very favorable," signifying a response of less than 1 percent. With the exception of Turkey, the news was hardly any better elsewhere.

When asked specifically about the September 11 attacks, pluralities or bare majorities in most of the nine countries did say they found them "totally unjustifiable"—but much *higher* proportions condemned the U.S. military action in Afghanistan as itself totally unjustifiable. The most startling results were for Kuwait, where a mere 26 percent of respondents found the attacks on the World Trade Center and Pentagon totally unjustifiable, while over twice that number, 55 percent, applied this judgment to America's actions in Afghanistan. It would have been fascinating to see how Saudis assessed the September 11 attacks, but the presumptively pro-American Saudi government forbade Gallup to ask the question, as did the government of Jordan.

To make matters worse, even where substantial numbers found the September 11 attacks unjustifiable, there was widespread denial—except in Turkey—that they had been carried out by Arabs. In Pakistan, deniers outnumbered believers 86 percent to 4, in Kuwait 89 percent to 11—and this was *after* the release of the infamous videotape in which Osama bin Laden had boasted of having planned the attack. Some respondents who denied Arab involvement did (confusingly) name bin Laden or al Qaeda as the responsible party, but among Lebanese, Kuwaitis, and Moroccans the favored culprit was Israel, and for Iranians, America itself.

The import of these stark numbers was soon brought into question by news items challenging the methodology of the Gallup survey and the presentation of its findings. The main target of criticism was a press release, echoed by CNN and *USA Today*, that aggregated the data for the nine countries, thereby yielding numbers that were statistically meaningless since they ignored the wide disparities in the size of the various populations. But the flaw in Gallup's press release was quite irrelevant. However erroneous the procedure, the aggregated numbers did not make the data any more appalling than they would be if taken country by country, which is how I have cited them here.

Another complaint was that the group of nine—Indonesia, Turkey, Morocco, Iran, Kuwait, Saudi Arabia, Pakistan, Jordan, and Lebanon—do not necessarily represent the diversity of the Islamic world as a whole. This argument too is hard to credit. Not only does the list include a rather disparate array of polities, but the sample is hardly weighted toward the anti-American side. Within the Muslim Middle East, which is the focus of concern in the war against terrorism, one would be foolish to imagine more comforting results than these in, say, Syria, Iraq, Yemen, Libya, Algeria, or Egypt.

Finally, the government of Kuwait, a country liberated by American power from the clutches of Saddam Hussein only a decade ago, has looked for a way out of its embarrassment over the Gallup figures by complaining that the pollsters sampled residents at large rather than only citizens. (In Kuwait, noncitizens outnumber citizens.) But, as it happens, Gallup did ask respondents in that country to indicate their status; as between citizens and noncitizens, the answers differed hardly at all. In fact, if Kuwaiti citizens alone had been tallied, the percentage finding the September 11 attacks morally justified would have *risen*, from 36 to 40 percent.

Confronted with the Gallup figures, President Bush exclaimed, in a masterpiece of understatement: "We've got work to do."

How is the work to be done? Basically, public diplomacy comprises two broad functions, both of which have traditionally been carried out by specially trained foreign-service officers, mostly stationed in U.S. missions abroad. One is short-term public relations: explaining current U.S. policy, circulating speeches by the President and the Secretary of State, flacking for them on their visits. The other is long-term: academic exchanges, sustaining U.S. libraries and American-studies programs, cultivating relationships with writers and editors receptive to America and its values, even publishing intellectual magazines in local languages.

For decades, both of these functions were the responsibility of the United States Information Agency. Opinion differs as to how successfully they were performed—better in some eras and under some directors than in others, obviously—but in any case, as I have already noted, the USIA is no longer in existence. It was abolished in 1999, with its functions being putatively taken over by the State Department.

This "reorganization" was pushed through by Republican Senator Jesse Helms in order to streamline what he called the "outrageously costly foreign-policy apparatus." But it was first proposed not by Helms but by Bill Clinton's Secretary of State, Warren Christopher, and other former Secretaries of State hurried to endorse it. (USIA's $2-billion annual budget would make a large addition to State's funding.) George P. Shultz, who served under Ronald Reagan, called it "bold and constructive," and James Baker, who served the elder Bush, found it "breathtaking in its boldness and visionary in its sweep."

The consequences of the reorganization were as swift in coming as they were predictable. For one thing, the promised savings never materialized: in its official implementation report, the Clinton administration was soon explaining that the merger of the agencies had instead led to an *increase* in costs, and one that would continue "over the next several fiscal years." For another thing, the longterm side of public diplomacy was eviscerated. This too was predictable: in the State Department, the main focus is not on the long-term but on the immediate; what enhances the Secretary's image is public relations, not libraries or exchange programs. No wonder that, in unveiling his Madison Avenue approach to public diplomacy, Colin Powell had gone out of his way to deprecate the USIA.

There is a third side, or complement, to public diplomacy—namely, international broadcasting. But here, too, such meager instruments as were once in our hands have been diminished in recent times. Post-cold-war budget cuts have weakened the Voice of America to the point where its Arabic service has been broadcasting only seven hours a day in a single dialect (the Arab world is notable for wide variations in pronunciation), reaching an audience estimated at only 2 percent of the population.

But the paucity of our means is not the sole or even the major problem we face. Nor is a solution to that problem to be found in enhancing our technique, either through "rebranding" programs or through attempts to do "a better job of telling the compassionate side of the American story," as the President has also suggested.

The key underlying premise of our entire publicity effort is that we and the Muslim Middle East inhabit the same moral and cognitive universe, and that our task is therefore to demonstrate the congruence of our goals and actions with those shared values. Yet nothing in Middle Eastern politics—from the nearly universal obsessive hatred of Israel, to the brutal conduct of relations among Arab states themselves and among factions within them, to the pitiless way rulers treat their subjects—

suggests that there is any truth to that premise, let alone that compassion is a prized value in this part of the world.

Take the one principal theme of our outreach efforts—that our enemy is not Islam but terrorism. To judge by the Gallup poll and other evidence, this is another subject on which we speak a different moral language from those we wish to reach. The numbers who told Gallup they found our war against terrorism even "somewhat" justifiable amounted to 1 percent in Morocco, 2 percent in Indonesia, 4 percent in Pakistan, 9 in Iran, 17 in Kuwait, 19 in Turkey, and 20 in Lebanon; Saudi Arabia and Jordan once again refused to allow Gallup even to ask the question.

UN Secretary General Kofi Annan—no hawk, he—discovered all this for himself when he proposed a world treaty against terrorism in the aftermath of September 11. Appealing for "moral clarity," Annan condemned "the deliberate taking of innocent life, regardless of cause or grievance. If there is one principle that all peoples can agree on," he added, "surely it is this." So cautious and anodyne was the wording of the proposed treaty that North Korea itself proclaimed its support. Not so the Islamic Conference, which turned it down flat. Even when Annan "gambled his moral authority" (in the words of a UN diplomat) by a personal appeal to a meeting of the Conference, the Islamic states would not budge or accept any compromise unless a blanket exemption were included for terrorist actions against Israel. At its meeting in Malaysia in early April, the Conference reaffirmed its stance.

If there is "one principle that all peoples can agree on," in short, it is not this one. For most Muslim states (Turkey again excepted), "terrorism" is a concept defined not by the nature of the act but by the cause in whose name it is undertaken, or by the identities of the perpetrators and the victims. Almost any military action *by* Israel is considered terrorism, almost any violence *against* Israel is resistance. For some large number of Muslims, the same would seem to apply if the term "United States" is substituted for "Israel."

This widespread acceptance of terrorism is only one sign of a larger syndrome. The political culture of the Muslim Middle East is mired in tyranny, violence, fanaticism, bigotry, and fantasy. As Fouad Ajami showed in *The Dream Palace of the Arabs*, this is not just a matter of regimes and rulers. It is also a matter of thinkers—academics, journalists, intellectuals, writers and artists, professionals of every stripe: the very people whose hearts and minds we are seeking to address. The widespread denial that it was Arabs who were responsible for the September 11 attacks, the credence given to the preposterous rumor that 4,000 Jewish employees at the World Trade Center stayed home from work on September 11 because the Mossad slipped them the word that it was about to blow up the towers, is evidence of a deficiency not merely in information but in the skills of reality-testing.

Changing this, if it is within our power at all, is not a matter for the short or even the medium term, and it cannot be accomplished by public diplomacy conceived along Madison Avenue lines. If we are going to chip away at the solid wall of hostility that Gallup found, we will have to proceed less by polishing our image than by improving the Arab-Muslim way of looking at things. The problem is not our "brand"; it is their buying habits.

FIRST THINGS first, then. What is needful above all (as Norman Podhoretz argued in these pages last month) is to prosecute the war against terrorism relentlessly until it is won. Our victory need not await local political change; indeed, we dare not risk making it contingent on such change. Rather, the inverse applies: a triumph of arms may facilitate a triumph of ideas that could obviate future resort to military measures.

Contemporary Islamism arose as an idea in response to political rather than religious yearnings. It was not an answer to the question, "what does my faith demand of me?" but rather to the question, "how can I overcome my sense of national humiliation?" And it battened on the image of an America defeated by the Iran of the ayatollahs and of an America and Israel driven from Lebanon by Hizbullah.

It is a cliché that you cannot kill an idea. But the defeat of an *armed* idea can indeed lead to its death. That is what happened to fascism, and we can hope it will happen to Islamic extremism in its turn. Just as we succeeded in imbuing Japan and Germany with liberalism and democracy after we had defeated them decisively on the battlefield, so the defeat of terrorism, which in practice means the defeat of the various regimes that sponsor terror and of the Islamist movement, may open the way to new thinking in the Middle East. Although it is unlikely that we will occupy any countries as long or as thoroughly as we did at the end of World War II, our goal ought to be the same: liberalizing and democratizing cultures that have previously proved resistant to it.

It is here that public diplomacy properly should be brought in—for it is true that, in the long run, if we are to foment some betterment of the political culture of the Muslim Middle East, we will have need of it. In lieu of reprising General MacArthur's role in Japan as an ersatz emperor, we will have to rely on instruments of "soft power" to effect lasting change. Nor need we wait until the moment of military victory to begin deploying those instruments.

On this front, there is good news and bad. The good news lies in the area of broadcasting, where Congress has funded plans, already in the testing stages, for a new Middle Eastern Radio Network (MERN) that promises to repair many of the defects of our current operation. The plan calls for a mixture of public affairs and music (both Arabic and Western) to be broadcast 24 hours a day on AM and FM bands rather than only on short wave as at present, and in five different regional dialects of Arabic. The network is scheduled to begin full operation this summer.

Plans for revitalizing public diplomacy per se offer a less encouraging picture. The fiasco of the Pentagon's short-lived Office of Strategic Influence, and the embarrassment that was the State Department's pamphlet on terrorism or the President's breakfast with supporters of Hamas and Hizbullah—all give witness to a vacuum of coherent, long-range thought. During the very week of the OSI scandal, the White House confirmed that it was working on its own plan to transform the wartime

Coalition Information Center into a permanent office that would be oriented toward a more distant horizon. There is much value in such an idea—the presidency is a bullier pulpit by far than the State Department—but the political pressures that weigh on the State Department weigh even more heavily on the White House. The same purpose would be better served by reinventing a semi-independent agency like the old USIA.

No initiative of public diplomacy is likely to succeed, however, unless it is informed by a spirit of honesty, however politically incorrect, about the depth of the problem we face, and of unapologetic directness in confronting the sordid political culture that gave rise to the attacks of September 11. We need an effective capability for disseminating information and influence, but if its message is one of "anxious propitiation" (in the phrase of the eminent Islamic scholar Bernard Lewis), it will not only fail on its own terms but it will undercut and compromise the very different and necessary message being sent by our awesome military forces. On this front, not only do we have much work to do, we have not even begun.

JOSHUA MURAVCHIK, *a resident scholar at the American Enterprise Institute, is the author of* Exporting Democracy *and, most recently,* Heaven on Earth: The Rise and Fall of Socialism *(Encounter Books).*

UNIT 2

Managers, Performance, and the Environment

Unit Selections

Key Points to Consider

- What do you think of the manager's job? Do you think it is only to plan, direct, organize, control, and staff, or does he or she do other things? Explain.
- Do you think the manager's job is likely to change in the twenty-first century? In what ways?
- How do you think the environment is going to change for business and other organizations in the coming years? Do you think that change will increase or decrease in speed? Explain your answer.

DUSHKIN ONLINE **Links: www.dushkin.com/online/**

These sites are annotated in the World Wide Web pages.

Design for Competitive Advantage
http://www.dfca.org/toc.html

Krislyn's Favorite Advertising & Marketing Sites
http://www.krislyn.com/sites/adv.htm

Sheffield University Management School
http://www.shef.ac.uk/uni/academic/I-M/mgt/research/research.html

Two Scenarios for 21st Century Organizations
http://ccs.mit.edu/21c/21CWP001.html

The need for management has been recognized since the early days of civilization. The concepts of leadership, administration, and management have existed since at least before the time of Plato. Some of the early modern writers in management include Frederick W. Taylor, Elton Mayo, and Mary Parker Follett. These people helped to establish the basis of modern management theory during the first part of the twentieth century.

Management has come a long way since the days of Taylor, Mayo, and Follett. The techniques and theories that they and their successors helped to develop have contributed to the establishment of industrialized countries as major forces in the world. These ideas helped American culture dominate the better part of the twentieth century, and the success of Western concepts is even now being seen in eastern Europe and the republics of the former Soviet Union. Management—the way people arrange their lives and businesses—is a major part of capitalism's success. The failure that the communist system experienced in the former Soviet bloc was not a failure of industrialism; rather, it was a failure of a system that unsuccessfully attempted to use that industrial base. This was not a failure of the machines or the workers in the system but of the way the system operated and managed the equipment and people. It was a situation that people of those countries would no longer tolerate as they rushed to embrace capitalism, democracy, pluralism, and finally management as keys to their future in the twenty-first century.

As a discipline, management faces new challenges. These challenges are mostly the result of management's success. They include the transformation of the American economy from one based upon industrialization to one based upon knowledge and the challenge of other economies, in particular, the newly integrated Europe. Another challenge is the new role of managers and management as more women, African Americans, Hispanic Americans, and other minorities, as well as more demanding groups of workers with different expectations, enter the workforce.

Management is responding to these challenges in various ways. New ideas are constantly being projected in the midst of the chaos that is the legacy of the post–cold war world. Times have indeed changed, and the tools necessary to meet those changes are only now being developed. Some of these tools and techniques will have lasting impact on the way managers perform their jobs, but others will be merely passing fads, as may be seen in the article "Managing From A to Z."

The new economy and the forms it will support will be very different from the environment of the past. "Management Lessons From the Bust," as to "Why Companies Fail," must be analyzed to determine the reasons why many organizations crashed during the burst in the stock market bubble. The dominating strength of corporations will be based on brains, not brawn; the economic system will be international, not national, in scope; and competition will be even more fierce while an organization's competitive advantage in the marketplace will be even more fleeting. Organizations will need managers who can think clearly to deal with the changes in all kinds of environments. This is a result of the dependence upon ideas and creativity that are necessary to build and sustain organizations. Future organizations that think, create, and adapt to the changing conditions of an increasingly fluid environment are the ones that will survive and be successful.

America's new economy and the managers who plan, direct, organize, control, and staff its businesses must provide new, different, and creative approaches to meet the new competitive global environment, as shown in "Reinventing How We Do Business." This will require better products and services, produced and marketed with improved, more efficient methods. Organizations no longer compete only domestically, as they did in the 1950s, when General Motors, Ford, and Chrysler dominated an American auto industry that also included such names as Studebaker, Packard, Hudson, DeSoto, and Nash. Today, Ford and GM must compete on an international basis with DaimlerChrysler and names like Nissan, Toyota, Honda, Volkswagen, and BMW. Corporations the world over must meet these new conditions or accept the fate of past organizations and follow Studebaker in its drive into oblivion.

The Manager's Job: Folklore and Fact

The classical view says that the manager organizes, coordinates, plans, and controls; the facts suggest otherwise.

Henry Mintzberg

Henry Mintzberg is the Bronfman Professor of Management at McGill University. His latest book is Mintzberg on Management: Inside Our Strange World of Organizations *(Free Press, 1989). This article appeared originally in HBR July–August 1975. It won the McKinsey Award for excellence.*

If you ask managers what they do, they will most likely tell you that they plan, organize, coordinate, and control. Then watch what they do. Don't be surprised if you can't relate what you see to these words.

When a manager is told that a factory has just burned down and then advises the caller to see whether temporary arrangements can be made to supply customers through a foreign subsidiary, is that manager planning, organizing, coordinating, or controlling? How about when he or she presents a gold watch to a retiring employee? Or attends a conference to meet people in the trade and returns with an interesting new product idea for employees to consider?

What do managers do? Even managers themselves don't always know.

These four words, which have dominated management vocabulary since the French industrialist Henri Fayol first introduced them in 1916, tell us little about what managers actually do. At best, they indicate some vague objectives managers have when they work.

The field of management, so devoted to progress and change, has for more than half a century not seriously addressed *the* basic question: What do managers do? Without a proper answer, how can we teach management? How can we design planning or information systems for managers? How can we improve the practice of management at all?

Our ignorance of the nature of managerial work shows up in various ways in the modern organization—in boasts by successful managers who never spent a single day in a management training program; in the turnover of corporate planners who never quite understood what it was the manager wanted; in the computer consoles gathering dust in the back room because the managers never used the fancy on-line MIS some analyst thought they needed. Perhaps most important, our ignorance shows up in the inability of our large public organizations to come to grips with some of their most serious policy problems.

Somehow, in the rush to automate production, to use management science in the functional areas of marketing and finance, and to apply the skills of the behavioral scientist to the problem of worker motivation, the manager—the person in charge of the organization or one of its subunits—has been forgotten.

I intend to break the reader away from Fayol's words and introduce a more supportable and useful description of managerial work. This description derives from my review and synthesis of research on how various managers have spent their time.

In some studies, managers were observed intensively; in a number of others, they kept detailed diaries; in a few studies, their records were analyzed. All kinds of managers were studied—foreman, factory supervisors, staff managers, field sales managers, hospital administrators, presidents of companies and nations, and even street gang leaders. These "managers" worked in the United States, Canada, Sweden, and Great Britain.

A synthesis of these findings paints an interesting picture, one as different from Fayol's classical view as a cubist abstract is from a Renaissance painting. In a sense, this picture will be obvious to anyone who has ever spent a day in a manager's office, either in front of the desk or behind it. Yet, at the same time, this picture throws into doubt much of the folklore that we have accepted about the manager's work.

Folklore and Facts About Managerial Work

There are four myths about the manager's job that do not bear up under careful scrutiny of the facts.

Folklore: The manager is a reflective, systematic planner. The evidence of this issue is overwhelming, but not a shred of it supports this statement.

Fact: Study after study has shown that managers work at a unrelenting pace, that their activities are characterized by brevity, variety, and discontinuity, and that they are strongly oriented to action and dislike reflective activities. Consider this evidence:

Half the activities engaged in by the five chief executives of my study lasted less than nine minutes, and only 10% exceeded one hour.[1] A study of 56 U.S. foremen found that they averaged 583 activities per eight-hour shift, an average of 1 every 48 seconds.[2] The work pace for both chief executives and foremen was unrelenting. The chief executives met a steady stream of callers and mail from the moment they arrived in the morning until they left in the evening. Coffee breaks and lunches were inevitably work related, and ever-present subordinates seemed to usurp any free moment.

How often can you work for a half an hour without interruption?

A diary study of 160 British middle and top managers found that they worked without interruption for a half hour or more only about once every two days.[3]

Of the verbal contacts the chief executives in my study engaged in, 93% were arranged on an ad hoc basis. Only 1% of the executives' time was spent in open-ended observational tours. Only 1 out of 368 verbal contacts was unrelated to a specific issue and could therefore be called general planning. Another researcher found that "in *not one single case* did a manager report obtaining important external information from a general conversation or other undirected personal communication."[4]

Is this the planner that the classical view describes? Hardly. The manager is simply responding to the pressures of the job. I found that my chief executives terminated many of their own activities, often leaving meetings before the end, and interrupted their desk work to call in subordinates. One president not only placed his desk so that he could look down a long hallway but also left his door open when he was alone—an invitation for subordinates to come in and interrupt him.

Clearly, these managers wanted to encourage the flow of current information. But more significantly, they seemed to be conditioned by their own work loads. They appreciated the opportunity cost of their own time, and they were continually aware of their ever-present obligations—mail to be answered, callers to attend to, and so on. It seems that a manager is always plagued by the possibilities of what might be done and what must be done.

When managers must plan, they seem to do so implicitly in the context of daily actions, not in some abstract process reserved for two weeks in the organization's mountain retreat. The plans of the chief executives I studied seemed to exist only in their heads—as flexible, but often specific, intentions. The traditional literature notwithstanding, the job of managing does not breed reflective planners; managers respond to stimuli, they are conditioned by their jobs to prefer live to delayed action.

Folklore: The effective manager has no regular duties to perform. Managers are constantly being told to spend more time planning and delegating and less time seeing customers and engaging in negotiations. These are not, after all, the true tasks of the manager. To use the popular analogy, the good manager, like the good conductor, carefully orchestrates everything in advance, then sits back, responding occasionally to an unforeseeable exception. But here again the pleasant abstraction just does not seem to hold up.

Fact: Managerial work involves performing a number of regular duties, including ritual and ceremony, negotiations, and processing of soft information that links the organization with its environment. Consider some evidence from the research:

A study of the work of the presidents of small companies found that they engaged in routine activities because their companies could not afford staff specialists and were so thin on operating personnel that a single absence often required the president to substitute.[5]

One study of field sales managers and another of chief executives suggest that it is a natural part of both jobs to see important customers, assuming the managers wish to keep those customers.[6]

Someone, only half in jest, once described the manager as the person who sees visitors so that other people can get their work done. In my study, I found that certain ceremonial duties—meeting visiting dignitaries, giving out gold watches, presiding at Christmas dinners—were an intrinsic part of the chief executive's job.

Studies of managers' information flow suggest that managers play a key role in securing "soft" external information (much of it available only to them because of their status) and in passing it along to their subordinates.

Folklore: The senior manager needs aggregated information, which a formal management information system best provides. Not too long ago, the words *total information system* were everywhere in the management literature. In keeping with the classical view of the manager as that individual perched on the apex of a regulated, hierarchical system, the literature's manager was to receive all important information from a giant, comprehensive MIS.

But lately, these giant MIS systems are not working—managers are simply not using them. The enthusiasm has waned. A look at how managers actually process information makes it clear why.

Fact: Managers strongly favor verbal media, telephone calls and meetings, over documents. Consider the following:

In two British studies, managers spent an average of 66% and 80% of their time in verbal (oral) communication.[7] In my study of five American chief executives, the figure was 78%.

These five chief executives treated mail processing as a burden to be dispensed with. One came in Saturday morning to process 142 pieces of mail in just over three hours, to "get rid of all the stuff." This same manager looked at the first piece of "hard" mail he had received all week, a standard cost report, and put it aside with the comment, "I never look at this."

Today's gossip may be tomorrow's fact—that's why managers cherish hearsay.

These same five chief executives responded immediately to 2 of the 40 routine reports they received during the five weeks of my study and to 4 items in the 104 periodicals. They skimmed most of these periodicals in seconds, almost ritualistically. In all, these chief executives of good-sized organizations initiated on their

Research on Managerial Work

In seeking to describe managerial work, I conducted my own research and also scanned the literature to integrate the findings of studies from many diverse sources with my own. These studies focused on two different aspects of managerial work. Some were concerned with the characteristics of work—how long managers work, where, at what pace, with what interruptions, with whom they work, and through what media they communicate. Other studies were concerned with the content of work—what activities the managers actually carry out, and why. Thus, after a meeting, one researcher might note that the manager spent 45 minutes with three government officials in their Washington office, while another might record that the manager presented the company's stand on some proposed legislation in order to change a regulation.

A few of the studies of managerial work are widely known, but most have remained buried as single journal articles or isolated books. Among the more important ones I cite are:

- Sune Carlson developed the diary method to study the work characteristics of nine Swedish managing directors. Each kept a detailed log of his activities. Carlson's results are reported in his book *Executive Behaviour*. A number of British researchers, notably Rosemary Stewart, have subsequently used Carlson's method. In *Managers and Their Jobs*, she describes the study of 160 top and middle managers of British companies.
- Leonard Sayles's book *Managerial Behavior* is another important reference. Using a method he refers to as "anthropological," Sayles studied the work content of middle and lower level managers in a large U.S. corporation. Sayles moved freely in the company, collecting whatever information struck him as important.
- Perhaps the best-known source is *Presidential Power,* in which Richard Neustadt analyzes the power and managerial behavior of Presidents Roosevelt, Truman, and Eisenhower. Neustadt used secondary sources—documents and interviews with other parties.
- Robert H. Guest, in *Personnel,* reports on a study of the foreman's working day. Fifty-six U.S. foremen were observed and each of their activities recorded during one eight-hour shift.
- Richard C. Hodgson, Daniel J. Levinson, and Abraham Zaleznik studied a team of three top executives of a U.S. hospital. From that study they wrote *The Executive Role Constellation.* They addressed the way in which work and socioemotional roles were divided among the three managers.
- William F. Whyte, from his study of a street gang during the Depression, wrote *Street Corner Society*. His findings about the gang's workings and leadership, which George C. Homans analyzed in *The Human Group,* suggest interesting similarities of job content between street gang leaders and corporate managers.

My own study involved five American CEOs of middle- to large-sized organizations—a consulting firm, a technology company, a hospital, a consumer goods company, and a school system. Using a method called "structural observation," during one intensive week of observation for each executive, I recorded various aspects of every piece of mail and every verbal contact. In all, I analyzed 890 pieces of incoming and outgoing mail and 368 verbal contacts.

own—that is, not in response to something else—a grand total of 25 pieces of mail during the 25 days I observed them.

An analysis of the mail the executives received reveals an interesting picture—only 13% was of specific and immediate use. So now we have another piece in the puzzle: not much of the mail provides live, current information—the action of a competitor, the mood of a government legislator, or the rating of last night's television show. Yet this is the information that drove the managers, interrupting their meetings and rescheduling their workdays.

Consider another interesting finding. Managers seem to cherish "soft" information, especially gossip, hearsay, and speculation. Why? The reason is its timeliness; today's gossip may be tomorrow's fact. The manager who misses the telephone call revealing that the company's biggest customer was seen golfing with a main competitor may read about a dramatic drop in sales in the next quarterly report. But then it's too late.

To assess the value of historical, aggregated, "hard" MIS information, consider two of the managers's prime uses for information—to identify problems and opportunities[8] and to build mental models (e.g., how the organization's budget system works, how customers buy products, how changes in the economy affect the organization). The evidence suggests that the manager identifies decision situations and builds models not with the aggregated abstractions an MIS provides but with specific tidbits of data.

Consider the words of Richard Neustadt, who studied the information-collecting habits of Presidents Roosevelt, Truman, and Eisenhower: "It is not information of a general sort that helps a President see personal stakes; not summaries, not surveys, not the *bland amalgams*. Rather… it is the odds and ends of *tangible detail* that pieced together in his mind illuminate the underside of issues put before him. To help himself he must reach out as widely as he can for every scrap of fact, opinion, gossip, bearing on his interests and relationships as President. He must become his own director of his own central intelligence."[9]

The manager's emphasis on this verbal media raises two important points. First, verbal information is stored in the brains of people. Only when people write this information down can it be stored in the files of the organization—whether in metal cabinets or on magnetic tape—and managers apparently do not write down much of what they hear. Thus the strategic data bank of the organization is not in the memory of its computers but in the minds of its managers.

Second, managers' extensive use of verbal media helps to explain why they are reluctant to delegate tasks. It is not as if they can hand a dossier over to subordinates; they must take the time to "dump memory"—to tell subordinates all about the subject. But this could take so long that managers may find it easier to do the task themselves. Thus they are damned by their own information system to a "dilemma of delegation"—to do too much or to delegate to subordinates with inadequate briefing.

Folklore: Management is, or at least is quickly becoming, a science and a profession. By almost any definition of *science* and *profession,* this statement is false. Brief observation of any manager will quickly lay to rest the notion that managers practice a science. A science involves the enaction of systematic, analytically determined procedures or programs. If we do not even know what procedures managers use, how can we prescribe them by scientific analysis? And how can we call management a profession if we cannot specify what managers are to learn? For after all, a profession involves "knowledge of some department of learning or science" (*Random House Dictionary*).[10]

The Manager's Roles

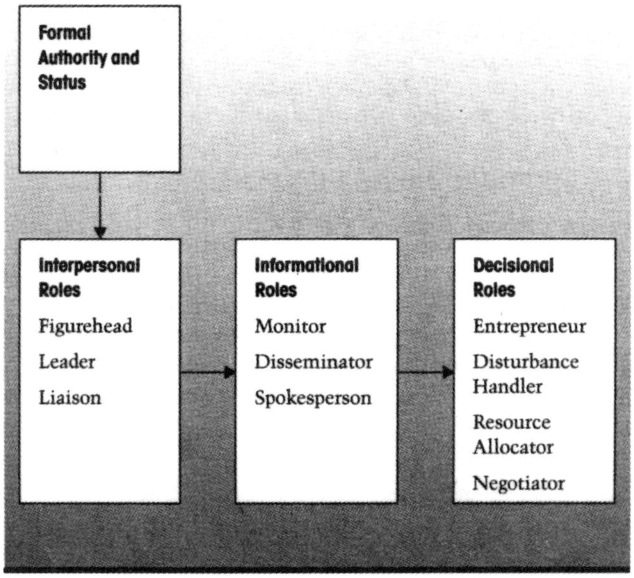

Fact: The managers' programs—to schedule time, process information, make decisions, and so on—remain locked deep inside their brains. Thus, to describe these programs, we rely on words like *judgment* and *intuition*, seldom stopping to realize that they are merely labels for our ignorance.

I was struck during my study by the fact that the executives I was observing—all very competent—are fundamentally indistinguishable from their counterparts of a hundred years ago (or a thousand years ago). The information they need differs, but they seek it in the same way—by word of mouth. Their decisions concern modern technology, but the procedures they use to make those decisions are the same as the procedures used by nineteenth century managers. Even the computer, so important for the specialized work of the organization, has apparently had no influence on the work procedures of general managers. In fact, the manager is in a kind of loop, with increasingly heavy work pressures but no aid forthcoming from management science.

Considering the facts about managerial work, we can see that the manager's job is enormously complicated and difficult. Managers are overburdened with obligations yet cannot easily delegate their tasks. As a result, they are driven to overwork and forced to do many tasks superficially. Brevity, fragmentation, and verbal communication characterize their work. Yet these are the very characteristics of managerial work that have impeded scientific attempts to improve it. As a result, management scientists have concentrated on the specialized functions of the organization, where it is easier to analyze the procedures and quantify the relevant information.[11]

But the pressures of a manager's job are becoming worse. Where before managers needed to respond only to owners and directors, now they find that subordinates with democratic norms continually reduce their freedom to issue unexplained orders, and a growing number of outside influences (consumer groups, government agencies, and so on) demand attention. Managers have had nowhere to turn for help. The first step in providing such help is to find out what the manager's job really is.

Back to a Basic Description of Managerial Work

Earlier, I defined the manager as that person in charge of an organization or subunit. Besides CEOs, this definition would include vice presidents, bishops, foremen, hockey coaches, and prime ministers. All these "managers" are vested with formal authority over an organizational unit. From formal authority comes status, which leads to various interpersonal relations, and from these comes access to information. Information, in turn, enables the manager to make decisions and strategies for the unit.

The manager's job can be described in terms of various "roles," or organized sets of behaviors identified with a position. My description, shown in "The Manager's Roles," comprises ten roles. As we shall see, formal authority gives rise to the three interpersonal roles, which in turn give rise to the three informational roles; these two sets of roles enable the manager to play the four decisional roles.

Interpersonal Roles

Three of the manager's roles arise directly from formal authority and involve basic interpersonal relationships. First is the *figurehead* role. As the head of an organizational unit, every manager must perform some ceremonial duties. The president greets the touring dignitaries. The foreman attends the wedding of a lathe operator. The sales manager takes an important customer to lunch.

The chief executives of my study spent 12% of their contact time on ceremonial duties; 17% of their incoming mail dealt with acknowledgments and requests related to their status. For example, a letter to a company president requested free merchandise for a crippled schoolchild; diplomas that needed to be signed were put on the desk of the school superintendent.

Duties that involve interpersonal roles may sometimes be routine, involving little serious communication and no important decision making. Nevertheless, they are important to the smooth functioning of an organization and cannot be ignored.

Managers are responsible for the work of the people of their unit. Their actions in this regard constitute the *leader* role. Some of these actions involve leadership directly—for example, in most organizations the managers are normally responsible for hiring and training their own staff.

In addition, there is the indirect exercise of the leader role. For example, every manager must motivate and encourage employees, somehow reconciling their individual needs with the goals of the organization. In virtually every contact with the manager, subordinates seeking leadership clues ask: "Does she approve?" "How would she like the report to turn out?" "Is she more interested in market share than high profits?"

The influence of managers is most clearly seen in the leader role. Formal authority vests them with great potential power; leadership determines in large part how much of it they will realize.

The literature of management has always recognized the leader role, particularly those aspects of it related to motivation. In comparison, until recently it has hardly mentioned the *liaison* role, in which the manager makes contacts outside the vertical chain of command. This is remarkable in light of the finding of virtually every study of managerial work that managers spend as much time with peers and other people outside their units as they do with their own subordinates—and, surprisingly, very little time with their own superiors.

In Rosemary Stewart's diary study, the 160 British middle and top managers spent 47% of their time with peers, 41% of their time with people inside their unit, and only 12% of their time with their superiors. For Robert H. Guest's study of U.S. foremen, the figures were 44%, 46%, and 10%. The chief executives of my study averaged 44% of their contact time with people outside their organizations, 48% with subordinates, and 7% with directors and trustees.

The contacts the five CEOs made were with an incredibly wide range of people: subordinates; clients, business associates, and

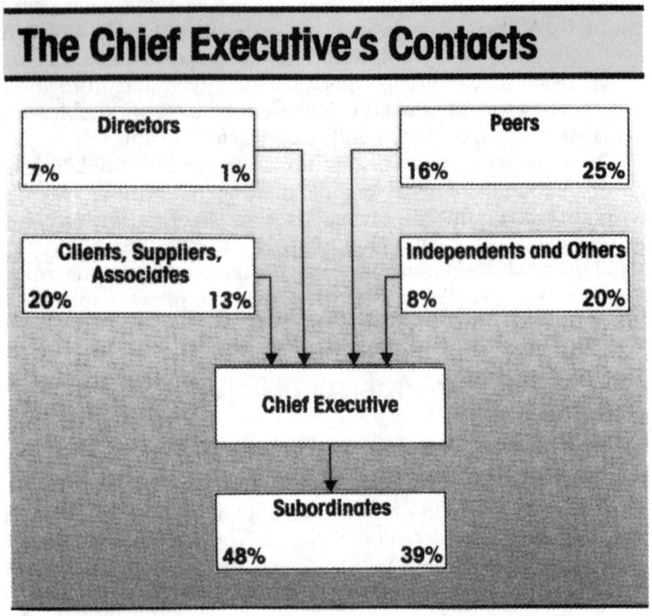

Note: The first figure indicates the proportion of total contact time spent with each group and the second figure, the proportion of mail from each group.

suppliers; and peers—managers of similar organizations, government and trade organization officials, fellow directors on outside boards, and independents with no relevant organizational affiliations. The chief executives' time with and mail from these groups is shown in "The Chief Executive's Contacts." Guest's study of foremen shows, likewise, that their contacts were numerous and wide-ranging, seldom involving fewer than 25 individuals, and often more than 50.

Informational Roles

By virtue of interpersonal contacts, both with subordinates and with a network of contacts, the manager emerges as the nerve center of the organizational unit. The manager may not know everything but typically knows more than subordinates do.

Studies have shown this relationship to hold for all managers, from street gang leaders to U.S. presidents. In *The Human Group*, George C. Homans explains how, because they were at the center of the information flow in their own gangs and were also in close touch with other gang leaders, street gang leaders were better informed than any of their followers.[12] As for presidents, Richard Neustadt observes: "The essence of [Franklin] Roosevelt's technique for information-gathering was competition. 'He would call you in,' one of his aides once told me, 'and he'd ask you to get the story on some complicated business, and you'd come back after a couple of days of hard labor and present the juicy morsel you'd uncovered under a stone somewhere, and *then* you'd find out he knew all about it, along with something else you *didn't* know. Where he got this information from he wouldn't mention, usually, but after he had done this to you once or twice you got damn careful about *your* information.'"[13]

We can see where Roosevelt "got this information" when we consider the relationship between the interpersonal and informational roles. As leader, the manager has formal and easy access to every staff member. In addition, liaison contacts expose the manager to external information to which subordinates often lack access. Many of these contacts are with other managers of equal status, who are themselves nerve centers in their own organization. In this way, the manager develops a powerful database of information.

Processing information is a key part of the manager's job. In my study, the CEOs spent 40% of their contact time on activities devoted exclusively to the transmission of information; 70% of their incoming mail was purely informational (as opposed to requests for action). Managers don't leave meetings or hang up the telephone to get back to work. In large part, communication *is* their work. Three roles describe these informational aspects of managerial work.

As *monitor*, the manager is perpetually scanning the environment for information, interrogating liaison contacts and subordinates, and receiving unsolicited information, much of it as a result of the network of personal contacts. Remember that a good part of the information the manager collects in the monitor role arrives in verbal form, often as gossip, hearsay, and speculation.

In the *disseminator* role, the manager passes some privileged information directly to subordinates, who would otherwise have no access to it. When subordinates lack easy contact with one another, the manager may pass information from one to another.

In the *spokesperson* role, the manager sends some information to people outside the unit—a president makes a speech to lobby for an organization cause, or a foreman suggests a product modification to a supplier. In addition, as a spokesperson, every manager must inform and satisfy the influential people who control the organizational unit. For the foreman, this may simply involve keeping the plant manager informed about the flow of work through the shop.

The president of a large corporation, however, may spend a great amount of time dealing with a host of influences. Directors and shareholders must be advised about finances; consumer groups must be assured that the organization is fulfilling its social responsibilities; and government officials must be satisfied that the organization is abiding by the law.

Decisional Roles

Information is not, of course, an end in itself; it is the basic input to decision making. One thing is clear in the study of managerial work: the manager plays the major role in the unit's decision-making system. As its formal authority, only the manager can commit the unit to important new courses of action; and as its nerve center, only the manager has full and current information to make the set of decisions that determines the unit's strategy. Four roles describe the manager as decision maker.

As *entrepreneur*, the manager seeks to improve the unit, to adapt it to changing conditions in the environment. In the monitor role, a president is constantly on the lookout for new ideas. When a good one appears, he initiates a development project that he may supervise himself or delegate to an employee (perhaps with the stipulation that he must approve the final proposal).

The scarcest resource managers have to allocate is their own time.

There are two interesting features about these development projects at the CEO level. First, these projects do not involve single decisions or even unified clusters of decisions. Rather, they emerge as a series of small decisions and actions sequenced over time. Apparently, chief executives prolong each project both to fit

Retrospective Commentary

Henry Mintzberg

Over the years, one reaction has dominated the comments I have received from managers who read "The Manager's Job: Folklore and Fact": "You make me feel so good. I thought all those other managers were planning, organizing, coordinating, and controlling, while I was busy being interrupted, jumping from one issue to another, and trying to keep the lid on the chaos." Yet everything in this article must have been patently obvious to these people. Why such a reaction to reading what they already knew?

Conversely, how to explain the very different reaction of two media people who called to line up interviews after an article based on this one appeared in the *New York Times*. "Are we glad someone finally let managers have it," both said in passing, a comment that still takes me aback. True, they had read only the account in the *Times*, but that no more let managers have it than did this article. Why that reaction?

One explanation grows out of the way I now see this article—as proposing not so much another view of management as another face of it. I like to call it the insightful face, in contrast to the long-dominant professional or cerebral face. One stresses commitment, the other calculation; one sees the world with integrated perspective, the other figures it as the components of a portfolio. The cerebral face operates with the words and numbers of rationality; the insightful face is rooted in the images and feel of a manager's integrity.

Each of these faces implies a different kind of "knowing," and that, I believe, explains many managers' reaction to this article. Rationally, they "knew" what managers did—planned, organized, coordinated, and controlled. But deep down that did not feel quite right. The description in this article may have come closer to what they really "knew." As for those media people, they weren't railing against management as such but against the cerebral form of management, so pervasive, that they saw impersonalizing the world around them.

In practice, management has to be two-faced—there has to be a balance between the cerebral and the insightful. So, for example, I realized originally that managerial communication was largely oral and that the advent of the computer had not changed anything fundamental in the executive suite—a conclusion I continue to hold. (The greatest threat the personal computer poses is that managers will take it seriously and come to believe that they can manage by remaining in their offices and looking at displays of digital characters.) But I also thought that the dilemma of delegating could be dealt with by periodic debriefings—disseminating words. Now, however, I believe that managers need more ways to convey the images and impressions they carry inside of them. This explains the renewed interest in strategic vision, in culture, and in the roles of intuition and insight in management.

The ten roles I used to describe the manager's job also reflect management's cerebral face, in that they decompose the job more than capture the integration. Indeed, my effort to show a sequence among these roles now seems more consistent with the traditional face of management work than an insightful one. Might we not just as well say that people throughout the organization take actions that inform managers who, by making sense of those actions, develop images and visions that inspire people to subsequent efforts?

Perhaps my greatest disappointment about the research reported here is that it did not stimulate new efforts. In a world so concerned with management, much of the popular literature is superficial and the academic research pedestrian. Certainly, many studies have been carried out over the last 15 years, but the vast majority sought to replicate earlier research. In particular, we remain grossly ignorant about the fundamental content of the manager's job and have barely addressed the major issues and dilemmas in its practice.

But superficiality is not only a problem of the literature. It is also an occupational hazard of the manager's job. Originally, I believed this problem could be dealt with; now I see it as inherent in the job. This is because managing insightfully depends on the direct experience and personal knowledge that come from intimate contact. But in organizations grown larger and more diversified, that becomes difficult to achieve. And so managers turn increasingly to the cerebral face, and the delicate balance between the two faces is lost.

Certainly, some organizations manage to sustain their humanity despite their large size—as Tom Peters and Robert Waterman show in their book *In Search of Excellence*. But that book attained its outstanding success precisely because it is about the exceptions, about the organizations so many of us long to be a part of—not the organization in which we actually work.

Fifteen years ago, I stated that "No job is more vital to our society than that of the manager. It is the manager who determines whether our social institutions serve us well or whether they squander our talents and resources." Now, more than ever, we must strip away the folklore of the manager's job and begin to face its difficult facts.

---

it into a busy, disjointed schedule, and so that they can comprehend complex issues gradually.

Second, the chief executives I studied supervised as many as 50 of these projects at the same time. Some projects entailed new products or processes; others involved public relations campaigns, improvement of the cash position, reorganization of a weak department, resolution of a morale problem in a foreign division, integration of computer operations, various acquisitions at different stages of development, and so on.

Chief executives appear to maintain a kind of inventory of the development projects in various stages of development. Like jugglers, they keep a number of projects in the air; periodically, one comes down, is given a new burst of energy, and sent back into orbit. At various intervals, they put new projects on-stream and discard old ones.

While the entrepreneur role describes the manager as the voluntary initiator of change, the *disturbance handler* role depicts the manager involuntarily responding to pressures. Here change is beyond the manager's control. The pressures of a situation are too severe to be ignored—a strike looms, a major customer has gone bankrupt, or a supplier reneges on a contract—so the manager must act.

Leonard R. Sayles, who has carried out appropriate research on the manager's job, likens the manager to a symphony orchestra conductor who must "maintain a melodious performance,"[14] while handling musicians' problems and other external distur-

Self-Study Questions for Managers

1. Where do I get my information, and how? Can I make greater use of my contacts? Can other people do some of my scanning? In what areas is my knowledge weakest, and how can I get others to provide me with the information I need? Do I have sufficiently powerful mental models of those things I must understand within the organization and in its environment?

2. What information do I disseminate? How important is that information to my subordinates? Do I keep too much information to myself because disseminating it is time consuming or inconvenient? How can I get more information to others so they can make better decisions?

3. Do I tend to act before information is in? Or do I wait so long for all the information that opportunities pass me by?

4. What pace of change am I asking my organization to tolerate? Is this change balanced so that our operations are neither excessively static nor overly disrupted? Have we sufficiently analyzed the impact of this change on the future of our organization?

5. Am I sufficiently well-informed to pass judgment on subordinates' proposals? Can I leave final authorization for more of the proposals with subordinates? Do we have problems of coordination because subordinates already make too many decisions independently?

6. What is my vision for this organization? Are these plans primarily in my own mind in loose form? Should I make them explicit to guide the decisions of others better? Or do I need flexibility to change them at will?

7. How do my subordinates react to my managerial style? Am I sufficiently sensitive to the powerful influence of my actions? Do I fully understand their reactions to my actions? Do I find an appropriate balance between encouragement and pressure? Do I stifle their initiative?

8. What kind of external relationships do I maintain, and how? Do I spend too much of my time maintaining them? Are there certain people whom I should get to know better?

9. Is there any system to my time scheduling, or am I just reacting to the pressures of the moment? Do I find the appropriate mix of activities or concentrate on one particular function or problem just because I find it interesting? Am I more efficient with particular kinds of work, at special times of the day or week? Does my schedule reflect this? Can someone else schedule my time (besides my secretary)?

10. Do I overwork? What effect does my work load have on my efficiency? Should I force myself to take breaks or to reduce the pace of my activity?

11. Am I too superficial in what I do? Can I really shift moods as quickly and frequently as my work requires? Should I decrease the amount of fragmentation and interruption in my work?

12. Do I spend too much time on current, tangible activities? Am I a slave to the action and excitement of my work, so that I am no longer able to concentrate on issues? Do key problems receive the attention they deserve? Should I spend more time reading and probing deeply into certain issues? Could I be more reflective? Should I be?

13. Do I use the different media appropriately? Do I know how to make the most of written communication? Do I rely excessively on face-to-face communication, thereby putting all but a few of my subordinates at an informational disadvantage? Do I schedule enough of my meetings on a regular basis? Do I spend enough time observing activities first-hand, or am I detached from the heart of my organization's activities?

14. How do I blend my personal rights and duties? Do my obligations consume all my time? How can I free myself from obligations to ensure that I am taking this organization where I want it to go? How can I turn my obligations to my advantage?

bances. Indeed, every manager must spend a considerable amount of time responding to high-pressure disturbances. No organization can be so well run, so standardized, that it has considered every contingency in the uncertain environment in advance. Disturbances arise not only because poor managers ignore situations until they reach crisis proportions but also because good managers cannot possibly anticipate all the consequences of the actions they take.

The third decisional role is that of *resource allocator*. The manager is responsible for deciding who will get what. Perhaps the most important resource the manager allocates is his or her own time. Access to the manager constitutes exposure to the unit's nerve center and decision maker. The manager is also charged with designing the unit's structure, that pattern of formal relationships that determines how work is to be divided and coordinated.

Also, as resource allocator, the manager authorizes the important decisions of the unit before they are implemented. By retaining this power, the manager can ensure that decisions are interrelated. To fragment this power encourages discontinuous decision making and a disjointed strategy.

There are a number of interesting features about the manager's authorization of others' decisions. First, despite the widespread use of capital budgeting procedures—a means of authorizing various capital expenditures at one time—executives in my study made a great many authorization decisions on an ad hoc basis. Apparently, many projects cannot wait or simply do not have the quantifiable costs and benefits that capital budgeting requires.

Second, I found that the chief executives faced incredibly complex choices. They had to consider the impact of each decision on other decisions and on the organization's strategy. They had to ensure that the decision would be acceptable to those who influence the organization, as well as ensure that resources would not be overextended. They had to understand the various costs and benefits as well as the feasibility of the proposal. They also had to consider questions of timing. All this was necessary for the simple approval of someone else's proposal. At the same time, however, the delay could lose time, while quick approval could be ill-considered and quick rejection might discourage the subordinate who had spent months developing a pet project.

One common solution to approving projects is to pick the person instead of the proposal. That is, the manager authorizes those projects presented by people whose judgment he or she trusts. But the manager cannot always use this simple dodge.

The final decisional role is that of *negotiator*. Managers spend considerable time in negotiations: the president of the football team works out a contract with the holdout superstar; the corporation president leads the company's contingent to negotiate a new strike issue; the foreman argues a grievance problem to its conclusion with the shop steward.

These negotiations are an integral part of the manager's job, for only he or she has the authority to commit organizational resources in "real time" and the nerve-center information that important negotiations require.

The Integrated Job

It should be clear by now that these ten roles are not easily separable. In the terminology of the psychologist, they form a gestalt, an integrated whole. No role can be pulled out of the framework and the job be left intact. For example, a manager without liaison contacts lacks external information. As a result, that manager can neither disseminate the information that employees need nor make decisions that adequately reflect external conditions. (This is a problem for the new person in a managerial position, since he or she has to build up a network of contacts before making effective decisions.)

Here lies a clue to the problems of team management.[15] Two or three people cannot share a single managerial position unless they can act as one entity. This means that they cannot divide up the ten roles unless they can very carefully reintegrate them. The real difficulty lies with the informational roles. Unless there can be full sharing of managerial information—and, as I pointed out earlier, it is primarily verbal—team management breaks down. A single managerial job cannot be arbitrarily split, for example, into internal and external roles, for information from both sources must be brought to bear on the same decisions.

To say that the ten roles form a gestalt is not to say that all managers give equal attention to each role. In fact, I found in my review of the various research studies that sales managers seem to spend relatively more of their time in the interpersonal roles, presumably a reflection of the extrovert nature of the marketing activity. Production managers, on the other hand, give relatively more attention to the decisional roles, presumably a reflection of their concern with efficient work flow. And staff managers spend the most time in the informational roles, since they are experts who manage departments that advise other parts of the organization. Nevertheless, in all cases, the interpersonal, informational, and decisional roles remain inseparable.

Toward More Effective Management

This description of managerial work should prove more important to managers than any prescription they might derive from it. That is to say, *the managers' effectiveness is significantly influenced by their insight into their own work*. Performance depends on how well a manager understands and responds to the pressures and dilemmas of the job. Thus managers who can be introspective about their work are likely to be effective at their jobs. The questions in "Self-Study Questions for Managers" may sound rhetorical; none is meant to be. Even though the questions cannot be answered simply, the manager should address them.

Let us take a look at three specific areas of concern. For the most part, the managerial logjams—the dilemma of delegation, the database centralized in one brain, the problems of working with the management scientist—revolve around the verbal nature of the manager's information. There are great dangers in centralizing the organization's data bank in the minds of its managers. When they leave, they take their memory with them. And when subordinates are out of convenient verbal reach of the manager, they are at an informational disadvantage.

The manager is challenged to find systematic ways to share privileged information. A regular debriefing session with key subordinates, a weekly memory dump on the dictating machine, maintaining a diary for limited circulation, or other similar methods may ease the logjam of work considerably. The time spent disseminating this information will be more than regained when decisions must be made. Of course, some will undoubtedly raise the question of confidentiality. But managers would be well advised to weigh the risks of exposing privileged information against having subordinates who can make effective decisions.

If there is a single theme that runs through this article, it is that the pressures of the job drive the manager to take on too much work, encourage interruption, respond quickly to every stimulus, seek the tangible and avoid the abstract, make decisions in small increments, and do everything abruptly.

Here again, the manager is challenged to deal consciously with the pressures of superficiality by giving serious attention to the issues that require it, by stepping back in order to see a broad picture, and by making use of analytical inputs. Although effective managers have to be adept at responding quickly to numerous and varying problems, the danger in managerial work is that they will respond to every issue equally (and that means abruptly) and that they will never work the tangible bits and pieces of information into a comprehensive picture of their world.

To create this comprehensive picture, managers can supplement their own models with those of specialists. Economists describe the functioning of markets, operations researchers simulate financial flow processes, and behavioral scientists explain the needs and goals of people. The best of these models can be searched out and learned.

In dealing with complex issues, the senior manager has much to gain from a close relationship with the organization's own management scientists. They have something important that the manager lacks—time to probe complex issues. An effective working relationship hinges on the resolution of what a colleague and I have called "the planning dilemma."[16] Managers have the information and the authority; analysts have the time and the technology. A successful working relationship between the two will be effected when the manager learns to share information and the analyst learns to adapt to the manager's needs. For the analyst, adaptation means worrying less about the elegance of the method and more about its speed and flexibility.

Analysts can help the top manager schedule time, feed in analytical information, monitor projects, develop models to aid in making choices, design contingency plans for disturbances that can be anticipated, and conduct "quick and dirty" analyses for those that cannot. But there can be no cooperation if the analysts are out of the mainstream of the manager's information flow.

The manager is challenged to gain control of his or her own time by turning obligations into advantages and by turning those things he or she wishes to do into obligations. The chief executives of my study initiated only 32% of their own contacts (and another 5% by mutual agreement). And yet to a considerable extent they seemed to control their time. There were two key factors that enabled them to do so.

First, managers have to spend so much time discharging obligations that if they were to view them as just that, they would leave no mark on the organization. Unsuccessful managers blame failure on the obligations. Effective managers turn obligations to advantages. A speech is a chance to lobby for a cause; a meeting is a chance to reorganize a weak department; a visit to an important customer is a chance to extract trade information.

Second, the manager frees some time to do the things that he or she—perhaps no one else—thinks important by turning them into obligations. Free time is made, not found. Hoping to leave some time open for contemplation or general planning is tantamount to hoping that the pressures of the job will go away. Managers who want to innovate initiate projects and obligate others to report back to them. Managers who need certain environmental information establish channels that will automatically keep them informed. Managers who have to tour facilities commit themselves publicly.

The Educator's Job

Finally, a word about the training of managers. Our management schools have done an admirable job of training the organization's specialists—management scientists, marketing researchers, accountants, and organizational development specialists. But for the most part, they have not trained managers.[17]

Management schools will begin the serious training of managers when skill training takes a serious place next to cognitive learning. Cognitive learning is detached and informational, like reading a book or listening to a lecture. No doubt much important cognitive material must be assimilated by the manager-to-be. But cognitive learning no more makes a manager than it does a swimmer. The latter will drown the first time she jumps into the water if her coach never takes her out of the lecture hall, gets her wet, and gives her feedback on her performance.

In other words, we are taught a skill through practice plus feedback, whether in a real or a simulated situation. Our management schools need to identify the skills managers use, select students who show potential in these skills, put the students into situations where these skills can be practiced and developed, and then give them systematic feedback on their performance.

My description of managerial work suggests a number of important managerial skills—developing peer relationships, carrying out negotiations, motivating subordinates, resolving conflicts, establishing information networks and subsequently disseminating information, making decisions in conditions of extreme ambiguity, and allocating resources. Above all, the manager needs to be introspective in order to continue to learn on the job.

No job is more vital to our society than that of the manager. The manager determines whether our social institutions will serve us well or whether they will squander our talents and resources. It is time to strip away the folklore about managerial work and study it realistically so that we can begin the difficult task of making significant improvements in its performance.

References

1. All the data from my study can be found in Henry Mintzberg, *The Nature of Managerial Work* (New York: Harper & Row, 1973).
2. Robert H. Guest, "Of Time and the Foreman," *Personnel*, May 1956, p. 478.
3. Rosemary Stewart, *Managers and Their Jobs* (London: Macmillan, 1967); see also Sune Carlson, *Executive Behaviour* (Stockholm: Strombergs, 1951).
4. Francis J. Aguilar, *Scanning the Business Environment* (New York: Macmillan, 1967), p. 102.
5. Unpublished study by Irving Choran, reported in Mintzberg, *The Nature of Managerial Work*.
6. Robert T. Davis, *Performance and Development of Field Sales Managers* (Boston: Division of Research, Harvard Business School, 1957); George H. Copeman, *The Role of the Managing Director* (London: Business Publications, 1963).
7. Stewart, *Managers and Their Jobs;* Tom Burns, "The Directions of Activity and Communication in a Departmental Executive Group," *Human Relations 7*, no. 1 (1954): 73.
8. H. Edward Wrapp, "Good Managers Don't Make Policy Decisions," HBR September–October 1967, p. 91. Wrapp refers to this as spotting opportunities and relationships in the stream of operating problems and decisions; in his article, Wrapp raises a number of excellent points related to this analysis.
9. Richard E. Neustadt, *Presidential Power* (New York: John Wiley, 1960), pp. 153–154; italics added.
10. For a more thorough, though rather different, discussion of this issue, see Kenneth R. Andrews, "Toward Professionalism in Business Management," HBR March–April 1969, p. 49.
11. C. Jackson Grayson, Jr., in "Management Science and Business Practice," HBR July–August 1973, p. 41, explains in similar terms why, as chairman of the Price Commission, he did not use those very techniques that he himself promoted in his earlier career as management scientist.
12. George C. Homans, *The Human Group* (New York: Harcourt, Brace & World, 1950), based on the study by William F. Whyte entitled *Street Corner Society*, rev. ed. (Chicago: University of Chicago Press, 1955).
13. Neustadt, *Presidential Power*, p. 157.
14. Leonard R. Sayles, *Managerial Behavior* (New York: McGraw-Hill, 1964), p. 162.
15. See Richard C. Hodgson, Daniel J. Levinson, and Abraham Zaleznik, *The Executive Role Constellation* (Boston: Division of Research, Harvard Business School, 1965), for a discussion of the sharing of roles.
16. James S. Hekimian and Henry Mintzberg, "The Planning Dilemma," *The Management Review*, May 1968, p. 4.
17. See J. Sterling Livingston, "Myth of the Well-Educated Manager," HBR January–February 1971, p. 79.

Managing from A to Z

By Leigh Buchanan

I NEVER METAPHOR I DIDN'T LIKE. Poets use metaphor to help readers see familiar objects in new and provocative ways. Business authors use metaphor to help themselves sell books in new and provocative ways. Ever since Sun Tzu stoked fires in the well-padded bellies of corporate leaders with *The Art of War* (which for 2,500 years wasn't marketed as a business book, Tzu's original publishers having missed a trick), metaphor-laden books have sold briskly. Managers look to battle, sport, science, the arts, and—sadly—cheese to reveal truths not present in more literal-minded texts. The best way to understand what business is really like is to study things that aren't really like business. The following A-to-Z rundown of business metaphors is by no means exhaustive: in the interest of limiting ourselves to 26 examples we've left out many items, from football to rocket science. But compiling any kind of alphabetical primer requires making trade-offs. In that sense, it's a lot like business.

A IS FOR ANTARCTIC EXPLORATION

In the eat-or-be-eaten world of business you'd expect the Donner Party to win the Most Admired Explorers title hands down. Instead, business readers are devouring the exploits of **Sir Ernest Shackleton**, the intrepid commander who used a rowboat, penguin meat, and benchmarkable management practices to save 27 men from freezing to death in the Antarctic. Yes, there is an I in ice, but that didn't stop Shackleton from forming effective teams and exhorting the personal best from each individual. *Shackleton's Way: Leadership Lessons From the Great Antarctic Explorer*, by Margot Morrell and Stephanie Capparell, has been embraced by everyone from *Fortune* 500 to the CEOs of Internet start-ups, who presumably see in the disintegration of the floes beneath Shackleton's feet a situation analogous to their own. Except Shackleton got his people out in one piece.

B IS FOR BASEBALL

You couldn't ask for a better turnaround artist than **Billy Martin**, the baseball manager and longtime George Steinbrenner nemesis who spun into gold a succession of hapless teams. With his ferocious temper and penchant for infuriating people, **Martin comes off like the Al Dunlap of professional athletics**. But Michael DeMarco, author of *Dugout Days: Untold Tales and Leadership Lessons From the Extraordinary Career of Billy Martin,* considers his subject closer in style to Jack Welch. DeMarco also compares Martin to General Patton, who was famous for his boldness, discipline, and embrace of the warrior spirit. And who wrote the preface to *Patton on Leadership: Strategic Lessons for Corporate Warfare*? Why, George Steinbrenner, of course.

C IS FOR COMMANDO

War is hell. Business is war. Ergo, business is hell. And into the fray where lesser men hesitate and are lost drops Richard Marcinko, presumably lowering himself on a rope made of hair hacked from his enemies' scalps. *Leadership Secrets of the Rogue Warrior: A Commando's Guide to Success* is no sedate screed on the elegance of well-wrought strategy. **Marcinko, who earned his tough-bastard stripes as a Navy SEAL and burnished them as a consultant, barks and swears and talks about killing the competition.** He means that metaphorically, of course. Probably. Perhaps.

D IS FOR DANCE

Dance is about timing; business is about timing. Dance is about movement; business is about movement. Dance is about rhythm; business is about rhythm. That's about as far as the metaphor extends in Jeffrey C. Shuman's *The Rhythm of Business: The Key to Building and Running Successful Companies.* Despite dance-instruction diagrams plastered across the cover and occasional references in subject headers ("The Cash Flow Tango," "Leveling the Dance Floor"), Shuman's terpsichorean allusions are superficial at best. We ache for the lost chance to explore the graceful waltz of a well-formed alliance, the jig of an animated brainstorming session, the minuet of thoughtful process design, and the tap of fast, flawless execution. Bring in da noise, Mr. Shuman. Bring in da funk.

E IS FOR ELIZABETH I

You're out of cash. Your competitors are hungrily eyeing your assets. And although you've broken through the glass ceiling, your followers doubt that a woman can handle the job. You're... **Queen Elizabeth I**, leader of one of the most dysfunctional family businesses in history. Elizabeth's life is a thoroughly modern managerial-success story. The new queen triumphed by mastering the facts of a situation, assembling a brilliant advisory board, tracking every penny, and rigorously controlling her image, explains Alan Axelrod in *Elizabeth I, CEO: Strategic Lessons From the Leader Who Built an Empire.* By definition, the personal affairs of the "Virgin Queen" were less satisfactory. Those desiring a role model for work-life balance should look elsewhere.

F IS FOR FRACTALS

At first glance, the illustrations in *Leadership and the New Science: Learning About Organization From an Orderly Universe* look like psychedelic gift wrap. But they are, in fact, *fractals*—which Margaret J. Wheatley defines as objects that repeat "a similar pattern or design at ever-smaller levels of scale." In other words (and other words are very, very helpful here), fractals result when a shape or an equation or an organization's values are processed repeatedly in an endless feedback loop with each iteration producing similarities but also new levels of complexity. Something like that. Anyway, fractals are ubiquitous in nature, but they also characterize companies whose employees "trust in the power of guiding principles or values, knowing that they are strong enough influencers of behavior to shape every employee into a desired representation of the organization," writes Wheatley. So having a fractal organization is good. We think.

G IS FOR GEESE

Forget the eagle. Yes, Donald H. Weiss knows that entrepreneurs like to imagine themselves as spiritual kin to the Great Bald: independent, fierce, soaring. But greatness "doesn't come to people perched in an aerie high above the world they seek to conquer," argues Weiss in *Secrets of the Wild Goose: The Self-Management Way to Increase Your Personal Power and Inspire Productive Teamwork.* Rather, Weiss is smitten with the collegial Canadian wild goose who "flies alone in full command of its own wing power ... individually contributing to the flock's progress, while relying on the other geese to do their share." Geese are like successful business leaders in that they manage resources well, effectively motivate their troops, and apparently practice a primitive form of succession planning. Sadly, geese score lower on planning and "visioning." And the book makes no allusion to their core competency, which blankets lawns and golf courses everywhere.

H IS FOR HOLLYWOOD

Hoo-ray for: an information-intensive industry whose evolution into a project-based structure presaged the emergence of our technology-reliant networked economy. *Dah dah dah dah dah dah dah...Hollywood!* Tinseltown, historically ruled by all-powerful studios, has morphed into an amalgam of "loose, temporary project groups that draw from a central talent pool," explain Mark London Williams and Steve Barth in *Knowledge Management* magazine. That model—in which intellectual capital (the acting talent of **Ben Affleck**, say) bounces from knowledge-based project to knowledge-based project (*Pearl Harbor* to *Jay and Silent Bob Strike Back*)—is de rigueur in companies that rely on outsourcing and independent contractors. "Hollywood's network economy isn't unique," explain Joel Kotkin and David Friedman in a 1995 article for *Inc.* "Eventually every knowledge-intensive industry will end up in the same flattened, atomized state." As one executive whose function was outsourced put it, "It's only the companies that got small."

I IS FOR IMPROVISATIONAL THEATER

All Sun Microsystems is a stage, and all its entrepreneurial leaders and flexible product groups merely players. So suggests Rosabeth Moss Kanter in *Evolve! Succeeding in the Digital Culture of Tomorrow.* "The drama of management was once like traditional theater," writes Kanter, who blasts both for their reluctance to innovate. On the other hand, the companies best positioned to make hay of the Web operate like "improvisational theater," the author notes. "A general theme is identified to get the actors started. Then the actors try out different moves, develop the story as they interact with the audience, and create a better experience with each round." **Too bad so many audience members shouted suggestions like "online advertising" and "premium-tier services."**

J IS FOR JAZZ

In John Kao's *Jamming: The Art and Discipline of Business Creativity*, **Charlie Parker** is the essence of a talented innovator, and bebop is the killer app. Jam sessions are the perfect metaphor for creativity management, Kao believes, because in "today's global marketplace—turbulent, 'spacey,' and endlessly demanding of the new, the experimental, the faster, the better, and the cheaper—there's no time for business managers to look for solutions in the archives of corporate sheet music." OK, organizations do need some sheet music—in the form of budgets, agendas, and the like—but they also need the freedom to improvise, to innovate, to feed and channel inspiration. Jazz artists walk the line in music that managers walk in business: "to locate the ever-mobile sweet spot somewhere between systems and analysis on the one hand and the free-flowing creativity of the individual on the other," writes Kao. Take five.

K IS FOR KIDDIE STORIES

In his classic book, *The Uses of Enchantment*, Bruno Bettelheim revealed the psychological and existential truths that animate classic fairy tales. But a mine of management principles also lies beneath all those happily-ever-afters. In *Goldilocks on Management: 27 Revisionist Fairy Tales for Serious Managers*, Gloria Gilbert Mayer and Thomas Mayer translate what are essentially Aesopian morals into basic business sense. So, for example, ***Little Red Riding Hood* demonstrates that competitors will take advantage of inexperience.** *The Pied Piper* teaches us that consultants should be carefully managed. *The Bremen Town Musicians* is about the importance of functional teams. And *The Emperor's New Clothes* proves that the only reliable sources of accurate information are individuals without a vested interest. Like, say, the authors of business books.

L IS FOR LEAR

King Lear may be the definitive work on succession management. But it is also about the failure of authority and the ability of omnipotent executives to destroy organizations with one poor decision. "One of Shakespeare's clearest lessons is that when this much power is placed in one person, there is a great chance that the power will be used in a capricious or whimsical way," writes Paul Corrigan in *Shakespeare on Management: Leadership Lessons for Today's Managers.* And though today's organizations are less feudal than the England of Shakespeare's plays, Corrigan sees no shortage of modern Lears. One sign of progress: When contemporary business leaders blow it, their followers end up without jobs. When Shakespeare's leaders blew it, their followers ended up without heads.

M IS FOR MARTIAL ARTS

From the jujitsu-schooled warriors of feudal Japan to cinema's crouching tigers, practitioners of martial arts are celebrated for their agility, speed, and ability to use an opponent's power against him or her. For business leaders, what's not to like? Judo strategy is particularly important for small companies, explain David Yoffie and Mary Kwak in *Judo Strategy: Turning Your Competitors' Strengths to Your Advantage,* because "it values skill over size and strength." The business world is awash in successful *judokas:* for example, Charles Schwab turned Fidelity's fee-collection strength against the giant by eliminating many of Schwab's own charges. Then there's Netscape, which initially outfoxed Microsoft in the browser wars by championing cross-platform technology. Of course, the outcome of that battle was predictable to anyone who's seen *Raiders of the Lost Ark.* All the fancy fighting in the world won't help you if the other guy has a gun.

N IS FOR NEWTONIAN PHYSICS

The influence of **Sir Isaac Newton** has been pervasive in business—and not just in the years when Apple's sales were falling. Newton's rationalist view of the universe influenced everything from the mechanical models that underlie organizations to modern accounting systems. But the juiciest management meat is in the laws of motion and gravitation, says Richard Koch, author of *The Natural Laws of Business: How to Harness the Power of Evolution, Physics, and Economics to Achieve Business Success.* For example, entrepreneurs guided by the principle of action and reaction will stake out not the hot market of the moment but rather the hot market destined to emerge in opposition to it. The business equivalent of gravity is competition. And intense competition imitates the forces that create black holes. But black holes are an Einstein thing. And we already have an entry for "E."

O IS FOR ORGANIZED CRIME

Wise guy is an imperfect synonym for *guru.* So Bob Andelman has an excuse to seek management lessons in the wiretapped conversations and court testimony of mobsters. (See *Context* magazine, February/March 2001.) Take this bit of advice from Boston capo Ilario Zannino: **"If you're clipping people ... make sure you clip the people around him first. Get them together, 'cause everybody's got a friend. He could be the dirtiest [bleep] in the world, but someone likes this guy, that's the guy that sneaks you."** Andelman makes the management connection by telling leaders to use a "killer app" to "knock off an entire class of competitors"—much the way that Home Depot sent hundreds of hardware stores to sleep with the fishes. The entrepreneur's viewpoint comes from *The Sopranos'* ***Paulie Walnuts: "How did we miss out on this? Espresso, cappuccino, we [bleeping] invented this!"***

P IS FOR PHILOSOPHY

Who'd a thunk that Tom Chappell, founder of Tom's of Maine, used the works of theologian Martin Buber to get his toothpaste company back on track? Or that pre-Socratic philosopher Heraclitus may have introduced change management? Philosophy ***is*** relevant to business, and not just the Hobbesian stuff that floats the boats of masters-of-the-universe types. In his book *If Aristotle Ran General Motors: The New Soul of Business,* Tom Morris asserts that certain elemental truths "undergird any sort of human excellence or flourishing." The goal is to reinvent corporations along the principles of truth, beauty, goodness, and unity. And what would **Aristotle** do at General Motors? He'd make sure all the employees find their work personally fulfilling. That is, if his busy lecture-circuit schedule let him.

Q IS FOR QUANTUM MECHANICS

The Newtonian world is rational, predictable, ruled by numbers. The quantum world—governed by the motion of subatomic particles—is uncertain, unpredictable, prone to paradox. Which better describes *your* business? Probably the latter, says Ralph H. Kilmann, author of *Quantum Organizations: A New Paradigm for Achieving Organizational Success and Personal Meaning.* Kilmann prefers the quantum model because companies are made up of human beings (which he calls "self-motion monads") with minds of their own. Managers cannot predict human behavior in the same way they can predict, say, what will happen to a billiard ball when you hit it from a certain angle. Consequently, Kilmann argues, they should design strategies, processes, and reward systems with particulate care. (It is tempting to suggest that the quantum view is most appropriate for small companies because they are somewhat closer in size than large organizations to the atom. Tempting but silly.)

R IS FOR RELIGION

In this religious country, who better to dispense business wisdom than the results-oriented leaders of the Bible? Laurie Beth Jones has turned *Jesus, CEO: Using Ancient Wisdom for Visionary Leadership* into a mini consulting-and-publishing empire based on her subject's motivational and managerial strengths. But Jesus has some Old Testament competition, as evidenced by *Moses on Management: 50 Leadership Lessons From the Greatest Manager of All Time.* The authors of *The Wisdom of Solomon at Work: Ancient Virtues for Living and Leading Today* urge managers to also consider Ruth, Job, David, and especially Solomon, who may be the most relevant for entrepreneurs. "The great buildings of Solomon's reign serve as a monument to traditional ideas about prosperity and material wealth," the authors write. "However, if we reflect more deeply, we may face the question, 'for whom do you build up and why?'"

S IS FOR STAR TREK

Great leadership is about the future, not the past. So **why bother with long-dead heroes when you can study someone who won't be born for 200 years? Jean-Luc Picard**, captain of the starship *Enterprise*, epitomizes strong, caring leadership, say Wess Roberts and Bill Ross in *Make It So: Leadership Lessons From Star Trek: The Next Generation.* Readers will marvel at Picard's focus during run-ins with the Borg and at his deft management of challenging employees, including Data, a humanoid android, and Worf, a Klingon. (This is the definitive book about managing diversity.) Jean-Luc is also a font of inspiration: "We must recognize that in the most dire circumstances, an officer must retain a sense of hope—trusting in his own ability and in the competence of others to stand firm against what would otherwise be an overpowering tide of helplessness and gloom." Go boldly, Captain Picard. Go boldly.

T IS FOR TYRANNOSAURUS REX

Jurassic Park was released in 1993, so the 1994 publication of William Lareau's *Dancing With the Dinosaur: Learning to Live in the Corporate Jungle* was probably unavoidable. Lareau's focus on the jungle primeval, a conceit achieved chiefly by slapping suffixes such as "-asaurus" or "-adon" onto office stereotypes, is as elegant as it is effective (which is to say, not at all). A metaphor-translation chart explains that a "hotshotadon" is a hotshot and an "executiv-adon bloatasaurus" is an executive. Little can be learned by imagining employees pursued by a Faceupadon Tofailureasaurus, however, since Lareau chose his metaphor for its ability to cause "cognitive dissonance" rather than because corporate types are more like dinosaurs than, say, circus performers or roving packs of baboons. Honest to Godasaurus.

U IS FOR U.S. MARINES

Business loves boot camps. But bull-dogged drill sergeants and shorn recruits are not all that the U.S. Marines offer companies. "Everything about the marines—their culture, their organizational structure, their management style, their logistics, their decision-making process—is geared toward high-speed, high-complexity environments," writes David H. Freedman in *Corps Business: The 30 Management Principles of the U.S. Marines.* Marines make decisions quickly but never irresponsibly. Their range of capabilities allows them to handle any assignment. Most important, they get the job done even when the mission is poorly defined and the environment chaotic—status quo for business today. The marine ethos is embodied by such business leaders as Robert Lutz, now of General Motors, and Fred Smith of FedEx. Of course, other branches of the armed forces have also spawned corporate leaders. But as Freedman reminds us, Ross Perot—who built rigid, conservative EDS—was a *navy* man.

V IS FOR VOODOO

Back when Internet companies were pulling sky-high valuations out of zero-profit hats, the new economy seemed magical. Even now that many of those businesses have vanished back up their conjurers' sleeves, we yearn for mystery, insist René Carayol and David Firth, authors of *Corporate Voodoo: Principles for Business Mavericks and Magicians.* Specifically, say the authors, we need voodoo. Originally, voodoo flourished among slaves, who drew strength in captivity from their Afro-Caribbean religion. The book's whimsy is that **voodoo, in its corporate incarnation, "releases people from the slavery of old ways of being, thinking about and leading organizations"** and "connects people with what is important, meaningful and instinctual." In practice, voodoo seems interchangeable with *new economy*. Voodoo's followers may march to the beat of a different tribal drummer, but we've heard the song before.

W IS FOR *WIZARD OF OZ*

Business gurus promise magical transformation. But most are just ordinary folks pulling strings behind a curtain. In *The Oz Principle: Getting Results Through Individual and Organizational Accountability,* Roger Connors, Tom Smith, and Craig Hickman disdain business thinkers who—like Oz—promise a "solution" that doesn't exist. Fortunately, managers and employees—much like a certain fictional quartet—hold within themselves the power to achieve the desired results. First, though, they need the courage to see reality, the heart to "own" their circumstances, and the brain—er, *wisdom*—to overcome obstacles. They find those things on the road—picture one with an ocher cast—of change. "People relate to the theme of a journey from ignorance to knowledge, from fear to courage, from insensitivity to caring, from paralysis to powerfulness, from victimization to accountability," the book points out. That goes for Toto, too.

X IS FOR X-PRESIDENTS

The great thing about U.S. presidents is that, as chief executives of the most complex organization on earth, their wisdom is invaluable to business leaders. The great thing about *dead* ex-presidents is that you don't have to shell out $10 million to publish that wisdom. Past prezes with business tomes include **Theodore Roosevelt** (youthful, dynamic, progressive) and Ulysses S. Grant (hard-drinking, indecisive, and inconsistent—but his "lessons" come chiefly from the battlefield, so it's OK). James M. Strock's *Theodore Roosevelt on Leadership* renders its subject as an aggressive, risk-taking master of PowerPoint-friendly advice. John Barnes's *Ulysses S. Grant on Leadership: Executive Lessons From the Front Lines* praises the general as an innovator, communicator, and delegator. Of course, Grant's chief claim to sage status is that he won a war. But winning isn't everything: Robert E. Lee has at least two leadership books to his name.

Y IS FOR YACHT RACING

Is there anything so heartwarming as a business mogul and his sailboat? Ted Turner and *Courageous.* Larry Ellison and *Sayonara.* Roy Disney and *Pyewacket.* And wouldn't you know it, while those titans of industry are battling churning seas and screaming winds, they are also exercising valuable management insight, according to Peter Isler and Peter Economy, authors of *At the Helm: Business Lessons for Navigating Rough Waters.* The book compares the early days of an America's Cup campaign to an entrepreneurial start-up, but bootstrappers, beware: it costs, on average, $25 million to compete in sailing's most prestigious event. In addition, "it's often said that the perfect racing sailboat is one that has pushed the limits of what is humanly and technologically possible so far that it falls apart and sinks just after it wins the regatta," write the authors. So much for built to last.

Z IS FOR ZEUS

Just what company leaders need: another reason to think of themselves as gods. But that's what Charles Handy gives them in *Gods of Management: The Changing Work of Organizations.* The Greek gods personify traits that characterize people and, Handy argues, corporate cultures. **Do you run a small entrepreneurial company where decisions are quickly made and intuitively based on powerful empathy? Then yours is a Zeus culture**, making you the top dog among top gods. The new economy, clearly, was a hotbed of Zeusian enterprises, most of which fell from Olympus. In the Internet age, even immortality won't save you from early death.

Leigh Buchanan is a senior editor at *Inc.*

Why companies fail

CEOs offer every excuse but the right one: their own errors. Here are ten mistakes to avoid.

By Ram Charan and Jerry Useem

HOW MANY MORE MUST FALL? EACH MONTH SEEMS TO BRING the sound of another giant crashing to earth. Enron. WorldCom. Global Crossing. Kmart. Polaroid. Arthur Andersen. Xerox. Qwest. They fall singly. They fall in groups. They fall with the heavy thud of employees laid off, families hurt, shareholders furious. How many? Too many; 257 public companies with $258 billion in assets declared bankruptcy last year, shattering the previous year's record of 176 companies and $95 billion. This year is on pace, with 67 companies going bust during the first quarter. And not just any companies. Big, important, FORTUNE 500 companies that aren't supposed to collapse. If things keep going like this, we may have trouble filling next year's list.

Why do companies fail? Their CEOs offer every excuse in the book: a bad economy, market turbulence, a weak yen, hundred-year floods, perfect storms, competitive subterfuge—forces, that is, very much outside their control. In a few cases, such as the airlines' post–Sept. 11 problems, the excuses even ring true. But a close study of corporate failure suggests that, acts of God aside, most companies founder for one simple reason: managerial error.

We'll get to the errors in a moment. But first let's acknowledge that, yes, failures usually involve factors unique to a company's own industry or culture. As Tolstoy said of families, all happy companies are alike; every unhappy company is unhappy in its own way. Companies even collapse in their own way. Some go out in blinding supernovas (Enron). Others linger like white dwarfs (AT&T). Still others fizzle out over decades (Polaroid). Failure is part of the natural cycle of business. Companies are born, companies die, capitalism moves forward. Creative destruction, they call it.

It was roughly this sentiment that Treasury Secretary Paul O'Neill was trying to convey when he said that Enron's failure was "part of the genius of capitalism." But aside from sounding insensitive, O'Neill got one thing wrong. Capitalism's true genius is to weed out companies that no longer serve a useful purpose. The dot-coms, for instance, were experiments in whether certain businesses were even viable. We found out: They weren't. Yet many recent debacles were of companies that could have lived long, productive lives with more enlightened management—in other words, good companies struck down for bad reasons. By these lights, Arthur Andersen's fall is no more part of the "genius of capitalism" than the terrorism on Sept. 11 was part of the "genius of evolution."

By "failure," we don't necessarily mean bankruptcy. A dramatic fall from grace qualifies too. In the most recent bear market, for instance, 26 of America's 100 largest companies lost at least two-thirds of their market value, including such blue chips as Hewlett-Packard, Charles Schwab, Cisco, AT&T, AOL Time Warner, and Gap. In the 1990 bear market, by contrast, none did, according to money management firm Aronson & Partners.

The sheer speed of these falls has been unnerving. Companies that were healthy just moments ago, it seems, are suddenly at death's door. But this impression may be misleading. Consider, for instance, a certain Houston institution we've heard so much about. There was no one moment when its managers sat down and conspired to commit wrongdoing. Rather, the disaster occurred because of what one analyst calls "an incremental descent into poor judgment." A "success-oriented" culture, mind-numbing complexity, and unrealistic performance goals all mixed until the violation of standards *became* the standard. Nothing looked amiss from the outside until, boom, it was all over.

It sounds a lot like Enron, but the description actually refers to NASA in 1986, the year of the space shuttle *Challenger* explosion. We pull this switch not to conflate the two episodes—one, after all, involved the death of seven astronauts—but to make a point about failures: Even the most dramatic tend to be years in the making. At NASA, engineers noticed damage to the crucial O-rings on previous shuttle flights yet repeatedly convinced themselves the damage was acceptable. Companies fail the way Ernest Hemingway wrote about going broke in *The Sun Also Rises*: gradually, and then suddenly. (For some solutions, see box "Three Quick Fixes.")

What undoes them is the familiar stuff of human folly: denial, hubris, ego, wishful thinking, poor communication, lax oversight, greed, deceit, and other *Behind the Music* plot conventions. It all adds up to a failure to execute. This is not an exhaustive list of corporate sins. But chances are your company is committing one of them right now.

Softened by success

"Those whom the gods would destroy," Euripides wrote nearly 2,500 years ago, "they first make mad." In the modern update, the gods send their victims 40 years of success. Actually, it's a proven fact: A number of studies show that people are less likely to make optimal decisions after prolonged periods of success. NASA, Enron, Lucent, WorldCom—all had reached the mountaintop before they ran into trouble. Someone should have told them that most mountaineering accidents happen on the way down.

Consider the case of Cisco Systems. While by no means a failure, Cisco suffered a remarkable comedown in the spring of 2001—remarkable not only for its swiftness (its shares lost 88% of their value in one year) but also because Cisco, more than any other company, was supposed to be able to see into the future. The basis of this belief was a much vaunted IT system that enabled Cisco managers to track supply and demand in "real time," allowing them to make pinpoint forecasts. The technology, by all accounts, worked great. The forecasts, however, did not. Cisco's managers, it turned out, never bothered to model what would happen if a key assumption—growth—disappeared from the equation. After all, the company had recorded more than 40 straight quarters of growth; why wouldn't the future bring more of the same?

The rosy assumptions, moreover, persisted even when evidence to the contrary started piling up. Customers began going bankrupt. Suppliers warned of a coming dropoff in demand. Competitors stumbled. Even Wall Street wondered if the Internet equipment market was falling apart. "I have never been more optimistic about the future of our industry as a whole or of Cisco," CEO John Chambers declared in December 2000, still projecting 50% annual growth.

What was Chambers thinking? In *The Challenger Launch Decision*, her definitive book on the disaster, Boston College sociologist Diane Vaughan notes that people don't surrender their mental models easily. "They may puzzle over contradictory evidence," she writes, "but usually succeed in pushing it aside—until they come across a piece of evidence too fascinating to ignore, too clear to misperceive, too painful to deny, which makes vivid still other signals they do not want to see, forcing them to alter and surrender the world-view they have so meticulously constructed."

Even when a boss doesn't intend to quash dissent, subtle signals can broadcast the message that bad news is not welcome.

For the perpetually sunny Chambers, that "piece of evidence" did not come until April 2001, when cratering sales forced Cisco to write down $2.5 billion in excess inventory and lay off 8,500 employees. Chambers may have been operating in real time, but he wasn't operating in the real world.

See no evil

With $6.5 billion in cash and a strong competitive position, Cisco will live to fight another day. Polaroid may not be so lucky. Like its fellow old-economy stalwart Xerox, Polaroid was a once-highflying member of the Nifty Fifty group of growth stocks that lost their luster over the years. Eventually the question "What does Polaroid make?" became a latter-day ver-

Ten big mistakes

They are the standard stuff of corporate folly.
Chances are, your company has made at least one.

	Slave to Wall Street	See no evil	Overdosing on risk	Dysfunctional board	Softened by success	Strategy du jour	Acquisition lust	Fearing the boss	Dangerous culture	Death spiral
◆ Enron	●	●	●	●	●			●	●	●
Arthur Andersen		●	●						●	●
◆ Global Crossing	●	●	●	●						
Lucent	●		●	●	●					
◆ Warnaco	●	●		●				●		
◆ Kmart		●		●		●				
Providian	●		●		●					
◆ Sunbeam	●	●						●		
Tyco	●					●	●			
WorldCom			●		●		●			
Xerox	●	●		●						
AT&T						●	●			
◆ Polaroid		●			●					
Qwest	●		●							

◆ Filed for bankruptcy

FORTUNE TABLE

sion of "Who's buried in Grant's tomb?" Polaroid, that is, made Polaroid cameras—period.

Time had passed the company by, you might say. Not exactly. Think about another company that once seemed doomed to fail: Intel. Back in 1985, competition from Japan was turning Intel's memory chips into cheap commodities, and observers were all but writing the company's obituary. Instead of going the way of Polaroid, though, Intel decided to exit the memory business entirely and become a maker of microprocessors. The key insight occurred when Intel founders Andy Grove and Gordon Moore sat down and asked themselves some tough questions. "If we got kicked out and the board brought in a new CEO," Grove asked Moore, "what do you think he would do?" Get out of memory chips was the answer. From there, they said later, it was just a matter of doing what needed to be done.

Polaroid and Xerox, by contrast, were slow to confront the changing world around them. Executives at both companies repeatedly blamed poor results on short-term factors—currency fluctuations, trouble in Latin America—rather than the real cause: a bad business model. By the time Xerox President (and now CEO) Anne Mulcahy came out and spoke the truth—the company had "an unsustainable business model," she told analysts in 2000—Xerox was flirting with bankruptcy.

Jim Collins, author of the influential management books *Built to Last* and *Good to Great*, has spent years studying what separates great companies from mediocre ones. "The key sign—the litmus test—is whether you begin to explain away the brutal facts rather than to confront the brutal facts head-on," he says. "That's sort of the pivot point." By forcing themselves to think like outsiders, Grove and Moore recognized the brutal facts before it was too late. Polaroid and Xerox didn't.

Fearing the boss more than the competition

Sometimes CEOs don't get the information they need to make informed decisions. The main reason, says Daniel Goleman, a psychologist and author of the book *Primal Leadership*, is that subordinates are afraid to tell them the truth. Even when a boss doesn't intend to quash dissent, subtle signals—a sour expression, a curt response—can broadcast the message that bad news isn't welcome. That's why, according to a study by Goleman and two associates, higher-ranking executives are less likely to have an accurate assessment of their own performance.

Three quick fixes

THE RECENT CORPORATE COLLAPSES HAVE INvolved many breakdowns: in ethics, in trust, in common sense, to name a few. But perhaps the most troubling breakdown is in corporate oversight. Directors, senior executives, and Wall Street analysts all failed miserably by missing—or concealing—danger signals until it was too late. Regulators will no doubt have plenty to say on the issue, but the most zealous reformers should be the companies themselves. They can begin with three changes that, taken together, will provide a better early-warning system against failure:

1 **Reengineer the board**. Remember reengineering? It was applied to every corner of the corporation at one point or another—except the board. That needs to change. Incompetence is not the problem. Boards can be full of very capable people yet be totally ineffective as a group. The problem is that directors are too nice. Boards seldom convene without the CEO, and raising troubling questions can simply seem rude—which is often the way the CEO wants it. Directors need a forum where they can talk frankly *without* the CEO. Ten minutes at the end of each meeting would be a good start. Better yet, an annual retreat where the board can assess its own performance as well as the CEO's. Collectively, the directors are supposed to serve as a company's peripheral vision. Often at least one director suspects trouble before it becomes a crisis. The trick is getting him or her to say it out loud.

Boards should also appoint the chairperson of the governance committee as lead director. This especially makes sense when the CEO and chairman are the same person, as is the case with most U.S. companies. The lead director would be from the outside, reappointed every two years or so, and authorized to convene a meeting anytime, any place, with or without management.

2 **Turn employees into corporate governors**. As the Enron debacle has proven, regular employees—not executives, not directors, not shareholders—have the most to lose when a company fails. With their jobs, pensions, and stock-option wealth on the line, it follows that they have a greater incentive than anyone to act as company watchdogs. Yet few companies tap this built-in alarm system. Too often, front-line employees smell something rotten but do not, or cannot, convey the message upward. That's why companies need a mechanism to make it happen.

Whistle-blowing does not count as a mechanism. Whistle-blowing is a last resort—one that's frequently harmful to the whistle blower's health. What's really needed is a survey, carefully designed and administered by an outside agency, that regularly solicits employee feedback on sensitive questions. Do people trust management? Is there any reason to doubt the reported revenue numbers? Are the company's values out of whack? Think of it as a human audit. Send the results directly to the board. And give employees a chance to inspect company finances directly—say, by holding Q&A sessions with the CFO. Corporate governance should ideally include all a company's stakeholders, and employees hold the biggest stake of all.

3 **Banish Ebitda**. Companies hit the skids for all sorts of reasons, but it's one thing that ultimately kills them: They run out of cash. Yet most managers are too preoccupied with measures like Ebitda (earnings before interest, taxes, debt, and amortization) and return on assets to give cash much notice. Boards don't ask for it. Analysts don't analyze it. Corporate financial statements do typically include a statement of cash flow, but it's a crude snapshot that excludes off-balance-sheet items and doesn't show where the cash comes from. The solution is a detailed, easily readable cash-flow report. Give it to the board. Give it to employees. Break out cash flow by division, letting people track the company's blood flow themselves. Warren Buffett pays close attention to cash flow because, among other reasons, he knows cash is hard to fudge. That's why creative accountants hate it—and why you should learn to love it.

No system survives for long without feedback and controls. So corporate America has a choice: It can implement these controls itself. Or it can wait for regulators and politicians to impose them. Which sounds better to you?

Fear can have its uses, of course; Andy Grove has long espoused the value of competitive paranoia. But in unhealthy situations, employees come to worry more about internal factors—what the boss might say, what management might do—than about threats from the outside world. Certainly this was the case at Enron, where even alarm-ringer Sherron Watkins chose to express her concerns anonymously rather than hazard one of CEO Jeff Skilling's famous tongue-lashings. And she was one of the brave ones.

The same problem hampered Samsung Chairman Lee Kun Hee in 1997 when he decided to take Samsung into the auto business. Knowing the car industry was a crowded field plagued by overcapacity, many of Samsung's top managers silently opposed the $13 billion investment. But Lee was a forceful chairman and a car buff to boot. So when Samsung Motors folded just a year into production, forcing Lee to spend $2 billion of his own money to placate creditors, he expressed surprise: How come nobody had spoken up about their reservations?

During World War II, Churchill set up an office outside the chain of command whose main job was to tell him the unvarnished truth.

During World War II, Winston Churchill worried that his own larger-than-life personality would deter subordinates from bringing him bad news. So he set up a unit outside his generals' chain of command, the Statistical Office, whose primary job was to feed him the starkest, most unvarnished facts. In a similar vein, Richard Schroth and Larry Elliott, authors of the forthcoming book *How Companies Lie*, suggest designated "counterpointers," whose function is to ask the rudest questions possible. Such mechanisms take information and turn it into information that can't be ignored.

Overdosing on risk

Some companies simply live too close to the edge. Global Crossing, Qwest, 360networks—these telecom flameouts chose paths that were not just risky but wildly imprudent. Their key mistake: loading up on two kinds of risk at once.

The first might be called "execution risk." In their race to band the earth in optical fiber, the telco upstarts ignored some key questions: Namely, would anyone need all of this fiber? Weren't there too many companies doing the same thing? Wouldn't, uh, most of them fail? "People seemed to say, 'Maybe—but it's not going to be us,'" says Darrell Rigby, a Bain & Co. consultant who studies managing during times of turbulence. "Everyone thought they were immune."

Ebbers liked to eat. He ate MCI. He ate MFS. Wall Street helped him wash it all down with cheap capital and a soaring stock.

On top of execution risk was another kind, which we'll call liquidity risk. Global Crossing—run by Gary Winnick, formerly of the junk-bond house Drexel Burnham Lambert—loaded up on $12 billion of high-yield debt. This essentially limited Winnick to a cannonball strategy: one shot, and if you miss, it's bankruptcy.

Bankruptcy it was. Given the utter violence of the telecom shakeout, you might say it was inevitable. But other telcos did manage to escape the carnage. BellSouth, dismissed as hopelessly conservative during the Wild West years, emerged with a pristine balance sheet and a strong competitive position. Its gentlemanly CEO, Duane Ackerman, was guided by a radical idea: "being good stewards of our shareholders' money." What a concept.

Acquisition lust

WorldCom founder Bernard Ebbers liked to eat. He ate MCI. He ate MFS and its UUNet subsidiary. He tried to eat Sprint. Wall Street helped him wash it all down with cheap capital and a buoyant stock price. Pretty soon WorldCom was tipping the scales at $39 billion in revenues. But there was a problem: Ebbers didn't know how to digest the things he ate. A born dealmaker, he seemed to care more about snaring new acquisitions than about making the existing ones—all 75 of them—work together. At least Ebbers was up front about it: "Our goal is not to capture market share or be global," he told a reporter in 1997. "Our goal is to be the No. 1 stock on Wall Street."

The results were frequently chaotic. For a time, sales reps from UUNet competed head-to-head with WorldCom sales teams for corporate telecom contracts. Smaller customers complained they had to call three different customer-service reps for their Internet, long-distance, and local-phone inquiries. If there is such a thing as negative synergy, WorldCom may have discovered it.

Not that acquisitions are always so bad. General Electric combines its acquisitive nature with an impressive ability to break down acquisitions and integrate them into existing operations. But too often CEOs succumb to an undisciplined lust for growth, accumulating assets for the sake of accumulating assets. Why? It's fun. There are lots of press conferences. It's what powerful CEOs do. And like Ebbers, whose WorldCom stock has lost 98% of its value, few wonder if their eyes might be bigger than their stomachs.

Listening to Wall Street more than to employees

No one likes a good growth story better than Wall Street. And in the late 1990s, no one was telling a better one than Lucent CEO Rich McGinn. He knew how to give Wall Street what it wanted—explosive top-line growth—and in return, Wall Street turned McGinn and his team into rock stars. For a bunch of former Bellheads, it was intoxicating stuff.

Says an ex-Xerox executive: "I could not present to the board unless things were perfect. Everything had to be prettied up."

But while McGinn was busy performing for the Street, there were at least two groups he wasn't listening to. The first was Lucent's scientists, who feared the company was missing out on a new optical technology, OC-192, that could transmit voice and data faster. They pleaded in vain for its development, then watched as rival Nortel rolled out OC-192 gear to thunderous success. At the same time McGinn was neglecting Lucent's salespeople, who might have told him that his growth targets were becoming increasingly unrealistic. To meet them, employees were pulling forward sales from future quarters by offering steep discounts and wildly generous financing arrangements, largely to dot-coms. "As we got further and further behind," Chairman Henry Schacht later explained, "we did more and more discounting."

It could only last so long. After Lucent stock had lost more than 80% of its value and he had replaced McGinn as CEO, Schacht sat down with FORTUNE to ponder some hard-earned lessons. "Stock price is a byproduct; stock price isn't a driver," he said. "And every time I've seen any of us lose sight of that, it has always been a painful experience." Top management needs to understand what the folks on Wall Street want—but not necessarily give it to them.

Strategy du jour

When companies run into trouble, the desire for a quick fix can become overwhelming. The frequent result is a dynamic that Collins describes in *Good to Great*: "A&P vacillated, shifting from one strategy to another, always looking for a single stroke to quickly solve its problems. [It] held pep rallies, launched programs, grabbed fads, fired CEOs, hired CEOs and fired them yet again." Lurching from one silver bullet solution to another, the company never gained any traction.

Collins calls it the "doom loop," and it's a killer. Kmart is another victim. In the 1980s and early '90s, Kmart was all about diversification, shifting away from discounting to acquire stakes in chains like Sports Authority, OfficeMax, and Borders bookstores. But in the 1990s a new management team divested those stores and decided to revamp Kmart's supply chain by investing heavily in IT. That lasted for a while, until a new CEO, Chuck Conaway, decided that, actually, Kmart would try to beat Wal-Mart at its own game. This unleashed a disastrous price war that in the end proved to be one mistake too many. "When you look at companies that get themselves into trouble," says Collins, "they're often taking steps of great, lurching bravado rather than quiet, deliberate understanding." Did somebody say AT&T?

A dangerous corporate culture

Arthur Andersen, Enron, and Salomon Brothers were all brought down, or nearly so, by the rogue actions of a tiny few. But the bad apples in these companies grew and flourished in the same kind of environment: a rotten corporate culture. It's impossible to monitor the actions of every employee, no matter how many accounting and compliance controls you put in place. But either implicitly or explicitly, a company's cultural code is supposed to equip front-line employees to make the right decisions without supervision. At Salomon Brothers the culture did just the opposite. The transgressor there was Paul Mozer, a trader who in February of 1991 improperly overbid in auctions of U.S. Treasury bonds. While it was another improper bid on May 22 that finally did him in, the critical event occurred in April, when Salomon Chairman John Gutfreund learned of the February overbid by Mozer and failed to discipline him. Mozer evidently took Gutfreund's lack of action as a green light.

Salomon's culture of swashbuckling bravado encouraged risk taking without accountability. Enron's culture encouraged profit taking without disclosure. Andersen's culture engendered conflicts of interest without safeguards. Rotten cultures produce rotten deeds.

The new-economy death spiral

Alan Greenspan has his own theory on failure. Testifying about Enron in February, he noted, "a firm is inherently fragile if its value-added emanates more from conceptual as distinct from physical assets.... Trust and reputation can vanish overnight. A factory cannot." The speed of some recent crackups would seem to confirm his thesis. The first domino falls when questions are raised, sometimes anonymously. Wrongdoing is suspected. Customers delay new orders. Rating agencies lower their debt ratings. Employees head for the exits. More customers defect. And *voilà*, you have what former Enron CEO Jeff Skilling has called "a classic run on the bank."

Is it possible to halt one? Yes, but only if you stop the spiral from building up speed. Salomon broke the cycle by hiring Warren Buffett as interim CEO —essentially a giant credibility infusion. By waiting several months to step down, on the other hand, Arthur Anderson CEO Joseph Berardino lost whatever chance he had to avoid disaster. Once started, the spiral can bring a company whose main assets are people and ideas to its knees with breathtaking finality.

A dysfunctional board

What was Enron's board thinking? Of all the infamous moments in the company's demise, perhaps the least explicable was the board's decision to waive Enron's code of ethics to accommodate CFO Andrew Fastow's partnerships. "A red flag the size of Alaska," says Nell Minow, founder of the board watchdog group Corporate Library. Even Enron directors belatedly agreed with this assessment. "After having authorized a conflict of interest creating as much risk as this one," the board's special investigation committee wrote in a February report, "the board had an obligation to give careful attention to the transactions that followed. It failed to do this... In short, no one was minding the store."

"The great companies don't make excuses," said Treasury Secretary Paul O'Neill recently. "They do well anyway."

Despite a decade's worth of shareholder activism, Enron's board was not an anomaly. The sorry fact is that most corporate boards remain hopelessly beholden to management. "I was never allowed to present to the board unless things were perfect," says a former senior executive at Xerox, whose board includes Vernon Jordan and former Senator George Mitchell. "You could only go in with good news. Everything was prettied up." At many boards, the CEO oversees meetings, hand-picks directors, and spoon-feeds them information. "Directors know relatively little apart from what management tells them," says John Smale, a former CEO of Procter & Gamble and onetime chairman of General Motors.

Unless, that is, the board demands more. "The CEO is always going to want to turn the board meeting into a pep rally," says Minow. "You've got to say to him 'Look, I'm a busy person. I don't have time for the good news. What I need for you to tell me is the bad news.' It's like what Robert Duvall says in *The Godfather*: 'I have to go to the airport. The Godfather is a man who likes to hear bad news immediately.' That should be emblazoned on every corporate governance policy sheet."

Paul O'Neill may have been wrong about his assessment of Enron, but he was right about something else. "The great companies don't make excuses," he said recently, "including excuses about how they didn't do well because the economy was against them or prices were not good. They do well anyway." It's true. And it's something to think about the next time you hear a CEO railing at the gods.

RAM CHARAN *advises* FORTUNE *500 CEOs and is co-author, with Larry Bossidy, of* Execution: The Discipline of Getting Things Done.

REPORTER ASSOCIATE *Ann Harrington*

AMERICA'S FUTURE

MANAGEMENT LESSONS FROM THE BUST

Surprisingly, industry stalwarts reacted nimbly to the slowdown. Here's what they can teach the fallen tech stars

By **Joseph Weber**

Only a year ago, Cisco Systems Inc. was widely hailed as the shining exemplar of the New Economy. Management gurus viewed Cisco as the prototype of the 21st century corporation, an organization where information technology linked suppliers and customers in ways that allowed the company to nimbly respond to every market nuance.

Cisco had flattened the corporate pyramid, outsourced capital-intensive manufacturing, and forged strategic alliances with suppliers that were supposed to eliminate inventory almost entirely. Sophisticated information systems gave its managers real-time data, allowing them to detect the slightest change in current market conditions and to forecast with precision. If anyone had the "vision thing" nailed for the new digital era, it was supposed to be Cisco CEO John T. Chambers.

Oops! The surprising abruptness and severity of Cisco's downturn—marked by a shocking $2.2 billion write-off of inventory in April—showed that it was just as vulnerable as any other company to an economic slowdown. And it wasn't just Cisco. Motorola, Lucent Technologies, and Oracle also failed to see the downturn until it had all but engulfed their operations. Indeed, some of the hardest hit have been companies that were supposed to show Corporate America the way into the new century. What happened?

Good eye
Eaton CFO Adrian Dillon saw a "short, sharp shock" in the economy in October, giving Eaton time to prepare

Blindsided by hubris, too much success, and an overreliance on their world-class computer systems, some of the most successful companies of the dot-com era discovered that even the best information is only as good as the minds interpreting it. The revolution in computer technology has put near-perfect financial information within the reach of almost every manager. Yet no amount of information can ever offset simple human judgment. When that judgment is clouded, as it was in some cases by the irrational exuberance of the high-tech bubble, it may not be possible to see what the numbers are telling you. "A bubble is like a gravitational field," says Adrian J. Slywotzky, a partner with Mercer Management Consulting. "It robs you of your ability to think clearly."

So perhaps it is not surprising that some industry stalwarts, from DuPont and Eaton Corp. to the Big Three carmakers, responded more quickly to the slowing economy. Months before Silicon Valley stars realized that they, too, could fall prey to the business cycle, these Old Economy players were downshifting to tough out a manufacturing recession that is still idling assembly lines all across Corporate America.

Their market-intelligence systems flashed warning signals that their executives—veterans of past downturns—were savvy enough to recognize. "In those kinds of organizations, memories are pretty long," says Harvard Business School professor David A. Garvin. "You have to have a jaundiced eye and say, 'Wait. This can't last forever.'"

Lessons From the Bust

Good Info Requires Good Judgment

1 Information systems can put the numbers in front of you in real time. But you need experienced managers with skepticism and judgment to figure out what it all means.

Stay Flexible

2 Using the Internet to forge closer links with suppliers and customers, outsourcing nonessential work, and contract manufacturing are ways to lower inventories and fixed overhead costs. Those management ideas are more important than ever in a downturn.

Know Your Customers' Customers

3 The further you are from the final customer, the harder it is to see a swing in the economic cycle. The trick is to monitor consumption by the end users and produce to their needs.

Look Beyond a Backlog in Orders

4 Basing a forecast just on order backlogs is a fool's game. In boom times, your customers may double- or triple-order to avoid shortages. You need to track your customers' revenues.

Planning Goes Only So Far

5 Predicting the future with precision is nearly impossible. Forecasts based on consumer confidence and economic output are important, but avoid tying yourself to one economic world view. Instead, consider a range of possibilities and prepare for all of them.

Don't Just Sell Them, Serve Them

6 Building a service business can bring long-term contracts that produce more predictable streams of revenue and income. Product service can be a life-saving fallback with times get tough.

CHEAP FINANCING. Many managers insist that the falloff in business was so sudden and so severe that no one could have foreseen the depth of the abyss. "We saw the same signs as everybody else, but we viewed it as an inflection point and an opportunity to gain market share," says Claudia Ceniceros, a Cisco spokesperson. "We were ultimately wrong about the severity of the downturn." Indeed the order flow did screech into reverse with astonishing speed. And it's always harder to gauge the market in young, fast-growing industries. Still, once you look beyond the order book, there were signs that in a less giddy period might have signalled trouble ahead.

Lessons from the fallout abound. In some cases, cheap financing distorted real demand, underscoring the need to look to the end users, particularly if a company is not directly selling to them. How much are they actually consuming of your product? And no company, no matter how high-flying, is divorced from the larger economy. If earnings are dropping elsewhere, falling demand is likely to follow. Above all, forecasting is hard. No one does it perfectly. So companies have to constantly plan for less likely scenarios. It's also important to remember that even highly accurate forecasts have their limitations. Knowing that your business is about to get slammed by a falling market doesn't shield you from the blow; it only helps you limit the damage.

Perhaps the biggest lesson is to look behind the numbers. Companies such as Cisco, Nortel Networks, and JDS Uniphase, which sell telecom equipment, clearly misread the market, in part because they weren't analyzing their customers' businesses. A good chunk of their sales came from alternative phone companies that had relied on venture capitalists and Wall Street for funding equipment purchases rather than using cash flow from their own operations. When that money abruptly dried up, the shortfall drove many of the new phone companies out of business.

Some of the artificial demand should have been even easier to spot. In the case of both Cisco and Nortel, significant funding came from the equipment makers themselves, skewing real demand. Both companies looked at their 40%-plus revenue gains, took a gander at their mountains of customer orders, and figured the good times would just keep on rolling.

Simply projecting the past gains forward cost the telecom equipment giants dearly. JDS Uniphase reported in July a $7.9 billion fourth-quarter loss and a $50.6 billion loss for its 2001 fiscal year, the largest in corporate history. A month earlier, Nortel announced one of the biggest quarterly losses ever—a $19.4 billion hit—and ratcheted up its planned layoffs to 30,000. Nortel Chief Executive John Roth warned that "the market is contracting at an alarming rate," and he cautioned that Internet traffic, still thought to be in its infancy, was even declining. While these Goliaths still refuse to fault their forecasting systems for missing the slide, some critics argue that they failed to do the most basic homework. The customer orders they relied on to measure demand, for instance, could have been checked to screen out the double- and triple-ordering that had become common because of past scarcities.

What's more, they should have taken careful measure of the health of their customers to see whether they really were in a position to buy. "People started to believe too much in technology vs. their common sense," says Wojtek Uzdelewicz of Bear Stearns & Co. "You can't look at what your customer is telling you, you have to look at what is going on with the customer's revenues."

Managers can't stop with their own customers, either. No company exists in a vacuum. Until early last year, it was all too easy to believe that New Economy outfits were different, somehow outside the normal forces of the economy. Managers who fell into that trap learned the hard way that ultimately the same forces that drive down demand for old-line companies curb the sales of everything from fiber-optic cable to PCs.

PANIC-ORDERING. DuPont—whose products are used in everything from medical equipment to clothing, carpeting, and paint—has been through countless economic swings. Managers there have learned to pay close attention to such macroeconomic factors as oil prices, currency fluctuations, inflation, and Federal Reserve policies. That's how DuPont was able to figure out as far back as July, 2000, that business was deteriorating. DuPont cut back early, keeping layoffs and write-offs to a minimum. The main warning signals then: high energy prices, lackluster apparel sales, and government-reported declines in new factory orders.

Even for the most experienced hands, forecasting demand is an inexact science. At Massachusetts Institute of Technology's Sloan School of Management, students and executives for years have played "the beer game," where they take the roles of brewer, distributor, wholesaler, and retailer and try to estimate demand across economic cycles. Nearly everybody gets it wrong—especially those who are farthest from the customer. The trick, says MIT Professor John D. Sterman, is to figure out how the ultimate consumers are behaving and produce to suit them, not the manufacturers, distributors, or retailers in-between. So-called panic-ordering and other distortions only confuse everyone. Says Sterman: "If you are in the pasta business, you want to know how much pasta people are cooking and eating, not how much they're buying, and certainly not how much supermarkets and distributors are ordering from the factory."

Strong ties

Sun tries to help its partners when demand falls. Treat suppliers decently, and "they remember," says exec Marissa Peterson

Gathering good information, of course, doesn't guarantee acting wisely on it. Carmakers, for instance, regularly get a better-than-average fix on overall demand as their in-house economists pore over such time-tested data as household formation rates and consumer confidence surveys. "The forecasting is pretty good," says David J. Andrea of the nonprofit Center for Automotive Research. The problem, he says, is "industry behavior."

Detroit still winds up during a slowdown with at least some excess inventory—as it did in January. Why? Each carmaker bets that its models will outsell the rest and produces accordingly. Lately, too, the Big Three carmakers have sullied their profit margins and clouded forecasting by offering steep incentives to buyers. Much like the networking industry's vendor financing, such market-distorting inducements make it tough to gauge real demand—even if the carmakers can boast of better results than, say, the producers of networking equipment.

Other companies, though, were able to use a sound forecast as an intellectual framework for smart decision-making. Eaton Corp., with $8 billion in annual sales and products that range from truck transmissions to circuit breakers for homes, started getting cautious last October when Adrian T. Dillon, Eaton's chief financial and planning officer, warned of an impending "short, sharp shock" in the economy.

Dillon's insights didn't save Eaton from the consequences of the downturn; no forecast can do that. But it did allow the company to cushion against the coming drop. As demand for its products shriveled, Eaton halted a stock-buyback program to save cash and pulled the plug on a couple of planned acquisitions. Although this year's first-half earnings have plunged by 64%, the decline could have been steeper had the company not prepared its managers—and Wall Street—early on. In fact, Eaton's stock is up 11% since early January.

FOOL'S GAME. Sun Microsystems Inc. doesn't rely on long-range forecasts in its purchasing but instead tries to buy supplies—often over the Internet—as needed. Its top operations and sales staffers meet weekly in supply-demand gatherings to make sure their work is balanced. And they try to ensure that their partners don't get left in the lurch when demand moves south. Twice last year, Sun asked supplier Celestica Inc. to delay deliveries of memory devices that Sun had ordered, but when it came time in April for Celestica to either take a charge for the goods or deliver, Sun took them. "Sun treats suppliers more decently and they remember," says Sun operations chief Marissa Peterson.

Regrettably for many in Silicon Valley, the ability to make accurate forecasts can depend on how well-established a company's products are. Young industries on steep growth curves are almost always surprised by how well their products do in the first few years, and then they're taken aback when demand ebbs. Says Stanford University business strategy professor Kathleen M. Eisenhardt, "in a highly dynamic, ambiguous, and unpredictable market people are going to make mistakes. It's inherent in the type of business."

In many corners of Silicon Valley—and elsewhere—unpredictability is inevitable. One solution: keep innovating but develop sound service businesses to sell with products. "I break the world into two segments—one is creating demand and the other is servicing demand," says Craig H. Muhlhauser, president of the cutting-edge power-storage systems maker, Exide Technologies. Building a "very robust service business," he says, smooths out the rough spots between innovations.

No matter how well companies try to forecast demand, they will almost always be off the bull's eye. Chaos is simply more the norm than orderly, predictable patterns. Indeed, Wharton

School adjunct professor Paul J.H. Schoemaker argues that sticking too closely to a forecast is a fool's game. Better to use scenario planning, in which you prepare to handle different sets of circumstances. "You can't reduce the uncertainty, but you can manage it by having options," says Schoemaker.

No business, of course, is recession-proof. But managers who understand that markets go down as well as up are a lot more likely to read the tea leaves correctly. Better to see the warning signs and ratchet down early than find yourself stuck with billions in equipment that suddenly no one wants. Just ask Cisco. By Joseph Weber

---

With Ben Elgin and Peter Burrows in Silicon Valley and Michael Arndt in Chicago

What's **right** with the US economy

The secret behind the new economy isn't information technology but old-fashioned competition and managerial innovation.

William W. Lewis, Vincent Palmade, Baudouin Regout, and Allen P. Webb

As companies attempt to cope with an economic downturn and the United States fights a war on terrorism, many wonder whether the long-term health of the US economy will be undermined. The answer depends on what happens to the productivity growth rate—the main determinant of how fast the economy can grow. At issue is whether the near doubling of US productivity growth rates during the late 1990s, from 1.4 percent (1972–95) to 2.5 percent (1995–2000), can continue.

Our yearlong research[1] indicates that many of the product, service, and process innovations underlying the productivity acceleration of the late 1990s will continue to generate productivity growth rates above the 1972–95 trend for the next several years, although probably not as high as those of 1995 to 1999. Higher productivity, in turn, will boost economic growth.

Surprisingly, the primary source of the productivity gains of 1995 to 1999 was not increased demand resulting from the stock market bubble, as some economists have claimed. Nor was information technology the source, though companies accelerated the pace of their IT investments during those years.[2] Rather, managerial and technological innovations in only six highly competitive industries—wholesale trade, retail trade, securities, semiconductors, computer manufacturing, and telecommunications—-were the most important causes (Exhibit 1).[3] The other 70 percent of the economy contributed a mix of small productivity gains and losses that offset each other. In addition, cyclical demand factors were important in some parts of the economy.

It is not unusual, we found, for only a small number of sectors to experience a productivity jump during any four-year period. But in the late 1990s, these six sectors, departing from the norm, either enjoyed extremely large leaps in productivity (for instance, semiconductors and computer manufacturing) or accounted for a large share of employment (retail and wholesale).

At the national level, the relationship between IT spending and productivity is unclear. Many sectors other than the six jumping ones increased their pace of IT investment but experienced stagnant or even *slower* productivity growth (Exhibit 2). We found an inconclusive correlation between the acceleration of IT investments and changes in productivity growth. In fact, taken as a group, the other 53 economic sectors had almost no productivity growth.

The challenge, then, was to understand what caused the productivity acceleration in the six key sectors. We did a detailed study of these sectors, as well as three others that invested heavily in IT but failed to boost productivity—hotels, long-distance data telephony, and retail banking.

Explaining the 1995 productivity acceleration

Within the six jumping sectors, the most important cause of the productivity acceleration after 1995 was fundamental changes in the way companies deliver products and services. Sometimes these innovations were aided by technology (whether new or old), sometimes not. In all six sectors, high or increasing competitive intensity was essential to the spread of innovation, and in two sectors, regulatory changes played an important role in raising that intensity. Cyclical demand factors and a shift in consumer purchasing patterns toward higher-value goods were important in explaining the acceleration of productivity in retail, wholesale, and securities.

EXHIBIT 1

Six sectors led the way

Contributions of selected sectors to 1995-99 US labor productivity growth acceleration,[1] compound annual growth rate (CAGR), percent

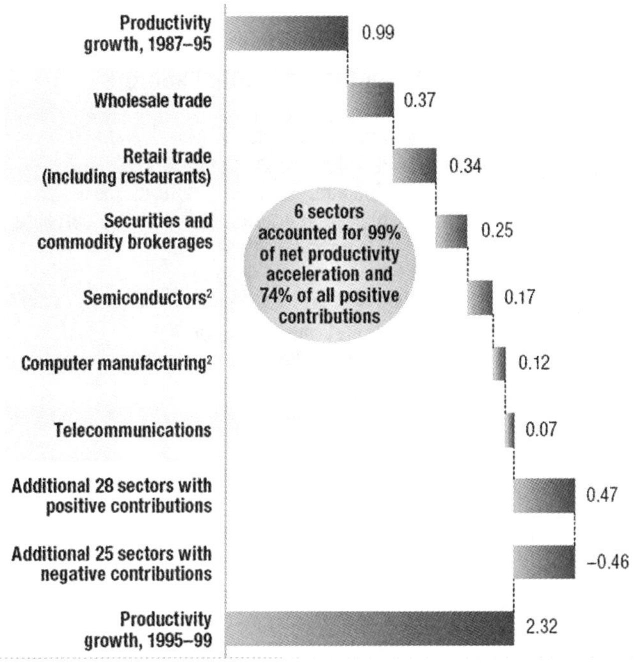

[1]Analysis based on US Bureau of Economic Analysis (BEA) sector data, which differ slightly from widely publicized US Bureau of Labor Statistics (BLS) aggregate data. BLS labor productivity growth figures show 1.4% CAGR for 1987-95 and 2.5% CAGR for 1995–2000.

[2]Semiconductors industry (representing 20% of overall productivity growth) is a subset of Electronic and Electric Equipment, which as a group contributed 17%; computer manufacturing (representing 10% of overall productivity growth) is a subset of Industrial Machinery and Equipment, which as a group contributed 12%.

Source: US Bureau of Economic Analysis, McKinsey analysis

Structural factors: Competition and innovation

The bulk of the acceleration in productivity after 1995 can be traced to managerial and technological innovations that improved the basic operations of companies. These innovations were structural and are likely to persist. Sometimes, the catalyst was a dominant player with a superior business model; other times, it was managers using new technology to redesign core operations.

In general-merchandise retailing, productivity growth more than tripled after 1995 because competitors started more rapidly adopting Wal-Mart's innovations—including the large-scale ("big-box") format, "everyday low prices," economies of scale in warehouse logistics and purchasing, and electronic data interchange (EDI) with suppliers. As a result, Wal-Mart's competitors increased their productivity by 28 percent from 1995 to 1999, while Wal-Mart itself raised the bar further by increasing its own productivity by an additional 22 percent. Although e-commerce grew rapidly during this period, its penetration (0.9 percent of retail sales in 2000) was too low to make a difference in overall retail productivity. We estimate that Internet commerce contributed less than 0.01 percentage points to the 1.33 percent jump in economy-wide productivity growth.

The operations of wholesalers underwent similarly dramatic changes during the middle of the 1990s as new warehouse-management systems were adopted (Exhibit 3). Pharmaceuticals wholesalers, for instance, responded to increasing price pressure from large retailers by automating distribution centers. Because each center keeps an inventory of tens of thousands of different items, stocking, picking, and shipping have traditionally been highly labor-intensive. The combination of pre-1995 hardware (bar codes, scanners, picking machines) and software for tracking and controlling inventory allowed wholesalers to automate their flow of goods partially and to increase their labor productivity greatly.

In computer manufacturing, nearly all of the productivity acceleration was due to innovations outside the sector itself. Technological improvements in microprocessors and other components (memory, storage devices), as well as the integration of new components (CD-ROMs, DVDs), caused an acceleration in the value of computers produced. At the same time, the popularization of the Internet and the accelerating processing requirements of Microsoft's Windows operating systems (Exhibit 4) caused a spike in demand for more powerful personal computers. These two factors further contributed to the high productivity growth in the manufacture of computers and semiconductors.

Productivity growth in the semiconductor industry accelerated mainly because the performance of the average chip did. Largely in response to competitive pressure from Advanced Micro Devices, Intel took less time to bring out new and better chips than it had done previously.

The securities industry was the only sector we studied in which the Internet materially boosted productivity. At the end of 1999, roughly 40 percent of retail securities trades were being conducted on-line, up from virtually zero in 1995, and a given number of frontline employees can now broker ten times as many trades as they could then. Competition from on-line discount brokers, such as E*Trade and Charles Schwab, was critical to the rapid dif-

EXHIBIT 2

It takes more than just IT

Correlation between US labor productivity and information technology (IT) capital intensity in selected sectors, 1987–95 to 1995–99, compound annual growth rate (CAGR), percent

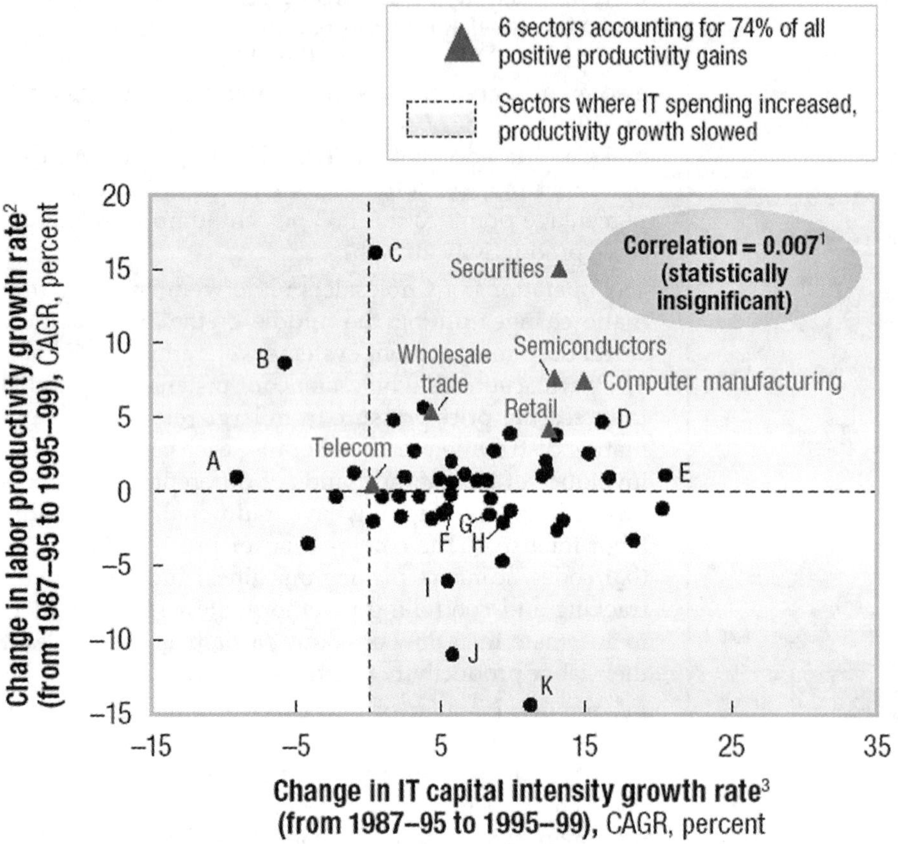

Selected additional sectors

A. Motion pictures
B. Petroleum and coal products
C. Pipelines (excluding natural gas)
D. Insurance agents, brokers, and services
E. Business services
F. Depository institutions
G. Hotels and lodging
H. Oil and gas extraction
I. Food and kindred products
J. Radio and television
K. Tobacco products

[1]Excludes coal mining, farms, and metal mining because of low initial levels of IT capital stock and excludes holding companies for measurement reasons, although weighting each sector by its share of employment yields a statistically significant correlation of 0.26, excluding the 6 jumping sectors yields statistically insignificant results.

[2]Measured as change in real value added - PEP (people employed in production).

[3]Measured as change in real IT capital stock - PEP

Source: US Bureau of Economic Analysis; McKinsey analysis

fusion of these innovations in the traditional brokerage houses.

Regulatory changes increased competition and had a significant effect on productivity in some cases. In the securities industry, the US Securities and Exchange Commission's order-handling and 16th rules[4] sharply reduced transaction costs, allowing institutional investors to take advantage of increasingly small price anomalies and boosting trading volumes. In the telecom sector, the licensing of new spectrum for mobile telephony heightened competition and sparked faster price decreases, lifting both penetration and usage. In both the securities industry and the telecom sector, larger volumes allowed industry players to leverage fixed costs.

Cyclical demand factors

Some of the acceleration in productivity after 1995 was due to demand factors that may not be sustainable. In the securities industry, the soaring stock market led to productivity advances in three different ways (Exhibit 5).

EXHIBIT 3

The changing warehouse

Sales of warehouse-management systems, $ million (nominal $)

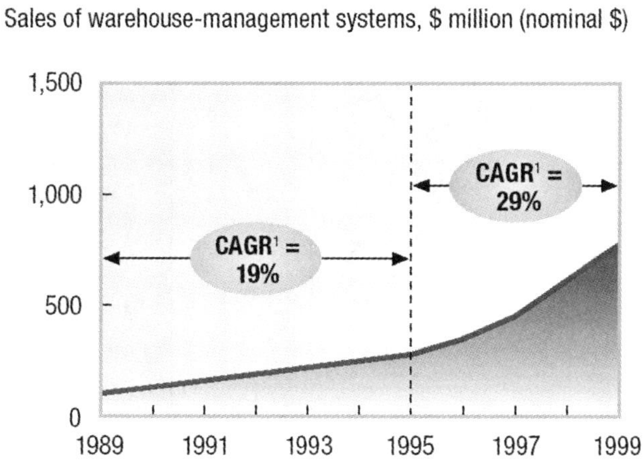

[1]Compound annual growth rate.

Source: AMR Research

First, lofty index values (particularly Nasdaq's) fueled a surge in on-line retail trading. Second, they also increased the value of assets under management, boosting the productivity of money managers. Finally, they increased the number and value of initial public offerings and of mergers. These factors explain half of the productivity jump observed in the securities industry.

In general-merchandise retailing, and most likely in the rest of retail and in wholesale, almost half of the measurable productivity jump reflected the higher value of the goods that consumers increasingly favored. Retailing experts believe that the shift was mainly the result of growing confidence, income, and wealth rather than a marked improvement in the retailers' techniques of enticement.

The role of information technology

Contrary to conventional wisdom, the widespread adoption of information and communications technology was not the most important cause of the acceleration in productivity after 1995. Our nine sector case studies clearly show that the relationship between IT and labor productivity is extremely variable.

In rare cases, IT can deliver truly extraordinary productivity improvements, expanding labor capacity by an order of magnitude. As mentioned above, on-line securities trading requires only a fraction of the frontline labor employed in traditional channels. In mobile telecommunications, cellular equipment employing new digital standards made better use of the available spectrum, spurring rapid price declines and a spike in usage. In both cases, the product or service itself, being intangible information that could easily be digitized, was highly susceptible to such improvements.

In most cases, however, IT was just one of many tools that creative managers used to redesign core business processes, products, or services. A significant portion of Wal-Mart's business innovations (such as the big-box format) was independent of IT. Where IT did play a role, it was a necessary but not a sufficient enabler of productivity gains. To reap the full productivity benefits of inventory-management systems or EDI, for instance, a business must implement operational-process changes. The same is true of the automation of warehouse and distribution centers in the wholesale sector.

To understand why IT is not a panacea, we looked at three sectors that invested heavily in IT but experienced no improvement in productivity growth: hotels, the long-distance data portion of the telecom sector, and retail banking. Some spending on IT in these sectors and elsewhere in the economy was designed to maintain capabilities, such as investments in Y2K compliance and more rapid upgrades of personal computers to ensure compatibility with emerging Windows standards. Other IT expenditures, on things such as Internet and corporate-networking equipment, were made to generate future rather than immediate productivity benefits. The confluence of these unusual demand factors explains most of the acceleration in IT spending from 1995 to 1999.

It is also possible that IT increases the consumer's convenience in ways that are not fully captured by government productivity measures. Even so, this would not be sufficient to explain the " IT paradox." Hotels invested heavily in creating central reservation systems that provided customers with some unquantifiable value (for instance, immediate, centralized information on the availability of rooms), but the increase in convenience was probably modest. The added convenience of on-line banking also doesn't appear in government productivity measures. But even if it were possible to correct for this measurement problem, the small number of on-line transactions would not have been enough to reverse the deceleration of productivity growth in retail banking.

Some IT investments do not appear to be delivering the intended results, and whether they ever will remains to be seen. Retail banks and hotels, for instance, have collected significant amounts of customer data that they have yet to use productively. Companies in the retail-banking industry bought an average of two PCs per employee from 1995 to 1999. Some of this computing power was not fully utilized and some, it is likely, never will be.[5] Long-distance telephone players made enormous investments in metropolitan and long-haul networks that are

EXHIBIT 4

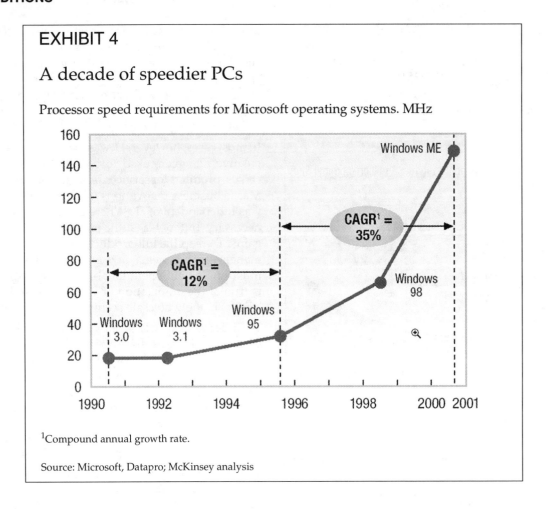

A decade of speedier PCs

Processor speed requirements for Microsoft operating systems. MHz

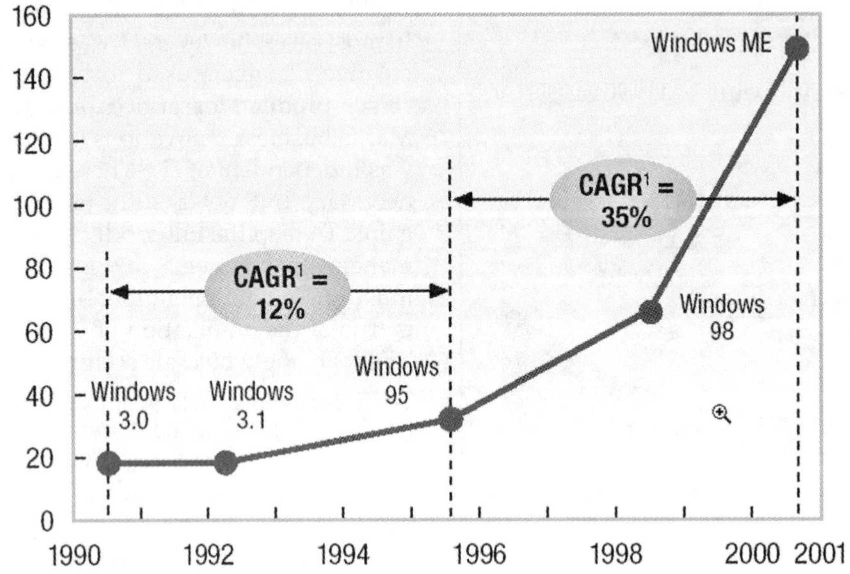

[1]Compound annual growth rate.

Source: Microsoft, Datapro; McKinsey analysis

currently underutilized and will probably remain so for several years to come.

Our conclusion about the effect of IT on productivity is straightforward. IT can be quite valuable when deployed as part of a management plan to reorganize specific core activities of a business. In this respect, it is not different from other forms of capital—new building designs, new materials-handling systems, new semiconductor production tools. But when generic IT solutions are applied to support functions, or when IT represents no more than a "me-too" investment, it is unlikely to move the needle on a company's productivity. A robust explanation of the recent acceleration in productivity must therefore go well beyond IT.

The future of US productivity

If the pattern of the two most recent recessions (1981–82 and 1991–92) holds, the impact of a recession on labor productivity over the next four years will be minimal. Even if the tragic attacks of September 11 cause a sharp decline in productivity growth, we would expect an economic recovery, and thus an uptick, prior to 2005.

The more important question for the longer term is whether the acceleration in productivity from 1995 to 1999 is sustainable. We estimate that at least half of what occurred in the six jumping sectors can be sustained over the next five years. Wal-Mart still enjoys a sizable productivity advantage over its competitors and will continue to force efficiency improvements in the industry. The limited penetration of warehouse automation (now at just 25 percent), and, to a lesser degree, of mobile telephony and on-line trading, leaves room for further growth, and thus productivity gains, in those sectors. Both the computer-manufacturing and semiconductor industries should benefit from a continuation of the current rate of improvement in the performance of microprocessors.

Clearly, however, some of this acceleration will be unsustainable. The burst in demand for personal computers is behind us, and the effects of the stock market bubble on asset valuations, M&A, and securities trading have already largely evaporated. We cannot judge whether consumers will continue to shift their purchasing patterns in favor of higher-value goods at the 1995–99 rate or know what will happen in the portions of the retail and wholesale sectors that we did not study.

A larger source of uncertainty about future productivity growth is the behavior of the rest of the economy. A review of the performance of the other 53 sectors over the past two decades reveals that both their contribution to national productivity growth and their average annual productivity growth rate have been quite small. Those

EXHIBIT 5

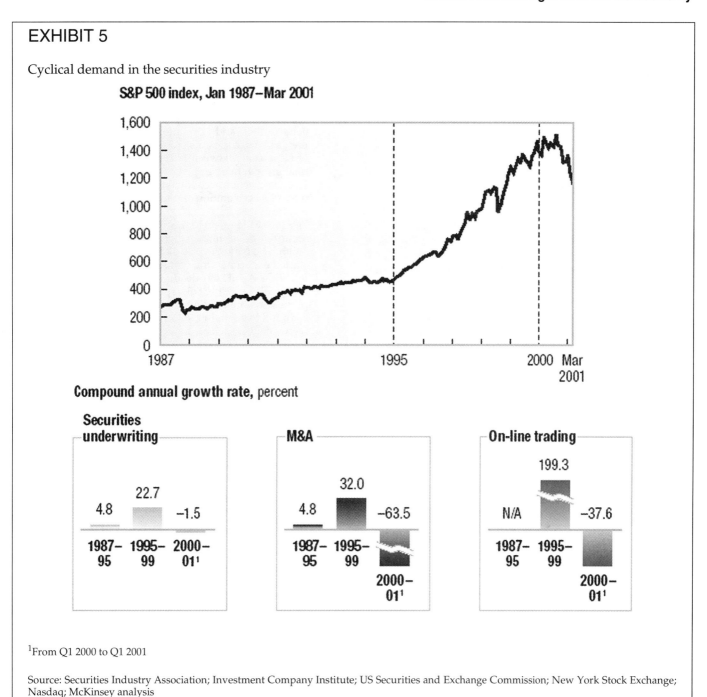

Cyclical demand in the securities industry

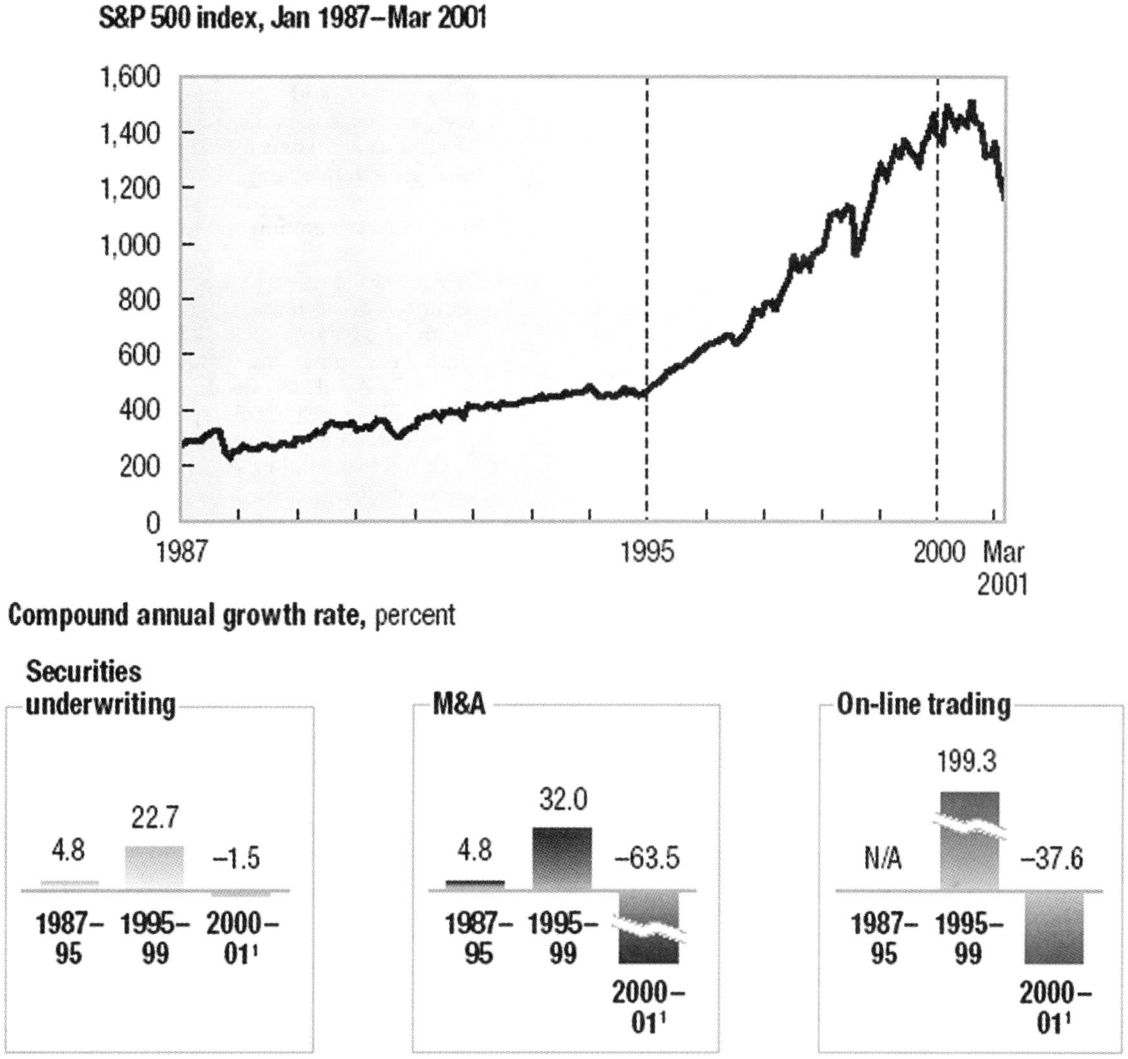

[1]From Q1 2000 to Q1 2001

Source: Securities Industry Association; Investment Company Institute; US Securities and Exchange Commission; New York Stock Exchange; Nasdaq; McKinsey analysis

figures, however, show considerable volatility—some of it caused by business cycles and some by changes in industry dynamics and structure. If historical precedents hold, this kind of noncyclical volatility could reduce the national rate of productivity growth over the next four years by 0.1 percentage points annually or increase it by as much as 0.4 percentage points annually.

It is possible that other sectors of the economy will defy the historical trend and experience extraordinary productivity jumps. The key contributor to such jumps would be innovations, such as Wal-Mart's improvements in its business system or on-line securities-trading technology, that streamlined labor-intensive activities or leveraged fixed labor costs. Competition, which could be triggered by regulatory changes, is required to diffuse innovation. A quick scan of the economy revealed several sectors showing the first signs of emerging innovators (such as software; media, including motion pictures; insurance carriers; and depository and nondepository institutions) and of promising regulatory changes (electric, gas, and sanitary services as well as pharmaceuticals). However, the number of these sectors, their share of total employment, and the potential magnitude of their jumps are not impressive. Therefore, we believe, continuing volatility in the rest of the economy's productivity growth rate is likely to encompass the effect of these innovations and regulatory changes.

Although uncertainty about the performance of all these factors makes precise predictions impossible, our analysis indicates that overall productivity growth could be as low as 1.6 percent or as high as 2.5 percent.[6]

Even our low estimate offers ample reason for optimism about the US economy, regardless of what happens in the short term. The six key sectors will continue to generate above-trend productivity growth for at least several more years. No one can predict when and where the next entrepreneurial initiative will strike outside of these sectors. But healthy levels of competition, 20 years of deregulation, and a long tradition of US ingenuity will allow the country's economy to continue to define the productivity frontier.

Notes

1. The study on which this article is based involved a collaboration of the McKinsey Global Institute, the Firm's high-technology practice, and the San Francisco office. Greg Hughes, James Manyika, Lenny Mendonca, and Mike Nevens helped lead the project. The research team, which deserves special recognition, included Angelique Augereau, Mike Cho, Brad Johnson, Brent Neiman, Gabriela Olazabal, Matt Sandler, Sandra Schrauf, Kevin Stange, Andrew Tilton, and Eric Xin. The full study is available on-line at www.mckinsey.com.
2. Between 1987 and 1995, information technology investments by US companies rose by a compound annual rate of 11 percent. Between 1995 and 1999, this compound annual growth rate jumped to 20.2 percent.
3. These six sectors accounted for virtually all of the net productivity acceleration and for 74 percent of all positive contributions.
4. The 16th Rule refers to the SEC's 1997 mandate to quote securities prices in increments of 1/16th rather than 1/8th. The New York Stock Exchange and the Nasdaq started experimenting with decimalization even before the SEC's April 2001 deadline.
5. From 1995 to 1999, banks spent a total of $5,253 per employee (in nominal dollars) on new PCs.
6. For a full explanation, see chapter 3 of the full report, at www.mckinsey.com.

Bill Lewis is the director of the McKinsey Global Institute, where **Vincent Palmade** is a principal; **Baudouin Regout** is a consultant in McKinsey's New York office; **Allen Webb** is a consultant in the Pacific Northwest office.

Reinventing How We Do Business

LEADERSHIP FOR DARWINIAN TIMES

JANET PERNA

Thanks to Merv Adrian and his team. It's great being at Giga World, and seeing so many customers, partners and friends of IBM.

It's an honor for me to follow President Bush, who opened this conference. I know President Bush talked to you yesterday about the challenge of leadership in a new global economy. I want to talk to you this morning about leadership on a far more familiar and practical level—how game-changing technologies are impacting business. Bob Weiler summed this up beautifully in his welcoming letter for this conference. Bob told us that "Darwin's theory is proving true in the world of e-business." Was Bob ever right about that! What a difference a year makes!

After the ups and downs of this past year, it's clear that Darwin wasn't just writing about "the origin of the species." He was writing about the evolution of e-business! We are in a Darwinian world where only the fastest, smartest, and most savvy companies and executives survive and thrive.

After a few years of trial-and-error, companies have no choice but to get serious about reinventing how they run their businesses using technology. Executives are getting serious about harnessing e-business to change fundamental work processes, like customer relationship management, supply chain, procurement and ERP.

They're focusing not just on quick wins, but on permanent fixes so they can go-to-market faster, cut costs, speed internal processes—all primed to help them win in the marketplace. That's why I'm delighted to be here today, to offer a perspective on how these things are happening and what's in it for you.

I'm going to focus on three things: how companies are reinventing how they work using the Internet; how e-business infrastructure is becoming the key enabler for business reinvention; and some key questions you should be considering so your organization can win in this Darwinian universe.

e-business Adaptation

Lest anybody feel too complacent or too threatened, it's important to keep in mind that we're still very early in the evolution of e-business. A recent study conducted by IBM on e-business adoption... which was based on 33,000 enterprises around the globe... revealed some fascinating results. We found 6 logical steps in the e-business adoption process.

Everybody doesn't take the same route, but if you follow the logical progression, you wind up with these steps:

1. First is Internet Access—accessing the Internet from your company. Fifty-four percent are still at this stage.
2. Second is Internet Publishing—making information about your company, products and services available on the Internet. Twenty-seven percent are at this point.
3. Third is Internet Transactions—buying and selling on the Web. Only 12 percent of those we surveyed are here.
4. Fourth is Internal Web Integration—enabling internal processes like customer order management and expense accounting. Four-and-a-half percent have gotten this far.
5. Fifth is External Integration—like connecting suppliers and distributors. Just two-and-a-half percent report progress in this area.
6. The last step is Dynamic e-business, which is over the horizon line for everyone we surveyed.

I think there are few interesting takeaways from this data. First, for all the talk and agitation about e-business, most companies are just getting serious about it. It's very early in the e-business adoption process.

Another implication is that as those of us who've worked with technology for many years know, e-business is a lot of really hard work. Technologists always knew it would be. It's not only tough technical work, but it requires major reinvention of the way work is done. You don't change fundamental business processes or company cultures overnight.

A third takeaway from this survey is that "the best is yet to come." Let me explain. Once you have integrated your work processes, we believe e-business is going to take on a "dynamic" of its own.

You can start to think about using IT as a "Web Service"—as easily and flexibly as you purchase. power from an electric utility, telecom from a phone company, or water from a municipal utility. You pay for what you use, and nothing more. Turn on the IT spigot, and there it is, whenever and wherever you need it. Turn it off, and it goes away, along with the expense.

"Web Services" are the logical next step for companies that have moved from proprietary to open architectures, and achieved an integrated e-business infrastructure. It's still very early in this evolution, but we think Web Services are going to be increasingly attractive. Why? Because they make good business sense.

The Data Explosion

Another indication of how early it is in the roll out of e-business has to do with is the explosion of data… or what you might call the electronic version of the "Big Bang" theory of the universe. As you well know, for years companies have been collecting huge amounts of transaction data, which flops around inside corporations, often lost in "black holes."

All of a sudden the Internet and e-business have come on the scene, and everything from e-mail to catalogs and transactions are exploding the capacity of the existing information infrastructure and bang! All of a sudden you have to rethink how to store, analyze and digitize all the data streaming into your enterprise.

This isn't just about centralized data, but decentralized data; and not just about structured data, but the 85 percent that is unstructured. Now, you begin to appreciate the dimensions of this data explosion when you put it in historical context. Researchers at the University of California at Berkeley have predicted that people will create more data in the next three years than in all of recorded history. Imagine that! I'm not sure if they included caveman drawings, but you get the idea.

We're at a turning point in how we manage information. Either we move rapidly to manage the data explosion, or we're going to be buried by it. Either we learn to leverage it, or we're going to be left on the sidelines. Smart companies are finding ways to turn data into business intelligence. They are finding ways to leverage data to drive decision making, speed work processes, cut costs, enhance customer loyalty and grab market share.

At IBM, we believe strongly that leveraging information is how companies win in the marketplace, because information is the jet fuel for e-business success. We're betting on a future where all information is digitized, secure and easily accessed anywhere it resides from any device; a future where our customers gain significant competitive advantage by leveraging all of their information.

Our vision is to be the leader in providing companies with software products that enable them to leverage all of their information. And I'm really excited about this future… and I hope you are too! The next few years are going to offer great opportunity to our customers, employees and partners.

Reinventing Global Package Delivery: UPS

Now, I want to spend a few moments telling you about some companies we're working with—companies that are stepping up to the need to use technology to reinvent themselves, and achieving impressive results.

UPS is a great example. They're using technology to reinvent the global package delivery business. They touch everyone in this room, probably many hundreds of times every day. They handle over 12 million packages daily, making them the biggest package delivery firm in the world.

Now, in the late 90s, UPS got serious about leveraging information to build their industry leadership. They wanted to improve dramatically their supply chain so they could speed service to customers, and really drive costs out of their business.

As their business customers started moving to the Web, UPS moved to the Web in a big way. They built an e-business infrastructure that automated package tracking and offered multi-channel customer self-service. They figured out that a "live" phone call costs them $1.04, compared to four cents when customers self-serve over the Web. All told, harnessing the Web eliminated $450,000 a day for UPS!

They followed some business fundamentals to get there that are worth remembering. They targeted the right customers—business customers—making it easy for them to provide their customers with real-time package-tracking—using e-mail, the Web, and a touch-tone phone.

They streamlined business processes impacting their customers and their customers' customers. End users no longer had to remember their tracking number or log onto the UPS Web site. They could go directly to the seller's Web site and get an instant update on where their package is and when it will arrive. By the way, UPS's quick-response Web site manages over 700,000 tracking requests every day!

How did UPS achieve these dramatic results? First and foremost, they built a world-class e-business infrastructure. This enabled them to upgrade their 60 customer service telephone centers so information could be scanned and ready for their 7,000 customer service reps whenever it was needed. Their plan called for this upgrade to pay for itself in two years. In fact, it paid for itself in 10 months.

UPS was also the first package-tracking company to digitize recipients' signatures, making them available electronically for delivery verification, which is what their customers wanted. Remember the TV ad where the delivery guy tells the customer his package was not only delivered, but signed for—"and here's your signature." Case closed!

They also started capturing data earlier in the supply chain, at the point of shipment, helping business customers improve their own shipping processes, which also increased their loyalty to UPS.

UPS started scanning packages en route, with the aid of overhead scanners and more than 17,000 wearable scanners used by their shipping personnel. Constant tracking technology gave them the added advantage of rerouting packages on the fly, to speed delivery.

Now, at the end of the day, UPS automated something every business has to deal with—moving physical stuff from one place to another, and doing it fast and at lowest cost. How did they do it? They did it by leveraging information to automate work every step of the way. Did it pay off? You bet it did! UPS retained their position as the premier supplier of global package distribution services.

Reinventing Retail—Safeway

Let's take a look at how Safeway in the UK has been reinventing retailing, especially by leveraging customer information. Like a lot of grocers, Safeway has been collecting product data at the point-of-sale for a long time. They then introduced a loyalty card that helped them connect customers to what they were buying, which gave them a market basket for every customer.

That enabled them to do some interesting things, like finding out who their most profitable customers were, and what they were buying. They found, for example, that only eight of the 28 orange juices they carried were profitable. So, they reduced their orange juices, and increased their profitability.

They started analyzing other products, and found out they were carrying 200 different cheeses, and only a few of them were profitable. So, if you follow the orange juice example, your natural inclination would be to reduce the number of cheeses. However, when they connected their product data with their customer data, they found out that their most profitable customers were buying their least profitable cheeses.

Based on this analysis, they decided it was important for them to carry these unprofitable cheeses. Knowing who your most profitable customers are is an invaluable competitive edge, whether they buy your most profitable products or not.

Safeway also found out that a typical customer buys roughly 125 products with a predictable frequency. They used this understanding to develop another competitive weapon, customized shopping lists for customers, which they made available at store kiosks.

Customers could put their Loyalty Card into the kiosk, and get a personalized shopping list… along with up-to-date product promotions. Safeway then ordered the shopping list in the same way that items were laid out in the store.

Safeway took another bold step by analyzing what customers hated most about shopping. It turns out waiting on line at check-out tops the shoppers' most-hated list. So, Safeway started giving customers PDAs that they could use to scan products as they shopped. All customers had to do was put items in their bag and get an itemized receipt as they left the store. No more lines, no more checkout.

The next thing shoppers really hate about shopping is not being able to buy out-of-stock items. At first, they tried suggesting substitute items that were available. But shoppers didn't go for it. So, Safeway started doing something they had been reluctant to do for years, for fear of giving away competitive information. They started sharing their customer database with their suppliers, turning their suppliers into collaborators. By doing this, they could have just-in-time inventory, and be able to do things like forecast spikes in demand timed to store promotions.

Leveraging information enabled Safeway to close the loop with their stores, customers and suppliers, which improved customer service and reduced cost. Lately, Safeway has taken another big step into the future by giving their preferred customers wireless devices, which they can use to shop at home. Customers can access their personalized shopping list, scan products they want to replenish, and submit their order to Safeway using their wireless device. The customer can then pick up the order at the store when it's convenient.

Now, all of these things—from personalized shopping lists, to loyalty cards, PDAs, instant receipts, and home shopping—have one thing in common. They tie the customer to Safeway, to the supply chain, and back out to the customer. We think Safeway is not only reinventing themselves, but reinventing the retailing business.

Reinventing Manufacturing and Marketing: Whirlpool

Whirlpool is another great example of how a company is reinventing itself around the Internet. Like most companies, their operational and business applications are in their data center. They have installed SAP as their ERP to manage their internal inventory.

One of their major challenges has been servicing their mid-tier trading partners, which are small to midsize businesses. They wanted to reduce the cost of servicing this partner segment, at the same time that they expanded their reach into these partners.

In order to do that, they installed a business-to-business commerce server. This enabled Whirlpool's business partners to access the inventory data and manufacturing data that was in the SAP system. And this helped Whirlpool reduce the cost of filling an order to less than $5, representing a cost-savings of 80 percent. It also paid for itself in eight months.

Next, Whirlpool used a commerce server to provide consumers with direct access into their inventory management system. Consumers can do things like register appliances online, as well as buy accessories and small parts, and have these orders fulfilled directly through the SAP system. Whirlpool is also doing a number of imaginative things to tie its appliances closer to its customer, using the Web.

For example, their refrigerators include pervasive devices that collect diagnostic and operational data that is fed back to Whirlpool. Whirlpool can then do things like schedule preventive maintenance for its appliances.

You may have seen the TV commercial where the Whirlpool repairman shows up at a customer's front door. The customer says, "I didn't call anyone." The repairman says, "I'm here to repair your refrigerator," and the customer says, "But it's not broken." And the repairman says, "Not yet."

Well, this kind of preventive maintenance takes the ability to collect and analyze lots of information, and come up with the right course of action. Going forward, Whirlpool sees its appliances becoming Internet devices. For example, a refrigerator will become a portal to the Internet. Customers will be able to scan food products that need to be replenished into a Web-enabled refrigerator. This data can then be fed to an online grocer, which will take the guesswork out of shopping and save loads of time.

In similar fashion, a washing machine will become a portal for dispensing helpful consumer information. Like how to remove a tough clothing stain. You won't have to reach for "Hints From Heloise." You'll be able to ask your washing machine for the answer. Turning appliances into information devices will have a big payoff for Whirlpool, including improving customer service, driving new sources of revenue, and reducing cost.

Beyond that, imagine what would happen if we applied "preventive maintenance" to things like cars, air craft, energy generators, respirators, pacemakers, and even the human heart. We're no longer talking about science fiction. These things are real, and they are happening!

Reinventing The Life Sciences

They're happening in really amazing ways right now in the life sciences, which is a major new area of focus for IBM. We're working to reinvent the life sciences, with our core strengths in data and storage management, supercomputing, knowledge management and e-business.

This isn't just about changing business; it's about changing how we live, in the most literal sense. Imagine the lives we could save by shrinking the time it takes to discover a miracle drug from 15 years to a few months! Now, the heart of the discovery process is collecting and analyzing vast amounts of data.

I spoke to you a moment ago about the data explosion, and how data is doubling every 18 months. In the life sciences, data is growing three times that fast, doubling every 6 months.

For example, the human genome, which is the sum of all genetic material encased in nearly every cell of the human body, is at least 3 billion chemical letters long—as many letters as you would find in 10,000 copies of the Sunday New York Times.

All of this genetic data is worthless without the information technology that can help scientists manage and analyze it, to unlock the pathways that will lead to new cures for disease.

IT has become the "language" of the life sciences, the key to managing, analyzing and sharing massive amounts of life sciences data. We're using our strengths in supercomputing, database and storage management, and services to foster collaboration among leading researchers around the world, including institutions like Johns Hopkins University, Duke University and the Georgia Institute of Technology.

We're also working with emerging companies in the life sciences, like Incyte Genomics, Structural Bioinformatics and MDS Proteomics, in addition to leading pharmaceutical companies.

This is a massive effort, and we believe the payoff will be enormous. The potential for change based on innovation in the life sciences will be bigger than the change caused by the digital circuit. More important, progress in the life sciences is going to save lives and prevent disease. It doesn't get better than that.

e-business Infrastructure: Premier Global Online Broker

All of these organizations recognized the importance of having a robust technology infrastructure in support of a new way of doing business. Now, I'd like to drill down into that infrastructure by sharing one more customer story, this time using e-business infrastructure to demonstrate how one of the premier global online brokers actually operates.

We rearchitected their e-business infrastructure so they could better manage the explosive growth in their business. To do that, we put in place a new kind of multitier infrastructure. The objective was to support millions of wireless devices, and high transaction volumes, ranging from simple transactions like looking up market research, to very complex transactions like buying or selling stock. These wireless devices are going to need to connect to content, data, and transactions.

The infrastructure we developed consisted of: 1. Edge servers that provide workload balancing, caching and security; 2. Mid-tier application servers, messaging servers, directory and security servers and database servers; and at the back end; 3. Transaction and content servers, which provide the business critical processing and in many cases, consist of legacy applications.

Now, there are a number of key lessons to keep in mind in building this kind of infrastructure, like: designing for scalability and 24x7 availability; linking to existing systems; and evolving non-disruptively. Finally, the Internet's open standards are vital because they provide a base for rapid integration and business agility.

The implementation of this new infrastructure has shown some impressive results in handling thousands of Web transactions per second: fifty-five percent of requests are satisfied at the edge and presentation server layer, doing sign ons, market statistics and quotes. Twenty-seven percent are light transactions, like a customer portfolio look-up or a trade confirmation—and they never have to go to the back half of the system. Only 18 percent of the hits pass through as full business transactions, where stock trades and money actually changes hands.

That kind of flexible infrastructure allows you to build customer loyalty through fast service, while managing the volatility inherent in the business. The secret is that each level of the infrastructure performs the class of processing that it has been optimized for.

IBM's Value Proposition

Now, we think the real challenge ahead is building open, flexible e-business infrastructures—so businesses can easily integrate their work processes internally and externally; infrastructures that are a natural extension of the organization's existing IT infrastructure, and that can grow flexibly with the business; infrastructures that open up dynamic new possibilities, like buying IT the way you buy electricity, telecom and water.

Buy what you need whenever and wherever you need it, and leave the rest to the service provider.

All of IBM's offerings are built on this e-business infrastructure value proposition, which includes: our software, which is built on open standards so you can integrate across multiple operating systems, platforms and devices; our DB2 database software, so you can turn data into information that helps you improve customer relations, supply chain, and that links to business intelligence and content management; our WebSphere middleware, so you can Web-enable your work processes and conduct high volume transactions; our Lotus collaboration software, so you can build a continuous e-Learning organization; our Tivoli systems management software, so you can build a secure, manageable infrastructure, and IBM's integrated family of eServers, so your e-business infrastructure is bullet-proof, robust, scalable, flexible and highly reliable.

Key Challenges

Let me close by asking some key questions that can help you win in the marketplace, because at the end of the day, this is about your business and your success:

First: How well do you know your customers? Do you know who your most profitable customers are, and can you anticipate their purchasing behavior? Can you forecast demand, and make sure you have adequate supply during peak demand periods? Are you building secure, collaborative relations with your suppliers? Consider the lessons from Safeway.

Second: Are you leveraging the Web so customers can self-serve, speed execution and drive costs out of your business? Have you fully automated your supply chain? Consider the lessons from UPS.

Third: Is your company's Web site a portal for partners, distributors and customers? Could you adapt your Web site flexibly for this purpose, without starting from scratch? Is your Web site profitable, and if not, when will it be? Are your call center and sales force integrated with your Web site? Consider the lessons from Whirlpool.

Fourth: Are you building a continuous learning organization that leverages all the data inside your organization, and that allows you to set up collaborative relations with business partners? Consider the lessons of the nome project and the life sciences.

Fifth: Can your Web site manage record high transaction volumes with customers, at the same time that you provide flexibility and availability to millions of others who are just visiting? Consider the lessons of leading online brokers.

Like many of you, I've been in business in good times and bad. This is an exceptional moment, without question. The challenge is to reinvent how we do business, to speed innovation, to increase efficiency, to enhance collaboration inside and outside the enterprise, and to leverage information more effectively than ever before.

I hope that what I've suggested today gives you the courage to take a fresh look at your business, just as we're taking a fresh look at ours. In times of challenge like this, leaders find a way to win. As you well know, challenge is just another word for opportunity.

Let's take the next step of this incredible journey together. Believe me, IBM is ready when you are, and so am I. Thank you, and have a great conference!

Address by JANET PERNA, *General Manager, Data Management Solutions, IBM Software Group Delivered to the Giga World IT Forum 2001, Las Vegas, Nevada, May 23, 2001.*

From *Vital Speeches of the Day*, July 15, 2001, pp. 587-591.

Case: *Robin Hood*

Robin Hood awoke just as the sun was creeping over the crest of the hill in the very middle of Sherwood Forest. He was not the least rested, for he had not slept well that night. He could not get to sleep because of all the problems he was going to have to face today.

Certainly his campaign against the sheriff was going well, perhaps too well. It had all started out as a personal quarrel between the two of them, but now it was much more than just that. There was a price on his head of 1000 pounds, and there was no doubt that he was causing the sheriff a great deal of trouble, as taxes went uncollected or undelivered to the Crown, and rich men could not sleep soundly at night anywhere near Sherwood.

Things had changed since the early days, however. In those days it was just a small band of men, united in their cause against the sheriff, and for that matter, against Prince John, for the sheriff was simply doing John's bidding. But that was no longer the case. The fame of the Merry Men had grown and with it their numbers. He used to know each man as both a friend and companion, but now he didn't even know all of their names. Little John continued to keep discipline among the men as well as maintaining their skills with the bow, while Will Scarlet kept an eye on the sheriff, as well as any rich prospect who was foolish enough to travel Sherwood. Scarlock took care of the loot as he always had, and Much the Miller's Son continued to keep the men fed.

All this success was leading to problems. Game was, frankly, getting scarce as the number of men in the band increased, and the corresponding demand for food grew. Likely targets for the Merry Men were getting hard to find as more and more wealthy travelers were giving Sherwood a wide berth, as they were reluctant to part with their gold. Finally, the Sheriff and his men were getting better. Robin had always had the advantage of knowing Sherwood better than any man alive, but now there were at least several men who knew it almost as well as he, and some of them wore the colors of Prince John.

All this was leading Robin to reconsider his old ways. Perhaps a simple transit tax through Sherwood might be a part of the answer. But that might destroy his support among the people of the forest, and it had been rejected by the Merry Men, who were proud of their motto "Rob from the rich and give to the poor!" Besides, he needed the support of the poor, as they were his main source of information on the movements of the sheriff.

Killing the sheriff was not the answer. He would just be replaced, and, aside from quenching Robin's personal thirst for revenge, the new sheriff might be even more treacherous. Robin hated his enemy, but he had the advantage of knowing the sheriff's strengths and weaknesses. He would not know a new man's talents.

Prince John, on the other hand, was a vicious tyrant, a good part of which stemmed from his very weakness. The Barons were growing more restless every day, and the people simply hated him. They wanted King Richard back from his jail in Austria. Robin had been discreetly approached by several nobles loyal to Richard to join in the effort to free the King with the promise of a full pardon for him and all his men should they succeed. But Robin knew that if they failed, John would burn Sherwood and the rest of England to the ground to reap his vengeance. Theft and unrest in the provinces were one thing, intrigue at court was another.

Robin knew the days of the Merry Men were numbered. Even as they grew stronger, they grew weaker. Time was on the side of the sheriff, who would draw on all the power of the Crown if he had to, and, if Robin became too much of a threat, would surely do so.

Just then the horn blew for the traditional English breakfast of bread and ale. Robin would have breakfast with the Merry Men and then confer with Will Scarlet, Little John, and Scarlock.

Using the Case of *Robin Hood*

Robin Hood is a perfect example of a manager facing the problems of success. Robin's very success has created his problems.

Questions for Discussion

1. What are some of the problems facing Robin and the Merry Men?
2. What are some of the situations in the environment that will have an impact on whatever Robin decides to do?
3. What are some of the alternatives that Robin is considering for dealing with his problems? Can you identify some additional alternatives?
4. What do you think the reaction of Merry Men will be? The sheriff? The people?
5. What do you think Robin should do?

Exercise: *Managerial Development*

1. Identify the best manager with whom you personally have interacted within the last seven years:

2. Why did you select that person? I selected him/her because:
   a. s/he:
   b. s/he:
   c. s/he:
4. Of the attributes you listed above, which is the most important for you? A, B, or C?
5. Why do you feel that is the most important attribute of a manager?
6. Identify the best employee with whom you personally have interacted within the past seven years.
7. Why did you select that person? I selected him/her because:
   a. s/he:
   b. s/he:
   c. s/he:
4. Of the attributes you listed above, which is the most important? A, B, or C?
5. Why do you feel that is the most important attribute of an employee?

Using the Exercise for *Managerial Development*

This exercise has been developed to give you the opportunity to establish a role model for managerial and employee behavior. It provides a useful tool for determining your attitude toward what makes a good manager and a good employee.

It might be particularly useful to do the exercise during the first few days of class, discuss it, and then, at the end of the term, redo the exercise to determine if there has been any changes in your perception of the best manager and employee and what they did.

It is recommended that you keep the papers so that they can be used for reference during a class discussion of managerial and employee behavior. The names of the individuals are not important. The ideas, perceptions, and attitudes of those people are what count

Case: Robin Hood; Exercise: Managerial Development, Fred Maidment, McGraw-Hill/Dushkin, 2000.

UNIT 3

Planning

Unit Selections

Key Points to Consider

- What do you think is the best way to make decisions when other people have to implement them? Do you think some ways are better than others? Explain.
- Many organizations talk about thinking "out of the box," yet few seem able to do so. Why do you think this is? Why is timing critical to the implementation of any plan?
- Many organizations are seeking new ways to implement strategic management in the twenty-first century. What are some of the things that you might consider doing that have not been done in the past?

DUSHKIN ONLINE **Links: www.dushkin.com/online/**
These sites are annotated in the World Wide Web pages.

American Civil Liberties Union (ACLU)
http://www.aclu.org/issues/worker/campaign.html

Benchmarking Network
http://www.well.com/user/benchmar/tbnhome.html

GBN Scenario Planning
http://www.gbn.org/public/gbnstory/scenarios/

Innovation in the Workplace
http://www.managementfirst.com/articles/workplace.htm

Managers must plan. Planning must be accomplished before action takes place. The question is, how should managers plan and decide on a course of action?

There are various styles, methods, and techniques that a manager can call upon. As Victor Vroom demonstrates in his classic essay, "A New Look at Managerial Decision Making," the way that decisions are made will be a key factor in the implementation of the plan. People who feel that they have some participation in making important decisions that will affect them are far more likely to support the plan enthusiastically than are people who feel that the decision is a fiat from the upper reaches of the organization chart. Of course, a manager can make some decisions alone or in consultation with a few people. The important part is to select the appropriate planning/decision-making style, so that the action will have the greatest chance for success. The way to accomplish this is to involve the people who will be most directly concerned with the implementation of that decision.

It is basic to the function of a manager that he or she must make decisions. It is not possible for the policy manual to cover every situation that can arise. Managers must be able to interpret the goals and objectives of the plans for the good of the organization—not an easy task. Since there is always a degree of uncertainty in an important decision, the organization is also obligated to provide the manager with support and resources so that the decision will succeed. Support includes not only a recognition and knowledge of the firm and its plans, but an understanding of the organization's internal and external environment.

Planning must consider the internal strengths and weaknesses of the organization, including finance, human resources, manufacturing, distribution, and marketing. Capitalizing on strengths while minimizing the impact of weaknesses is vital to successful planning. Strategic decision making also involves an assessment of the environment as well as an understanding of the corporate culture. Organizations must interact with their surroundings and timing is important.

Those who manage and plan for organizations must recognize that the only constant is change. Everything is fluid—people, places, and things—and managing the strategic agenda will be a key to success.

Finally, there are many ways to plan and make strategy. The effectiveness of the plans depends on the nature and needs of the business, the styles of the people, and the goals and plans of the firm. The five basic questions in strategic planning are: (1) Where have we been? (2) Where are we now? (3) Where do we want to go? (4) How do we want to get there? (5) How will we know we have arrived? These questions must be answered by each firm's management as they plan for the organization in a changing and uncertain world. It is essential that students of management learn these principles and be able to put them into practice. Opportunities abound and are often found in what might be considered less than traditional areas of planning, as can be seen in "New Rules of the Game."

A NEW LOOK AT MANAGERIAL DECISION MAKING

Victor H. Vroom

All managers are decision makers. Furthermore, their effectiveness as managers is largely reflected in their track record in making the right decisions. These right decisions in turn largely depend on whether or not the manager has utilized the right person or persons in the right ways in helping him solve the problem.

Our concern in this article is with decision making as a social process. We view the manager's task as determining how the problem is to be solved, not the solution to be adopted. Within that overall framework, we have attempted to answer two broad sets of questions: What decision-making processes should managers use to deal effectively with the problems they encounter in their jobs? What decision-making processes do they use in dealing with these problems and what considerations affect their decisions about how much to share their decision-making power with subordinates?

The reader will recognize the former as a normative or prescriptive question. A rational and analytic answer to it would constitute a normative model of decision making as a social process. The second question is descriptive, since it concerns how managers do, rather than should, behave.

Towards a Normal Model

About four years ago, Philip Yetton, then a graduate student at Carnegie-Mellon University, and I began a major research program in an attempt to answer these normative and descriptive questions.

We began with the normative question: What would be a rational way of deciding on the form and amount of participation in decision making that should be used in different situations? We were tired of debates over the relative merits of Theory X and Theory Y and of the truism that leadership depends upon the situation. We felt that it was time for the behavioral sciences to move beyond such generalities and to attempt to come to grips with the complexities of the phenomena with which they intended to deal.

Our aim was ambitious—to develop a set of ground rules for matching a manager's leadership behavior to the demands of the situation. It was critical that these ground rules be consistent with research evidence concerning the consequences of participation and that the model based on the rules be operational, so that any manager could see it to determine how he should act in any decision-making situation.

Table 1 shows a set of alternative decision processes that we have employed in our research. Each process is represented by a symbol (e.g., AI, CI, GII) that will be used as a convenient method of referring to each process. The first letter in this symbol signifies the basic properties of the process (A stands for autocratic; C for consultative; and G for group). The Roman numerals that follow the first letter constitute variants on that process. Thus, AI represents the first variant on an autocratic process, and AII the second variant.

Conceptual and Empirical Basis of the Model

A model designed to regulate, in some rational way, choices among the decisions processes shown in Table 1 should be based on sound empirical evidence concerning the likely consequences of the styles. The more complete the empirical base of knowledge, the greater the certainty with which we can develop the model and the greater will be its usefulness. To aid in understanding the conceptual basis of the model, it is important to distinguish among three classes of outcomes that bear on the ultimate effectiveness of decisions. These are:

1. The quality or rationality of the decision.
2. The acceptance or commitment on the part of subordinates to execute the decision effectively.
3. The amount of time required to make the decision.

The effects of participation on each of these outcomes or consequences were summed up by the author in *The Handbook of Social Psychology* as follows:

TABLE 1 TYPES OF MANAGEMENT DECISION STYLES

AI	You solve the problem or make the decision yourself, using information available to you at that time.
AII	You obtain the necessary information from your subordinate(s), then decide on the solution to the problem yourself. You may or may not tell your subordinates what the problem is in getting the information from them. The role played by your subordinates in making the decision is clearly one of providing the necessary information to you, rather than generating or evaluating alternative solutions.
CI	You share the problem with relevant subordinates individually, getting their ideas and suggestions without bringing them together as a group. Then you make the decision that may or may not reflect your subordinates' influence.
CII	You share the problem with your subordinates as a group, collectively obtaining their ideas and suggestions. Then you make the decision that may or may not reflect your subordinates' influence.
GII	You share a problem with your subordinates as a group. Together you generate and evaluate alternatives and attempt to reach agreement (consensus) on a solution. Your role is much like that of chairman. You do not try to influence the group to adopt your solution and you are willing to accept and implement any solution that has the support of the entire group.

(GI is omitted because it applies only to more comprehensive models outside the scope of this article.)

The results suggest that allocating problem solving and decision-making tasks to entire groups requires a greater investment of man hours but produces higher acceptance of decisions and a higher probability that the decision will be executed efficiently. Differences between these two methods in quality of decisions and in elapsed time are inconclusive and probably highly variable.... It would be naive to think that group decision making is always more "effective" than autocratic decision making, or vice versa; the relative effectiveness of these two extreme methods depends both on the weights attached to quality, acceptance and time variables and on differences in amounts of these outcomes resulting from these methods, neither of which is invariant from one situation to another. The critics and proponents of participative management would do well to direct their efforts toward identifying the properties of situations in which different decision-making approaches are effective rather than wholesale condemnation or deification of one approach.

We have gone on from there to identify the properties of the situation or problem that will be the basic elements in the model. These problem attributes are of two types: 1) Those that specify the importance for a particular problem of quality and acceptance, and 2) those that, on the basis of available evidence, have a high probability of moderating the effects of participation on each of these outcomes. Table 2 shows the problem attributes used in the present form of the model. For each attribute a question is provided that might be used by a leader in diagnosing a particular problem prior to choosing his leadership style.

In phrasing the questions, we have held technical language to a minimum. Furthermore, we have phrased the questions in Yes-No form, translating the continuous variables defined above into dichotomous variables. For example, instead of attempting to determine how important the decision quality is to the effectiveness of the decision (attribute A), the leader is asked in the first question to judge whether there is any quality component to the problem. Similarly, the difficult task of specifying exactly how much information the leader possesses that is relevant to the decision (attribute B) is reduced to a simple judgment by the leader concerning whether or not he has sufficient information to make a high quality decision.

We have found that managers can diagnose a situation quickly and accurately by answering this set of seven questions concerning it. But how can such responses generate a prescription concerning the most effective leadership style or decision process? What kind of normative model of participation in decision making can be built from this set of problem attributes?

Figure 1 shows one such model expressed in the form of a decision tree. It is the seventh version of such a model that we have developed over the last three years. The problem attributes, expressed in question form, are arranged along the top of the figure. To use the model for a particular decision-making situation, one starts at the left-hand side and works toward the right asking oneself the question immediately above any box that is encountered. When a terminal node is reached, a number will be found designating the problem type and one of the decision-making processes appearing in Table 1. AI is prescribed for four problem types (1, 2, 4, and 5); AII is prescribed for two problem types (9 and 10); CI is prescribed for only one problem type (8); CII is prescribed for four problem types (7, 11, 13, and 14); and GII is prescribed for three problem types (3, 6, and 12). The relative frequency with which each of the five decision processes would be prescribed for any manager would, of course, depend on the distribution of problem types encountered in his decision making.

Rationale Underlying the Model. The decision processes specified for each problem type are not arbitrary. The model's behavior is governed by a set of principles intended to be consistent with existing evidence concerning the consequences of participation in decision making on organizational effectiveness.

There are two mechanisms underlying the behavior of the model. The first is a set of seven rules* that serve to protect the quality and the acceptance of the decision by eliminating alternatives that risk one or the other of these decision outcomes. Once the rules have been applied, a feasible set of decision processes is generated. The second mechanism is a principle for choosing among alternatives in the feasible set where more than one exists.

TABLE 2 PROBLEM ATTRIBUTES USED IN THE MODEL

	Problem Attributes	Diagnostic Questions
A.	The importance of the quality of the decision.	Is there a quality requirement such that one solution is likely to be more rational than another?
B.	The extent to which the leader possesses sufficient information/expertise to make a high-quality decision by himself.	Do I have sufficient information to make a high-quality decision?
C.	The extent to which the problem is structured.	Is the problem structured?
D.	The extent to which acceptance or commitment on the part of subordinates is critical to the effective implementation of the decision.	Is acceptance of decision by subordinates critical to effective implementation?
E.	The prior probability that the leader's autocratic decision will receive acceptance by subordinates.	If you were to make the decision by yourself, is it reasonably certain that it would be accepted by your subordinates?
F.	The extent to which subordinates are motivated to attain the organizational goals as represented in the objectives explicit in the statement of the problem.	Do subordinates share the organizational goals to be obtained in solving this problem?
G.	The extent to which subordinates are likely to be in conflict over preferred solutions.	Is conflict among subordinates likely in preferred solutions?

Let us examine the rules first, because they do much of the work of the model. As previously indicated, the rules are intended to protect both the quality and acceptance of the decision. In the form of the model shown, there are three rules that protect decision quality and four that protect acceptance.

1. *The Information Rule.* If the quality of the decision is important and if the leader does not possess enough information or expertise to solve the problem by himself, AI is eliminated from the feasible set. (Its use risks a low-quality decision.)

2. *The Goal Congruence rule.* If the quality of the decision is important and if the subordinates do not share the organizational goals to be obtained in solving the problem, GII is eliminated from the feasible set. (Alternatives that eliminate the leader's final control over the decision reached may jeopardize the quality of the decision.)

3. *The Unstructured Problem Rule.* In decisions in which the quality of the decision is important, if the leader lacks the necessary information or expertise to solve the problem by himself, and if the problem is unstructured, i.e., he does not know exactly what information is needed and where it is located, the method used must provide not only for him to collect the information but to do so is an efficient and effective manner. Methods that involve interaction among all subordinates with full knowledge of the problem are likely to be both more efficient and more likely to generate a high-quality solution to the problem. Under these conditions, AI, AII, and CI are eliminated from the feasible set. (AI does not provide for him to collect the necessary information, and AII and CI represent more cumbersome, less effective, and less efficient means of bringing the necessary information to bear on the solution of the problem than methods that do permit those with the necessary information to interact.)

4. *The Acceptance Rule.* If the acceptance of the decision by subordinates is critical to effective implementation, and if it is not certain that an autocratic decision made by the leader would receive that acceptance, AI and AII are eliminated from the feasible set. (Neither provides an opportunity for subordinates to participate in the decision and both risk the necessary acceptance.)

5. *The Conflict Rule.* If the acceptance of the decision is critical, and an autocratic decision is not certain to be accepted, and subordinates are likely to be in conflict or disagreement over the appropriate solution, AI, AII, and CI are eliminated from the feasible set. (The method used in solving the problem should enable those in disagreement to resolve their differences with full knowledge of the problem. Accordingly, under these conditions, AI, AII, and CI, which involve no interaction or only "one-on-one" relationships and therefore provide no opportunity for those in conflict to resolve their differences, are eliminated from the feasible set. Their use runs the risk of leaving some of the subordinates with less than the necessary commitment to the final decision.)

FIGURE 1
Decision Model

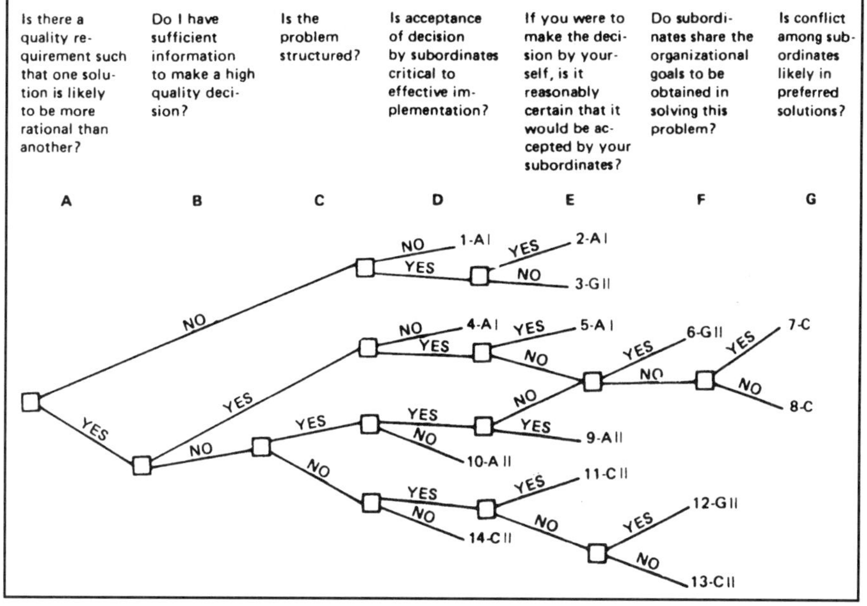

*The rules and figure 1 are reprinted from Leadership and Decision-Making, by Victor H. Vroom and Philip W. Yetton, by permission of the University of Pittsburgh Press. © 1973 by University of Pittsburgh Press

6. *The Fairness Rule.* If the quality of decision is unimportant and if acceptance is critical and not certain to result from an autocratic decision, AI, AII, CI, and CII are eliminated from the feasible set. (The method used should maximize the probability of acceptance as this is the only relevant consideration in determining the effectiveness of the decision. Under these circumstances, AI, AII, CI, and CII, which create less acceptance or commitment than GII, are eliminated from the feasible set. To use them is to run the risk of getting less than the needed acceptance of the decision.)

7. *The Acceptance Priority Rule.* If acceptance is critical, not assured by an autocratic decision, and if subordinates can be trusted, AI, AII, CI, and CII are eliminated from the feasible set. (Methods that provide equal partnership in the decision-making process can provide greater acceptance without risking decision quality. Use of any method other than GII results in an unnecessary risk that the decision will not be fully accepted or receive the necessary commitment on the part of subordinates.)

Once all seven rules have been applied to a given problem we emerge with a feasible set of decision processes. The feasible set for each of the fourteen problem types is shown in Table 3. It can be seen that there are some problem types for which only one method remains in the feasible set, others for which two methods remain feasible, and still others for which five methods remain feasible.

When more than one method remains in the feasible set, there are a number of ways in which one might choose among them. The mechanism we have selected, the principle underlying the choices of the model in Figure 1, utilizes the number of man-hours used in solving the problem as the basis for choice. Given a set of methods with equal likelihood of meeting both quality and acceptance requirements for the decision, it chooses that method that requires the least investment of man-hours. On the basis of the empirical evidence summarized earlier, this is deemed to be the method furthest to the left within the feasible set. For example, since AI, AII, CI, CII, and GII are all feasible as in Problem Types 1 and 2, AI would be the method chosen.

To illustrate application of the model in actual administrative situations, we will analyze four cases with the help of the model. While we attempt to describe these cases as completely as is necessary to permit the reader to make the judgments required by the model, there may remain some room for subjectivity. The reader may wish after reading the case to analyze it himself using the model and then to compare his analysis with that of the author.

CASE I. You are a manufacturing manager in a large electronics plant. The company's management has recently installed new machines and put in a new simplified work system, but to the surprise of everyone, yourself included, the expected increase in productivity was not realized. In fact, production has begun to drop, quality has fallen off, and the number of employee separations has risen.

You do not believe that there is anything wrong with the machines. You have had reports from other companies that are using them and they confirm this opinion. You have also had representatives from the firm that built the machines go over them and they report that they are operating at peak efficiency.

You suspect that some parts of the new work system may be responsible for the change, but this view is not widely shared among your immediate subordinates who are four first-line supervisors, each in charge of a section, and your supply manager. The drop in production has been variously attributed to poor training of the operators, lack of an adequate system of financial incentives, and poor morale. Clearly, this is an issue about which there is considerable depth of feeling within individuals and potential disagreement among your subordinates.

This morning you received a phone call from your division manager. He had just received your production figures for the last six months and was calling to express his concern. He indicated that the problem was yours to solve in any way that you think best, but that he would like to know within a week what steps you plan to take.

You share your division manager's concern with the falling productivity and know that your men are also concerned. The problem is to decide what steps to take to rectify the situation.

Analysis
Questions—
A (Quality?) = Yes
B (Manager's Information?) = No
C (Structured?) = No
D (Acceptance?) = Yes
E (Prior Probability of Acceptance?) = No
F (Goal Congruence?) = Yes
G (Conflict) = Yes
Problem Type—12
Feasible Set—GII
Minimum Man-Hours Solution (from Figure 1)—GII
Rule Violations—
AI violates rules 1, 3, 4, 5, 7
AII violates rules 3, 4, 5, 7
CI violates rules 3, 5, 7
CII violates rule 7

CASE II. You are general foreman in charge of a large gang laying an oil pipeline and have to estimate your expected rate of progress in order to schedule material deliveries to the next field site.

You know the nature of the terrain you will be traveling and have the historical data needed to compute the mean and variance in the rate of speed over that type of terrain. Given these two variables, it is a simple matter to calculate the earliest and latest times at which materials and support facilities will be needed at the next site. It is important that your estimate be reasonably accurate. Underestimates result in idle foremen and workers, and an overestimate results in tying up materials for a period of time before they are to be used.

TABLE 3 PROBLEM TYPES AND THE FEASIBLE SET OF DECISION PROCESSES

Problem Type	Acceptable Methods
1.	AI, AII, CI, CII, GII
2.	AI, AII, CI, CII, GII
3.	GII
4.	AI, AII, CI, CII, GII*
5.	AI, AII, CI, CII, GII*
6.	GII
7.	CII
8.	CI, CII
9.	AII, CI, CII, GII*
10.	AII, CI, CII, GII*
11.	CII, GII*
12.	GII
13.	CII
14.	CII, GII*

*Within the feasible set only when the answer to F is Yes.

Progress has been good and your five foremen and other members of the gang stand to receive substantial bonuses if the project is completed ahead of schedule.

Analysis
Questions—
A (Quality?) = Yes
B (Manager's Information?) = Yes
D (Acceptance?) = No
Problem Type—4
Feasible Set—AI, AII, CI, CII, GII
Minimum Man-Hours Solution (from Figure 1)—AI
Rule Violations—None

CASE III. You are supervising the work of 12 engineers. Their formal training and work experience are very similar, permitting you to use them interchangeably on projects. Yesterday, your manager informed you that a request had been received from an overseas affiliate for four engineers to go abroad on extended loan for a period of six to eight months. For a number of reasons, he argued and you agreed that this request should be met from your group.

All your engineers are capable of handling this assignment and, from the standpoint of present and future projects, there is no particular reason why anyone should be retained over any other. The problem is somewhat complicated by the fact that the overseas assignment is in what is generally regarded as an undesirable location.

Analysis
Questions—
A (Quality?) = No
D (Acceptance?) = Yes
E (Prior Probability of Acceptance?) = No
G (Conflict?) = Yes
Problem Type—3
Feasible Set—GII
Minimum Man-Hours Solution (from Figure 1)—GII
Rule Violations—
AI and AII violate rules 4, 5, and 6
CI violates rules 5 and 6
CII violates rule 6

CASE IV. You are on the division manager's staff and work on a wide variety of problems of both an administrative and technical nature. You have been given the assignment of developing a standard method to be used in each of the five plants in the division for manually reading equipment registers, recording the readings, and transmitting the scorings to a centralized information system.

Until now there has been a high error rate in the reading and/or transmittal of the data. Some locations have considerably higher error rates than others, and the methods used to record and transmit the data vary among plants. It is probable, therefore, that part of the error variance is a function of specific local conditions rather than anything else, and this will complicate the establishment of any system common to all plants. You have the information error rates but no information on the local practices that generate these errors or on the local conditions that necessitate the different practices.

Everyone would benefit from an improvement in the quality of the data; it is used in a number of important decisions. Your contacts with the plants are through the quality-control supervisors who are responsible for collecting the data. They are a conscientious group committed to doing their jobs well, but are highly sensitive to interference on the part of higher management in their own operations. Any solution that does not receive the active support of the various plant supervisors is unlikely to reduce the error rate significantly.

Analysis
Questions—
A (Quality?) = Yes
B (Manager's Information?) = No
C (Structured?) = No
D (Acceptance?) = Yes
E (Prior Probability of Acceptance?) = No
F (Goal Congruence?) = Yes
Problem Type—12
Feasible Set—GII
Minimum Man-Hours Solution (from Figure 1)—GII
Rule Violations—
AI violates rules 1, 3, 4, and 7
AII violates rules 3, 4, and 7
CI violates rules 3 and 7
CII violates rule 7

Short Versus Long-Term Models

The model described above seeks to protect the quality of the decision and to expend the least number of man-hours in the process. Because it focuses on conditions surrounding the making and implementation of a particular decision rather than any long-term considerations, we can term it a short-term model.

It seems likely, however, that the leadership methods that may be optimal for short-term results may be different from those that would be optimal over a longer period of time. Consider a leader, for example, who has been uniformly pursuing an autocratic style (AI or AII) and, perhaps as a consequence, has subordinates who might be termed "yes men" (attribute E) but who also cannot be trusted to pursue organizational goals (attribute F), largely because the leader has never bothered to explain them.

It appears likely, however, that the manger who used more participative methods would, in time, change the status of these problem attributes so as to develop ultimately a more effective problem-solving system. A promising approach to the development of a long-term model is one that places less weight on man-hours as the basis for choice of method within the feasible set. Given a long-term orientation, one would be interested in the possibility of a trade-off between man-hours in problem solving and team development, both of which increase with participation. Viewed in these terms, the time-minimizing model places maximum relative weight on man-hours and no weight on development, and hence chooses the style farthest to the left within the feasible set. A model that places less weight on man-hours and more weight on development would, if these assumptions are correct, choose a style further to the right within the feasible set.

We recognize, of course, that the minimum man-hours solution suggested by the model is not always the best solution to every problem. A manager faced, for example with the problem of handling any one of the four cases previously examined might well choose more time-consuming alternatives on the grounds that the greater time invested would be justified in developing his subordinates. Similar considerations exist in other decision-making situations. For this reason we have come to emphasize the feasible set of decision methods in our work with managers. Faced with considerations not included in the model, the manager should consider any alternative within the feasible set, and not opt automatically for the minimum man-hours solution.

As I am writing this, I have in front of me a "black box" that constitutes an electronic version of the normative model discussed on the preceding pages. (The author is indebted to Peter Fuss of Bell Telephone Laboratories for his interest in the model and his skill in developing the "black box.") The box, which is small enough to fit into the palm of one hand, has a set of seven switches, each appropriately labeled with the questions (A through G) used in Figure 1. A manager faced with a concrete problem or decision can "diagnose" that problem by setting each switch in either its "yes" or "no" position. Once the problem has been described, the manager depresses a button that illuminates at least one or as many as five lights, each of which denotes one of the decision processes (AI, AII, etc.). The lights that are illuminated constitute the feasible set of decision processes for the problem as shown in Table III. The lights not illuminated correspond to alternatives that violate one or more of the seven rules previously stated.

In this prototype version of the box, the lights are illuminated in decreasing order of brightness from left to right within the feasible set. The brightest light corresponds to the alternative shown in Figure 1. Thus, if both CII and GII were feasible alternatives, CII would be brighter than GII, since it requires fewer man-hours. However, a manager who was not under any undue time pressure and who wished to invest time in the development of his subordinates might select an alternative corresponding to one of the dimmer lights.

Toward a Descriptive Model of Leader Behavior

So far we have been concerned with the normative questions defined at the outset. But how do managers really behave? What considerations affect their decisions about how much to share their decision-making power with their subordinates? In what respects is their behavior different from or similar to that of the model? These questions are but a few of those that we attempted to answer in a large-scale research program aimed at gaining a greater understanding of the factors that influence managers in their choice of decision processes to fit the demands of the situation. This research program was financially supported by the McKinsey Foundation, General Electric Foundation, Smith Richardson Foundation, and the Office of Naval Research.

Two different research methods have been utilized in studying these factors. The first investigation utilized a method that we have come to term "recalled problems." Over 500 managers from 11 different countries representing a variety of firms were asked to provide a written description of a problem that they had recently had to solve. These varied in length from one paragraph to several pages and covered virtually every facet of managerial decision making. For each case, the manager was asked to indicate which of the decision processes shown in Table I they used to solve the problem. Finally, each manager was asked to answer the questions shown in Table II corresponding to the problem attributes used in the normative model.

The wealth of data, both qualitative and quantitative, served two purposes. Since each manager had diagnosed a situation that he had encountered in terms that are used in the normative model and had indicated the methods that he had used in dealing with it, it is possible to determine what differences, if any, there were between the model's behavior and his own behavior. Second, the written cases provided the basis for the construction of a standard set of cases used in later research to determine the factors that influence managers to share or retain their decision-making power. Each case depicted a manager faced with a problem to solve or decision to make. The cases spanned a wide range of managerial problems including production scheduling, quality control, portfolio management, personnel allocation, and research and development. In each case, a person could readily assume the role of the manager described and could indicate which of the decision processes he would use if he actually were faced with that situation.

In most of our research, a set of thirty cases has been used and the subjects have been several thousand managers who were participants in management development programs in the United States and abroad. Cases were selected systematically. We desired cases that could not only be coded unambiguously in the terms used in the normative model but that would also permit the assessment of the effects of each of the problem attributes used in the model on the person's behavior. The solution was to select cases in accordance with an experimental design so that they varied in terms of the seven attributes used in the model and variation in each attribute was independent of each other attribute. Several such standardized sets of cases have been developed, and over a thousand managers have now been studied using this approach.

To summarize everything we learned in the course of this research is well beyond the scope of this paper, but it is possible to discuss some of the highlights. Since the results obtained from the two research methods—recalled and standardized problems—are consistent, we can present the major results independent of the method used.

Perhaps the most striking finding is the weakening of the widespread view that participativeness is a general trait that individual managers exhibit in different amounts. To be sure, there were differences *among* managers in their general tendencies to utilize participative methods as opposed to autocratic ones. On the standardized problems, these differences accounted for about 10 percent of the total variance in the decision process observed. These differences in behavior between managers, however, were small in comparison with differences *within* managers. On the standardized problems, no manager indicated that he would use the same decision process on all problems or decisions, and most used all five methods under some circumstances.

Some of this variance in behavior within managers can be attributed to widely shared tendencies to respond to some situations by sharing power and others by retaining it. It makes more sense to talk about participative and autocratic situations than it does to talk about participative and autocratic managers. In fact, on the standardized problems, the variance in behavior across problems or cases is about three times as large as the variance across managers!

What are the characteristics of an autocratic as opposed to a participative situation? An answer to this question would constitute a partial descriptive model of this aspect of the decision-making process and has been our goal in much of the research that we have conducted. From our observations of behavior on both recalled problems and on standardized problems, it is clear that the decision-making process has been our goal in much of the research that we have conducted. From our observations of behavior on both recalled problems and on standardized problems, it is clear that the decision-making process employed by a typical manager is influenced by a large number of factors, many of which also show up in the normative model. Following are several conclusions substantiated by the results on both recalled and standardized problems: Managers use decision processes providing less opportunity for participation (1) when they possess all the necessary information than when they lack some of the needed information, (2) when the problem that they face is well-structured rather than unstructured, (3) when their subordinates' acceptance of the decision is not critical for the effective implementation of the decision or when the prior probability of acceptance of an autocratic decision is high, and (4) when the personal goals of their subordinates are *not* congruent with the goals of the organization as manifested in the problem.

So far we have been talking about relatively common or widely shared ways of dealing with organizational problems. Our results strongly suggest that there are ways of "tailoring" one's approach to the situation that distinguish managers from one another. Theoretically, these can be thought of as differences among managers in decision rules that they employ about when to encourage participation. Statistically, they are represented as interactions between situational variables and personal characteristics.

Consider, for example, two managers who have identical distributions of the use of the five decision processes shown in Table I on a set of thirty cases. In a sense, they are equally participative (or autocratic). However, the situations in which they permit or encourage participation in decision making on the part of their subordinates may be very different. One may restrict the participation of his subordinates to decisions without a quality requirement, whereas the other may restrict their participation to problems with a quality requirement. The former would be more inclined to use participative decision processes (like GII) on such decisions as what color the walls should be painted or when the company picnic should be held. The latter would be more likely to encourage participation in decision making on decisions that have a clear and demonstrable impact on the organization's success in achieving its external goals.

Use of the standardized problem set permits the assessment of such differences in decision rules that govern choices among decision-making processes. Since the cases are selected in accordance with an experimental design, they can indicate differences in the behavior of managers attributable not only to the existence of a quality requirement in the problem but also in the effects of acceptance requirements, conflict, information requirements, and the like.

The research using both recalled and standardized problems has also enabled us to examine similarities and differences between the behavior of the normative model and the behavior of a typical manager. Such an analysis reveals, at the very least, what behavioral changes could be expected if managers began using the normative model as the basis for choosing their decision-making processes.

A typical manager says he would (or did) use exactly the same decision process as that shown in Figure 1 in 40 percent of the situations. In two thirds of the situations, his behavior is consistent with the feasible set of methods proposed in the model. In other words, in about one third of the situations his behavior violates at least one of the seven rules underlying the model.

The four rules designed to protect the acceptance or commitment of the decision have substantially higher probabilities of being violated than do the three rules designed to protect the quality or rationality of the decision. One of the acceptance rules, the Fairness Rule (Rule 6) is violated about three quarters of the time that it could have been violated. On the other hand, one of the quality rules, the Information Rule (Rule 1), is violated in only about 3 percent of occasions in which it is applicable. If we assume for the moment that these two sets of rules have equal validity, these findings strongly suggest that the decisions made by typical managers are more likely to prove ineffective due to deficiencies of acceptance by subordinates than due to deficiencies in decision quality.

Another striking difference between the behavior of the model and of the typical manager lies in the fact that the former shows far greater variance with the situation. If a typical manager voluntarily used the model as the basis for choosing his methods of making decisions, he would become both more autocratic and more participative. He would employ autocratic methods more frequently in situations in which his subordinates were unaffected by the decision and participative methods more frequently when his subordinates' cooperation and support were critical and/or their information and expertise were required.

It should be noted that the typical manager to whom we have been referring is merely a statistical average of the several thousand who have been studied over the last three or four years. There is a great deal of variance around that average. As evidenced by their behavior on standardized problems some managers are already behaving in a way that is highly consistent with the model, while others' behavior is clearly at variance with it.

A New Technology for Leadership Development

The investigations that have been summarized here were conducted for research purposes to shed some light on the causes and consequences of participation in decision making. In the course of the research, we came to realize, partly because of the value attached to it by the managers themselves, that the data collection procedures, with appropriate additions and modifications, might also serve as a valuable guide to leadership development. From this realization evolved an important by-product of the research activities—a new approach to leadership development based on the concepts in the normative model and the empirical methods of the descriptive research.

This approach is based on the assumption stated previously that one of the critical skills required of all leaders is the ability to adapt their behavior to the demands of the situation and that one component of this skill involves the ability to select the appropriate decision-making process for each problem or decision he confronts.

Managers can derive value from the model by comparing their past or intended behavior in concrete decisions with that prescribed by the model and by seeing what rules, if any, they violate. Used in this way, the model can provide a mechanism for a manager to analyze both the circumstances that he faces and what decisions are feasible under these circumstances.

While use of the model without training is possible, we believe that the manager can derive the maximum value from a systematic examination of his leadership style, and its similarities to and dissimilarities from the model, as part of a formal leadership development program.

During the past two years we have developed such a program. It is not intended to "train" participants in the use of the model, but rather to encourage them to examine their own leadership style and to ask themselves whether the methods they are using are most effective for their own organization. A critical part of the program involves the use of a set of standardized cases, each depicting a leader faced with an administrative problem to solve. Each participant then specifies the decision-making process that he would use if faced with each situation. His responses are processed by computer, which generates a highly detailed analysis of his leadership style. The responses for all participants in the course are typically processed simultaneously, permitting the economical representation of differences between the person and other participants in the same program.

In its present form, a single computer printout for a person consists of three 15 x 11 pages, each filled with graphs and tables highlighting different features of his behavior. Understanding the results requires a detailed knowledge of the concepts underlying the model, something already developed in one of the previous phases of the training program. The printout is accompanied by a manual that aids in explaining results and provides suggested steps to be followed in extracting full meaning from the printout.

Following are a few of the questions that the printout answers:

1. How autocratic or participative am I in my dealings with subordinates in comparison with other participants in the program?
2. What decision processes do I use more or less frequently than the average?
3. How close does my behavior come to that of the model? How frequently does my behavior agree with the feasible set? What evidence is there that my leadership style reflects the pressure of time as opposed to a concern with the development of my subordinates? How do I compare in these respects with other participants in the class?
4. What rules do I violate most frequently and least frequently? How does this compare with other participants? On what cases did I violate these rules? Does my leadership style reflect more concern with getting decisions that are high in quality or with getting decisions that are accepted?
5. What circumstances cause me to behave in an autocratic fashion; what circumstances cause me to behave participatively? In what respects is the way in which I attempt to vary my behavior with the demands of the situation similar to that of the model?

When a typical manager receives his printout, he immediately goes to work trying to understand what it tells him about himself. After most of the major results have been understood, he goes back to the set of cases to reread those on which he has violated rules. Typically, managers show an interest in discussing and comparing their results with others in the program. Gatherings of four to six people comparing their results and their interpretation of them, often for several hours at a stretch, were such a common feature that they have recently been institutionalized as part of the procedure.

We should emphasize that the method of providing feedback to managers on their leadership style is just one part of the total training experience, but it is an important part. The program is sufficiently new so that, to date, no long-term evaluative studies have been undertaken. The short-term results, however, appear quite promising.

Conclusion

The efforts reported in this article rest on the conviction that social scientists can be of greater value in solving problems of organizational behavior if their prescriptive statements deal with the complexities involved in the phenomena with which they study. The normative model described in this paper is one step in that direction. Some might argue that it is premature for social scientists to be prescriptive. Our knowledge is too limited and the issues too complex to warrant prescriptions for action, even those that are based on a diagnosis of situational demands. However, organizational problems persist, and managers cannot wait for the behavioral sciences to perfect their disciplines before attempting to cope with them. Is it likely that models that encourage them to deal analytically with the forces impinging upon them would produce less rational choices than those that they now make? We think the reverse is more probable—reflecting on the models will result in decisions that are more rational and more effective. The criterion for social utility is not perfection but improvement over present practice.

Victor H. Vroom, Professor, Yale University

From *Readings in Management,* 1986, pp. 132-148. Published by South-Western Publishing Company. Originally from *Organizational Dynamics,* Spring 1972, pp. 66-80.

MANAGEMENT ACCOUNTING MASTER: CLOSING THE GAP BETWEEN MANAGERIAL ACCOUNTING AND EXTERNAL REPORTING

Soeren Dressler

Times of significant market adjustments and an uncertain economy spotlight the need for effective decision-support systems. Leadership must have the ability to promptly identify issues and make adjustments based on benchmarks. Financial professionals, however, especially those for multinationals, are challenged to align management accounting with legal reporting requirements. A globally harmonized management accounting master (MAM) can be the answer. It becomes the blueprint for organizational alignment and provides benchmarking for management decision-making. To make it work, the current assortment of business unit structures must be supplemented with local centers comprised of comparable units across divisions and countries. The result is integrated local reporting for management information and control that effectively steers the business from both the local and corporate perspectives, while meeting the various financial reporting requirements.

INTRODUCTION

Especially during a softening economy, finance departments of international corporations are challenged in closing their books—monthly, quarterly, and on a yearly basis. This challenge is basically twofold: on one side, a community of financial analysts thirsts for disclosure of financial figures to guide recommendations for investors and on the other side, management seeks indications of underperforming units and opportunities to streamline its business. The biggest challenge is delivering a set of harmonized and integrated data. Financial professionals and managers, both corporate and of local subsidiaries, are challenged to simplify and harmonize accounting approaches to meet financial reporting requirements and management needs, while balancing diverse, entrepreneurial independence and corporate goals.

In their effort to ensure data transparency for investors, the SEC and the U.S. GAAP have established rigid reporting requirements, relying on standardization and a consistent methodology of profit and loss statements (P&Ls) to derive accurate reporting of corporate business conditions. But even if the investment community is satisfied with the level of detail provided on a corporation and business segment level, the need for information to effectively manage the business is much greater. In particular, international, diversified organizations suffer from inconsistent data provided by their subsidiaries scattered around the globe. Although subsidiaries generally develop and deploy effective internal accounting principles, management reports must be integrated with external reporting, which is based on country-specific legal requirements. The consequence of a global presence is, therefore, a multitude of diverse external reports defined by legal entities. International corporations, however, are not managed according to legal structures but by divisions or product and market segments. The result is financial reporting confusion and inadequate management information.

EXECUTIVE SUMMARY

- *Business leaders, especially those at multinational firms, need effective decision-support systems.*
- *A globally harmonized management accounting master can integrate multiple accounting systems, serving as a "blueprint" for organizational alignments, and providing benchmarks for management decision making.*
- *To make it work, current business units must be reconfigured or supplemented with local centers comprised of comparable units across divisions and countries.*
- *The result is integrated local reporting for management information and control.*

Local management usually does not understand corporate reporting as its core business.

For a number of reasons, this lack of integration between management reporting and financial reporting often results in reduced impact for deploying corporate objectives and strategies in decentralized units and entities. The primary root of this problem is that management reporting figures have to be derived from financial statements, which are often not detailed enough to identify urgent needs for management intervention.[1] Additionally, local management usually does not understand corporate reporting as its core business, and often resources are not available beyond preparation of consolidated financial statements. The consequences impact both corporate leadership and local management[2]:

- Without appropriately detailed and integrated management information, local managers often make suboptimal decisions.
- Local management is unable to benefit from benchmarking against other local units.
- Corporate leadership cannot optimize its international operations due to missing comparable benchmarking insights.
- Corporate leadership lacks a reliable and accurate overall financial picture.
- Tracking of corporate strategy deployment in decentralized units is quite limited.

This research reviews issues that contribute to financial professionals' challenges in reporting at multinationals, provides a case study example, and suggests and approach based on an MAM and an organizational design of local centers.

This article uses a case study of a construction supply company. We worked with the company for one year, during which time we helped assess their situation and implement numerous changes. The project was guided by the following question: how can corporate reporting be simplified and harmonized to meet financial reporting requirements and management needs, while balancing entrepreneurial independence and corporate goals?

CASE STUDY: CONSTRUCTION SUPPLY COMPANY

The company is a concrete and brick manufacturer based in France that operates across Europe in six countries. It is organized according to two basic principles: each country is an individual operating unit, and the business is organized into four divisions. Overall sales in 2000 were approximately $485 million, with the strongest division contributing nearly $290 million (concrete) and the smallest division $55 million (brick components). The company is headquartered in France, its strongest local market, with Poland and Spain considered emerging markets.

In the last three years, the organizational structure and size of the construction supply company have changed due to massive merger and acquisition activities. The brick business is relatively new to the portfolio and still has to be fully integrated. Overall, the company is well positioned in the market and possesses well-known brands in its industry. As the examples will illustrate, the construction supply company is forced to operate on a global basis, because of transportation costs and access to raw materials. And as a result, harmonizing its management reporting systems has been a significant challenge. This study, reinforced by similar work with other companies during the past three years,[3] is the basis for the local-center accounting model. Details of the construction supply company's business, organization, and reporting provide the examples throughout.[4]

PROBLEMS WITH NONINTEGRATED REPORTING

Consolidated financial statements must be prepared in the United States according to U.S. GAAP. Most international corporations in Europe use the International Accounting Standards (IAS) in order to apply one harmonized standard throughout their entire corporation. Financial reporting normally must meet both legal requirements of each respective country and internationally chosen principles, usually either U.S. GAAP or IAS (for non-U.S. based corporations).[5]

Because management structures rarely are aligned with legal structures, any additional insights that could be gained from consolidated financial statements are quite limited, even if the U.S. GAAP or IAS is applied consistently. The development of international management and cost accounting has not yet succeeded, as external accounting has, in introducing generally accepted principles and guidelines.[6] The lack of convergence is further exacerbated in international corporations by cultural, linguistic, and technological disparities among countries.[7]

Example of Reporting Complications

The France-based construction supplier was challenged by the massive complexity of its reporting structure, which was basically driven by the chosen business unit model and legal entity structure. Because of continuously shrinking margins, especially in the concrete segments, however, cost efficiency needed significant improvement across all countries. Furthermore, as a result of M&A activities, reporting was not fully aligned with corporate principles. The objective was integration for efficiencies and cost savings. Exhibit 1 illustrates why the construction supply company's reporting could not be reconciled with its country-specific consolidated financial statements.

The company experienced numerous business problems that potentially could have been avoided with a better decision-support system. The general manager in Poland, for example, maintained two production units but only one sales organization, which sold products belonging to the brick elements division. His key performance measure was overall revenue growth achieved in Poland; therefore, it was in his interest not to disclose latent underuse in his plants that produced products for the brick division. He kept production at a high level even if these products could not reach the profitability benchmark. If he succeeded in negotiating a transfer price to sell his products to the sales organizations in Austria, Germany, and France as the brick division allowed, he would show an appropriate profitability and continue production levels. The corporate goal, however, is to optimize asset productivity by identifying underutilized production capacities. One essential indicator is profitability; from a corporate perspective, the nonprofitable production of Poland's brick division was not being identified, and value for the corporation further diminished.

EXHIBIT 1

Lack of Integration of Management Reporting and Consolidated Financial Statements

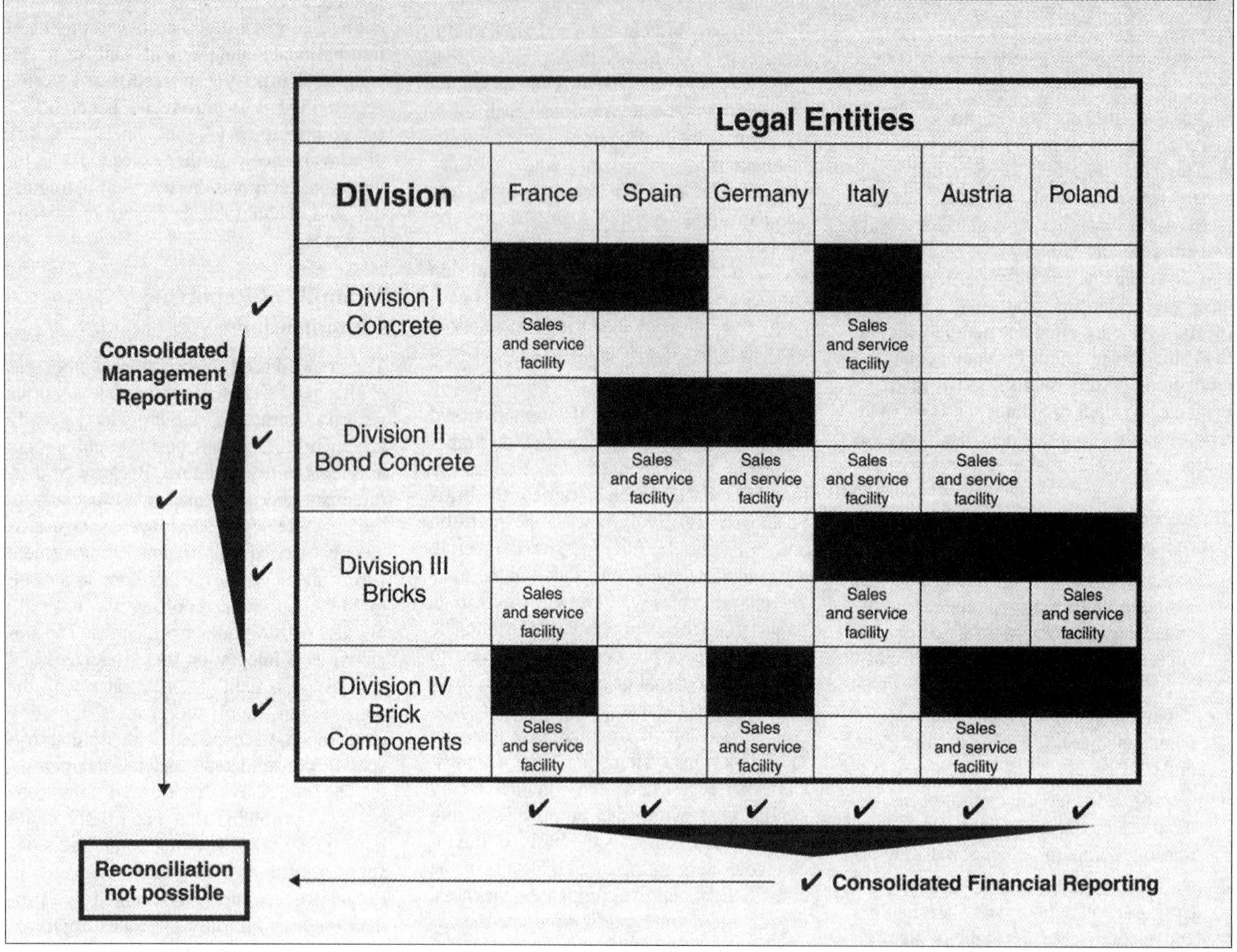
Legal Entities
Division
France
Spain
Germany
Italy
Austria
Poland
Division I Concrete
Division II Bond Concrete
Division III Bricks
Division IV Brick Components
Sales and service facility
Consolidated Management Reporting
Reconciliation not possible
Consolidated Financial Reporting

LOCAL-CENTER ACCOUNTING MODEL

This case example illustrates the usual business problems that can result when normal financial reporting does not produce the information necessary for management's decision-making. Along with the case company's corporate leaders and local managers, a local center accounting model was developed and implemented, based on the MAM—a blueprint for integrating management accounting and external financial reporting.

This local-center accounting model is most effective in corporations with homogeneous business divisions. If the divisions are significantly dissimilar, a refocused accounting model will not result in comparable best practices. If big corporations maintain business units that belong to completely different industry sectors, for example, such as the finance and leasing business automotive companies, it is more appropriate to develop segment-specific MAMs by industry.

If the divisions are significantly dissimilar, a refocused accounting model will not result in comparable best practices.

This approach for integrating financial and managerial accounting for improved business decision-making and simplified reporting has three key elements. Because they are interdependent, the elements are developed concurrently:

1. Management Accounting Master.
2. Center-oriented organizational design.
3. Integrated legal-entity reporting.

MANAGEMENT ACCOUNTING MASTER

The MAM is developed to cope with requirements of both local and corporate management. It is both a conceptual blueprint that guides organizational redesign and a reporting framework that defines key performance indicators and decision rules for alignment across business units, their subunits, and external financial requirements.[8] In particular, it generates information needed to manage the business from a local perspective. An MAM is defined by the following characteristics:

- Harmonized center accounting schemes according to the center function (e.g., manufacturing, sales, and administration).
- Performance indicators of center heads thoroughly linked to their functional roles, responsibilities, and accountabilities.
- Consistent and sustainable transfer pricing rules between cost centers and profit centers based on standard cost mechanism.
- Profit center accounting scheme closely aligned to the country P&Ls.
- Consistent bridging methodologies between profit center accounting and country P&Ls.

Example of Management Accounting Information

The case company example helps explain the purpose of the MAM. The European division head of the bond concrete division, for example, maintains two production facilities that supply its four European sales organizations. Because the plant in Spain is quite remote and is clearly disadvantageous in transportation costs, its use has dropped recently. In addition, Spain has only a small sales organization. Due to more streamlined production and newer machinery and equipment, however, the plant in Spain is more productive than the facility in Germany.

The MAM becomes the blueprint.

Germany's financial statements indicate an overall strong profit position. In fact, its higher profitability is based on an extremely successful sales team and less competitive and price-sensitive market, which compensate for the relative poor productivity of its plant. Even with significant transportation costs, the facility in Spain performs stronger than the one in Germany. Without detailed insights about sales organization effectiveness and plant productivity, however, the division head will not identify these differences or effectively manage assets.

THE BLUEPRINT

As the previous section illustrates, detailed and useful management accounting information is critical for making viable local and corporate business decisions. The division head mentioned above has to make major decisions based on six center reports and four country-specific financial statements. This manager needs clearly defined key performance indicators and decision rules for his center heads and general managers.

The MAM becomes the blueprint for both creating the centers with aligned responsibility for that information, and at the same time, extracting relevant data from financial statements. In all cases where center reports are created, consistent bridging to financial accounts has to be maintained. The added management capability derives from information consistency across centers, not added data.

Example of Management Account Master Benefits

By implementing the MAM, the division head (DH) of bond concrete will receive two reports from the production center that, structure-wise and content-wise, are 100% comparable. The DH will see the same line items, and per line item, will get insights about actual costs and standard cost deviations. In addition, it will be easy for the DH to investigate the root causes for deviations because the major categories, such as bill of material variances or deviations in use, will appear automatically on his or her monthly report. Despite not being an expert in management accounting, the DH will be able to compare cost structures and assess productivity of its plants. In conjunction with the operations head for the country responsible, the DH can work on leveraging efficiency advantages or shifting use for overall value creation.

Furthermore, the MAM will help to separate functional-specific efficiencies. That means, in the situation just described, the relatively poor production efficiency of the Germany-based bond concrete plant was hidden by overperforming sales results. The MAM will reinforce the split of production units and sales units to clearly address improvement potentials. The performance of the sales team will be mirrored primarily in profit-center accounting, whereas plant productivity will be shown in cost center accounting. Because the plant performance is displayed at standard values, the real strength of the German sales team will be visible, and the production team will need to cope with its predefined standard costs. Higher actual costs are the proof of inefficiencies and have to be scrutinized. If necessary, utilization has to be shifted to more productive units such as the one in Spain. Consequently, asset reduction (e.g., line closing) or shut-down of the German operations will have to be considered.

To formulate the MAM, its definitions, rules, and responsibilities must be continually played out against perceived organizational designs and reporting structures. With all of these factors in play and through various modelling exercises, an aligned blueprint will result, leading to the implementation of a center-oriented organizational design across the corporation.

Center-Oriented Organizational Design

An organizational redesign is necessary to create local centers, which supplement and hone the current assortment of business unit structures. Center-oriented organizations are not new, however, their alignment with a harmonized management accounting system is essential. They provide a unique advantage for implementing harmonized structures in a business unit and legal-entity environment without adding a third organizational dimension. The center model is simply used on the level below country entities to provide uniform organizational standards that integrate existent business segments in the respective country. This redesign or refinement forces the development of independent and self-guided organizational centers. Each center head should have the opportunity to optimize his or her center results based on clearly aligned responsibilities.[9] Only when center heads have the ability and opportunity to influence performance and success will they be highly motivated. As well, they will have clear responsibility for major deviations from planned corporate objectives. In any case, a manager should not be able to avoid responsibility by being a great negotiator of internal transfer prices. The management objective is clearly aligned responsibility and control of balance sheet items.

Example of Nonaligned Responsibility

In reality, the opposite of clearly aligned responsibilities is often the case. The construction supply company must often operate relatively small production units, located near its raw-material suppliers and customers. In addition, concrete or brick production is primarily asset intensive, except for the manual concrete reinforcement activities. In the cases of bondless concrete and brick production units, the headcount is on average below 100; for brick production in Austria, it is below 20. To foster the entrepreneurial thinking of its center heads, corporate management decided to assign "virtual" profits to all production units. For the manager of a workforce of 20, this creates quite a challenge. An accurate management accounting system had to be developed that allowed the manager to build in theoretical revenue streams; the manager had to understand the implications of revenue and cost effects on his profitability; and, finally, the manager needed to ensure that appropriate transfer prices had been negotiated. Imagine a production supervisor with an engineering brick processing background. He or she would probably not be able to cope with all of these reporting tasks; more importantly, focus on his core objectives—to process high-quality products at the lowest cost possible and in a timely manner—might be lost.

The MAM can guide necessary redesign across all divisions and countries in the entire corporation.

Local Centers of Responsibility

Local centers are the means to align individual managers' responsibility with their area of highest competence. With this alignment, managers are most able to leverage their creative influence and leadership and, therefore, positively control outcomes. Local centers fall into two basic types according to their primary role in the value chain[10]:

- Profit centers—Have revenue streams and significant costs related directly to the center activities.
- Cost centers—Generate no external revenues but cause significant costs, mostly production costs.

With these basic types of centers, the MAM can guide necessary redesign across all divisions and countries in the entire corporation. The specific design of each center cannot be determined by corporate defaults. Corporate-led redesign guidelines contain only a set of modules and definitions that will drive country-specific center solutions. These guidelines focus on standardization of elements to develop local conformity and therefore overall visibility of information for corporate control. For each center, core activities need to be clarified. And to ensure comparability, it is critically important that equal center types manage equal proportions of the value chain so that insightful cross-country benchmarking analyses can be conducted.

Units below the centers can be structured and organized according to local specifics and the taste of local management. The starting point for tracking the needs of a decentralized management is mapping the decentralized processes and structures. By creating transparency in the basic designs of local units and their interactions, the plausibility of the redesigned organizational structure can be cross checked. Additional reorganization efforts to further harmonize the organizations will be identified.

Exhibit 2 shows the needed redesign of basic center structures for the case company's sales (profit centers) and operations (cost centers). These basic models served as the redesign framework and then were further refined according to country specifics.

Profit Centers

Because of external revenue streams, sales organizations are predestined to be measured according to profits. They are in charge of the margin between revenues and costs of goods sold plus selling costs. Potentially, a relative high profit could be displayed because charges for materials are lower than the effective cost of goods sold. For this reason, profit-center accounting for the major sales organizations in a country is run as part of the P&L-accounting for the respective country. This approach implies that values for overhead such as administration or R&D have to be considered as part of profit center accounting. Because the sales force cannot directly influence overhead costs, however, the values taken should be based on planned figures. The sales organization is only responsible for its "actual" selling costs and will take notice of other "planned" administrative costs that are charged on its profit center account. Exhibit 3 illustrates the basic structure of a profit-center account.

For the profit center organization in France, the case company has developed the following organizational solution. From a sales perspective, only the bricks division requires a regional structure. The current organization according to regions for all divisions, therefore, is not very useful. Instead, the former solution of a countrywide operation sales team for concrete and brick components was reintroduced. Exhibit 4 illustrates the new profit center structure compatible to the basic-center model.

Cost Centers

Cost centers are established for all units without external revenues. Typical cost centers are production, R&D, and administration. Production centers require an effective production control system that monitors productivity, quality, and time. Indicators, such as product cost, the cost effects of different utilization levels, and cost and quality relations are the required bare minimum. For administrative cost centers, it is important to determine the necessary level of quality to be provided. Otherwise, a cost center head might try to stay within budget just by cutting down on certain services.

To apply the basic center model for operation units in France, management agreed on the following center structure, as illustrated in Exhibit 5.

Using the cost center template, the structure could be significantly streamlined. For historical reasons, logistics was previously located in two different parts of the organization. The concrete division maintained logistics resources because of the company's roots in the concrete business. In addition, procurement had its own logistic department that covered issues for the acquired brick component plant. Quality control was also duplicated. The MAM, with its local center model, uncovered these organizational issues, which the agreed on template has solved.

Center Contentions and Balance-Sheet Alignment

The creation of a center-based management accounting approach often brings to light contentions over responsibility for balance sheet items. Through the process of designing and implementing this approach, clear responsibility should be determined, leading to increased corporate value. Commonly, agreement needs to be reached around fixed assets, working capital, and inventories.

As a general rule, cost centers for production should be in charge of fixed assets, in particular, plants, property and equipment. Although cost centers for production have to carry all productive assets, nonpro-

EXHIBIT 2
Basic Center Models

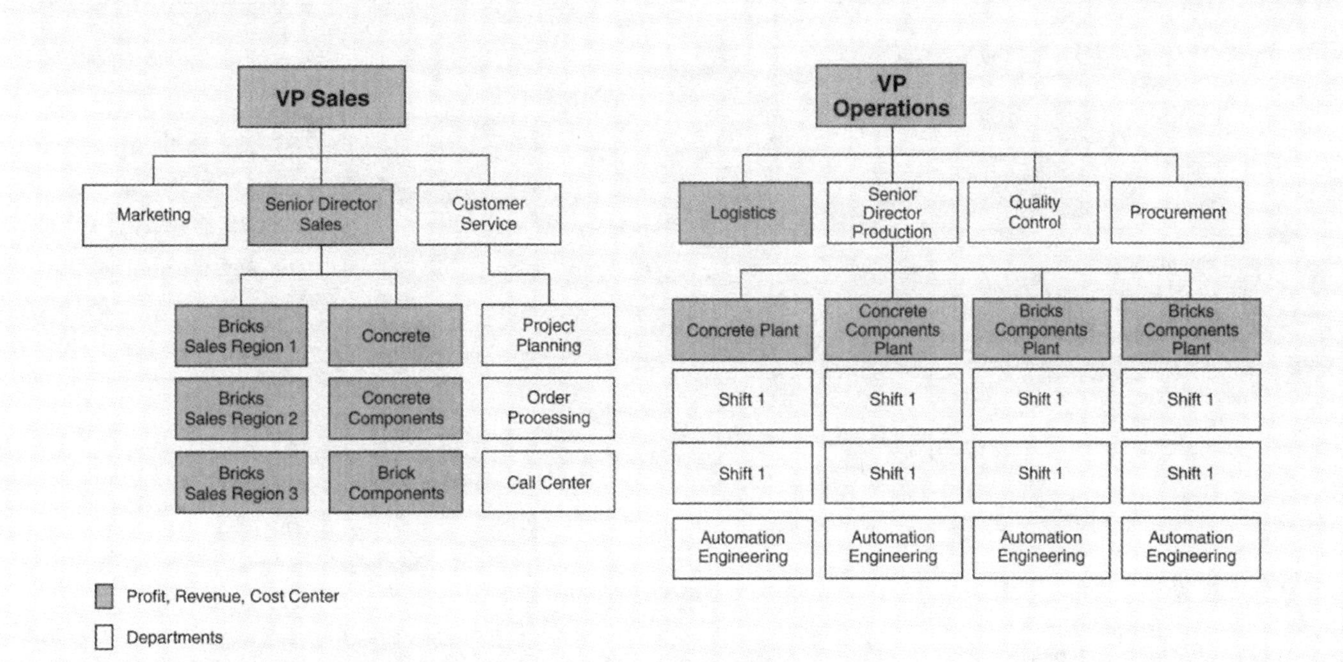

ductive assets, such as nonused real estate or administrative buildings should appear in the cost center account of administrative units.[11]

Often, responsibility for working capital is disputed. Accounts receivable is the easy part; since sales teams normally "own" the customer, they should ensure timely cash inflow. Accounts payable is heavily dependent on supplier relationships. The procurement organization normally negotiates prices and terms and conditions, but actual purchases are made by others. In particular, organizations with a very decentralized sourcing approach face problems in assigning responsibility of accounts payable. Therefore, case-by-case decisions are appropriate for assigning responsibility.

Contentions most often occur around inventories. Plant managers frequently try to improve their profitability on a product basis by ramping up their use—even with significant decreases in demand. When the sales organization is in charge of inventories, plant managers have no problem applying this approach. If the production centers have to carry the inventories, however, they will try to lower inventory levels to a minimum extent. Volatile or even surge customer demand might not be supplied. In both cases, the value of the overall corporation is threatened. As a general rule, the average level of inventory should be agreed upon at the beginning of each planning cycle.[12] Then the production centers will have to optimize their utilization and production costs against this predetermined inventory level, and the sales team will have to cope with unpredicted rises in demand above these levels.

INTEGRATED LEGAL-ENTITY REPORTING

As local centers are implemented, the decision-support system will naturally induce increased demand by the profit center heads for performance indicators. As a result, the potential develops for these self-guided and self-optimizing units to generate a multitude of different reporting formats. Although the MAM is the tool to ensure consistent reporting of comparable business transactions across all centers and countries, it can also drive the development and use of a set of lean, standardized reports that cover most information needs. Close integration of management reporting with legal financial statements is a useful lever to streamline reporting.

Although external reporting according to legal principles has a somewhat different purpose than management reporting, the information can be harmonized as far as format and content. The different purposes will remain: financial statements are primarily prepared to provide investors with a true and fair view about business conditions, management accounting provides insights into the profitability of the business itself and helps identify cost, revenue, and profit drivers. Moreover, the formal harmonization helps center heads, especially those without an accounting background, to correctly understand the financials and derive from them the appropriate business decisions. Any deviations between external reporting figures and management accounting will still be seen and tracked on a country level.

Accurate definitions should be used according to the legal principles.

The following three major steps can be used as a guide for achieving this harmonization:

1. The starting point of the integration is a set of P&L-statement items that should appear in the MAM without any deviation. Normally, these include the revenue items and the major cost items. In the future, the center heads will manage these items. Accurate definitions

EXHIBIT 3
Illustrative Profit Center Account

Profit Center Account Country: France Sales Unit: Concrete Month: November 2001	Actual ($ MM)	Plan ($ MM)	Δ ($) MM)	Sources	Comments
Revenue	29.6	30.3	- 0.7	Financial statements	Actual
— Costs of goods sold	20.1	18.2	+ 1.9	Management Accounting	Standard
— Selling costs	5.2	5.4	- 0.2	Financial statements	Actual
— Administration costs	2.8	2.8	-	Management Accounting	Plan
— General management	1.1	1.1	-	Management Accounting	Plan
— Finance department	0.8	0.8	-	Management Accounting	Plan
— ...	0.9	0.9	-	Management Accounting	Plan
Profit Center total (standard values)	1.5	3.9	2.4		

EXHIBIT 4
Sales Organization — France

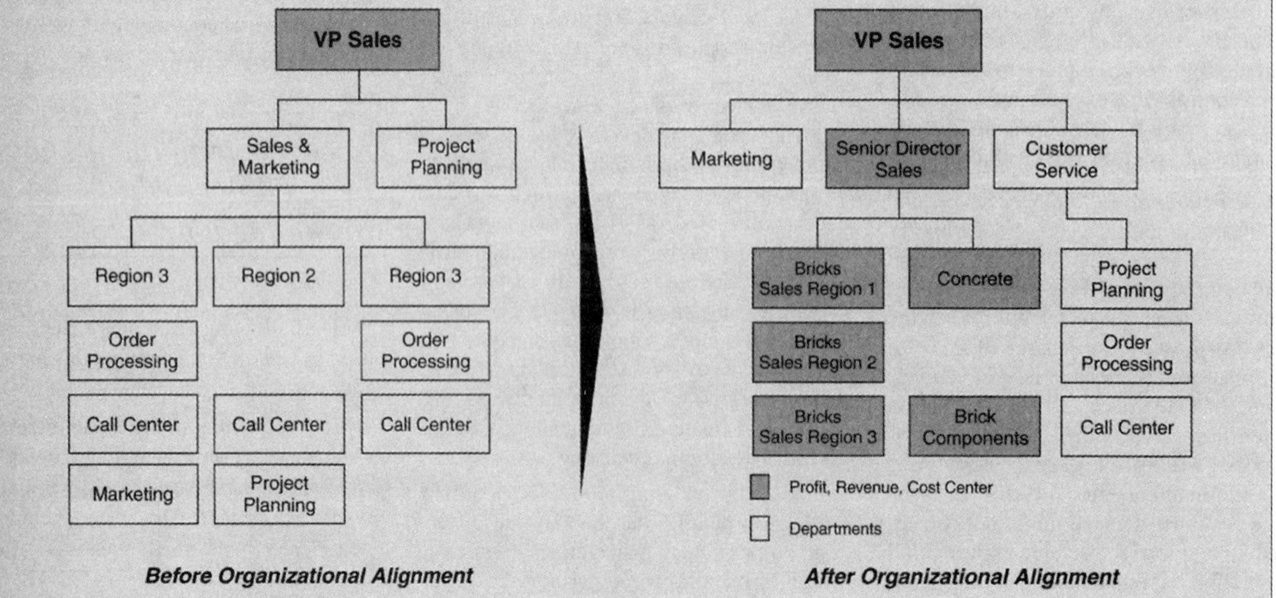

EXHIBIT 5
Operations Organization — France

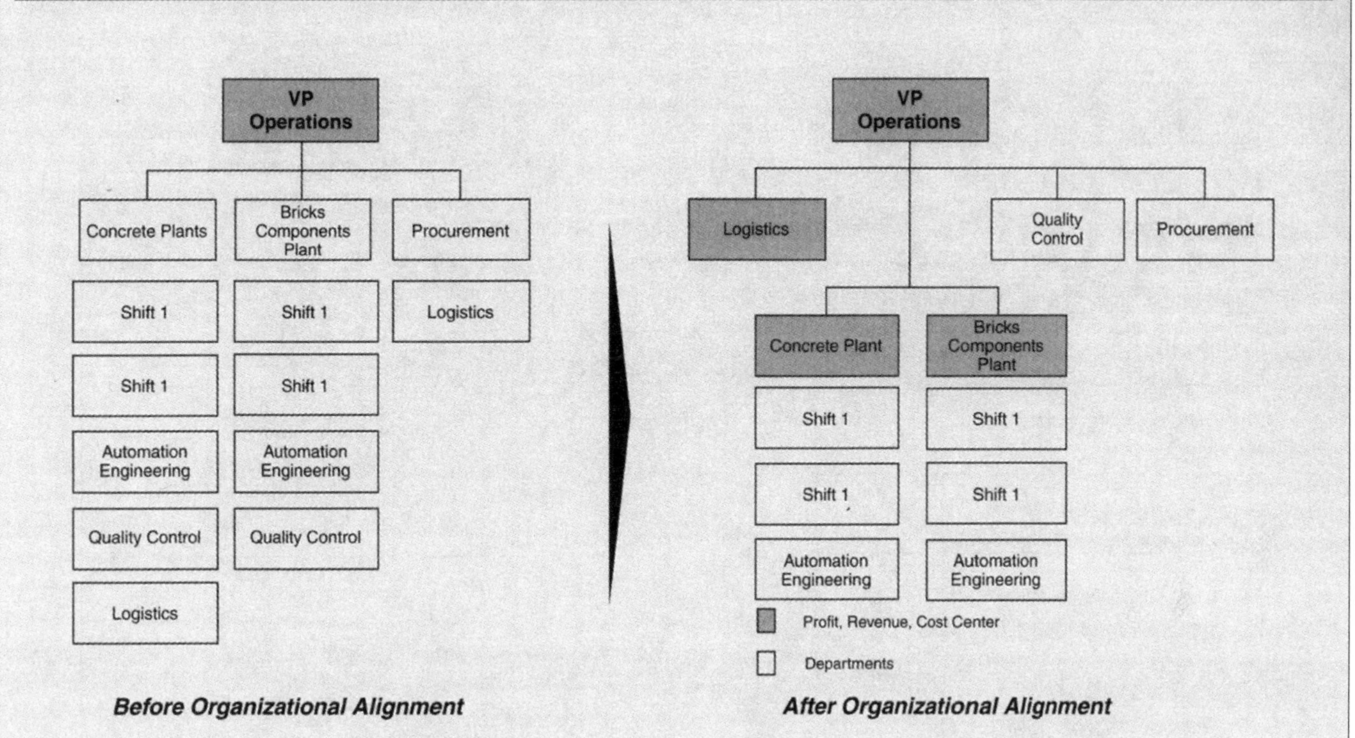

should be used according to the legal principles.

2. The next step is to identify indicators that are not part of the center heads' responsibility. Examples include non-operating revenues and expenses not under the immediate control of the respective center manager, such as sales of fixed assets.

3. Finally, deviations to the financial statements have to be determined. These deviations must be based on the required level of detail or content. The following examples describe potential content-related deviations:

- Profit centers will value the cost of goods sold in their profit center account based on standard costs.[13] The actual costs for the costs of goods sold will be tracked in the cost center accounts of the supplying cost centers (production). Because the profit center should not be responsible for deviating production cost, it will only be charged with a predetermined standard cost rate per unit taken times the volume of units. The production cost centers will be measured against this standard cost rate. If the actual costs deviate, it will have an immediate impact on the production cost centers' performance evaluation. The cost deviations, however, are not transferred to the profit center; they will be directly tracked in the profit & loss statement of the respective country. This principle ensures comparability and continuity across different centers.
- Internal service charges at actual costs can create a tremendous administrative burden. To simplify the system, accounting can valuate internal service charges with planned figures instead of actual costs.[14] Service and cost receiving centers only have to deal with predetermined planned charges and, therefore, have no deviations in their account caused by service charges. The effective difference between planned service costs and actual service costs will only occur in the center account of the delivering center (e.g., administration or customer support). These centers are in charge of deviations, and as in the other example, they will be tracked directly in the P&L account of the respective country.

The major objective of the integration is to eventually connect all center reports to the single line items of the P&L statement. To create maximum transparency and to keep the financial and accounting systems as streamlined as possible, it is important to use a harmonized approach across the entire corporation on a worldwide level. The system in itself will be greatly efficient, and the foundation is laid for effective benchmarking. Exhibit 6 shows the basic principles of integration.

Example of Bridging Accounting Systems

The essential steps in developing and implementing the MAM at the case company were assessment, concept development, and implementation. Although assessment and concept development required less than four months, the implementation took nearly eight months. Implementation was the most difficult part as well. The local management and division management had to buy into the basic principles and to own the new accounting approach. Implementation of this mindset with managers is not an easy task because they all have concerns about giving up certain local and divisional independence. It is crucial to identify, early in the process, the appropriate performance indicators and to commu-

EXHIBIT 6
Bridging Proft Center Accounting and Profit & Loss Accounting

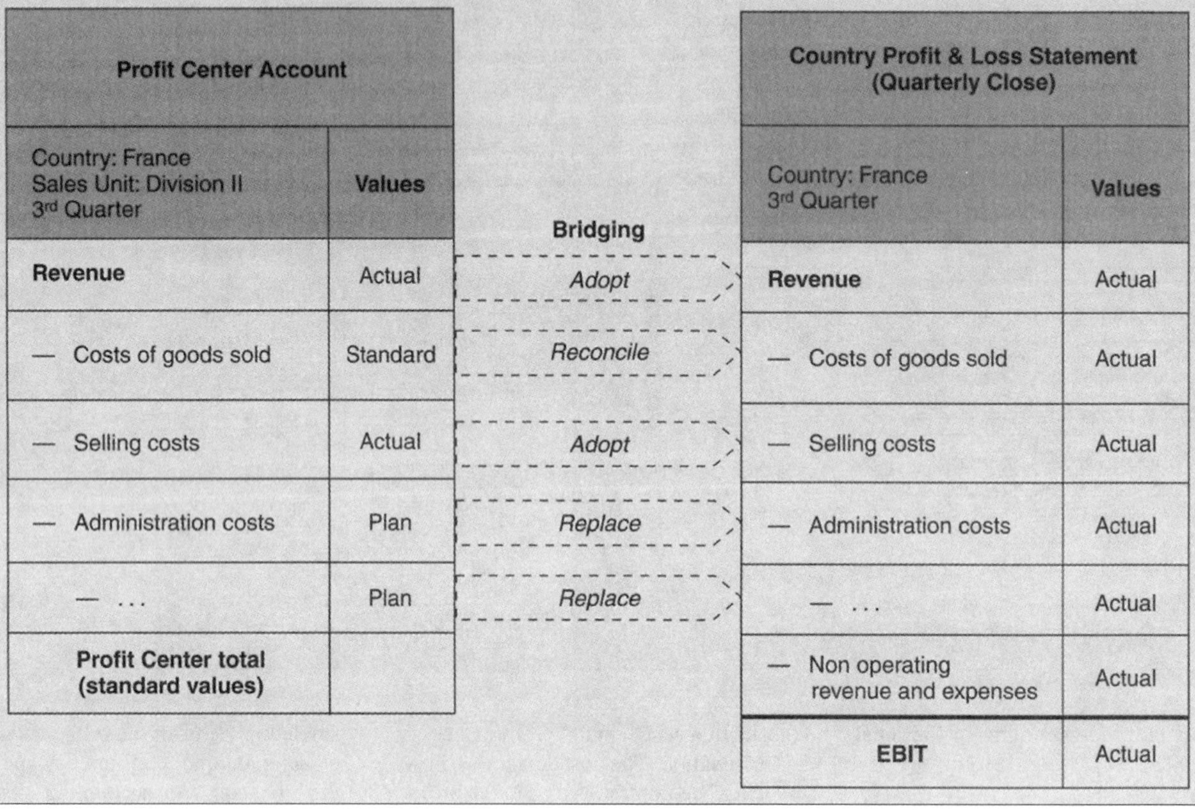
Profit Center Account
Country: France
Sales Unit: Division II
3rd Quarter
Values
Revenue
Actual
— Costs of goods sold
Standard
— Selling costs
Actual
— Administration costs
Plan
— ...
Plan
Profit Center total (standard values)
Bridging
Adopt
Reconcile
Adopt
Replace
Replace
Country Profit & Loss Statement (Quarterly Close)
Country: France
3rd Quarter
Values
Revenue
Actual
— Costs of goods sold
Actual
— Selling costs
Actual
— Administration costs
Actual
— ...
Actual
— Non operating revenue and expenses
Actual
EBIT
Actual

nicate and agree on them. The construction supply company has chosen the right path to integrate the MAM in its corporation-wide SAP/R3 configuration, although it was necessary to extend the implementation. If done right, however, the benefits are tremendous. Today, the case company has an integrated center logic in which center reports are created in SAP/R3 CO (controlling) by using primarily data from the modules FI (finance), MM (material management), and SD (sales and delivery). With only minor manual interventions, P&L statements are produced based on the profit center reports for each country and consolidated for the entire corporation on a monthly basis. After conducting intensive training for all managers (including top management), everybody understands the meaning of all information and each report, and all data can easily be reconciled and performance measures can be applied consistently. The concerted initiative to implement the MAM approach has transformed a nightmare into a nearly perfect world of information provision, which has clearly led to an overall increase in productivity and value creation.

SIMPLIFYING FOR THE FUTURE

As businesses continue to globalize and internationally decentralized corporations to proliferate, the need to simplify, harmonize, and standardize corporate control systems becomes more urgent. The MAM and corresponding organizational redesign offer a feasible compromise for balancing local entrepreneurial freedom and strategically important corporation goals.

The concept can easily be implemented, even in small subsidiaries and units abroad. The core element is the MAM, which is used as a blueprint to create centers in all legal entities around the globe and to harmonize their reporting. When integration of management accounting and external financial reporting is managed well, a corporate control system emerges that can cope with the variety of international legal reporting requirements.

Notes

1. P. Sadler, *The Seamless Organization*, 4th Edition (London: Kogan Page, 2001).

2. W. Bay and H-G. Bruns, "Multinational Companies and International Capital Markets," in P. Walton, A. Haller, and B. Raffournier, *International Accounting* (London: Thomson, 1998), pp. 336–355.

3. We have found the problem of nonharmonized management accounting systems in a variety of sizes and industries. Common to all is the need for internationally diversified operations. We worked with an electronic manufacturer of consumer goods, with revenues of $15 billion in 2000, whose need for international production is simply driven by technological

requirements in target markets. In the case of a German automotive supplier of transmission systems and gearbox technology, with $1.6 billion in 2000, the company was forced by its customers to set up production facilities close to assembly plants, leading to unavoidable cost disadvantages.

4. Some structural detail and financial data have been sanitized.

5. T. M. Plank and L. R. Plank, *Accounting Desk Book,* 11th Edition (Upper Saddle River, New Jersey: Prentice Hall, 2000).

6. R. G. Schroeder and C. W. Myrtle, *Accounting Theory* (New York: Wiley, 1998); J. K. Skim and J. G. Siegel, *Modern Cost Management & Analysis,* 2nd Edition (New York: Barron Educational Series, 2000).

7. A. Haller and P. Walton, "Country Differences and Harmonization," in P. Walton, A. Haller and B. Raffournier, *International Accounting* (London: Thomson, 1998), pp. 1–30; S. Klimczuk, "Global Operations and National Roots," *Executive Agenda* (Chicago: AT Kearney, Second Quarter 2001).

8. Additionally, a Balanced Scorecard or Integrated Strategic Measurement Approach should be developed and implemented to fully deploy a value creating decision-culture across the entire organization. A. T. Kearney, Inc., "Making Strategies Pay: A White Paper on Integrated Strategic Measurement" (Chicago: A. T. Kearney, 1999).

9. A. De Waal, *Power of Performance Management: How Leading Companies Create Sustained Value* (New York: Wiley, 2001).

10. J. K. Shank and V. Govindarajan, *Strategic Cost Management* (New York: Wiley, 1993).

11. Schroeder and Myrtle.

12. D. R. Emery and J. D. Finnerty, *Corporate Financial Management* (New Jersey: Prentice Hall, 1997).

13. L. Oliver, *The Cost Management Toolbox* (New York: AMACOM, 1999).

14. Skim and Siegel.

SOEREN DRESSLER, Ph.D., is a principal with A. T. Kearney International Management Consultants and a member of its global strategy and organization practice. He is based in Chicago.

Michael Porter: What Is Strategy?

In an age when management gurus are both lauded by the faithful and hounded by the critics, Michael Porter seems to be one of the few who is well-accepted both academically and in the business world. Though he has his critics, Porter has generally been viewed as at the leading edge of strategic thinking since his first major publication, *Competitive Strategy* (1980), which became a corporate bible for many in the early 1980s.

Life and Career

Born in 1947, Porter completed a degree in aeronautical engineering at Princeton and took an economics doctorate at Harvard, joining the faculty there as a tenured professor at the age of 26. He has acted as consultant to companies and to governments and, like many academics, he set up a consulting company—Monitor.

Porter's Thinking

Porter's thinking on strategy has been supported by precision research into industries and companies, and has remained consistent as well as developmental. He has concentrated on different aspects at different times, spinning the threads together with a logic that is irrefutable.

Before *Competitive Strategy*, most strategic thinking focused either on the organisation of a company's internal resources and their adaptation to meet particular circumstances in the marketplace, or on increasing an organisation's competitiveness by lowering prices to increase market share. These approaches, derived from the work of Igor Ansoff, were bundled into systems or processes which provided strategy with its place in the organisation.

In *Competitive Strategy*, Porter managed to reconcile these approaches, providing management with a fresh way of looking at strategy—from the point of view of industry itself rather than just from the point of view of markets, or of organisational capabilities.

Internal Capability for Competitiveness—The Value Chain

Porter describes two different types of business activity—primary and secondary. Primary activities are principally concerned with transforming inputs (raw materials) into outputs (products), and delivery and after-sales support. These usual line management activities include Inbound Logistics (materials handling, warehousing), Operations (turning raw materials into finished products), Outbound Logistics (order processing, and distribution), Marketing and Sales (communication and pricing), and Service (installation and after-sales service).

Secondary activities support the primary and include Procurement (purchasing and supply), Technology Development (know-how, procedures and skills), Human Resource Management (recruitment, promotion, appraisal, reward and development), and Firm Infrastructure (general and quality management, finance, planning).

To be able to survive competition and supply what customers want to buy, the firm has to ensure that all these value-chain activities link together and fit, as a weakness in any one of them will impact on the chain as a whole and affect competitiveness.

The Five Forces

Porter argued that in order to examine its competitive capability in the marketplace, an organisation must choose between three generic strategies: cost leadership—becoming the lowest-cost producer in the market; differentiation—offering something different, extra or special; and focus—achieving dominance in a niche market. The question is to choose the right one at the right time. These generic strategies are driven by five competitive forces which the organisation has to take into account:

- the power of customers to affect pricing and reduce margins
- the power of suppliers to influence the organisation's pricing
- the threat of similar products to limit market freedom and reduce prices and thus profits
- the level of existing competition which impacts on investment in marketing and research and thus erode profits

- the threat of new market entrants to intensify competition and further impact on pricing and profitability.

In recent years, Porter has revisited his earlier work and emphasises the acceleration of market change that means companies now have to compete not just on a choice of strategic front, but on all fronts at once. Porter has also said that a company that tries to position itself in relation to the five competitive forces misunderstands his approach, since positioning is not enough. What companies have to do is ask how the five forces can help to re-write industry rules in the organisation's favour.

Diversification

Instead of going it alone, an organisation can spread risk and attain growth by diversification and acquisition. While the blue-chip consulting companies such as Boston Consulting Group (Market growth/market share matrix) and McKinsey (7-S framework) have developed analytical models for discovering which companies will rise and fall, Porter prefers three critical tests for success:

1. The attractiveness test. Industries chosen for diversification must be structurally attractive. An attractive industry will yield a high return on investment but entry barriers will be high, customers and suppliers will have only moderate bargaining power and there will be only a few substitute products. An unattractive industry will be swamped by a range of alternative products, high rivalry and high fixed costs.
2. The cost-of-entry test. If the cost of entry is so high that it prejudices the potential return on investment, profitability is eroded before the game has started.
3. The better-off test. How will the acquisition provide advantage to either the acquirer or the acquired? One must offer significant advantage to the other.

Porter devised seven steps to tackle these questions:

1. As competition takes place at the business unit level, identify the interrelationships among the existing business units.
2. Identify the core business which is to be the foundation of the strategy. Core businesses are those in attractive industries and where competitive advantage can be sustained.
3. Create horizontal organisational mechanisms to facilitate interrelationships among core businesses.
4. Pursue diversification opportunities that allow shared activities and pass all three critical tests.
5. Pursue diversification through transfer of skills if opportunities for sharing activities are limited or exhausted.
6. Pursue a strategy of restructuring if this fits the skills of management or if no good opportunities exist for forging corporate partnerships.
7. Pay dividends so that shareholders can become portfolio managers.

National Competitiveness

Why do some companies achieve consistent capability in innovation, seeking an ever more sophisticated source of competitive advantage? For Porter the answer lies in four attributes which affect industries: These attributes are: Factor Conditions (the nations skills and infrastructure to enable a competitive position), Demand Conditions (the nature of home-market demand), Related and Supporting Industries (presence or absence of supplier/feeder industries), and Firm Strategy, Structure and Rivalry (the national conditions under which companies are created, grow, organise and manage).

These are the chief determinants which create the environment in which firms flourish and compete. The points on the diamond constitute a self-reinforcing system, where the effect of one point often depends on the state of the others and any weaknesses at one point will impact adversely on an industry's capability to compete.

The New Strategic Wave

Somewhere between 1980 and 1990 strategic planning came unstuck. Old theories no longer worked as customers became more demanding and changeable, and markets and technologies rose and fell ever more rapidly. Even industries that were once distinct with definable products and services now converged and became blurred. A new wave of more subversive strategic thinking—with Gary Hamel and Strategy as Revolution, and Mintzberg with The Fall and Rise of Strategic Planning—emerged to replace the old rule-book. Porter's main contribution to date—What is strategy?—argues that strategic planning lost its way because managers failed to distinguish between strategic and operational effectiveness and confused the two. The old strategic model—which still held up in the 1980s—was based on productivity, increasing market share and lowering costs. Hence total quality management, benchmarking, outsourcing and re-engineering were all at the forefront of change in the 1980s as the key drivers of operational improvements. But continuing incremental improvements to the way things are done tend, over time, to bring different players up to the same level, not differentiate them. To achieve differentiation means that:

- Strategy rests on unique activities based on customers' needs, customers' accessibility or the variety of a company's products or services.
- The company's activities must fit and link together. In terms of the value chain, one link is prone to imitation but with a chain, imitation is very difficult.
- Making trade-offs: excelling at some things means making a conscious choice not to do others—a question of being a 'master of one trade' to stand out from the crowd as opposed to being a 'jack of all trades' and lost in the crowd. Trade-offs purposefully limit what a company offers. The essence of strategy lies in what not to do.

The Internet

In 2001 Porter addressed the assertion that the Internet renders strategy obsolete. He admits that the Internet is in its infancy, but observes that lack of strategy and reliance on Internet technologies to gain market penetration is already proving not to be a sound approach. In a Harvard Business Review article in March 2001 Porter says:

> 'In our quest to see how the Internet is different, we have failed to see how the Internet is the same' (pp 63–78)

Porter argues that many Internet companies are competing through unsustainable, artificial means, usually propped up by short-term capital investment. He also argues that while the excitement of the Internet appeared to throw up new rules of competition, the first wave of excitement is now clearly over, and the old rules and strategic principles appear to be re-establishing themselves. He gives examples such as:

1. The right goal—healthy long-term return on investment.
2. Value—a company must offer a set of benefits which set it apart from the competition.
3. A company's value chain has to do things differently or do different things from rivals to reflect, produce and deliver that value.
4. Trade-offs—make conscious deliberate sacrifices in some areas in order to excel, or even be unique, in others.
5. All the different components in the value chain must fit together, reinforcing each other to create uniqueness and value: it is this which makes a core competence—something that is difficult to imitate.
6. Continuity—not only from a customer perspective but also in order to build and develop skills that bring competitive edge.

Porter foresees that, as most businesses embrace the Internet, it will become nullified as a source of advantage, while traditional strengths such as uniqueness, design and service relationships will reemerge. For Porter the next phase of Internet evolution will be more holistic, with a shift from e-business to business, from e-learning to learning, within which the Internet will be a communications medium and not necessarily a source of advantage.

In Perspective

It is a mark of Porter's achievement that much of his work on Competitive Strategy, researched in the 1970s, still has high value and relevance in the late 1990s, and still shapes mainstream thinking on competition and strategy.

Although now much quoted, the following was intended to be as much a compliment as the Economist would muster: "His work is academic to a fault… Mr. Porter is about as likely to produce a blockbuster full of anecdotes and boosterish catchphrases as he is to deliver a lecture dressed in bra and stockings." (Professor Porter Ph.D., Economist, 8 October 1994, p 97)

While his work is academically rigorous, his ability to abstract his thinking into digestible chunks for the business world has given him wide appeal to both the academic and business worlds. It is now standard practice for organisations to think and talk Value Chains, and the Five Forces have entered the curriculum and every management programme. Porter's later thinking on strategy rides the new wave of revolutionary strategic thinking led by Hamel and links consistently with his earlier work. One suspects that there is not only more to come from Michael Porter, but also that it will be wholly consistent with what he has said in the past.

Key works by Porter

Books

Competitive strategy: techniques for analyzing industries and competitors New York: Free Press, 1980
Competitive advantage: creating and sustaining superior performance London: Collier Macmillan, 1985
Competitive advantage of nations London: Macmillan, 1990
Cases in competitive strategy London: Collier Macmillan, 1983
Competition in global industries (ed) Boston, Mass.: Harvard Business School Press, 1986

Journal Articles

From competitive advantage to corporate strategy Harvard Business Review, May/June 1987, vol. 65 no 3, pp 43–59
The competitive advantage of nations Harvard Business Review, Mar/Apr 1990, vol. 68 no 2, pp 73–93
What is strategy? Harvard Business Review, Nov/Dec 1996, vol. 74 no 6, pp 61–78
Corporate strategy: the state of strategic thinking Economist, 23 May 1998, pp 21–22, 27–28. Revised Apr 2002

TRADING

New Rules of The Game

Confronted with Japanese trading giants like Mitsui, Mitsubishi and Itochu, Asia's smaller merchants are reinventing themselves as integral parts of the global supply chain

By Neel Chowdhury/HONG KONG AND SINGAPORE

FROM THE RUGGED PLAINS of southern Bihar, one of India's poorest and most violent states, a profit margin is a distant glint in a trader's eye. Pockmarked by cavernous mines and labyrinthine tunnels, where labourers scour the soil with picks, shovels and plastic buckets, Bihar's mineral-rich earth offers up iron, alumina and coal to India and the rest of the world. But the landlocked and industrially backward state is also hundreds of miles from the nearest seaport, factory or commodity exchange and transporting its treasures to those places isn't easy.

WHEELING AND DEALING: Elman parlayed his experience in a scrap-metal yard into a billion-dollar business

But for a few plucky traders, who come to off-the-map places like these in search of cheap and coveted commodities, Bihar can be a gold mine. Richard Elman is one of them. Chairman and CEO of Hong Kong–based and Singapore-listed Noble Group, a 15-year-old trading company that deals in everything from cocoa to steel, 61-year-old Elman runs a pan-Asian operation that in 2000 generated a net profit of $21 million on total turnover of nearly $1.2 billion, despite working from a capital base that year that barely exceeded $100 million. More impressive, Noble's return on equity in 2000 stood at 20%, a margin centuries-old Japanese trading behemoths cannot achieve. In fiscal 2000–01, for instance, Japanese trading giant Mitsui chalked up $409 million in net profits on turnover exceeding $103 billion. But its return on equity hovered at roughly 6%, less than a third of Noble's.

How does Noble do it? Partly by reinventing the hallowed rules of the Asian trading game. The old Asian middlemen, either the solitary adventurer who greased palms and bargained without mercy in danger zones like Bihar, or the massive multinational like Mitsui, Mitsubishi or Itochu, which bought in tremendous volumes and traded on paper-thin margins, are both struggling to remain relevant. More imaginative criteria now measure the middleman's success: namely, the flexibility to wedge oneself into a product's supply chain and find ways to conjure up value, as Noble does so nimbly. "Nobody just buys and sells any more," as Elman puts it. "You've got to do something else."

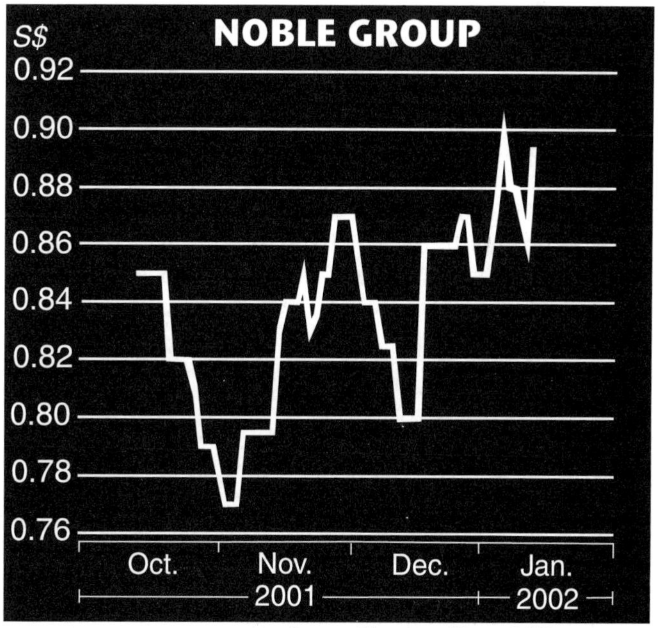

Source: Thomson Financial Datastream

The elaborate journey of Noble's Indian iron ore, worth roughly $1 million in its raw state, provides a glimpse into the industry's future. From Bihar's mines, Elman arranges for the iron ore to travel by train to a seaport near the Indian city of Bhubaneshwar. There, the iron ore is loaded onto a ship chartered by Noble, which charters roughly 400 ships a year. The ship's journey to the Chinese port of Qingdao, the first stop on the iron ore's long and complicated trip to its customer, will take 15 days and cost Noble more than $100,000.

At the Qingdao docks the iron ore leaves the hold of the ship and, simultaneously, the financial responsibility of Noble. Why? Elman has struck a deal with a state-owned steel mill in China to process the iron ore into steel. The terms are striking: For 60 days Elman has given all the iron ore to the Chinese mill—in this case, a typical money-bleeding, state-owned-enterprise—in return for $2 million worth of pig iron, billets and cold-rolled steel. Whatever excess iron ore is left over, the steel mill can keep for its own purposes.

For Noble, the advantages of the transaction are obvious: It transforms $1 million worth of iron ore into $2 million worth of steel at the stroke of a pen, without investing a penny. For the steel mill the deal is dicier: It must not only transport the iron ore from the docks of Qingdao to its mill in Shaanxi province, a journey of more than 1,000 kilometres, but the mill's managers are also betting global steel prices will remain lofty enough to justify the transaction. Admits Harindarpal "Harry" Banga, an executive director of Noble Group: "It doesn't always work out for them. Sometimes the end product is so cheap it doesn't cover their cost of production. But you just can't shut down these huge mills. Transactions keep carrying on regardless of price."

In this case, the iron ore is smoothly processed into steel that meets Noble's standards, and enough raw material is left to satisfy the Chinese steel mill's managers. Back the steel goes to Qingdao by train. So roughly two months after arriving in China, and more than two-and-a-half months after being coughed up from the mines of Bihar, the finished steel is reloaded onto another Noble-chartered ship to go to manufacturers in Japan, South Korea and Australia. Noble won't disclose how much it profited on this trade, but Banga says, "We collected a margin at five separate steps of this deal. So we can make five times the normal profit."

> "When I went out to India 30 years ago, I could tell the buyer and seller anything because their information was zero."
>
> RICHARD ELMAN

The middleman's new robes aren't exactly a natural fit for Elman. When Elman washed up in Tokyo in 1969, after a brief trip as a hippie in San Francisco, the middleman's job was simple: Spot a niche, charm your buyers and then scour Asia's darkest and dustiest corners to get your product. To Elman, business this way came naturally. A high-school drop-out who started as a self-described "coolie" at a scrap-metal yard in England, rising in his teens to yard manager, Elman knew his kingdom as a middleman lay in the knowledge gap between buyer and seller. "When I went out to India 30 years ago," he says, "I could tell the buyer and seller anything because their information was zero."

By the time Elman struck out on his own, founding Noble in Hong Kong in 1986 (Elman holds a 51% stake in the firm), the old Asian middleman's advantages were vanishing. To begin with, Asia's road, ports and airports were about to improve vastly, making the search for, and transport of, commodities far quicker and cheaper. No longer was it easy, therefore, for a middleman to keep his off-the-map product sources a secret.

Asian governments were also adopting globally uniform trade protocols, making a middleman's political connections less necessary. Last, but most important, the explosion of the Internet in Asia in the mid-to-late 1990s radically shrank the distance between buyer and seller, often to just a mouse click. "Everything became transparent," Elman explains. "You can't trade on lack of information anymore."

By the late 1990s the writing was on the wall for most Asian middlemen: Come up with more creative ways to add value, or get out. Hong Kong–based trading house Li & Fung is an instructive example of a middleman that successfully adapted to the new rules of the game. Traditionally a procurer of Asian textiles for Western clothing manufacturers, Li & Fung has in recent years become a one-stop shop for big Western retail stores like Abercrombie & Fitch and Esprit USA. From the design, tailoring and delivery of the clothes, Li & Fung manages the entire process on behalf of its clients.

"They just couldn't just sit around and do nothing," says Simon Lam, an analyst with Credit Suisse First Boston Securities in Hong Kong. "The current environment is too tough. So they've added more value in terms of their design and delivery services to maintain their operating margins."

Noble has followed Li & Fung's one-stop-shop strategy—but in the trickier realm of bulk commodities like steel, alumina, soya beans, grain and cocoa. Because it's not as simple to enhance the value of a shipment of Indonesian soya beans as it is to weave an Oxford shirt from a bolt of Pakistani cotton, Elman had to insert Noble into traditionally unexplored crevices of the supply chain. When a shipment of steel or grain is hoisted aboard one of Noble's ships, for example, a Noble subsidiary like Noble Finance or its risk-insurance arm, TradeVest Risk Services, offers to handle all the financing and insurance needs on behalf of the buyer.

Even more unusually, Noble often undertakes manufacturing jobs on behalf of its buyers, as it did in China with the Bihar-bought iron ore, or more recently for a European consumer-goods manufacturer with a craving for chocolate. Noble bought the cocoa from Sulawesi, processed it into chocolate bars at a nearby factory and then dispatched them to Switzerland on one of its Europe-bound vessels.

Finding such sweet spots in a customer's supply chain and then seizing them will be key to the new Asian middleman's future. "There's no question that the biggest potential source of operational efficiencies is not in the

STICK TO BASICS

Food, or the lack thereof, was the inspiration for Richard Elman's trading career. "When I was growing up in England, you never saw fresh fruit," Elman says, using an English child's craving for tropical fruits to illustrate the classic trader's dilemma: How to reduce a market's transaction costs to the point where even the arduous task of bringing Honduran or Thai bananas to drizzly markets in Leeds or Manchester would be a profitable endeavour.

Though greasing the commercial wheels of post-war England proved a tall order for Elman the toddler, he later earned his trading spurs as a teenager by trading steel, first in England, then, starting in the late 1960s, between Japanese steel producers and American manufacturers. In the 1970s Elman worked at Philbro, the commodity-trading house later bought by Salomon Brothers. It was at Philbro that Elman had his first brush with the most notorious trader in the business: Swiss fugitive Marc Rich, who in concert with the Malaysian government unsuccessfully tried to corner the global tin market in the mid-1980s. Elman does not recall those days of high-octane trading warmly. "If I had to keep hedging on commodities on futures exchanges, as Marc did," he says, "I'd have to be up 24 hours a day. No thanks."

Noble, which Elman founded in Hong Kong in 1986, is less exotic and more basic in its trading ambitions: It tries to shave transaction costs by undertaking all the steps—whether it be sourcing, marketing, processing or logistics—that lie between a product's seller and buyer. It is this simple formula that is at the heart of the trading house's success, whether it is dealing in steel, soybeans or coal.

NOBLE GROUP

$ million	*1st half '01*	*2000*	*1999*
Total sales	887.2	1,197.7	795.1
Net profit after tax	15.1	21.1	6.3
ROE	13.1%	20.0%	6.7%

Source: Noble Group

factory but in the linkages between the manufacturer and customer," says Ken Gibson, a Jakarta-based director with global management consultancy McKinsey & Co. "That is the challenge of the traditional Asian trader. He will die if he doesn't improve these linkages."

Elman the ex-hippie describes Noble's mission in similar—though more prosaic—terms. "We're the milkman," is how Elman puts it, drawing on a fond childhood memory. "When I was growing up in England you got the milk directly on your doorstep but you didn't know how it got there. The milk actually went through 40–50 different steps before it arrived on your doorstep. That's what we take care of."

HAPHAZARD ATTEMPTS TO DIVERSIFY WRECK A SINGAPORE WHOLESALER

HOW THAKRAL LOST THE PLOT

By Neel Chowdhury

The debt-ridden Thakral Corp., a once-prosperous Singaporean trading house, is an example of how tricky it can be for traders to lift their business to the next level. Thakral, owned and run by an Indian Sikh family settled in Singapore, was once one of the leading electronic-goods distributors in Asia. By selling Japanese stereos, televisions and videocassette recorders to consumers in Southeast Asia especially, the firm thrived, emblazoning its name on a bustling shopping mall across the road from Singapore's parliament.

But as profit margins thinned in the global consumer-electronics business over the past decade, largely because of cut-throat pricing by new manufacturers in South Korea and China, Thakral began to diversify into new businesses—haphazardly and regrettably, as it turned out.

> Thakral lacked in-house forex expertise to operate outside its home markets

Convinced that profits lay in controlling the retail arm of the consumer-electronics business, but possessing no retail experience, Thakral planned to open up a string of stores in China. It also launched itself into the Australian property market just as prices were set to tumble, and announced a joint venture in early 2000 with a Singaporean Internet service provider to form a technology-consulting company in China.

It had no track record to speak of in either business. Nor did Thakral possess any in-house foreign-exchange expertise, which became necessary as it ventured outside its home markets during a period of wild currency volatility. Investors, wary of Thakral's new moves, began dumping the company's shares, sending its share price from the S$10–15 ($5.5–8.3) range in 1996 to penny-stock levels today. Singaporean stockbrokers, who once touted Thakral as a promising China play, stopped covering it.

In the end, Thakral's new ventures saddled the company with roughly a quarter of a billion dollars in debt and, for the most part, could not generate sustainable cash flows. In late 2001 Thakral obtained permission from Singapore's High Court to temporarily waive claims from creditors as it entered the first stages of an arduous debt-restructuring plan. "For lack of a better word," admits Elie Baroudi, deputy CEO of Thakral, "we're doing what in America would be called a Chapter 11 bankruptcy."

Yet even as Noble has successfully adapted to the new rules, many older Asian middleman have not. In part, this is due to the growing need for scale in the trading business, which has effectively squeezed less nimble small to medium-sized traders out of the game. As trading in smaller volumes increasingly entails the agility and innovativeness of quasi-supply-chain managers like Noble, big Japanese trading houses like Mitsubishi, Mitsui and Itochu have largely receded to a domain where their dominance remains effectively unchallenged: The large-volume and low-margin industrial project. Because of their financial muscle and their almost incestuous links with Japanese manufacturers and banks, when it comes to large industrial projects like these, the Japanese behemoths possess advantages smaller trading operations could never secure.

A recent Black Sea gas-pipeline deal involving Mitsui is typical. The Black Sea project, a 760-kilometre undersea pipeline that will run from Russia to Turkey, will be largely financed by a syndicate of Japanese banks and built by a Japanese consortium assembled by Mitsui, and include such stalwart Mitsui partners as Nippon Steel, Kawasaki Steel and Sumitomo Metal. In return, Mitsui and its partners will source much of the steel required for the pipeline, an order amounting to some $1.8 billion.

Even so, money is only part of the problem facing the smaller trading shops; management is the tougher nut to crack. For most small to medium-sized Asian trading firms, the ubiquitous import-export shops that fill corporate registries in trading hubs like Hong Kong or Singapore simply don't possess the managerial talent to do anything but buy and sell. Says Milton Au, a Noble executive director who manages the firm's Singapore grain-trading division out of a leafy colonial bungalow: "In pure trading you don't need much managerial expertise. But the most important thing we need now is professional managers who know how to manage risk."

A CHANGING CULTURE

But not all traders in Asia fare so badly, not even the small companies that might seem automatically disadvantaged by the new rules of the game. Chris Baur, a recently minted Wharton MBA who returned to Singapore a few years ago, is carefully reinventing his family trading firm. The firm, which specializes in floor-covering products, has 50 employees spread across Europe, the Middle East and Asia. It's too small and capital-starved to become a manufacturer of flooring products in its own right, so the young heir faces a delicate task: How to change the trading culture of the firm from inside.

"My father followed a typical buy-and-sell model," Baur explains. "But when you're in a buying-and-selling culture, you can't attract people who can really think about processes and solutions. That's why I joined the firm. I'm the MBA. My father couldn't have done it on his own." Attracting more creative managers is Baur's hardest challenge, he says, as the company seeks to move closer to its buyers by taking on more logistical tasks. Adding lacquering to the floor products it imports, for example, is a small way to solidify its relationship with its buyers, for whom quality, not just price, is becoming more and more important. "I'm finding the transition very difficult," admits Baur. "You think as a hotshot MBA you can do it easily. But it's tough."

For his part, Elman has no doubts that the direction he's taking at Noble is not just opportunistic, but inevitable. "When I started out it was easy to make a living by trading in Asia if you just went to enough out-of-the-way places," he says, almost wistfully. "No more."

AUTOS

THE AMERICANIZATION OF TOYOTA

Its U.S. success is a lifeline, as other important markets languish

Since moving to the U.S. 15 years ago, Nicaragua-born Roberto Castillo has had a series of jobs at car dealerships—first Ford, then Pontiac, and eventually Hyundai. But two years ago, he landed the job he really wanted: selling Toyotas. "Toyotas are easier to sell than any other car," he says. "Everyone knows the reputation," he says. "So you never have to sell [people] on the benefits." Nowadays, Castillo works at Longo Toyota in the Los Angeles suburb of El Monte. Last year he piled up commissions worth more than $80,000. As he says: "You can make good money with Toyota."

Tell that to Tetsuo Kawano. He runs a Toyota dealership in a beachfront suburb of Yokohama, Japan. Recently Kawano held a promotion featuring FM deejay Haruhisa Kurihara. The event drew about 75 young Japanese with bleached hair, baggy pants, and goatees. The idea was to move a few Toyota Vitz subcompacts. The crowd enjoyed the music and free doughnuts, but there wasn't much interest in the product. "I'm here because I like the deejay," said Kidokoro Katsumi, 21. And the cars? "I just bought a Honda." Says a rueful Kawano: "We're selling into a shrinking market."

Booming in the U.S., but running out of gas in Japan? That was never Toyota Motor Corp.'s global strategy. Ten years ago the auto maker had a multipronged attack plan: grow steadily at home, make modest gains in the U.S., make money in Europe, and take over Southeast Asia. Well, things have changed. Japan has become the incredible shrinking market. The European conquest, though still possible, is a dream deferred. And Southeast Asia has stalled out. That leaves the U.S., the one market where sales remain robust. Toyota's American strategy, in short, has become Toyota's lifeline.

The importance of the U.S. raises questions about what kind of company Toyota will become. How far will the Japanese leadership let the Americanization of Toyota go? How will the importance of the North American market affect Toyota's international thrust? And most important, with future profits so dependent on the U.S., how easy will it be for Toyota to drive its current 10% share of the U.S. market to 15%—or even 20%?

Toyota, the world's third-largest auto maker—2001 sales are expected to hit $108 billion and operating profits $4.2 billion—will struggle with these and other questions over the next few years. Still, despite trepidation about the company's increasingly American tilt back at headquarters in Toyota City, about 100 km east of Nagoya, the way forward seems clear. Says Toyota Chief Executive Fujio Cho: "We must Americanize."

The process is already well under way. Consider the following facts, including some statistics that scare the wits out of Toyota's rivals in Detroit:

• Last year, Toyota sold more vehicles in the U.S. (1.74 million) than in Japan (1.71 million). Analysts figure that almost

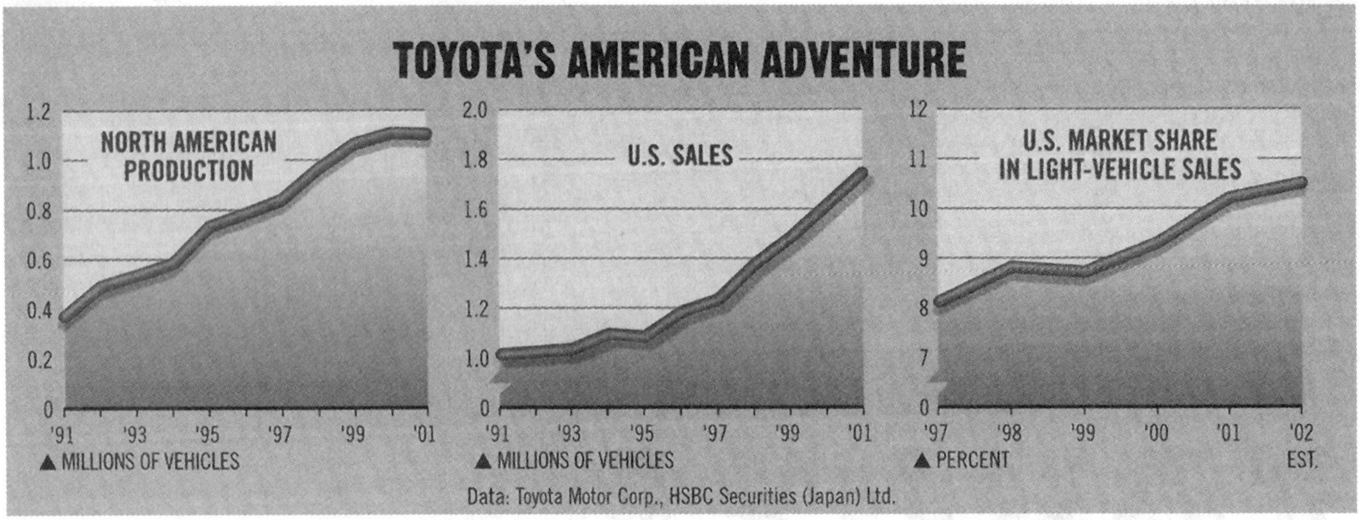

CHART BY ALBERTO MENA/BW

two-thirds of the company's operating profit comes from the U.S.

• Toyota's U.S. factories and dealerships currently employ 123,000 Americans—that's more than Coca-Cola, Microsoft, and Oracle combined.

• Toyota's top U.S. execs are, increasingly, local hires. The recently appointed manager of the key Georgetown (Ky.) plant, which makes the Camry, is Ford Motor Co. veteran Gary Convis. "Thirty years ago, we were more dependent on Japan," says James Press, chief operating officer of Toyota Motor Sales USA Inc. in Torrance, Calif. Now, Press says, "there's not much Japanese influence on a day-to-day basis."

• Toyota's big hits in the U.S.—the Camry sedan, Tundra pickup, and Sequoia sport-utility vehicle—were all designed with the American consumer in mind with significant input from U.S. design teams. Now, Toyota is launching a third brand: Scion, aimed at America's youth.

• With its 10% U.S. market share, Toyota is within striking distance of DaimlerChrylser's 14.5%. Some auto executives think it's only a matter of time before Toyota steals DaimlerChrysler's place in the Big Three.

It's easy to see why Toyota has become so focused on the U.S. While the company has never forfeited its dominant position in Japan, its market share is slipping steadily, while profit margins per vehicle are now an estimated 5%, vs. 13% in the U.S. In recessionary Japan, Toyota failed to shift production quickly enough into minivans and cheaper subcompacts. Its rivals, by contrast, have adapted to changing demand, putting unaccustomed pressure on Toyota. "The Japanese market has gotten much more competitive, with Nissan back on track and Honda on a roll," says Chris Richter, an analyst at HSBC Securities Inc. in Tokyo. And Toyota's move into Europe has been slower than expected.

Toyota's top brass won't discuss market-share goals—The last thing the company wants to do is ruffle feathers in Washington by publicly targeting DaimlerChrysler. However, "The American market is our top priority, bar none," says Cho, who in February became one of a few Japanese executives to be inducted into the U.S. Automotive Hall of Fame. "We'll do whatever it takes to succeed there." The company is already planning to ramp up production capacity in the U.S. to more than 1.45 million units by 2005, from 1.25 million now. In the next two to three years, Toyota hopes to be selling a total of 2 million vehicles a year, including imports, in the American market.

Of course, deep inside the company, ambivalence lingers about the growing clout of the U.S. division. Toyota traditionalists are reluctant to stray from the Toyota Way, a philosophy set forth by the company's legendary founder, Kiichiro Toyoda, a zealot for consensus-style decision-making, merciless cost-cutting, and fanatical devotion to quality and customer satisfaction. So, to ensure that Toyota doesn't lose the essence of what makes it great, the company in February opened the Toyota Institute, an internal, MBA-style program near Toyota City whose faculty will comprise Toyota execs and visiting professors from the University of Pennsylvania's Wharton School.

Fact is, Toyota and its U.S. subsidiaries don't always see eye to eye, especially when it comes to making design choices for the American market. Sometimes the conflicts are over small issues; one Toyota official in Japan, for example, says interior color schemes are a constant source of friction. At other times, there are clashes over crucial product-strategy decisions. "They have to be dragged kicking and screaming into bigger products," says Jim Olson, a senior vice-president at Toyota Motor North America Inc. in New York City.

In the late 1990s, Japanese product planners resisted their U.S. colleagues' idea that the company should produce a V8 pickup truck for the American market. To change their minds, U.S. executives took their Japanese counterparts to a Dallas Cowboys football game—with a pit stop in the Texas Stadium parking lot. There, the Japanese saw row upon row of full-size pickups. Finally, it dawned on them that Americans see the pickup as more than a commercial vehicle, considering it primary transportation. Result: the red-hot Tundra, which sells for about $25,000.

Now, it's harder than ever for executives in Japan to second-guess their American colleagues. "Once we started building products [in the U.S.]," says Donald V. Esmond, senior vice-president of the Torrance sales arm, "then the chief engineers started listening a lot closer in terms of what products we need in the market." The proof that American marketers know their business is in the numbers. March sales of the $20,000 Camry, a sedan revamped for the U.S., surged 24.1% over the same month last year. Sales of the Highlander SUV jumped 28.4%.

However successfully Toyota blends the essence of the Toyota Way with a dash of American salesmanship, increasing market share in the U.S. from now on will be a bigger challenge. "Toyota [has] very complete product coverage," says George Peterson, president of AutoPacific Group Inc., a market-research company in Tustin, Calif. "There are very few holes in its lineup." More ominously, Toyota could face in the U.S. the same problem it does in Japan: smaller rivals taking daring design steps that attract new customers. Already, Nissan Motor Co.'s redesigned Altima and Infiniti G35, with their head-turning styling, are luring Americans from the Camry and Lexus line. And South Korea's Hyundai is moving upscale with such cars as the XG350, a family sedan that is thousands of dollars cheaper than the Camry.

The average age of Toyota drivers in the U.S. is 45—the highest for any Japanese carmaker

Still, given Toyota's U.S. momentum, even stiffer competition from Honda and Nissan won't have a dramatic impact in the short term. Indeed, to increase market share, all Toyota needs to do is crank up U.S. production. Right now there is more demand for such models as the Lexus RX 300 and Highlander SUV than Toyota can fill. "They could get a full share point just by bringing Highlander production to the U.S.," says a well-placed analyst. The company already plans to make the RX 300 in Canada. As a result, Toyota should have no trouble "dialing up their U.S. sales through the remainder of the decade," says one analyst.

But Toyota does have an Achilles' heel: its aging customer base. The average age of a Toyota buyer in the U.S. is 45, the highest among Japanese carmakers. Press, the U.S. chief operating officer, says that Toyota has already halted the aging process by revamping the Celica coupe and MR2 Spyder roadster. Yet neither sold well last year. Nor did the Echo, the first Toyota subcompact aimed at Generation Y and younger. A moderate hit in Japan, it is a flop with young drivers in the U.S., who prefer the Ford Focus or any Volkswagen.

It's too early to tell, but the new $15,000 Matrix subcompact could be the winner Toyota is hoping for. The company's strongest prospect to close the generation gap, however, will be Scion, the new brand to be launched in California next summer. The first Scion models will be the bbX, a modified version of the bB—or black box—a particularly blocky looking van that is now being sold in Japan, as well as a car that is rumored to be derived from the Japanese-market Ist (pronounced "east"). In 2004, the Scion brand will go national in the U.S. and roll out models designed specifically for the American market. One prospect is the ccX, a sporty coupe with additional cargo space and not one, but two sunroofs to provide an open-air feeling.

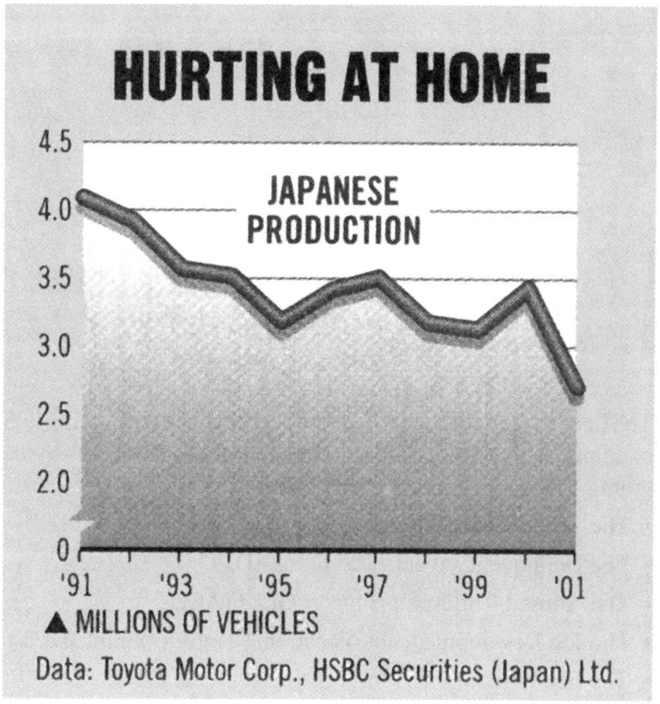

CHART BY ALBERTO MENA/BW

Will Scion work? Many analysts say that Toyota should have launched its youth-oriented line as part of the Toyota marque—and in doing so bring some verve to the whole brand. However, AutoPacific Group analyst James N. Hall believes that Scion has "no downside." With luck, he says, the brand will bring a new breed of buyers into Toyota showrooms. If it doesn't, he adds, the core Toyota franchise won't suffer. Besides, while the bbX may look bizarre to older buyers, some analysts are convinced that young Americans will like Scion products.

Toyota Chairman Hiroshi Okuda jokingly said last year that his company should move its headquarters to the U.S. That's unlikely. Still, this most Japanese of Japanese auto makers knows its U.S. strategy is crucial to its future. The company that Kiichiro Toyoda founded still has its roots in Japan, but Toyota's destiny is all-American.

By Chester Dawson in Toyota City, with Larry Armstrong in Los Angeles and Joann Muller and Kathleen Kerwin in Detroit

Case: *The Fairfax County Social Welfare Agency*

The Fairfax County Social Welfare Agency was created in 1965 to administer services under six federally funded social service grants:

- The Senior Citizens' Developmental Grant (SCD).
- The Delinquent Juvenile Act Grant (DJA).
- The Abused Children's Support Grant (ACS).
- The Job Development and Vocational Training Grant JDVT).
- The Food Stamp Program (Food).
- The Psychological Counseling and Family Therapy Fund (Counseling).

The agency's organizational structure evolved as new grants were received and as new programs were created. Staff members—generally the individuals who had written the original grants—were assigned to coordinate the activities required to implement the programs. All program directors reported to the agency's executive director, Wendy Eckstein, and had a strong commitment to the success and growth of their respective programs. The organizational structure was relatively simple, with a comprehensive administrative department handling client records, financial records, and personnel matters. (See below.)

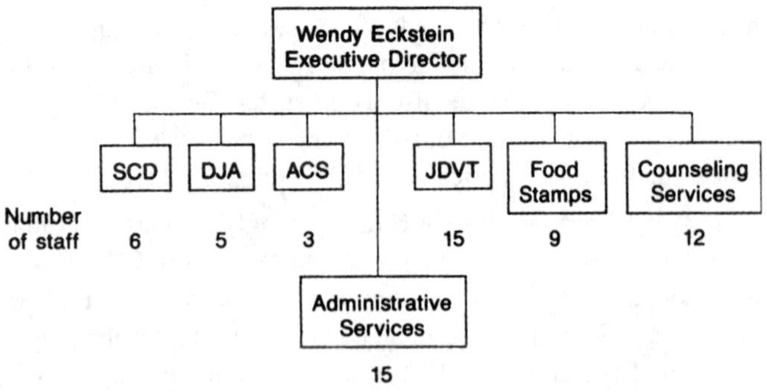

The sense of program "ownership" was intense. Program directors jealously guarded their resources and only reluctantly allowed their subordinates to assist on other projects. Consequently, there was a great deal of conflict among program directors and their subordinates.

The executive director of the agency was concerned about increasing client complaints regarding poor service and inattention. Investigating the matter, Eckstein discovered that:

1. Staff members tended to "protect" their clients and not refer them to other programs, even if another program could provide better services.
2. There was a total absence of integration and cooperation among program directors.
3. Programs exhibited a great deal of duplication and redundancy; program directors acquired administrative support for their individual programs.

Eckstein concluded that the present client or program-based structure no longer met the agency's needs. A major reorganization of this county social welfare agency is being considered.

Discussion Questions

1. What structural attributes of the agency could be causing the client complaints?
2. What actions could Eckstein take without actually changing the organization's structure?
3. Redesign the structure of the agency to improve cooperation and increase efficiency. How would you implement your newly designed structure?

Using the Case on *The Fairfax County Social Welfare Agency*

This case provides an outstanding opportunity to use Vroom's model of decision-making. Included with this discussion is some material developed by the Center for Creative Leadership, which takes Vroom's model and creates a schematic for decision purposes.

It is suggested that the instructor make a copy of the material for each of you or, perhaps, make an overhead for use in the classroom as you try to decide which decision-making approach would be best.

Questions for Discussion

1. How do you think Ms. Eckstein should proceed with making her decision?
2. What parts of the agency are going to be affected by the decision?
3. What are some of the likely outcomes from various decision-making approaches that Eckstein could use?

Exercise: *NASA Exercise*

As you approach the moon for a rendezvous with the mother ship, the lateral dissimilar malfunctions, forcing your ship and crew to land some 17 craters, or 145 Earth miles, from the mother ship. The touchdown results in a great deal of damage to the ship but, luckily, none to the crew. Survival is dependent upon reaching the mother ship. The most critical items must be chosen for the trip.

Instructions: Below are the only 15 items left intact after the landing. Rank the items in order of importance they hold to you and your crew in reaching the rendezvous point. Place 1 by the most important item, 2 by the next most important, and so on, through all fifteen items. You should complete this section in 10 minutes.

Your Decision	Articles	Group Decisions
_______	Box of matches	_______
_______	Food concentrate	_______
_______	50 feet of nylon rope	_______
_______	Parachute silk	_______
_______	Portable heating unit	_______
_______	Two .45 caliber pistols	_______
_______	One case of dehydrated Pet milk	_______
_______	Two 100-pound tanks of oxygen	_______
_______	Stellar map of the moon's constellation	_______
_______	Self-inflating life raft	_______
_______	Magnetic compass	_______
_______	Five gallons of water	_______
_______	Signal flares	_______
_______	First-aid kit containing injection needles	_______
_______	Solar-powered FM receiver/transmitter	_______

Because you have survived as a group, the most appropriate decision-making method is group consensus. Each member of the group has to agree upon the rank order. Because the consequence of a wrong decision is so severe—death—you want to be as logical as you can and avoid arguments. In addition, you want to be sure to agree with that ranking that somewhat meets your solution. Be sure not to employ any voting, averaging, or trading techniques that might stifle and embitter one of your companions on this survival journal. *(See answers below.)*

Scoring

1. Subtract the group score on each item from your individual score on each item. Write down the difference. For example, you put down an item as 3 on your list, and the group ended up ranking it 6. There is a net difference of 3.
2. Add all the net differences together to get your par score.
3. Collect all the scores in the group, add them, then divide by the number of people in the group. Your net difference-score ____________ Average Individual score ____________
4. Now take the NASA-computed rankings and compare the group's ranking with it, computing the net difference between the group's ranking and the correct ranking. Net Difference Score—Group and Correct ____________

What do these differences mean?

Answers:

15—Box of matches; 4—Food concentrate; 6—50 feet of nylon rope; 8—Parachute silk; 13—Portable heating unit; 11—Two .45 caliber pistols; 12—One case dehydrated Pet milk; 1—Two 100 lb. tanks of oxygen; 3—Stellar map of the moon's constellation; 9—Rubber life raft; 14—Magnetic compass; 2—Five gallons of water; 10—Signal flares; 7—First-Aid kit containing injection needles; 5—Solar-powered FM receiver-transmitter.

Case: The Fairfax County Social Welfare Agency; Exercise: NASA Exercise, Fred Maidment, McGraw-Hill/Dushkin, 2000.

UNIT 4

Organizing

Unit Selections

Key Points to Consider

- Some of the early work that was done by management theorists was in classifying and analyzing jobs. Do you think that this type of analysis style still applies? Explain.
- As different groups enter the labor force, they are going to have different demands than the more traditional sources of labor. What impact do you think this is going to have on organizations? How do you think employees from the more traditional sources of labor are going to react?
- Do you think that organizations are going to have to trust their employees more than they did in the past? Why or why not?

DUSHKIN ONLINE **Links: www.dushkin.com/online/**
These sites are annotated in the World Wide Web pages.

From Foosball to Flextime: Dotcommers Are Growing Up
http://www.fastcompany.com/invent/invent_feature/act_childcare.html

Sympatico: Careers
http://www.ntl.sympatico.ca/Contents/Careers/

U.S. Department of Labor (DOL)
http://www.dol.gov

Work and Organizational Psychology, Stockholm University
http://www.psychology.su.se/units/ao/ao.html

After the managers of an organization have planned a course of action, they must organize the firm to accomplish the goals. Many early writers in management were concerned with organization. Frederick W. Taylor was one of the first to apply scientific principles to organizing work. He was followed by Frank and Lillian Gilbreth, pioneers in the field of time and motion studies. Their work contributed to the development of the assembly line and other modern production techniques and is shown in the classic essay, "Classifying the Elements of Work."

The questions that constantly confront managers today are how best to organize the firm, given the internal and external environment, and how to approach the problem, not only from the company's perspective, but also from the perspective of the economy as a whole. Are large organizations better than small ones? Each has advantages and disadvantages. Which is better able to compete in the global environment against organizations from different countries with different expectations and rules? Add to this the fact that society is evolving, so that new types of organizations will be needed in the future as well as new forms of commerce, as seen in "Organizing for the New Economy."

There are several ways that a company can grow. One is to merge with and acquire other firms. The second is to expand the current business internally by building on its already established business units. A third is to utilize the new technology that is available as we start the twenty-first century. A recent trend in U.S. industry has been to grow via the merger and acquisition route, but growing internally or through the use of new technology can often be more rewarding.

People are not machines; they are looking for fulfilling and enjoyable work. Managers, therefore, must design jobs to be interesting and rewarding. The days of assembly-line workers doing the same task over and over are numbered. Such positions are being replaced by jobs that vary in the types of tasks the worker performs each day. The content is also changing for jobs that have traditionally required lower-level skills and less effort. Technology is forcing organizations to change the way that they do business and how people do their jobs.

Today, firms must be designed to meet the increasingly competitive environment of a global economy. Organizations must learn to do more with fewer resources and fewer people; management overlap and deadwood can no longer be tolerated. Organizations, therefore, try to be lean and mean; but is that necessarily the best way to go? As firms cut back, are they crippling the future of the organization by looking only at the short term? The opposite side of this coin is that the middle manager who is able to survive and prosper in this environment will be a better leader, having been tempered in a much hotter furnace than his or her predecessors.

To remain competitive in a rapidly changing environment, organizations must evolve to meet the rapidly developing global economy with which they will have to interact. "Creating a Learning Organization" will be a top priority for all organizations as new challenges appear for them to overcome. Managers will have to trust their employees more and share information with them that, in the past, they did not share, as seen in "Open Book Management—Optimizing Human Capital."

In the future, organizations will have the world as their market and their competitor. They must be able to foresee changes in their environment and to react quickly to turn those changes to their advantage. Organizations will need strength and flexibility to meet change or they will suffer the fate of the dinosaurs, which failed to adapt to new environments.

Classifying the Elements of Work

Frank B. Gilbreth and Lillian M. Gilbreth

This paper presents a complete method of visualizing a classification of all the subdivisions and the true motion-study elements of The One Best Way to Do Work.

NEED FOR SUCH A CLASSIFICATION

Such a classification is vitally necessary in order that fundamental super-standards shall be made by the scientific method of selecting and measuring the best units, for synthesis into methods of least waste.

This classification furnishes the basis of a definite mnemonic classification for filing all motion-study and time-study data for the work of the industrial engineer, the machine designer, and the behavior psychologist—that their various pieces of information, usually obtained through entirely different channels and methods of attack, may be automatically brought together, to the same filing folders, under the same filing subdivisions.

So far as we are able to learn, there are no other classifications or bases for filing that accomplish this purpose, and we have found that such a classification is absolutely necessary for our work of finding The One Best Way to Do Work, standardizing the trades, and making and enforcing standing orders for best management.

It is hoped that teachers of industrial engineering in our colleges will learn that *one* demonstration of building up The One Best Way to Do Work from the ultimate elements, in any kind of activity, will do more to teach a student the principles of motion study and most efficient methods of management than dozens of lessons dealing with generalities.

The coming generation should be taught a definite filing system for data of scientific management, laid out under a complete classification of all work; should be taught the method of selecting the right units to measure and the methods of measuring these units; and should be furnished with the devices for making the cost of measuring cheap, and with a method for synthesizing the resulting information. This would result in a general progress in world efficiency and an increase in quality of living that would mark an epoch in the history of industry and civilization.

USE OF FUNDAMENTAL ELEMENTS

The literature of scientific management abounds with examples of units of work improperly called "elements," which are in no sense elements. A classification for finding The One Best Way to Do Work must deal with *true elements,* not merely with subdivisions that are arbitrarily called "elements."

There has recently appeared a well-written biography of a great engineer[1] in which subdivisions of operations, requiring in many instances more than 30 seconds to perform, have been erroneously described as "elements." That error will again mislead many people. These so-called elements should be taken for what they really are, namely subdivisions and not elements, and not confused with true elements, or fundamental units which cannot be further subdivided.

SCOPE OF THE CLASSIFICATION

This classification for finding The One Best Way to Do Work is applicable to all kinds of work. It was used by one of the authors while serving as ranking officer in the field under the training committee of the General Staff, standardizing the methods of The Best Way to Do Work for teaching the five million men and officers in the World War. It has also been used in analyzing the work of the surgeon, nurse, hospital management, large department stores, selling a great many kinds of manufacturing, accounting, office work in general, and many other kinds of work.

TRUE ELEMENTS OF WORK

The classification of all work of any and all organizations for the purpose of finding The One Best Way to Do Work may be visualized as follows:

I. A complete organization, which consists of
II. Processes, such as
(a) Financing
(b) Advertising
(c) Marketing
(d) Distributing
(e) Selling
(f) Accounting
(g) Purchasing
(h) Manufacturing
(i) Planning
(j) Teaching
(k) Charting
(l) Maintaining
(m) Filing
These processes consist of
III. Operations, which consist of
IV. Cycles of motions, which consist of
V. Subdivisions, or events, or therbligs[2] of a cycle of motions which consist of
(a) Search
(b) Find
(c) Select
(d) Grasp
(e) Transport loaded
(f) Position
(g) Assemble
(h) Use
(i) Disassemble
(j) Inspect
(k) Pre-position for next operation
(l) Release load
(m) Transport empty
(n) Rest for overcoming fatigue
(o) Other periods of unavoidable delay
(p) Avoidable delay
(q) Plan
VI. Variables of motions
(a) Variables of the worker
1. Anatomy
2. Brawn
3. Contentment
4. Creed
5. Earning power
6. Experience
7. Fatigue
8. Habits
9. Health
10. Mode of living
11. Nutrition
12. Size
13. Skill
14. Temperament
15. Training
(b) Variables of the surroundings, equipment, and tools
1. Appliances
2. Clothes
3. Colors
4. Entertainment, music, reading, etc.
5. Heating, cooling, ventilating
6. Lighting
7. Quality of material
8. Reward and punishment
9. Size of unit moved
10. Special fatigue-eliminating devices
11. Surroundings
12. Tools
13. Union rules
14. Temperament
(c) Variables of the motion
1. Acceleration
2. Automaticity
3. Combination with other motions and sequences
4. Cost
5. Direction
6. Effectiveness
7. Foot-pounds of work accomplished
8. Inertia and momentum overcome
9. Length
10. Necessity
11. Path
12. "Play for position"
13. Speed

Under I, a complete organization, are included all kinds of organizations, including financial, industrial, commercial, professional, educational, and social.

Under II, processes, it should be noted that processes are divided in the same way from a motion-study analyst's standpoint, regardless in which department or in which function they are found.

Under III, operations, the operations include mechanical as well as physiological, and mental as well as manual. The reasons for these inclusions are:

1. From the motion-study standpoint there are not always clear dividing lines between the *operations of devices* and the *mental and manual operations of the human being*, for they are often mutually interchangeable, sometimes in part and sometimes as a whole.[3]

2. Records of many and probably all mental operations can now be obtained by the chronocyclegraph and micromotion photographic methods, and each year such photographic records can more and more be deciphered and used to practical advantage. Enough can already be read and used to serve our present needs. Careful examination of all our old micromotion and chronocyclegraph films taken under conditions of actual practice show that they are literally full of examples of such records of mental processes.

Under IV, cycles of motions are arbitrary subdivisions of operations. They have distinct and natural boundaries of beginning and ending. Usually and preferably there are certain sequences of therbligs that are especially suitable for standardization and transference to other kinds of work, and serve every purpose of finding The One Best Way to Do Work.

Under V, therbligs, we would emphasize that we do not place "motions" as the next subdivision under "cycle of motions" because "motions" have neither distinct and definite boundaries nor beginnings and endings. For example: It is difficult to determine correctly how many "motions" are required to take a fountain pen from the pocket and prepare to write with it. It will be found difficult to agree on just how many "motions" are made and as to where are located the boundaries of the "motions" of so simple a cycle as this, or of any other similarly common cycle of motions.

However, the 17 subdivisions, or events, or therbligs, as they are variously called, seem to be all that are necessary from which to synthesize all of the *cycles of motions* of all the *operations* of all the *processes* of all the *organizations* of every kind whatever. The science of motion study consists, therefore, of finding The One Best Sequence of therbligs for each kind of work and the science of management consists of deriving, installing, and enforcing the conditions that will permit the work to be done repeatedly in The One Best Way. It is conceivable that sometime in the future an eighteenth and possibly more therbligs will be found, and we seem near to their discovery at the present time. The discovery of additional therbligs pertaining to the phenomena of skill and automaticity seems inevitable.[4]

Under VI, variables of motions, provision is made for filing all information regarding any kind of motion made by either hand, device, or machine. It provides for all information regarding the structures in which work is performed. It provides for filing all data regarding human behavior—supernormal, normal, and subnormal. It supplies the basis of filing all data of the educator, psychologist, psychiatrist, and the expert in personnel, placement, and promotion problems.

This classification can be carried on and subdivided indefinitely. It furnishes an efficient and quickly usable plan for synthesizing the components of The One Best Way to Do Work in such shape that they can be cumulatively improved.

However, our present information regarding the 17 therbligs is sufficient to revolutionize all kinds of work, and if the industries of the various nations would eliminate the obviously unnecessary therbligs and standardize the kinds, sequences, and combinations of the remaining efficient therbligs, the resulting savings each year would be sufficient to pay the outstanding debts of most nations.

HISTORY OF THIS CLASSIFICATION

For many years we have used these therbligs as divisions for dissecting cycles of motions of a great many different kinds of work, but it was not until we began to use photography in motion study in 1892 that we made our greatest progress. It was not until 1912, when we used our first micromotion processes intensively, that we were able to make such great advances as projecting the motions of experts faster and slower, as well as at the speed of experts' demonstration. We were then also able to project and examine therbligs backwards, or in the reversed directions. This enabled us to get a new fund of information that resulted in many suggestions from seeing, measuring, and comparing the therbligs performed in the reversed sequence and opposite directions. This was used to great advantage in finding the methods of least waste and especially in the process of taking machines apart and putting them together again in front of a motion picture camera, and then running the film backwards, showing the films of assembling as dissembling and vice versa.

EXAMPLES OF PROFITABLE USE

Running films of superexperts backwards, to see what we could get for automatically suggesting inventions, or as "thought detonators" when seeing the operation done thus, presented peculiarities and combinations of therbligs never seen before. This was, of course, supplemented by examining one picture, or frame, at a time which, with motion study experts, will always be the most efficient method for getting facts from the films. Great progress was made, for example, in *pre-positioning for next operation* (therblig *k*) parts and tools so that *grasp* (therblig *d*) was performed with quite the same motions and actions and performed within a time equal to that of *release load* (therblig *l*).

As an example of the importance of recognizing the therblig as the fundamental element, the result of that particular study in 1912 was that our organization enabled a client to have his machine assemblers put together 66 machines per day with less fatigue than they had previously accumulated while assembling 18 machines per day. Because this method was synthesized from fundamentally correct units, the same methods are still in use today in this same factory.[5]

This increase in output should not be considered as an exceptional case. On the contrary, it is quite typical. In fact we have a great many illustrations that we could give where the savings were much greater. For example: One large motion-study laboratory, as a result of this method of attack, synthesized and demonstrated new methods which averaged an output of five times as much product per man. This method used in assembling carburetors enabled messenger boys to do the work in one-tenth the time required by skilled mechanics.[6] It has been used on work of assembling pumps with still greater results.[7]

THERBLIG SEQUENCES

It was early recognized that certain similar operations have similar sequences of therbligs. For example: The operations of feeding pieces into a drill press or into a punch press, time tickets into a time stamp, and paper into a printing press, have practically the same sequence of therbligs. A typical sequence of therbligs for one complete cycle of handling one piece on a drill press is *search, find, select, grasp, transport loaded, position, assemble, use, disassemble, inspect, transport loaded, pre-position for next operation, release load* and *transport empty*. This cycle of motions can and should be done with the following therbligs: *grasp, transport loaded, position, assemble, use, release load* and *transport empty*, which are half the number of therbligs of the usual method.

While the former is the usual sequence of therbligs on a drill press, it is by no means the best one. There is The One Best Sequence of therbligs on each machine and each kind of work, and it should always be found, standardized, taught, and maintained.

Table 1

PAIRED THERBLIG USUALLY PERFORMED BEFORE USE		PAIRED THERBLIG USUALLY PERFORMED AFTER USE
d. Grasp	Use	*l.* Release load
e. Transport loaded	Use	*m.* Transport empty
f. Position	Use	*k.* Pre-position for next operation
g. Assemble	Use	*i.* Disassemble
q. Plan	Use	*j.* Inspect

Table 2 Unpaired Therbligs

ORDER NO. 4		ORDER NO. 5
a. Search	Use	*n.* Rest for overcoming fatigue
b. Find	Use	*o.* Other forms of unavoidable delay
c. Select	Use	*p.* Avoidable delay

ANOTHER WORK CLASSIFICATION

Now let us look at another method of subdividing and classifying all work. There is another and better known type of division and classification for visualizing all activity which was early recognized. The importance of considering this simple classification can be seen in the unfairness and trouble that have been caused by giving the same piece rate for large lots as for small. This classification divides all work, both large and small, into three parts, as follows:

1. Get ready
2. Do it, or make it.
3. Clean up.

Now, applying this division to one piece on the drill press, we have:

1. *Get ready*, or pick up the piece and put it under the drill. This consists of all therbligs that come before *use* (therblig *h*).
2. *Drill it* (do it or make it). This consists of only one therblig, namely *use* (therblig *h*).
3. *Clean up*, or take the piece out from under the drill and inspect it and lay it down. This consists of all therbligs that come after *use* (therblig *h*).

THE IMPORTANCE OF USE

It should be recognized that the therblig *use* is the difficult one to learn in mastering a trade. It is the most productive and, therefore, the most important therblig of all.

All other therbligs of all kinds of work are desirable and necessary only so far as they facilitate, prepare for, or assist in increasing *use*. Any therbligs that do not foster *use* should be under suspicion as being unnecessary. Use is the highest paid therblig, because it usually requires the most skill. The more of the therbligs of "get ready" and "clean up" that are performed by less skilled and consequently lower priced workers the better for all workers, for they all will be employed a larger portion of the day at the highest priced work at which they are each individually capable. This is true not only in the consideration of the therbligs

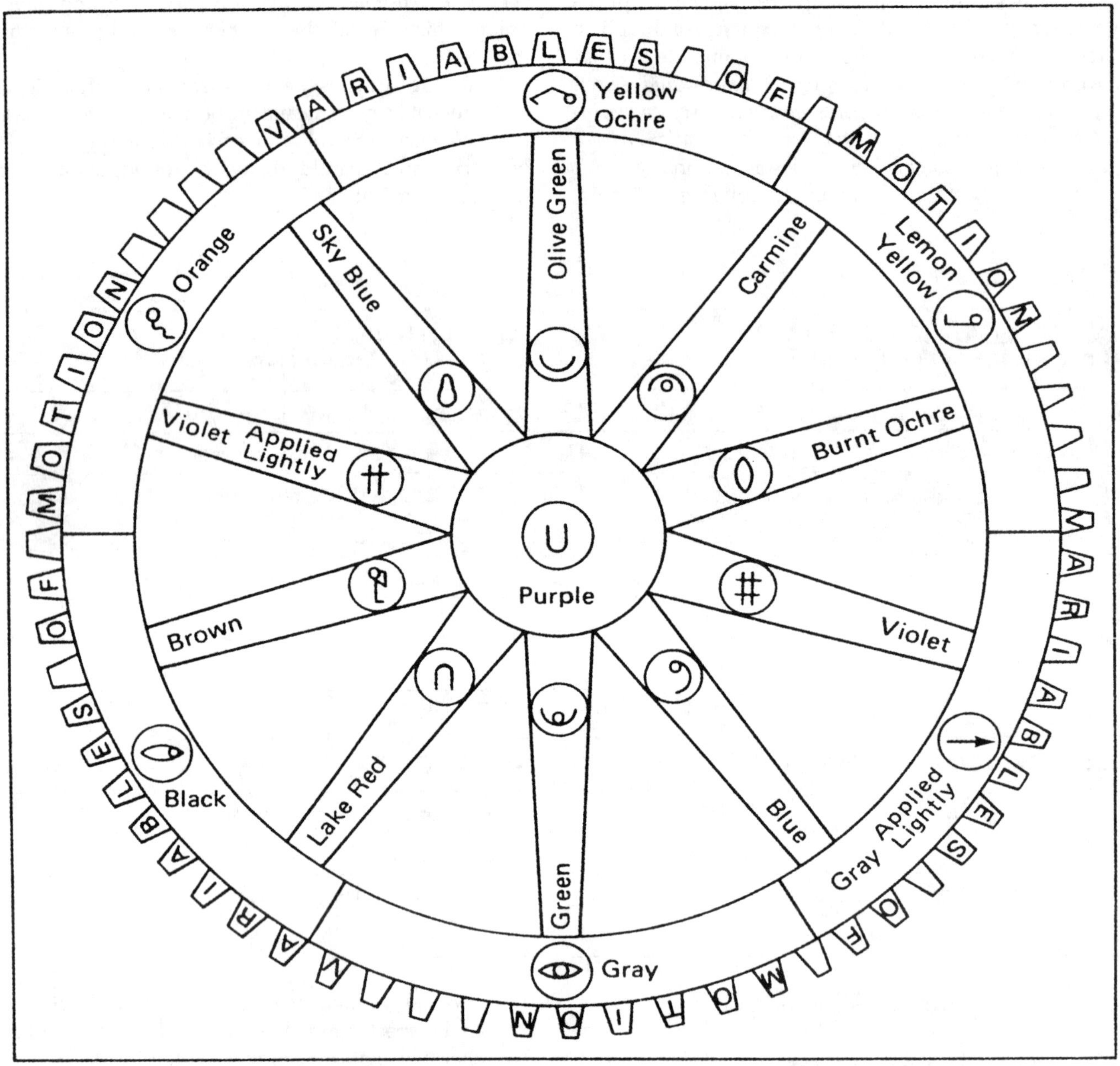

Figure 1. The Wheel of Motion

but also in the trades in general. For example: The bricklayer, the plumber, the steamfitter, the office executive, and many others, each have their specially assigned helpers, but they still habitually do much pay-reducing work for which in the long run they suffer a loss due to less personal activity. It will help to analyze and classify all work if it is recognized that the hod carrier bears the same relation to the bricklayer, and the secretary to the executive, as do the therbligs that compose "get ready" bear to the therblig *use;* and the laborer's work of "clean up" after the work of the bricklayer, is quite the same as the therbligs that compose "clean up" after therblig *use.*

Further investigations of a typical sequence of therbligs, such as on the drill press or other examples cited, from the standpoint of the classification of the therbligs show that *grasp* (therblig *d*) of "get ready" is used before *use* (therblig *h*) and that *release load* (therblig *l*) done after *use* may be quite the same except that it is performed in motions that are the reverse of those of *grasp.*

PAIRED THERBLIGS

There are a number of such paired therbligs which are almost always separated by the therblig *use.*

For example:

It was the absence of a therblig on the other side of *use* to pair with *inspect,* together with the fact that *plan* is actually found in the photographic records regardless of how much planning may be done prior to the beginning of an operation, that caused us to add to the list of therbligs, *plan* (therblig *q*). The therblig *plan* may occur in any place in the sequence of therbligs, but we have put it last in the list before cited because it was added last, and also to distinguish it from the "planning" that should be done before any "performing" of the operation is begun.

There are two more kinds of divisions, or orders, making a total of five orders of therbligs, namely one consisting of *search, find* and *select* (therbligs *a, b,* and *c*) which usually come before *use,* and *rest for overcoming fatigue, other forms of unavoidable delay* and *avoidable delay* (therbligs *n, o,* and *p*) which usually come after *use.* Thus we have two orders of unpaired therbligs separated by *use,* as follows:

In analyzing an operation of any kind a simultaneous motion cycle chart is prepared. The therbligs of motion are applied to this chart in studying it for present methods and determining the altered sequence which should be adopted to establish The One Best Way to Do Work. This brought up the problem of graphic presentation of the therbligs for ready identification.

To make these 17 therbligs more real, tangible, and easier to visualize and remember, different colors are used to distinguish them on the simultaneous motion cycle chart.[8] One member of our organization, Paul M. Vanderhorst, who conceived the idea of adding *plan* to our list of therbligs, also suggested the idea of showing the 17 therbligs in the design of a wheel, and we have adopted a "Wheel of Motion" not altogether unlike the "Wheel of Life" of Hindus, for explaining therblig study to the employees of our

STANDARD SYMBOLS, COLORS AND PENCILS FOR SIMO-CHARTS
(Simultaneous Motion Cycle Charts)

Symbol	Name of Symbol	Symbol Color	Name of Color	Name and Number of Pencil or Crayon
	Search		Black	Dixon's Best Black #331
	Find		Gray	Dixon's Best Gray #352½
	Select		Light Gray	Dixon's Best Gray #352½ Applied Lightly
	Grasp		Lake Red	Dixon's Best Lake Red #321½
	Transport Loaded		Green	Dixon's Best Green #354
	Position		Blue	Dixon's Best Blue #350
	Assemble		Violet	Dixon's Best Violet #323
	Use		Purple	Dixon's Best Purple #323½
	Dis-assemble		Light Violet	Dixon's Best Violet #323 Applied Lightly
	Inspect		Burnt Ochre	Dixon's Best Burnt Ochre #335½
	Pre-position for Next Operation		Sky Blue	Dixon's Best Sky Blue #320
	Release Load		Carmine Red	Dixon's Best Carmine Red #321
	Transport Empty		Olive Green	Dixon's Best Olive Green #325
	Rest for Over-coming Fatigue		Orange	Ruben's "Crayola" Orange
	Unavoidable Delay		Yellow Ochre	Dixon's Best Yellow Ochre #324½
	Avoidable Delay		Lemon Yellow	Dixon's Best Lemon Yellow #353½
	Plan		Brown	Dixon's Best Brown #343

Figure 2. Symbols, Colors, and Pencils for Simo-Charts. In practice, column 3 is solid colors, not crosshatching.

clients. Each part of the wheel representing a therblig has its own individual color, and each of the colors has a special meaning and is also mnemonic. See Figs. 1 and 2.

It should be noted that *use* is the hub of the wheel. *Use* is the most important therblig. The more *use,* the more production.

The therbligs that have like characteristics, although they may represent reversed action, are shown as paired spokes on opposite sides of the wheel.

The rim of the wheel consists of two different kinds, or orders, of three parts each, and the cogs on the rim are shaped like the letter V and are to remind the motion-study student that the variables affect all of the therbligs and must be all carefully considered in order to obtain The One Best Way to Do Work. There are at least a hundred variables that are important on nearly all kinds of work and our complete list contains several thousand variables. It is extremely important to recognize that information relating to the variables is applicable to all kinds of work. The application of this information is simply a matter of degree required in the particular study in hand.

The same colors are always used on the same therbligs wherever they are represented or shown. This permits instant visualization of all the therbligs of any one kind. These colors are specially important in connection with quickly visualizing, grouping, comparing, and interpreting the behavior and happenings on simultaneous motion cycle charts. The use of the standard colors enables the micromotion study engineer to acquire a proper sense of the proper time for each therblig, even before a new study is made. This is particularly important when studying an operator for his first time, as it will show whether or not he is fully cooperating.

In fact, too much stress can hardly be laid on the importance of showing each and every therblig and all possible happenings on the simultaneous motion cycle chart in finding The One Best Way to Do Work. We know of no other method in finding The One Best Way to Do Work. It answers all purposes satisfactorily.

After sufficient experience and study, preferably in a motion-study laboratory, the interrelations, peculiarities, and suitabilities of the therbligs on several simultaneous motion cycle charts of different kinds of work will be recognized by an engineer trained in motion study. When he has the proper training he is invariably able to improve and completely revolutionize any work on which the micromotion study method of attack has not already been used.

RELATION OF THERBLIG STUDY TO STOPWATCH TIME STUDY

The symbols here shown furnish a sort of shorthand which makes for greater speed in making notes regarding best sequences of therbligs and motion study in general, and for remembering the therbligs easily. The results of careful study of the peculiarities of the therbligs individually and in combination with those that immediately precede and immediately follow, as well as those that are executed simultaneously by other anatomical members, will remove for all time any idea that scientific motion study of the behavior of the workers can be accomplished with any such obsolete device as a stopwatch, or that time study and motion study are the same thing or even similar.

The literature of scientific management is full of examples where time study and motion study are confused. This confusion abounds even in books that are considered classics. It should be recognized that "Time study is the art of finding how long it takes to do work." This was Taylor's original definition, and it is still good. Time study is the great invention of Dr. Taylor. Taylor never did any motion study[9] of any kind whatever.[10]

The definition of motion study is: "Motion study is the science of finding The One Best Way to Do Work." Of course micromotion study gives records in indisputable permanent form of the motions and behavior of the demonstrator of the methods and of the individual errorless times of each therblig of each cycle of motions and of the overall times of the operator.

TRANSFERABLE DATA

Intensive study of the resulting therbligs furnishes information that is interchangeable in all kinds of work for finding The One Best Way to Do Work. It is this feature of the great value of the interchangeability of the indisputable detailed data that makes it most desirable to select as demonstrator of a method that person only who is *the best demonstrator obtainable* of the best methods extant or the best known, and in a motion-study laboratory[11] equipped for the purpose, and under controlled conditions.

It is obvious that records of the methods of recognized champions are most desirable. It must be recognized, however, that champions are usually champions because others are so inefficient. The synthesis of the best components of the methods of two or more champions will make a method better than that of the method of the champion of champions and better than the method of *the one best demonstrator obtainable.*

Data regarding the therbligs of a champion or a superexpert in any one kind of work are usable on a great many different kinds of work, for the times and skill on each therblig are transferable. It is also desirable, but not absolutely necessary, that *the best demonstrator obtainable,* of the best method extant, shall have sufficient experience to perform the cycles of motions and the complete operation in the shortest time for that operation. However, it is often difficult to obtain anyone who can demonstrate the combination of the *best method known* and also the *best speed of performance.* Oftentimes the expert of motion study can demonstrate the sequence of therbligs which constitute The One Best Way to Do Work, yet, because of his lack of practice and speed, is not able at first to equal the times nor the relativity of simultaneity of therbligs performed by different anatomical members of those with a much poorer method, but with much greater natural dexterity who have had so much practice that they have arrived at a state of motion automaticity.

The usual standards obtained by rule-of-thumb methods will always be temporary and transitory.

It is here that the method of recording lateness of therbligs previously cited is of importance. Here again the detailed records of the therbligs are of great value for the correct times of individual therbligs and the proper relativity of simultaneity can be obtained even from inferior sequences where great dexterity and automaticity have been recorded under the wrong method. When the best sequence is known, the correct time for task management for performing The One Best Way to Do Work *can be prophesied before anyone can demonstrate it.* The importance of prophesying the time for accomplishing The One Best Way to Do Work before it can be demonstrated will be appreciated when it is realized that there is not a single case on record where The One Best Way to Do Work has been derived by the wasteful fumbling methods of evolution.

RELATION OF THIS CLASSIFICATION TO FATIGUE STUDY

Much has been written in generalities regarding unnecessary fatigue. Because of the dreadful working conditions in nearly all factories, some improvements can almost always be made by anyone with good intentions and authority together with sufficient continuity of purpose. However, such improvements are only part of what could be done and often lapse after the passing of the regime of the untrained enthusiast who is merely interested in the elimination of unnecessary fatigue. The One Best Way to Do Work is that sequence of therbligs which permits the work to be done in least time, with least fatigue, and entails having the periods of *unavoidable delay* (therblig *o*) and *avoidable delay* (therblig *p*) utilized for *rest for overcoming fatigue* (therblig *n*).

The data relating to therbligs that cause or eliminate unnecessary fatigue can be filed in orderly fashion for future use under the classification shown herein.

Unnecessary fatigue should be recognized as the badge of ignorance of the therbligs and consequently of motion study. To eliminate unnecessary fatigue, there must be complete recognition that the therbligs are the fundamental elements of The One Best Way to Do Work, and are units for the application of the laws of motion study and fatigue study.

RELATION TO STANDARDIZATION

Much has been written also of standardization, and The One Best Way to make standards is to proceed from the standpoint that the best standard is the one that best complies with the laws of motion study. It is quite impossible to standardize a method for quickest achievement of the state of automaticity without recognition and standardization of the individual therbligs involved and their combinations and sequences.

Automaticity of the wrong method, so prevalent in highly repetitive vocations like those of the textile trades, is the shame and disgrace of industry today. However, it will be quite useless for executives and managers to talk standardizations of the correct sequences of the therbligs for The One Best Way to Do Work until they know from personal experience the possibilities of micromotion study and set the example in their own duties. For this purpose the simplest device is the executive's cross-sectioned desk which serves as a permanent reminder, and if used properly will furnish a permanent proof. It permits doing all manual work with almost exactly the same motions every time. It soon becomes strikingly evident how much faster work can be accomplished when the motions are made over the same locations each and every time. The next step is the search for The One Best Way to Do Work.

... the evils of deadening monotony do not exist where there is sufficient knowledge of the therblings ...

Because of the rule-of-thumb methods used in the past for obtaining standards, almost anyone can make improvements in the present state of standardization encountered in all organizations. The usual standards obtained by rule-of-thumb methods will always be temporary and transitory. If standards are based upon the permanent records of indisputable knowledge of the ultimate components of the cycles obtained by the micromotion methods, they will be in shape for cumulative improvement without any additional study. Comparatively few organizations have given proper attention to the possibilities of standardization built upon indisputable measured elements, and but few standards have been made with due regard to the extra outputs in the savings of time and fatigue that result if the standards are made to conform with the laws of automaticity, which is the greatest free asset of the working man, whatever his occupation.

RELATION TO THE LEARNING PROCESS

For greatest speed with least effort and fatigue in learning, The One Best Sequence of therbligs should be used whenever possible from the very beginning of the learning period so that automaticity may be achieved in the shortest possible learning period and with least habit interference. The study of the 17 therbligs of this classification furnishes a means to shorten the period required to learn any kind of art, trade, profession, or other activity. Hence, there will be more time available to learn more jobs and thus gain promotion, and, by reason of more knowledge of the theory combined with the practice, prolong one's earning periods by teaching others, when one is too old to do a young man's total quantity of output.

Finally, the evils of deadening monotony do not exist where there is sufficient knowledge of the therbligs and the variables affecting them. As two cycles of motions can never be made exactly alike, the quest of perfection of methods is much more interesting and absorbing than the desire to know which part of the whole structure is the piece which is being worked upon, although the latter is supposed to be the millennium by the academic enemies of standardization.

Knowledge of measuring, selecting, and studying of therbligs makes all work fascinating, for while the best method known and performed under given conditions may be called for practical purposes "The One Best Way to Do Work," a still better method with new tools and conditions is ever possible. There is no instance or example that cannot be improved with greater knowledge of the therbligs pertaining to that work. There are so many possible combinations of therbligs that the skilled worker with the knowledge of therbligs performing any work ordinarily considered monotonous has the opportunity to improve the temporary One Best Way to Do Work almost without limit.

It is not the fault of the skilled worker, if he has not been taught to visualize the therbligs, that he has not been given sufficient incentives to enlist and hold all of his zeal continuously, has not been taught the science that underlies his work, has not been induced to search for the scheme of perfection, has not been taught a filing method for his knowledge that he may have systematized improvement from his additional experience, and has not desired to teach the apprentices and other learners the best way that he knew.

The results derived under the method of attack that this classification embodies have been successful in every kind of work in which it has been used.

It is hoped that this description of this filing classification will be of service to those who are interested in efficiency, in making waste elimination attractive, and in finding and enforcing the managerial conditions which will permit The One Best Way to Do Work.

NOTES AND REFERENCES

1. See *Frederick W. Taylor* by E B. Copley.
2. This word was coined for the purpose of having a short word which will save the motions necessary to write such long descriptions as "The 17 categories into which the motion-study elementary subdivisions of a cycle of motions fall."
3. In 1910 and the years following, we collected and specially devised in our own laboratory, many devices for supplying, mechanically, the therbligs of cycles of motions that the crippled soldiers could not perform, due to their injuries. Such collections should be made by all museums and colleges that intend to teach motion study.
4. See Society of Industrial Engineers Bulletin, November 1923, pp. 6-7. "A Fourth Dimension for Recording Skill," by Frank B. Gilbreth and L. M. Gilbreth. The lateness in starting or finishing of a therblig performed by any one anatomical member as compared with the time of beginning or finishing of a therblig performed by another anatomical member is a most important unit for measuring skill and automaticity.
5. See *Management Engineering*, February 1923, p. 87. "Ten Years of Scientific Management," by John G. Aldrich, M. E., and also his discussion of paper 1378 on page 1131, vol. 34, 1912, American Society of Mechanical Engineers Transactions.
6. See Proceedings of the Institution of Automobile Engineers (English), "The Fundamentals of Cost Reduction," by H. Kerr Thomas, Member of the Council.
7. See Society of Industrial Engineers Transactions, vol. 2, 1920, "The One Best Way to Do Work," by Frank B. Gilbreth and L. M. Gilbreth.
8. See "Applied Motion Study" by Frank B. Gilbreth and L. M. Gilbreth, p. 138.
9. See Bulletin of The Taylor Society, June 1921.
10. This can easily be proved by reading Taylor's own writings, and it is also a matter of record in our own office. This fact is entirely missed, perhaps unintentionally, by Taylor's biographer, Copley.
11. Laboratory motion study has been criticized as being done under conditions of the shop. The conditions of the shop should be changed until they duplicate the most desirable conditions of the laboratory.

Frank Bunker Gilbreth graduated from the English high school in Boston in 1885, passed the entrance examinations at M.I.T., but decided to work for a firm of consulting engineers and to complete his technical training at night. In 1911, he established Gilbreth, Inc., an engineering consulting firm, which advanced the specialty of Motion Study. His achievements in scientific engineering were recognized by the University of Maine, which conferred on him an LL.D. degree in 1920. Gilbreth died in 1925.

Lillian Moller Gilbreth married Frank Gilbreth in 1904. Her education included a Bachelor of Letters and a Master of Letters from the University of California and a Ph.D. from Brown University (1915). She traveled widely as a lecturer on technology and human relations problems, served as president of Gilbreth, Inc., and received numerous awards and medals. Lillian Gilbreth died in 1972.

From *Management Classics*, 1977, pp. 150–165. Published by Goodyear Publishing Company. Originally from *Management and Administration*, August 1924, pp. 151–154, and September 1924, pp. 295–298.

Organizing for the New Economy

The changing role of management

By Ray Suutari

In the early 1970s, during a job interview, I asked the CEO of a major company about his organization. He took out an organization chart and outlined the various areas of functional responsibility and levels of authority, the hierarchy of the company. Then he added, "Of course, that is not the way that it works." He then proceeded to draw a number of dotted lines across the various functional divisions and levels of authority, explaining that these were the lines of communication which really governed day-to-day operations. He was astute enough to recognize that while organization charts are necessary to define responsibility and accountability, they cannot be allowed to define channels of communication and even the responsibility for taking action. Otherwise, the company would be so slow and cumbersome in making decisions and taking action that it would be almost totally ineffective.

What was true thirty years ago is even truer today. While we must still have organization charts to define the ultimate accountability, three inter-related developments have intervened to push the conventional organization chart into the background and change the role of management. These developments have been the increasing volatility of the environment in which a company does business, the increased speed of business and the advent of information and communications technology.

Many traditional managers have found it difficult to surrender the control inherent in the centralized structure

The volatility and unpredictability of the business environment emerged in the 1970s. A series of blunders in economic policy by the Nixon administration, natural forces and the politically-motivated OPEC oil embargo unleashed a wave of inflation upsetting the competitive balance in many industries. This led to a severe recession with a recovery compounded by liberalized trade, globalization and the rapid advent of new technologies. The traditional " smokestack" industries have been eclipsed by knowledge industries.

The increase in the speed of business has arisen because of the need to respond to this volatility by adapting products and services to changing market needs. Further, advances in information technology provide almost instant feedback on performance and market developments making quick response necessary.

The advent of information and communications technology has made possible the extensive automation of a wide range of clerical and production functions. It has also made possible the rapid dissemination of data through an organization, which has pre-empted one of middle management's traditional functions—the gathering, analysis and selective dissemination of information.

Companies have adapted to these changes in a number of ways. Starting in the 1970s, the first of these, triggered by volatile economic conditions, was "empowerment." This change saw decision-making authority move downward to the level that understood the situation best and could cope quickly.

The second change, primarily a response to the need for speed, was the creation of multifunctional teams. Initially, teams were used in the area of product development in which multifunctional groups produced dramatic reductions in the lead times necessary to bring forth new products. However, the concept has also been successfully applied to operating processes such as order generation and material handling. In the latter, the process integrates previously separate functions such as purchasing and manufacturing. Teams are essentially self-managing and leadership in the decision-making process is based on expertise in the issue on hand, rather than on rank. This has changed the organization from its traditional vertical structure to a horizontal one, thus flattening the organizational triangle.

Advances in information technology have had their most visible effect on the automation of clerical and production functions. This technology, however, has also made it possible for corporations to focus their activities in the area of their core competence, hence outsourcing supply and service functions. This has concentrated both management attention and resources where they can be the most productive.

However, this does not mean that the traditional hierarchical structure with its top down command structure is totally obsolete. It is still necessary to cope with routine functions although it cannot be expected to be able to deal with strategic issues. Corporations are managed by a combination of centralized and decentralized practices.

Perhaps the best way to understand the differences between the traditional and new organizations is to use an analogy from sports drawn up by Noel Tichy of the University of Michigan, in which he contrasts American football with rugby. Football is a "set" game that mirrors traditional management thinking. It has a hierarchy with the quarterback calling the play. After the ball is snapped, each player follows a predetermined course of action in accordance with the playbook (budget). Once the play is finished (end of accounting period) and the results measured (profit or loss), the situation is re-evaluated and a new play is called. The strategy is therefore periodic, the measurement of short-term results and the course of action, once decided upon, inflexible. The strategic decisions are made at the top and each player is a specialist in some function with a well-defined but limited role.

The limitations of traditional management practices have resulted in stagnation or slow erosion of competitive position

Conversely, rugby is a "flow" game. It requires tremendous communication, continuous adjustment to a changing environment, and problem solving without a hierarchy. The game therefore requires flexibility and the individual is empowered to take whatever action is necessary to move the ball downfield. Each rugby player is a generalist who must be able to perform all functions and must therefore have a sense of the strategy of the game and knowledge of the capabilities of his teammates.

The differences between the games extend to the roles of management. In football, the head coach has total control, usually to the extent of calling the plays from the sidelines. This is the traditional command-and-control structure. In rugby the role of the coach is one of educator, motivator and facilitator, and he has little control once the play has started.

The ever-perceptive Peter Drucker considers that the model for the new industrial organization can also be found in symphony orchestras and hospitals. Neither of these has a rigid hierarchy and their leaders are educators, motivators and coordinators. Each operates effectively based upon the employees' understanding of their respective roles and where they fit into the whole.

Not surprisingly, many traditional managers have found it difficult to surrender the control inherent in the centralized structure. While there are a large number of organizational arrangements that can meet the need for flexibility and speed, these must all have three essential elements:

1. The company must have a coherent strategy that is understood in its underlying logic and intent by all of its management. This serves to co-ordinate the action in a decentralized management situation and serves as a basis of reference for understanding priorities in making day-to-day decisions. The instant availability of information provided by modern technology creates the risk that managers will tend to respond by way of short-term expedients unless they have the broader perspective provided by the capability of thinking strategically. It is therefore important that companies give priority to developing strategic thinking skills in their management.
2. The organization must make available the information necessary to do the job. This is often difficult for the traditional manager who has been exercising control by the selective dissemination of information and doling out information on a need-to-know basis.
3. Horizontal communication and consultation, along with the authority to make relevant decisions, must be encouraged if not formalized. Often, this should extend beyond the walls of the company by having production personnel visit customers so that they understand their requirements and create a channel of communication capable of ironing out problems without drawing them to the attention of more senior management.

It has been difficult for many managers to recognize the characteristics of the new organization because the changes in conditions that make them necessary have been evolutionary. Thus, there has not been any crisis that has forced a rethinking of the way things are done. Consequently, the limitations of traditional management practices have resulted in stagnation or slow erosion of competitive position. But the need to adapt is essential to survival, as the dinosaurs found out. Are you still playing football when your competitors are playing rugby?

Ray Suutari (rsuutari@interLog.com) is the author of *Business Strategy and Security Analysis* (1996, Irwin Publishing, Burr Ridge, Ill.) and currently coaches CEOs on strategy formulation.

CREATING A learning organization

Creating a learning environment in the workplace is not only vital to keeping employees up to date on rapidly changing technology, but can also help to bring revenue to the company.

by Neal McChristy

JOE MILLER OWNS AN office supply store in a midsize town in the Midwest with a restaurant next door and a drugstore across the street. Joe is manager over a copier salesman, two clerks who handle requests for office supplies, and two technicians who work on the machines. When a customer comes in, Joe notices that he goes directly to Betty, one of his clerks, and starts asking her questions. In fact, at other times, Joe has noticed that when Georgette, his other clerk, is there alone, this customer will ask about when Betty will return so he can talk to her.

Joe notices that Betty listens with care to the customer and shows him two types of paper, he picks one and buys a box. This day, Joe asks the customer to come into his office saying, since he's a long-time customer, he'd like to ask him a few questions about customer service. The customer complies, and Joe asks him why he seems to prefer having Betty wait on him rather than Georgette, the newest employee of the two.

"She tells me everything I need about every product," the customer said. "I've asked her about paper, toner, pens—everything. She knows the latest about each product in the store—soup to nuts." Joe nodded.

"She just saved me money, too, by showing me a new type of paper that's processed chlorine free. Our company wants to try that to help the environment. She also knew where to find the partially recycled paper, and that's also something we're going towards. "She's the best salesman you have, Joe. She knows her stuff."

After the customer left, Joe brought Georgette into his office. "I'm going to see what I can do to help you learn about some of the supplies in this business. You're a good employee, but I think a little training will help you and the store even more."

It's likely that Georgette, in this fictional account, has already learned a lot in her years with the company by watching Betty and asking her questions, then doing it herself. This type of learning is one of the most effective learning tools available in the workplace.

Should Joe add a new employee, Georgette would likely find the new employee would bring new ideas and knowledge, maybe even challenging her own. And if Joe would face a complete shift in the office supplies or equipment he carries, his training process would need to be accelerated to accommodate a rapid, substantial change in how he does business. It's all part of learning in the workplace, and visible managers like Joe need knowledge to stay ahead of the competition.

In spite of the crucial role of training in an industry changing as much as office equipment, service, and supplies, an owner looking at cost reduction often considers training expendable, especially in these times of recession. But providing a learning environment adds real dollars to the company. "I believe if your people are learning something every day, most of it will translate into better service for clients and that translates into revenue growth real quickly," says Warren Whitlock, president of Landmark Printer Service, Rialto, California.

Learning is critical

Learning is "absolutely vital" in the process of having loyal employees who will stay with a company, according to Ronelle Ingram, director of technical service for FKM Copier Products, Irvine. Calif. So how do you keep employees as motivated at work on Monday morning as Friday afternoon? Or, put another way, "Are they as motivated about work as what they do on Saturday?" asks Tim Conlon, Rochester, N.Y., chief learning officer for Xerox Corp.

Regardless of whether you are a multinational corporation or a small startup, educating and training employees remain a key element of your business' health and future.

"Nothing kills a learning plan quicker than some boring lecturer droning on about things people already know," says Paul Schwartz, president of CopierCareers.com, Minneapolis, Minn., which specializes in working with technicians and employers for copier-industry placement. "Dry, factual, elementary material delivered by uninspired instructors can put your brightest stars in a coma. Spice it up and it will sink in," he advises.

Various studies done in workplaces have shown that:

- learning new skills are crucial to keep employees on the job—not for helping them go somewhere else. Employees will gauge a large amount of job satisfaction on the training opportunities in a job. "There's a tremendous employee value associated with learning," says Conlon.
- employees learn more easily by interacting with each other than in classroom-type teaching. Schwartz suggests employees read, study, and report on materials that are proven winners, such as gurus in the training world, before undertaking training. "This exercise 'limbers up' the employees' minds, preparing them to receive the training you are paying for, thus making it eventually more effective," Schwartz says.
- people learn by doing much more readily than through traditional training. "Instructor-based training—one of our traditional training methods—is not one of the best training modes," says Conlon.

Schwartz states that a learning plan must be tailored to the students. And, he says, ask which employees have "a fire in their belly to do the best by you, your customers, and their fellow employees. Those are the people who will benefit from the training you provide." You can't exactly discriminate against those who can't, or won't, learn and grow, but you don't have to throw good resources out the window, either.

"The bottom line is there are buffalo and there are steers," Schwarz says. "Buffalo roam the prairie, play in the snow, they have spirit and verve, and they thunder. Steers stand around munching and complaining."

Creating a future

Sometimes outcomes-based learning needs to be configured a different way in order to make it seem more attainable. Conlon uses the example of the person wanting to diet whose focus is on his or her weight. To turn this around, he says, the person could think about building a healthier lifestyle. Weight then becomes just one of the outcomes instead of the main drive for the diet. He calls this "creating a future instead of solving a problem."

Rapidly rising technology always creates a challenge that needs an immediate training solution. A majority of the office equipment and supplies training of late was first on the transition to digital sales and service and then the convergence of printers and copiers. "As many businesses look to transit from products to service to solutions," Conlon says, "this is where knowledge comes into play."

In the process of teaching people, Katherine Richard, regional director for the Kansas Small Business Development Center at Pittsburg State University, Pittsburg, Kan., says those training need to be aware that people have different traits and ways of learning; some learn by seeing, some by hearing, and some by doing. "Hands-on learning is really critical to making *what is learned* an everyday part of our mode of operation," she says.

It's a truism that if someone needs something bad enough to survive in the workplace, they'll do it. "Real learning occurs," Conlon states, "at the point of need in the work you do."

Schwartz says any educational endeavor should be field-tested and proven before being applied internally. "One must get employees to collaborate, endorse, and embrace," he says, "and there must be real-time evaluation of effectiveness while the teaching happens, plus long-term measurement of tangible results."

Some employers have resisted training because they're afraid their trained employees will then seek work elsewhere. But FKM's Ingram says they've retained most of their employees who have gained new certifications. FKM service technicians who succeed at acquiring Microsoft Certified Systems Engineer (MCSE)or A+ certification status receive not only recognition and their name on the wall, but also bonuses and raises. FKM requires a signed one-year noncompete agreement, Ingram says, and "it works out well for everybody." And she says the accomplishment and recognition from their peers has been a powerful positive force for those who complete it. Of the 23 technicians who have taken A+ certification, only one has left, Ingram says.

Employees who internalize effective practices in the workplace will lead the business to productivity and profit and gain personal satisfaction, Schwartz says. "They have to make it something that lives in their guts 24/7," he says. "Passion isn't conjured: it's electrified by a mystical combination of the individual's predisposition to excellence and the organization's genius in nurturing, inspiring, and challenging individuals to higher levels of performance."

Lessons from larger companies

For larger companies, one of the ideas floating around is that teams meet the needs of people in the organization. Ron Armstrong, Hardy, Va., of R.V. Armstrong and Associates, says the top executive must make the commitment to such an organizational structure. Learning provided by the organization helps the team members perform and achieve at the level sought by management, according to Armstrong, and there's an accompanying return on the training investment by increasing productivity, quality, and customer satisfaction.

"Execs have more time for making strategic decisions," Armstrong states, "managers make better decisions regarding their functional responsibilities, and supervisors don't carry the burden of accountability for large groups of people (teams carry the responsibility, authority, and accountability for their performance) —they become the resource persons and the coaches; staff employees' expertise is needed; *and* clerical, production, and service employees develop a sense of self-worth, ownership, and satisfaction in their work."

Peter Senge, author of *The Fifth Discipline: The Art and Practice of the Learning Organization*, was suggested as a resource by both Whitlock and Conlon.

Senge advocates a learning structure that differs from what he calls the current assembly-line model of schools and emphasizes an organic-like learning process that creates, acquires, and transfers knowledge, changing with the acquisition of new knowledge.

Conlon says Xerox has done work with Senge's model as well as the Center for Creative Leadership (CCL) model. (The CCL overview Web page states, "... we believe leadership development is the cornerstone of organizational effectiveness").

Much of the Xerox training has departed from classroom training toward e-learning, Conlon says, which gives everyone at Xerox access to training and feedback. In addition, mentors and chat rooms enhance the ability for employees to interact.

But Xerox's e-learning matrix doesn't have to be just for larger companies. An innovative manager or owner with a computer and access to the Internet has access to resources that can be used for learning, Conlon adds. "E-learning is available in a lot of different avenues out there."

Mom and pop need to stay current

Many of the old-timers who have owned stores in the copier and printer industry for 10–30 years are street savvy and don't necessarily have college training, Ingram says, and may not be as convinced of the value of teaching and training. "They've learned through the school of hard knocks," she says. But all that's changing as others join the office equipment area. Says Ingram, "The new generation is willing to learn, take the lead, and ask questions."

In the technical area such as Ingram's, the training is from within and uses a template. This is because of the task-oriented nature of office equipment service, she says. With competition for the customer as close as the nearest computer, Richard says there's a real need for mom-and-pop stores to stay current on what's going on in their industry and how to compete with it. A lot of this is customer service, she says—staying abreast of current technology and what products the customer wants. She adds, "And if you don't have it, they'll go somewhere else."

Training opportunities are readily available through classes offered by junior colleges or vo-tech schools and from places such as small-business development centers throughout the United States, Richard says. The centers can offer in-store seminars on improving customer service.

Learning and training doesn't have to be formal. "Brown bag" lunches and sharing ideas among employees, making sure everyone participates in some way, are easily done. And such get-togethers foster not only education, but also interaction, which it seems is a vital conduit to learning.

Whatever the setting, think of training that has inspired and motivated in order to keep the attention of your audience and then do likewise, say experts on training.

"Learning plans should be full of real-life stories, emotional word pictures, and compelling and inspiring examples of what real people accomplished when they applied time-tested principles and practices," Schwartz says.

Neal McChristy is a freelance writer from Pittsburg, Kan. He may be contacted by e-mail at freelance9@kscable.com.

Open Book Management—Optimizing Human Capital

Raj Aggarwal and Betty J. Simkins

"People acting together as a group can accomplish things which no individual acting alone could ever hope to bring about."

—Franklin D. Roosevelt

When President Roosevelt spoke these words, he probably was not thinking specifically about managing a business. Nevertheless, his statement seems to capture the essence of open-book management, or OBM. What is OBM? It is a way of managing a company demonstrably, without concealment, that motivates all employees to focus on helping the business grow profitably and increasing the return on its human capital. Literally, it means opening a company's financial statements to all employees and providing the education that will enable them to understand how the company makes money and how their actions affect its success and bottom line.

The case of Manco Inc. shows how a company can open up "confidential" information and motivate all of its employees to focus on business growth and profitability.

A crucial component of OBM is that employees have a direct stake in the company's success. The goal is to persuade every employee to think and act like an owner in the business. As a result, employees' goals and actions can be more closely aligned with those of the owners, greatly reducing the agency problem (inadequate goal congruence) between employees and owners. Wal-Mart is probably the first well-known company to embrace OBM, which is often described as a philosophy of running a business. However, Springfield Remanufacturing Corporation (SRC) in Springfield, Missouri is undoubtedly the first company to enthusiastically promote the technique, which it calls the "Great Game of Business."*

Here we will review the strategic nature of OBM in optimizing the deployment of human capital by illustrating its application at Manco Inc., a successful supplier of consumer products to major U.S. retailers. And we shall offer suggestions as to how other firms may implement OBM.

OBM AND STRATEGIC ADVANTAGE

Open book management as a term has been credited to John Case of *Inc.*, who began using it in 1993 to refer to this business approach. The method itself became popular in the early 1980s as many North American companies were losing their competitive edge and experiencing weak financial performance due to stepped-up foreign competition, high inflation, increased borrowing costs, and recessionary conditions. The many management fads developed during this period generally improved only a particular aspect of the business, such as quality, rather than the overall business, because their focus was limited to that one aspect without considering the entire operation. Moreover, although many of these management techniques recommend empowering people in their jobs, unlike OBM they fail to address the limitations that arise from the significant differences in power between managers and employees when it comes to access to financial and other information. OBM, then, can be viewed as the "missing link" in making many managerial methods more effective over the long run.

The ideas that form the basis of OBM have been developed further in recent years by management and finance experts. Johnson and Kaplan (1987), for example, showed that existing management accounting systems are inade-

Figure 1
Manco Inc. Product Lines

Manco's three strategic business units supply products throughout the U.S. and in 59 foreign countries. The products are sold in commercial office supply stores and superstores, hardware stores, home centers, food and drug stores, and discount store chains.

Office Stationery
- CareMail mailing and shipping supplies
- Carton sealing tapes
- Mailing and packaging tapes
- KID'sCRAFT creative learning products

DIY
- Pressure-sensitive tapes, including Duck® Brand duct tape
- Mounting products
- Weatherization products

Home Solutions
- Easy Liner, Smooth Top, and self-adhesive Easy Liner
- Softex houseware products

quate and that new systems are needed to help managers better in long-term planning. Johnson (1992) emphasized the importance of informed "bottom-up empowerment" in developing high levels of customer satisfaction and long-run competitiveness. OBM is a clear and essential aspect of such empowerment. It is also an essential prerequisite to the use of such measures as economic profit (EP) or economic value added (EVA), which can optimize the use of capital assets in a company. Traditional management literature recognizes that OBM can contribute to organizational efficiency and effectiveness as well. It is not only an important aspect of culture and communication systems, but also of building trust in management—a key component of organizational social capital, flexibility, entrepreneurship, and competitive advantage.

OBM is a way to optimize the use of human capital. Because of revolutionary advances in technology, the sources of wealth creation have been shifting to intangible assets, high-tech capabilities, and human capital. As a result, variable costs such as direct labor and material have been declining as a proportion of total costs. Fixed costs, which are difficult to allocate and may lead to mistakes in assessing product line and customer profitability, now make up increasing portions of the costs of goods and services. They can be attributed primarily to "people costs"—overhead, product development, technology and so on. Effective use and management of intangible resources relies on the efficient use and deployment of human capital, which in turn relies on empowerment and information—an alignment between information structure and decision rights in a business. OBM, then, is clearly becoming more important for corporate strategy.

Given their focus on managing company information, the accounting and finance functions must also play a key role in optimizing human capital. The recent adoption of new accounting and finance technology means that traditional transaction-focused activities are now close to their optimal level of efficiency in most modern firms. Thus, developing and implementing OBM procedures designed to optimize human capital can be a new leadership focus for accounting and finance groups. Whereas OBM can be useful for a wide range of businesses, it is particularly important in private firms and in divisions of public companies in which financial and other performance data are not readily or widely available.

To optimize the use of human and other capital in a firm, the distribution of decision rights among employees must be aligned with the employees' access to appropriate information. Proper alignment requires that management practices satisfy a number of conditions. First, employees need adequate information appropriate for business decisions combined with the power to make such decisions. Second, although such empowered individuals may be motivated by different factors, they need to work toward a goal or goals consistent with the rest of the organization. Third, they need similar information on corporate performance and goals to reduce incongruence and prevent losses that may result from conflicting goals. OBM adds the necessary elements of business literacy and widespread information sharing so that all employees know the performance drivers and can participate in making the business more profitable. Openly sharing information and rewards among employees can also lead to peer pressure for improving performance, thereby reducing supervisory costs.

Moving to OBM can be a challenge, however. It entails changes to corporate culture, especially if the firm has a tradition of centralized command and control. Such changes require the enthusiastic leadership of the CEO, in addition to one or more highly visible and active champions in the firm. Initial attempts to move to OBM may be met with skepticism, suspicion, or even out-right hostility. Many employees may not have the desire or the ability to take on the responsibility that comes with it. Managers may be uncomfortable with sharing information (and power). In fact, managerial roles may have to be redefined before OBM can be introduced. And many managers may be reluctant or unable to make the behavioral changes associated with such a move, often to the point of changing organizations.

Figure 2
Sales Growth for Manco, Inc. from 1971 to 1997

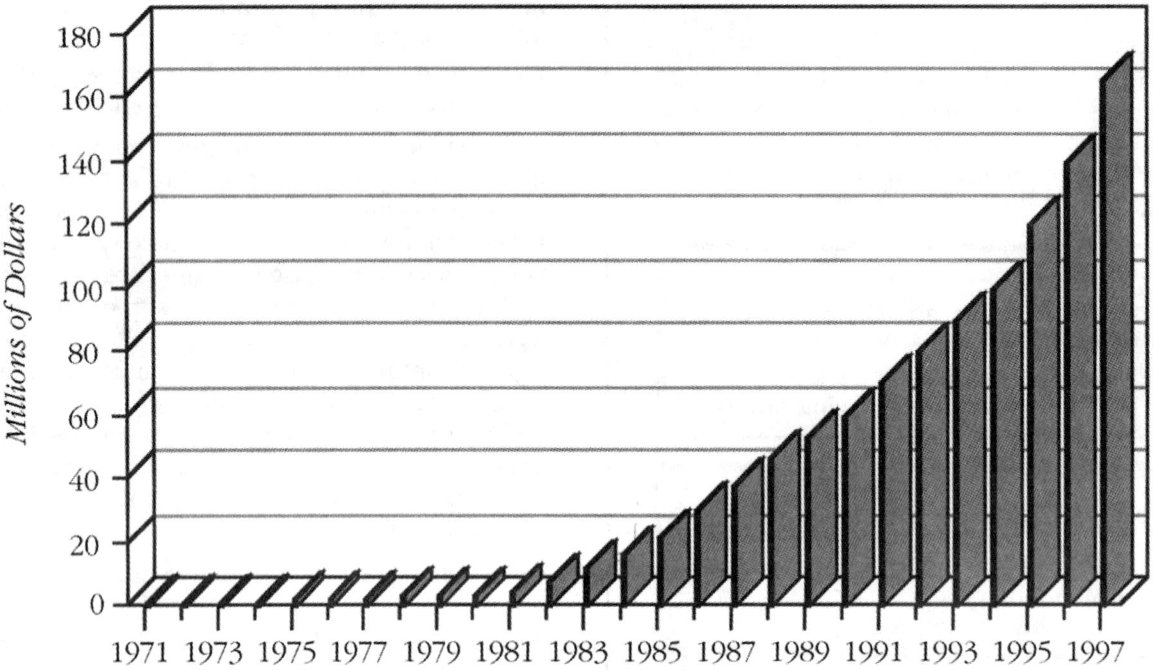

As people closest to an activity receive information and are empowered to make decisions, the focus of management shifts from giving orders to facilitating information flows for optimum decision making. Indeed, the practice of OBM is consistent with the practice of servant-leadership, whereby the job of senior managers and company leaders is to serve and support front-line employees in their efforts to serve customers. At Manco, Inc., the style of servant-leadership involves open communication, constant learning, high goal-setting, and a roll-up-your-sleeves attitude that puts the consumer first.

In light of all these challenges and potential changes, a move to an OBM system requires considerable preparation and training—and most important, a sustained commitment on the part of senior management.

IMPLEMENTING OBM: THE CASE OF MANCO

Manco Inc., a medium-sized supplier to the retail industry, is a private company headquartered in Avon, Ohio that processes and distributes a broad line of branded consumer products for retail and office product channels. Its products, outlined in **Figure 1**, include adhesive tapes, DIY (do-it-yourself) products, mailing and office supplies, and children's craft supplies. Jack Kahl, Manco's CEO and founder, bought out the original owner of the Melvin A. Andersen Company in 1971 and changed the name to Manco. As shown in **Figure 2**, the company has achieved high growth rates since Kahl acquired it. Annual revenues have risen from $800,000 in 1971 to nearly $167 million for fiscal 1997, and the employee count grew from one to more than 300 in the same period.

Much of this growth has undoubtedly been driven by Manco's focus on customer service. Kahl realized back in 1978 just how important the partnership between Manco and the customer was when he called on the then up-and-coming discount chain Wal-Mart. He saw firsthand how Sam Walton viewed suppliers as close associates—people who worked with Wal-Mart for mutual benefit—and truly treated them as such. Says Kahl, "Sam Walton will give [me] inspiration until my last breath." The feeling must have been mutual because Walton told Kahl in 1991, "Jack, I now know what makes Manco great. It's your people" (Hyatt 1991). Wal-Mart has been and remains an important customer and strategic partner for Manco.

Manco competes with much larger and highly admired companies such as 3M and Rubbermaid, yet it has the dominant market share in its product lines. **Figure 3** shows the market share for DIY tape in 1997. At the end of that year, Manco held 53.4 percent of the market versus 3M's share of 36.8 percent. The company is also known for its speed of product introduction and rapid market penetration with new products. **Figure 4** illustrates its rapid market share growth in 1997, when the company introduced its Softex Bath and Kitchen Product Line. Its expansion from 4 percent of the bath mat industry in 1996 to 26 percent the next year represents a one-year growth of 550 percent.

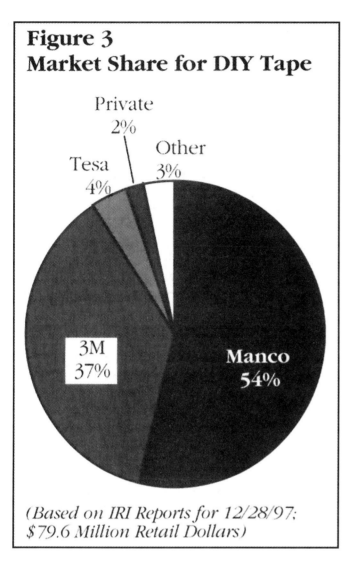

Figure 3
Market Share for DIY Tape

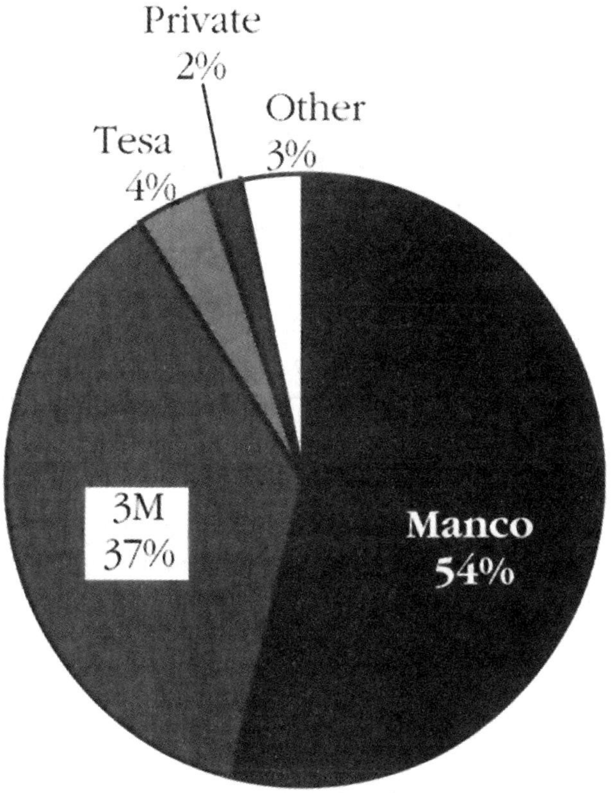

(Based on IRI Reports for 12/28/97; $79.6 Million Retail Dollars)

Excellence in customer service, speed to market in new product development, and other corporate attributes of success are possible only with committed, dedicated, and motivated employees. OBM, says Jack Kahl, is one of the keys to Manco's success and the primary means of motivating its people. Kahl is a widely respected top executive who, among other honors, has been selected by *Industry Week* as one of America's most admired CEOs and by *Inc.* as one of the top three CEOs in America to benchmark for business leadership. As he puts it, "At Manco, we grow people. They grow profits." Kahl started using many of his OBM ideas from the very early days of Manco, having observed the implementation of similar ideas firsthand at Wal-Mart stores. "Wal-Mart has taught me the most," he says.

Four Essential Steps in Implementing OBM

In Open-Book Management: The Coming Business Revolution, John Case (1995) recommends four essential steps to implementing OBM. **Figure 5** extends these steps and provides useful tips and practical examples for each one. The steps are described below and illustrated by the experiences of Manco.

Step 1: Get the information out there.

Tell employees not only what they need to know to do their jobs effectively, but also how the division or the company as a whole is doing. In essence, reduce the internal differences between the information available to owners and management and that available to lower-level employees.

At Manco, learning is important and informing employees is a top objective. The company's highest honor, the Spirit Award, recognizes curiosity. Instead of window offices apart from other employees, its vice presidents work in offices clustered in the middle of the room, called "Action Alley." The cafeteria is a perfect example of getting information out. On one wall, different colors of duct tape trace sales growth over the past three years. On another wall, year-to-date daily sales are compared against the previous year's on a chalkboard. Though a private firm, Manco knows that its 30 percent employee stock ownership is a crucial motivating factor for employees. A bar graph on one wall of the cafeteria tracks the company's estimated share price since 1985, showing its "partners" (what Manco calls its employees) how its success is translated into each individual's personal wealth. Employees never need to ask "What's in this for me?" when they work hard to make the company more profitable. The answer is right on the wall.

LED displays are strategically placed throughout Manco to share company news instantly. On one afternoon, the signs flashed the news, "We cracked a 750-store drug chain," and employees throughout the company burst into applause. "If you want to move fast, you have to trust people," insists Kahl. "You give people power with information, and you ask them to hold it in their confidence and use it on your behalf. It's not an easy thing for a lot of executives to do."

These are just some examples of the many ways of getting information out. A company committed to OBM could and should come up with other creative ways that are more suited to its specific situation.

Step 2: Teach the basics of finance and business.

The decision to convert to OBM requires a serious and ongoing commitment from management and employees to engage in continuing education and training, The director of human resources at Manco estimates that it takes about two planning cycles (years) before employees become financially literate. OBM implementation can take a long time, and the effect on the bottom line may not be apparent for a while.

The role of the Chief Financial Officer in an open-book company differs markedly from tradition. The CFO is the "gatekeeper," the firm's key financial expert who maintains the store of information necessary for OBM. Because OBM relies heavily on the financial talents and cooperation of the CFO, he must often become a leader in the OBM process and prepare the finance function for its new role. The CFO generally needs to become more open with information and should be able to communicate, motivate, and coach employees. Fortunately, the finance organization at Manco reflects these attributes and has been an effective leader for the OBM effort there.

Various techniques have been used to teach employees about the basics of business. Typically, groups of 30 or so at a time are trained in a classroom. A company may have a six-hour course in which simplified income statements and balance sheets are covered. At this time or during another session, more complex issues such as inventory costs and labor and how they affect the bottom line can be covered. But classroom lessons must be reinforced every day on the job if employees are to comprehend the concepts fully.

Jack Kahl, who has been called a tireless advocate of educational excellence, believes that Manco should be a crucible of lifelong learning. As the company has moved to progressively larger headquarters, a large portion of each new building has been dubbed "Manco University" and dedicated to employee learning. In addition to in-house training programs, Manco has generous programs to support self-education for employees at area colleges and universities; its "partners" are encouraged to sign up for any type of education, and reimbursement for an accredited course does not depend on its relevance for work at Manco. When implementing OBM, Kahl put managers and employees through an intensive financial and business education program and introduced a similar system of weekly performance reviews. He regularly holds meetings for all employees, using the time to talk to them about the company. He explains where Manco is going and walks people through the financials to show them how it is performing. As a result, people understand the business better, rather than just their jobs. All of the "partners" have access to all of the financials, from gross sales and gross margins to net profit.

Clearly, effectiveness is the result when policies for getting the information out are combined with activities designed to make the often arcane financial information more understandable to all employees. This process is especially effective when corporate financial information is explained in terms of personal financial activities.

Step 3: Empower people to make decisions based on what they know.

Companies should turn departments into business centers whenever possible. They should define goals at the unit level instead of the corporate level, so that employees understand the impact they can have on these goals. Manco has made each product line and department responsible for achieving specific financial and performance objectives. All of its "partners" working in shipping and distribution, for example, are authorized to stop shipment of an order that does not meet corporate quality standards. According to Garfield (1997), Manco understands

> that service, like quality, cannot be mandated; it must be volunteered. As a result, instead of focusing on service policies and procedures, [Jack Kahl] strives to build within Manco a caring culture that will naturally elicit high—quality service.

This culture, emphasizing high levels of customer service, encourages employees to focus on solving problems instead of trying to fix blame. The "partners" feel free to do whatever is necessary—within reason—to restore good service without necessarily seeking permission or approval from senior managers.

Step 4: Make sure everyone shares directly in the company's success, as well as in the risk of its failure.

OBM bonus systems vary widely, but the overall message is the same: Reward employees for business success. Traditional bonus systems do a poor job of communicating this critical link. In fact, employees often begin to expect the annual bonus and view it as a regular part of their compensation. OBM bonuses, in contrast, are pegged to numbers that employees see regularly, numbers they understand and on which they know they have an impact. Manco sets annual targets for net earnings and return on operating assets. If employees hit both targets, the company pays bonuses ranging from 10 percent to 50 percent of their total compensation.

"Achieving corporate goals at Manco can be fun, with the successes being celebrated widely and wildly."

Employee stock ownership is also a powerful tool for rewarding employees. Current research shows that equity-based incentives (stock option plans, restricted stock plans, and direct stock purchase plans) motivate employees to maximize shareholder value and are more effective in reducing agency costs than retirement incentives.[1] At Manco, the "partners" own 30 percent of the company. There is also a profit-sharing program. While Manco stock is not publicly traded, it is valued annually by an independent investment banking firm for transactions with its participating employees.

Achieving corporate goals at Manco can be fun, with the successes being celebrated widely and wildly. A few years ago, Jack Kahl had his head shaved at the company's annual "Duck Challenge Day." His senior management team had dared him to do so if they achieved his stretch goal for sales that year. The event ended up in the local and national press, and even had a spot on the Late Show with David Letterman. Of course, the attention also provided Manco with invaluable publicity and a brand image that no amount of advertising dollars could buy. Even the company's Web site, www.manco.com, is fun.

Manco's mission statement, included on the Web site, sums up how OBM transforms a firm:

> Manco's mission is to build a consumer products company that offers products and services to our customers that will bring quality and care to their lives. Our backyard, the United States, is our foundation for growth, and we will strive always to build new buying and selling partnerships globally. Quality products and caring personal relationships will always be the formula used for delivering extraordinary value to our only boss, the Customer.

Getting Started with OBM

Other companies can replicate Manco's success with OBM. Because of the need for a major change in the way a company is managed, it may be best to start experimenting with small steps and move on to bigger ones as the company and its employees gain experience and become comfortable with the new culture.

Based on recommendations by others as well as our own assessment, the following procedures are recommended for those firms wishing to test the water before taking the plunge. Some of the procedures are easier to implement than others, and a company may want to try progressively more difficult methods and policies as it gains experience. Whenever appropriate, examples of how Manco has implemented these procedures are used to illustrate these concepts further.

1. Play a game to get employees thinking about key numbers such as "guess the cost."

Just because financial information is made widely available does not mean employees will understand its meaning or importance. Most are often shocked to see how small a company's net income is as a percent of each dollar of sales. So it may be useful to make a game or a contest in which employees guess or estimate net profit or other important financial data as a way for them to become familiar with the numbers.

2. Start OBM with the managers first.

For example, ensure that certain managers understand what the assets, liabilities, and other key financial variables are and how they relate to the relative profitability of their area. If managers are not convinced of the value of OBM, it will be much more difficult to involve lower-level employees in the concept. Once managers are trained in OBM, they will be key players in disseminating information to their subordinates.

3. Start distributing information and attach a cash reward to its understanding and use.

Employees should be able to collect (relatively small amounts of) cash rewards for demonstrating an understanding of company financial information—and more if they can show they were able to use the information to improve their performance. Manco presents a "Thrifty Duck Award" to an outstanding "partner" for his or her cost "re-duck-tions" and improvements.

4. Play a business game that gets the employees' attention.

Manco has a wealth of examples to illustrate this technique. Consider its Duck Challenge Day, which started with a bet in 1990 between Kahl and his two sons, John and Bill. John, who was in charge of sales at the time, was explaining his sales projections for the rest of the year, which happened to fall just short of $60 million. Always raising the bar, Kahl said, "If we reach $60 million in sales this year, I'll jump in the pond out in front of the building." Kahl's sons knew the pond would be cold that time of year, so they immediately communicated the bet to the rest of the company.

With all employees doing their best to reach the sales goal, Kahl ended up taking a swim in the 45-degree water in the Manco duck pond. From then on, a new challenge was issued each year. By 1995, 59 "partners" had joined Jack for a celebratory swim. The Duck Challenge Day has since become an annual event. In addition to having his head shaved, Kahl has performed other stunts each year to motivate partners to reach sales and other goals.

5. Set up an Employee Stock Ownership Plan (ESOP) and use it to implement OBM.

Thirty percent of Manco is owned by its long-term employees. In addition, all "partners" participate in a profit-sharing or bonus plan.

Figure 4
Market Share for the Bath Mat Industry, 1996–97

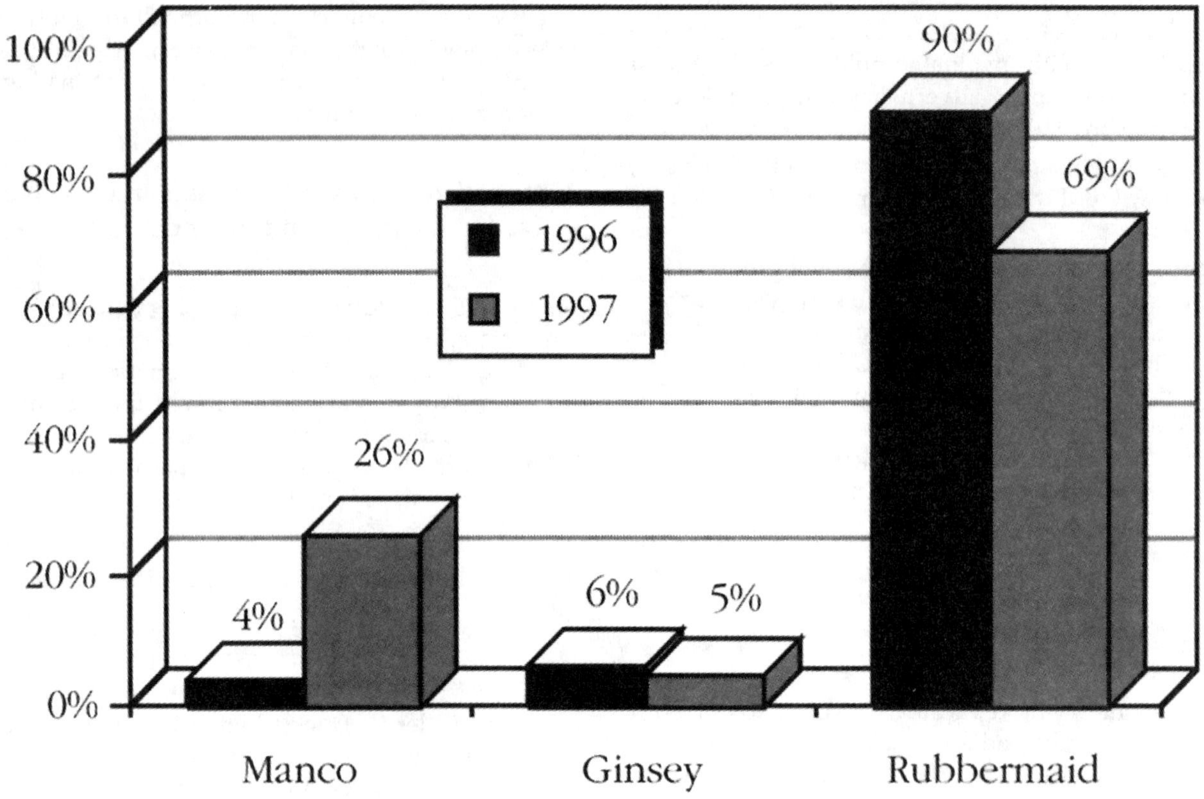

Total market size is $31.6 million in retail dollars.

6. Ask employees to show how they make money for the company.

Employees at Manco, for example, are required to indicate the ways in which they serve internal and external customers.

7. Make learning about the business a game.

Manco once held a contest to see who could create the cleverest name for excess inventory. The originator of SCUD, or "Still Collecting Unwanted Dust," won $200.

8. Play a game that gets customers or suppliers involved in your business.

This step not only shows customers how much you care about their business, it also reminds the firm's "partners" (sometimes in a humorous way) how important the products are to the customers. Manco once held a contest in which it asked customers to reveal their best uses for duct tape. One winner, reports Palmeri (1997), was a zoo in Kansas that used the tape to keep a newborn kangaroo in its mother's pouch.

"Under such conditions, it is natural that many managers are fearful of it. If this is the case, starting with small steps is a good way to try out OBM."

Concerns and Potential Problems with Implementing OBM

What if top management has a hard time sharing the financials with employees and is fearful of delegating decision-making? Top management must be willing and ready to share previously private financial data if it chooses to implement

Figure 5
The Four Essential Steps to Open-Book Management

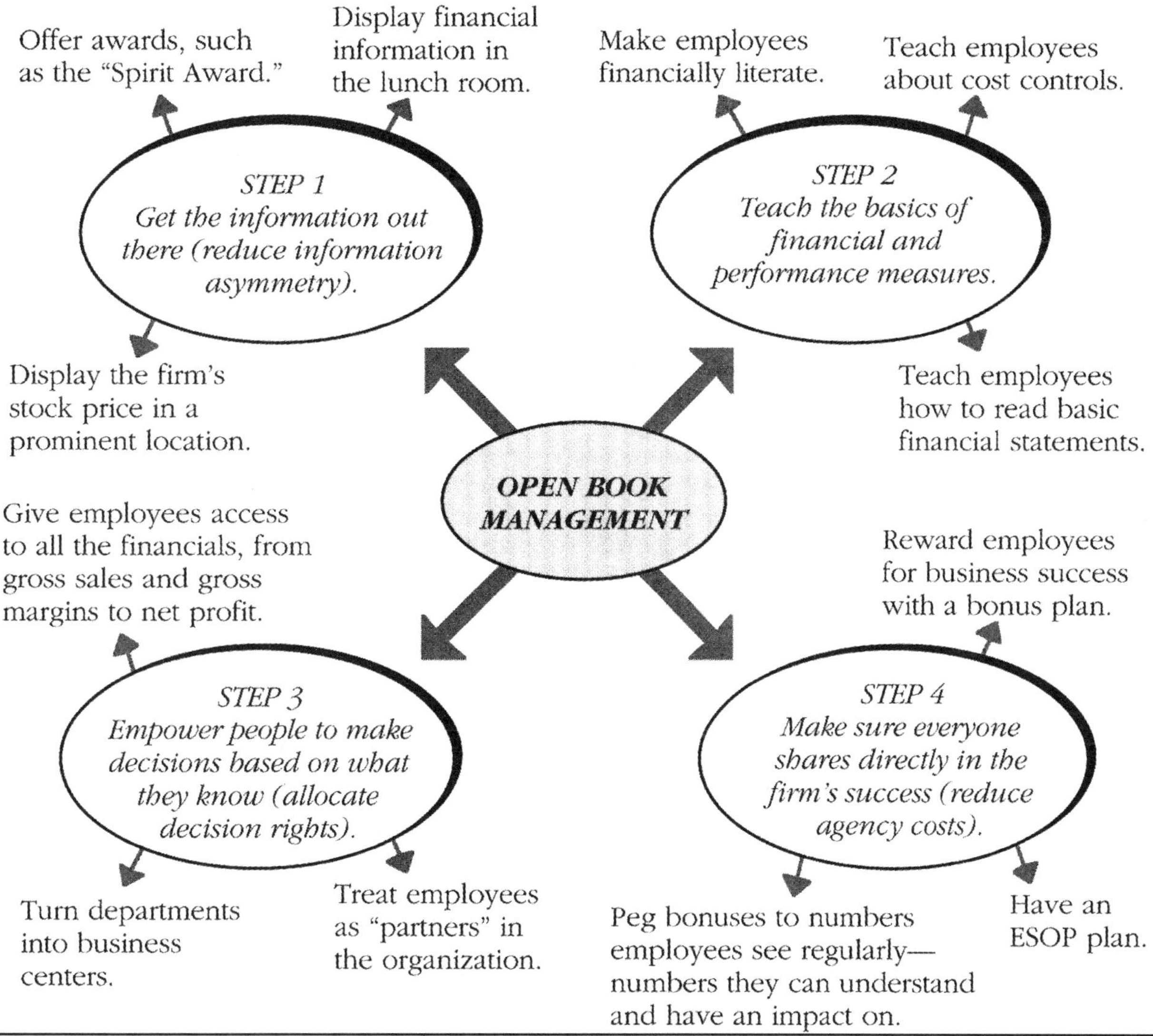
Offer awards, such as the "Spirit Award."
Display financial information in the lunch room.
Make employees financially literate.
Teach employees about cost controls.
STEP 1
Get the information out there (reduce information asymmetry).
STEP 2
Teach the basics of financial and performance measures.
Display the firm's stock price in a prominent location.
Teach employees how to read basic financial statements.
OPEN BOOK MANAGEMENT
Give employees access to all the financials, from gross sales and gross margins to net profit.
Reward employees for business success with a bonus plan.
STEP 3
Empower people to make decisions based on what they know (allocate decision rights).
STEP 4
Make sure everyone shares directly in the firm's success (reduce agency costs).
Turn departments into business centers.
Treat employees as "partners" in the organization.
Peg bonuses to numbers employees see regularly— numbers they can understand and have an impact on.
Have an ESOP plan.

OBM. Traditional management is generally hierarchical and managers often use their preferential access to information to wield power. So introducing OBM can alter traditional sources of influence and power in a company. Under such conditions, it is natural that many managers are fearful of it. If this is the case, starting with small steps is a good way to try out OBM.

What if customers (suppliers) obtain cost data about our products and try to use them to negotiate lower (higher) prices? Manco has taken a bold position by sharing financial information with retail and wholesale customers and vendors. Jack Kahl's philosophy is to build trust, not only with employee-partners but with all business partners, including suppliers and customers. As a sign posted at Manco says: "Trust is our foundation for growth, and the best way to create trust is to earn it every day."

What if our competitors get our financial statements and try to use this information to gain a competitive advantage? Financial information is the history of how a company has been performing. The financial statements show how it has been operating, but do not contain its business strategies. If a company is performing efficiently, it is unlikely that competitors will gain any competitive advantage from these statements. However, if a firm remains concerned about this, the company should evaluate whether the potential benefits of OBM outweigh the potential costs. Even though Manco is a private company, its financials have been widely available for a long time, and so far it is gaining market share in a highly competitive business. External availability of financial information generally does little if anything to alter a firm's competitiveness.

Can a firm give away too much information about its business? Yes, and this is not what OBM is intended to do. For example, a firm should share financial results but not salaries, which are personal data. Information on classified projects and patented products and processes also should not be shared.

Do all firms benefit equally from OBM or is it better for certain types? While OBM potentially holds benefits for all companies in competitive industries, a large number of firms practicing this technique are privately held. Traditionally, such firms share less financial information than public ones. Moreover, annual and quarterly reports, proxy statements, and other financial documents are available for all publicly held companies. Because of this "internal asymmetric information" between the owners and employees, private firms stand to benefit significantly from the practice of OBM. Publicly held firms can also benefit, especially considering that financial and operating data are not generally available in adequate detail for divisions of public companies. Large corporations such as Wal-Mart and Sprint, for example, have used OBM successfully. Firms in certain industries may benefit more, particularly those operating in competitive or oligopolistic industries. Finally, firms in some countries, regions, or industries may not have the cultural orientation necessary for OBM to take root.

Although there may be some concerns with sharing information under OBM, the success stories at firms like Manco demonstrate that the benefits can outweigh the potential costs in many cases. Manco is just one company reaping the many benefits of such a culture. Any company can start implementing OBM progressively using the steps outlined here. But implementation involves a transformation in corporate culture—a significant step and one that should be undertaken only after much deliberation. The many benefits of OBM are likely to appear only gradually as cultural changes take place slowly. So it is important to remember that once OBM is accepted, it requires sustained commitment by senior management.

The burgeoning role of technology and human capital in business success is making the practice of open book management ever more useful—perhaps even critical—for modern organizations. OBM is based on the principle that managers and employees who know and understand financial performance and goals and share a stake in organizational success are more apt to be highly effective and motivated in meeting those goals. As a result, management overhead and the agency problems between employees, managers, and owners will be much lower.

As the case study of Manco shows, not only can the practice of OBM lead to financial and organizational success, it can also make work fun and exciting. Its implementation is often considered a management process, but OBM addresses traditional finance issues of asymmetric information, agency costs, compensation, and corporate governance. With the success of technology in optimizing transaction-focused financial activity, OBM can be a useful new focus of leadership for the finance function.

Although OBM offers significant advantages and has been available for more than 20 years, its rate of adoption is only now picking up. Because it requires changes in hierarchical management styles and leads to shifts in sources of authority and power, it has not been very popular with many traditional managers. But with technological changes transforming business and the concurrent rise of intangible and human capital as the main sources of wealth creation, OBM has begun to find its place in the business world.

**Editor's note. In addition to Stack (1994), D. Keith Denton discusses SRC's culture of openness in at least two of his BH articles, "Entrepreneurial Spirit" (May–June 1993) and "Open Communication" (September–October 1993).*

Notes

1. Frye (1999) offers empirical evidence that finds shorter-term equity-based incentives more effective in motivating employees to maximize shareholder value. ESOPs are becoming increasingly popular and, according to Capell (1996) ,more than 2,000 firms adopted such plans between 1989 and 1996. However, there is some evidence that their benefits may be greater for high-growth companies and companies with a large ownership block (to offset the negative effects of managerial entrenchment). Park and Song (1995) provide more details.

References and Selected Bibliography

R. Aggarwal, "Technology and Globalization as Mutual Reinforcers in Business," *Management International Review*, 39, 2 (1999): 83–104.

R. Aggarwal, "Using Economic Profit to Assess Performance: A Metric for Modern Firms," *Business Horizons*, January–February 2001, pp. 55–60.

J.B. Barney and M.H. Hansen, "Trustworthiness as a Source of Competitive Advantage," *Strategic Management Journal*, Winter 1994 (special issue), pp. 174–189.

T.L. Barton, W.G. Shenkir, and T.N. Tyson, *Open-Book Management: Creating an Ownership Culture* (Morristown, NJ: Financial Executives Research Foundation, 1998).

R.D. Blackwell, *From Mind to Market: Reinventing the Retail Supply Chain* (New York: HarperBusiness, 1997).

J.A. Brickley, C.W. Smith, and J.L. Zimmerman, *Organizational Architecture: A Managerial Economics Approach* (Homewood, IL: Irwin, 1996).

A.D. Brown and K. Starkey, "The Effect of Organizational Culture on Communication and Information," *Journal of Management Studies*, November 1994, pp. 807–828.

J.K. Butler, "Toward Understanding and Measuring Conditions of Trust," *Journal of Management*, September 1991, pp. 643–663.

K. Capell, "Options for Everyone," *Business Week*, July 22, 1996, pp. 80+.

J. Case, *Open-Book Management: The Coming Business Revolution* (New York: HarperBusiness, 1995).

J. Day and J.C. Wendler, "The New Economics of Organization," *McKinsey Quarterly*, 1 (1999): 4–18.

M.B. Frye, "Equity-Based Compensation for Employees: Firm Performance and Determinants," working paper, Georgia Institute of Technology, Atlanta, GA, 1999.

C. Garfield, *Second to None: How Our Smartest Companies Put People First* (Homewood, IL: Business One Irwin, 1992).

D.F. Hastings, "Lincoln Electric's Harsh Lessons from International Expansion," *Harvard Business Review* May-June 1999, pp. 162–178.

L.T. Hosmer, "Trust: The Connecting Link Between Organizational Theory and Philosophical Ethics," *Academy of Management Review*, April 1995, pp. 379–403.

J. Hyatt, "Steal This Strategy," *Inc.*, February 1991, pp. 48+.

M.C. Jensen and W.H. Meckling, "Theory of the Firm: Managerial Behavior, Agency Costs, and Ownership Structure," *Journal of Financial Economics*, October 1976, pp. 305–360.

H.T. Johnson, *Relevance Regained: From Top-Down Control to Bottom-Up Empowerment* (New York: Free Press, 1992).

H.T. Johnson and R.S. Kaplan, *Relevance Lost: The Rise and Fall of Management Accounting* (Boston: Harvard Business School Press, 1987, 1991).

C.R. Leana and H.J. Van Buren III, "Organizational Social Capital and Employment Practices," *Academy of Management Review*, July 1999, pp. 538–555.

H. Leland and D. Pyle, "Informational Asymmetries, Financial Structure, and Financial Intermediation" *Journal of Finance*, May 1977, pp. 371–387.

T.J. McCoy, *Creating an "Open Book" Organization* (New York: AMACOM, 1996).

J.F. McKenna, "America's Most Admired CEOs," *Industry Week*, December 6, 1993, pp. 22–32.

C. Palmeri, "Believe in Yourself, Believe in the Merchandise," *Forbes*, September 8, 1997, pp. 118–124.

S. Park and M.H. Song, "Employee Stock Ownership Plans, Firm Performance, and Monitoring by Outside Blockholders," *Financial Management*, Winter 1995, pp. 52–65.

J.P. Schuster and J. Carpenter, with P. Kane, *The Power of Open-Book Management* (New York: Wiley, 1996).

T. Singer, "Sharer Beware: Are You Giving Away Too Much Information About Your Business?" *Inc.*, April 1, 1999, pp. 38–48.

S.W. Smith and J.D. Castille, "Customer and Product Profitability: Manco, Cleveland, Ohio," in S. Player and R. Lacerda (eds.), *Arthur Andersen's Global Lessons in Activity-Based Management* (New York: Wiley, 1999), pp. 187–198.

J. Stack, *The Great Game of Business* (New York: Currency Doubleday, 1994).

E.M. Whitener, S.E. Brodt, M.A. Korsgaard, and J.M. Werner, "Managers as Initiators of Trust," *Academy of Management Review*, July 1998, pp. 513–530.

Raj Aggarwal is the Firestone Chair and professor of finance at Kent State University, Kent, Ohio. **Betty J. Simkins** is an assistant professor of finance at Oklahoma State University, Stillwater, Oklahoma. Raj Aggarwal thanks his fellow board members at Manco for useful discussions on OBM. In addition, the authors wish to thank the following people: Jack Kahl and his staff at Manco for providing access to the company; Tom Coughlin of Wal-Mart for clarifying the nature of servant-leadership in an address to one of the author's classes; two anonymous referees; and J. Byers, M. Fedor, R. Johnson, J. Mariotti, N. Modani, R. Storey, M. White, J. Williamson, and participants at the Eastern Finance Association and the Financial Management Association Annual Meetings for useful comments. The authors remain solely responsible for the contents.

Case: *Resistance to Change*

What This Incident Is About: Employees face the threat of the unknown when consultants arrive to study their performance. The incident involves the process of successful change: gaining acceptance, coordination, use of consultants, attitudes, and morale.

As office manager of the Duncan Paper Products Corporation, Robert Hale was responsible for the work of approximately 45 employees, of whom 26 were classified as either stenographers or file clerks. Acting under instructions from the company president, he agreed to allow a team of outside consultants to enter his realm of responsibility and make time and systems-analysis studies in an effort to improve the efficiency and output of his staff.

The consultants began by studying job descriptions, making observations, and recording each detail of the work of the stenographers and file clerks. After three days, they indicated to Hale and his employees that they were prepared to begin more detailed studies, observations, and interviews on the following day.

The next morning, five employees participating in the study were absent. On the following day, 10 employees were absent. Concerned, Hale investigated the cause of the absenteeism by telephoning several absentees. Each employee related approximately the same story. Each was nervous, tense, and tired after being viewed as a "guinea pig" for several days. One stenographer told Hale that her physician had advised her to ask for a leave of absence if working conditions were not improved.

Shortly after the telephone calls, the chief of the systems-analysis team explained to Hale that, if there were as many absences on the next day, his team would have to drop the study and proceed to another department. He said that a valid analysis would be impossible to conduct with 10 employees absent. Realizing that he would be held responsible for the failure of the systems analysis, Hale began to create and evaluate alternative actions that would provide the conditions necessary for the study. He was also concerned about implementing the procedural changes that he knew would be mandated after the study was completed. Hale was astute enough to realize that policies declared and orders issued are not always followed by instant compliance, even in the military, and that this wasn't a military situation.

Using the Case on *Resistance to Change*

This case is a classic example of how people will react to situations that are imposed upon them as opposed to situations in which they themselves have been active in producing. These employees are responding in this manner because they fear for their jobs and their well-being. They have no input into the decisions leading to the study, and they are refusing to cooperate with the company by simply not showing up for work. This passive/aggressive behavior is typical in this type of situation, although mass absenteeism is a very strong form of protest, just short of mass resignation.

Questions for Discussion

1. How do you think the company could have handled the situation so as to get greater cooperation?
2. What are some of the alternatives that Robert Hale could implement to get greater cooperation from the employees?
3. What do you think Robert Hale and the company should do?

Exercise: *Organizing*

The purpose of this exercise is to increase your awareness of the importance of structure in organization. In addition, the exercise focuses on the importance of management in organizing a venture.

The Problem

Select one of the following situations to organize. Then read the background material before answering the questions.

- The registration process at your university or college
- A new hamburger fast-food franchise
- A Jet-ski rental in an ocean resort area

Do steps 1–7, below, as homework. In preparing your answers, use your own experience or think up logical answers to the questions.

Background

Organization is a way of gaining some power against an unreliable environment. The environment provides the organization with input, which includes raw materials, human resources, and financial resources. There is a service or product to produce that involves technology. The output is to be sold to a client, a group that must be nurtured. The complexities of the environment and the technology determine the complexity of the organization.

Planning Your Organization

1. In a few sentences, write the mission or purpose of your organization.

2. From the mission statement you should be able to write down specific things that must be done in order to accomplish the mission.
3. From the list of specifics that must be accomplished, an organizational chart can be devised. Each position on the chart will perform a specific task or is responsible for a specific outcome.
4. Add duties to each job position on your organizational chart. This will form a job description.
5. How would you ensure that the people you placed in these positions work together?
6. What degree of skill and abilities is required at each position and level in order to hire the right person for each position?
7. Make a list of the decisions that would have to be made while you planned and built the organization. Make a second list of those decisions you would have to make just after your organization began operating.

In Class

1. Form into groups of up to three members that organized the same project and share your answers to the questions.
2. Come to agreement on the way to organize, utilizing everyone's responses.
3. Present your group's approach to the class.

Case: Resistance to Change; Exercise: Organizing, Fred Maidment, McGraw-Hill/Dushkin, 2000.

UNIT 5

Directing

Unit Selections

Key Points to Consider

- Why do you think people have trouble managing agreement? Are they just trying to get along? Explain.
- To be effective, a leader has to be able to achieve results and be accountable for those results. Do you see that happening in today's world? Defend your answer.
- How much incentive is there for cooperation between supervisors in different departments in your organization? Do people cooperate or are they concerned with "turf"? Discuss.
- Communication is always a problem in any organization. How would you improve communication in your organization?

DUSHKIN ONLINE **Links: www.dushkin.com/online/**
These sites are annotated in the World Wide Web pages.

ADR (Alternative Dispute Resolution): General
http://www.opm.gov/er/adrguide/

Equity Compensation, Employee Ownership & Stock Options
http://www.fed.org

NewsPage
http://www.individual.com

Managers spend most of their time directing the organization. They have learned, however, that just telling people what to do is not good enough. To achieve the maximum possible results, people must first clearly understand the firm's goals, and then management must find a way to motivate them. Miscommunication and assumptions can often lead to poor choices and highly ineffective courses of action, as seen in the classic article by Jerry Harvey, "The Abilene Paradox: The Management of Agreement."

People enter business situations with a history of experiences, attitudes, and beliefs, and effectively communicating with them can be difficult. Open communication must be based upon trust. If there is fear, confusion, or lack of understanding, then communication will not be as effective as it could be. Managers must be able to communicate both in writing and orally. Effective communication involves the ability to design a letter, memo, or conversation so that both the sender and the receiver have a clear understanding of what was said and what is now expected of both parties. This frequently involves telling the receiver not only the message but also how the message was generated, because an employee's understanding of the reasons for an instruction can be the key to effective motivation. In today's environment, the problem is not a lack of ways to communicate, but, rather, selecting the important information. This can even be applied in situations where the subordinate does not agree with the instructions of his or her superior, as seen in "When You Disagree With the Boss's Order, Do You Tell Your Staff?"

Of all the various components of management, leadership is probably the most discussed, analyzed, and misunderstood. Indeed, some would argue that leadership and management are two separate and distinct activities. Leadership may be overdiscussed, but it is not well understood. Leaders come in all shapes and sizes and styles, but they need to be developed and they need to demonstrate leadership. There have been good leaders and evil leaders, saints and brutes, but they all share certain characteristics. One is the ability to communicate an idea to their followers and have them accept it as their own. This results in motivation of the followers. The second characteristic is genuine caring, enthusiasm, and dedication to the dream. A manager who is successful in communicating with, motivating, and leading people will experience enhanced performance and productivity. The Japanese have led other nations in this area with the application of many techniques, such as quality circles. However, not all forms of worker participation have resulted in enhanced productivity.

There are those who would say that there is a leadership crisis facing industry because not enough qualified people are available for these kinds of positions. But, there are also those who would disagree with that assumption, which would include John Nirenberg in his article, "What Leadership Crisis?" American firms have also been applying new ideas in a variety of industries and settings to motivate employees, but a cause for concern is whether American workers will continue to be motivated.

Effective managers are people who are able to direct an organization successfully. They know how to communicate, motivate, and lead, achieving enhanced productivity and performance that will accomplish the goals and mission of the organization in a fluid environment.

The Abilene Paradox: The Management of Agreement

Jerry B. Harvey

JERRY B. HARVEY *is professor of management science at the George Washington University in Washington, D.C. He is a graduate of the University of Texas in Austin, where he earned an undergraduate degree in business administration and a Ph.D. in social psychology. A member of the International Consultant's Foundation, a Diplomate of the American Board of Professional Psychology, and a member of the O.D. Network, he has served as a consultant to a wide variety of industrial, governmental, religious, and voluntary organizations. He has written a number of articles in the fields of organizational behavior and education and currently is involved in the exploration of moral, ethical, and spiritual issues of work. In the pursuit of that interest, his book,* The Abilene Paradox and Other Meditations on Management, *was published by Lexington Books in 1988.*

The July afternoon in Coleman, Texas (population 5,607) was particularly hot—104 degrees as measured by the Walgreen's Rexall Ex-Lax temperature gauge. In addition, the wind was blowing fine-gained West Texas topsoil through the house. But the afternoon was still tolerable—even potentially enjoyable. There was a fan going on the back porch; there was cold lemonade; and finally, there was entertainment. Dominoes. Perfect for the conditions. The game required little more physical exertion than an occasional mumbled comment, "Shuffle 'em," and an unhurried movement of the arm to place the spots in the appropriate perspective on the table. All in all, it had the makings of an agreeable Sunday afternoon in Coleman—this is, it was until my father-in-law suddenly said, "Let's get in the car and go to Abilene and have dinner at the cafeteria."

I thought, "What, go to Abilene? Fifty-three miles? In this dust storm and heat? And in an unairconditioned 1958 Buick?"

But my wife chimed in with, "Sounds like a great idea. I'd like to go. How about you, Jerry?" Since my own preferences were obviously out of step with the rest I replied, "Sounds good to me," and added, "I just hope your mother wants to go."

"Of course I want to go," said my mother-in-law. "I haven't been to Abilene in a long time."

So into the car and off to Abilene we went. My predictions were fulfilled. The heat was brutal. We were coated with a fine layer of dust that was cemented with perspiration by the time we arrived. The food at the cafeteria provided first-rate testimonial material for antacid commercials.

Some four hours and 106 miles later we returned to Coleman, hot and exhausted. We sat in front of the fan for a long time in silence. Then, both to be sociable and to break the silence, I said, "It was a great trip, wasn't it?"

No one spoke. Finally my mother-in-law said, with some irritation, "Well, to tell the truth, I really didn't enjoy it much and would rather have stayed here. I just went along because the three of you were so enthusiastic about going. I wouldn't have gone if you all hadn't pressured me into it."

I couldn't believe it. "What do you mean 'you all'?" I said. "Don't put me in the 'you all' group. I was delighted to be doing what we were doing. I didn't want to go. I only went to satisfy the rest of you. You're the culprits."

My wife looked shocked. "Don't call me a culprit. You and Daddy and Mama were the ones who wanted to go. I just went along to be sociable and to keep you happy. I would have had to be crazy to want to go out in heat like that."

Her father entered the conversation abruptly. "Hell!" he said.

He proceeded to expand on what was already absolutely clear. "Listen, I never wanted to go to Abilene. I just thought you might be bored. You visit so seldom I wanted to be sure you enjoyed it. I would have preferred to play another game of dominoes and eat the leftovers in the icebox."

After the outburst of recrimination we all sat back in silence. Here we were, four reasonably sensible people who, of our own volition, had just taken a 106-mile trip across a godforsaken desert in a furnace-like temperature through a cloud-like dust storm to eat unpalatable food at a hole-in-the-wall cafeteria in Abilene, when none of us had really wanted to go. In fact, to be more accurate, we'd done just the opposite of what we wanted to do. The whole situation simply didn't make sense.

At least it didn't make sense at the time. But since that day in Coleman, I have observed, consulted with, and been a part of more than one organization that has been caught in the same situation. As a result, they have either taken a side-trip, or, occasionally, a terminal journey to Abilene, when Dallas or Houston or Tokyo was where they really wanted to go. And for most of those organizations, the negative consequences of such trips, measured in terms of both human misery and economic loss, have been much greater than for our little Abilene group.

This article is concerned with that paradox—the Abilene Paradox. Stated simply, it is as follows: Organizations frequently take actions in contradiction to what they really want to do and therefore defeat the very purposes they are trying to achieve. It also deals with a major corollary of the paradox, which is that *the inability to manage agreement is a major source of organization dysfunction*. Last, the article is designed to help members of organizations cope more effectively with the paradox's pernicious influence.

As a means of accomplishing the above, I shall: (1) describe the symptoms exhibited by organizations caught in the paradox; (2) describe, in summarized case-study examples, how they occur in a variety of organizations; (3) discuss the underlying causal dynamics; (4) indicate some of the implications of accepting this model for describing organizational behavior; (5) make recommendations for coping with the paradox; and, in conclusion, (6) relate the paradox to a broader existential issue.

Symptoms of the Paradox

The inability to manage agreement, not the inability to manage conflict, is the essential symptom that defines organizations caught in the web of the Abilene Paradox. That inability to manage agreement effectively is expressed by six specific subsymptoms, all of which were present in our family Abilene group.

1. Organization members agree privately, as individuals, as to the nature of the situation or problem facing the organization. For example, members of the Abilene group agreed that they were enjoying themselves sitting in front of the fan, sipping lemonade, and playing dominoes.

2. Organization members agree privately, as individuals, as to the steps that would be required to cope with the situation or problem they face. For members of the Abilene group "more of the same" was a solution that would have adequately satisfied their individual and collective desires.

3. Organization members fail to accurately communicate their desires and/or beliefs to one another. In fact, they do just the opposite and thereby lead one another into misperceiving the collective reality. Each member of the Abilene group, for example, communicated inaccurate data to other members of the organization. The data, in effect, said, "Yeah, it's a great idea. Let's go to Abilene," when in reality members of the organization individually and collectively preferred to stay in Coleman.

4. With such invalid and inaccurate information, organization members make collective decisions that lead them to take actions contrary to what they want to do, and thereby arrive at results that are counterproductive to the organization's intent and purposes. Thus, the Abilene group went to Abilene when it preferred to do something else.

5. As a result of taking actions that are counterproductive, organization members experience frustration, anger, irritation, and dissatisfaction with their organization. Consequently, they form subgroups with trusted acquaintances and blame other subgroups for the organization's dilemma. Frequently, they also blame authority figures and one another. Such phenomena were illustrated in the Abilene group by the "culprit" argument that occurred when we had returned to the comfort of the fan.

6. Finally, if organization members do not deal with the generic issue—the inability to manage agreement—the cycle repeats itself with greater intensity. The Abilene group, for a variety of reasons, the most important of which was that it became conscious of the process, did not reach that point.

To repeat, the Abilene Paradox reflects a failure to manage agreement. In fact, it is my contention that the inability to cope with (manage) agreement, rather than the inability to cope with (manage) conflict, is the single most pressing issue of modern organizations.

Other Trips to Abilene

The Abilene Paradox is no respecter of individuals, organizations, or institutions. Following are descriptions of two other trips to Abilene that illustrate both the pervasiveness of the paradox and its underlying dynamics.

> *Case No. 1: The Boardroom.* The Ozyx Corporation is a relatively small industrial company that has embarked on a trip to Abilene. The president of Ozyx has hired a consultant to help discover the reasons for the poor profit picture of the company in general and the low morale and productivity of the R&D division in particular. During the process of investigation, the consultant be-

comes interested in a research project in which the company has invested a sizable proportion of its R&D budget.

When asked about the project by the consultant in the privacy of their offices, the president, the vice-president for research, and the research manager each describes it as an idea that looked great on paper but will ultimately fail because of the unavailability of the technology required to make it work. Each of them also acknowledges that continued support of the project will create cash flow problems that will jeopardize the very existence of the total organization.

Furthermore, each individual indicates he has not told the others about his reservations. When asked why, the president says he can't reveal his "true" feelings because abandoning the project, which has been widely publicized, would make the company look bad in the press and, in addition, would probably cause his vice-president's ulcer to kick up or perhaps even cause him to quit, "because he has staked his professional reputation on the project's success."

Similarly, the vice-president for research says he can't let the president or the research manager know of his reservations because the president is so committed to it that "I would probably get fired for insubordination if I questioned the project."

Finally, the research manager says he can't let the president or vice-president know of his doubts about the project because of their extreme commitment to the project's success.

All indicate that, in meetings with one another, they try to maintain an optimistic facade so the others won't worry unduly about the project. The research director, in particular, admits to writing ambiguous progress reports so the president and the vice-president can "interpret them to suit themselves." In fact, he says he tends to slant them to the "positive" side, "given how committed the brass are."

The scent of the Abilene trail wafts from a paneled conference room where the project research budget is being considered for the following fiscal year. In the meeting itself, praises are heaped on the questionable project and a unanimous decision is made to continue it for yet another year. Symbolically, the organization has boarded a bus to Abilene.

In fact, although the real issue of agreement was confronted approximately eight months after the bus departed, it was nearly too late. The organization failed to meet a payroll and underwent a two-year period of personnel cutbacks, retrenchments, and austerity. Morale suffered, the most competent technical personnel resigned, and the organization's prestige in the industry declined.

Case No. 2: The Watergate. Apart from the grave question of who did what, Watergate presents America with the profound puzzle of why. What is it that led such a wide assortment of men, many of them high public officials, possibly including the President himself, either to instigate or to go along with and later try to hide a pattern of behavior that by now appears not only reprehensible, but stupid? (*The Washington Star* and *Daily News*, editorial, May 27, 1973.)

One possible answer to the editorial writer's question can be found by probing into the dynamics of the Abilene Paradox. I shall let the reader reach his own conclusions, though, on the basis of the following excerpts from testimony before the Senate investigating committee on "The Watergate Affair."

In one exchange, Senator Howard Baker asked Herbert Porter, then a member of the White House staff, why he (Porter) found himself "in charge of or deeply involved in a dirty tricks operation of the campaign." In response, Porter indicated that he had had qualms about what he was doing, but that he "... was not one to stand up in a meeting and say that this should be stopped.... I kind of drifted along."

And when asked by Baker why he had "drifted along," Porter replied, "In all honesty, because of the fear of the group pressure that would ensue, of not being a team player," and "... I felt a deep sense of loyalty to him [the President] or was appealed to on that basis." (*The Washington Post*, June 8, 1973, p. 20.)

Jeb Magruder gave a similar response to a question posed by committee counsel Dash. Specifically, when asked about his, Mr. Dean's, and Mr. Mitchell's reactions to Mr. Liddy's proposal, which included bugging the Watergate, Mr. Magruder replied, "I think all three of us were appalled. The scope and size of the project were something that at least in my mind were not envisioned. I do not think it was in Mr. Mitchell's mind or Mr. Dean's, although I can't comment on their states of mind at that time."

Mr. Mitchell, in an understated way, which was his way of dealing with difficult problems like this, indicated that this was not an "acceptable project." (*The Washington Post*, June 15, 1973, p. A14.)

Later in his testimony Mr. Magruder said, ".... I think I can honestly say that no one was particularly overwhelmed with the project. But I think we felt that this information could be useful, and Mr. Mitchell agreed to approve the project, and I then notified the parties of Mr. Mitchell's approval." (*The Washington Post*, June 15, 1973, p. A14.)

Although I obviously was not privy to the private conversations of the principal characters, the data seem to reflect the essential elements of the Abilene Paradox. First, they indicate agreement. Evidently, Mitchell, Porter, Dean, and Magruder agreed that the plan was inappropriate. ("I think I can honestly say that no one was particularly overwhelmed with the project.") Second, the data indicate that the principal figures then proceeded to implement the plan in contradiction to their shared agreement. Third, the data surrounding the case clearly indicate that the plan multiplied the organization's problems rather than solved them. And finally, the organization broke into subgroups with the various principals, such as the President, Mitchell, Porter, Dean, and Magruder, blaming one another for the dilemma in which they found themselves, and internecine warfare ensued.

In summary, it is possible that because of the inability of White House staff members to cope with the fact that they agreed, the organization took a trip to Abilene.

Analyzing the Paradox

The Abilene Paradox can be stated succinctly as follows: Organizations frequently take actions in contradiction to the data they have for dealing with problems and, as a result, compound their problems rather than solve them. Like all paradoxes, the Abilene Paradox deals with absurdity. On the surface, it makes little sense for organizations, whether they are couples or companies, bureaucracies or governments, to take actions that are diametrically opposed to the data they possess for solving crucial organizational problems. Such actions are particularly absurd since they tend to compound the very problems they are designed to solve and thereby defeat the purposes the organization is trying to achieve. However, as Robert Rapaport and others have so cogently expressed it, paradoxes are generally paradoxes only because they are based on a logic or rationale different from what we understand or expect.

Discovering that different logic not only destroys the paradoxical quality but also offers alternative ways for coping with similar situations. Therefore, part of the dilemma facing an Abilene-bound organization may be the lack of a map—a theory or model—that provides rationality to the paradox. The purpose of the following discussion is to provide such a map.

The map will be developed by examining the underlying psychological themes of the profit-making organization and the bureaucracy and it will include the following landmarks: (1) Action Anxiety; (2) Negative Fantasies; (3) Real Risk; (4) Separation Anxiety; and (5) the Psychological Reversal of Risk and Certainty. I hope that the discussion of such landmarks will provide harried organization travelers with a new map that will assist them in arriving at where they really want to go and, in addition, will help them in assessing the risks that are an inevitable part of the journey.

Action Anxiety

Action anxiety provides the first landmark for locating roadways that bypass Abilene. The concept of action anxiety says that the reasons organization members take actions in contradiction to their understanding of the organization's problems lies in the intense anxiety that is created as they think about acting in accordance with what they believe needs to be done. As a result, they opt to endure the professional and economic degradation of pursuing an unworkable research project or the consequences of participating in an illegal activity rather than act in a manner congruent with their beliefs. It is not that organization members do not know what needs to be done—they do know. For example, the various principals in the research organization cited *knew* they were working on a research project that had no real possibility of succeeding. And the central figures of the Watergate episode apparently *knew* that, for a variety of reasons, the plan to bug the Watergate did not make sense.

Such action anxiety experienced by the various protagonists may not make sense, but the dilemma is not a new one. In fact, it is very similar to the anxiety experienced by Hamlet, who expressed it most eloquently in the opening lines of his famous soliloquy:

> To be or not to be; that is the question:
> Whether 'tis nobler in the mind to suffer
> The slings and arrows of outrageous fortune
> Or to take arms against a sea of troubles
> And by opposing, end them?...
> (*Hamlet*, Act III, Scene II)

It is easy to translate Hamlet's anxious lament into that of the research manager of our R&D organization as he contemplates his report to the meeting of the budget committee. It might go something like this:

> To maintain my sense of integrity and self-worth or compromise it, that is the question. Whether 'tis nobler in the mind to suffer the ignominy that comes from managing a nonsensical research project, or the fear and anxiety that come from making a report the president and V.P. may not like to hear.

So, the anguish, procrastination, and counterproductive behavior of the research manager or members of the White House staff are not much different from those of Hamlet; all might ask with equal justification Hamlet's subsequent searching question of what it is that

> makes us rather bear those ills we have than
> fly to others we know not of.
> (*Hamlet*, Act III, Scene II)

In short, like the various Abilene protagonists, we are faced with a deeper question: Why does action anxiety occur?

Negative Fantasies

Part of the answer to that question may be found in the negative fantasies organization members have about acting in congruence with what they believe should be done. Hamlet experienced such fantasies.

Specifically, Hamlet's fantasies of the alternatives to the current evils were more evils, and he didn't entertain the possibility that any action he might take could lead to an improvement in the situation. Hamlet's was not an unusual case, though. In fact, the "Hamlet syndrome" clearly occurred in both organizations previously described. All of the organization protagonists had negative fantasies about what would happen if they acted in accordance with what they believed needed to be done.

The various managers in the R&D organization foresaw loss of face, prestige, position, and even health as the outcome of confronting the issues about which they believed, incorrectly, that they disagreed. Similarly, members of the White House staff feared being made scapegoats, branded as disloyal, or ostracized as non-team players if they acted in accordance with their understanding of reality.

To sum up, action anxiety is supported by the negative fantasies that organization members have about what will happen as a consequence of their acting in accordance with their understanding of what is sensible. The negative fantasies, in turn, serve an important function for the persons who have them. Specifically, they provide the individual with an excuse that releases him psychologically, both in his own eyes and frequently in the eyes of others, from the responsibility of having to act to solve organization problems.

It is not sufficient, though, to stop with the explanation of negative fantasies as the basis for the inability of organizations to cope with agreement. We must look deeper and ask still other questions: What is the source of the negative fantasies? Why do they occur?

Real Risk

Risk is a reality of life, a condition of existence. John Kennedy articulated it in another way when he said at a news conference, "Life is unfair." By that I believe he meant we do not know, nor can we predict or control with certainty, either the events that impinge upon us or the outcomes of actions we undertake in response to those events.

Consequently, in the business environment, the research manager might find that confronting the president and the vice-president with the fact that the project was a "turkey" might result in his being fired. And Mr. Porter's saying that an illegal plan of surveillance should not be carried out could have caused his ostracism as a non-team player. There are too many cases when confrontation of this sort has resulted in such consequences. The real question, though, is not, Are such fantasized consequences possible? but, Are such fantasized consequences likely?

Thus real risk is an existential condition, and all actions do have consequences that, to paraphrase Hamlet, may be worse than the evils of the present. As a result of their unwillingness to accept existential risk as one of life's givens, however, people may opt to take their organizations to Abilene rather than run the risk, no matter how small, of ending up somewhere worse.

Again, though, one must ask, What is the real risk that underlies the decision to opt for Abilene? What is at the core of the paradox?

Fear of Separation

One is tempted to say that the core of the paradox lies in the individual's fear of the unknown. Actually, we do not fear what is unknown, but we are afraid of things we do know about. What do we know about that frightens us into such apparently inexplicable organizational behavior?

Separation, alienation, and loneliness are things we do know about—and fear. Both research and experience indicate that ostracism is one of the most powerful punishments that can be devised. Solitary confinement does not draw its coercive strength from physical deprivation. The evidence is overwhelming that we have a fundamental need to be connected, engaged, and related and a reciprocal need not to be separated or alone. Everyone of us, though, has experienced aloneness. From the time the umbilical cord was cut, we have experienced the real anguish of separation—broken friendships, divorces, deaths, and exclusions. C. P. Snow vividly described the tragic interplay between loneliness and connection:

> Each of us is alone; sometimes we escape from our solitariness, through love and affection or perhaps creative moments, but these triumphs of life are pools of light we make for ourselves while the edge of the road is black. Each of us dies alone.

That fear of taking risks that may result in our separation from others is at the core of the paradox. It finds expression in ways of which we may be unaware, and it is ultimately the cause of the self-defeating, collective deception that leads to self-destructive decisions within organizations.

Concretely, such fear of separation leads research committees to fund projects that none of its members want and, perhaps, White House staff members to engage in illegal activities that they don't really support.

The Psychological Reversal of Risk and Certainty

One piece of the map is still missing. It relates to the peculiar reversal that occurs in our thought processes as we try to cope with the Abilene Paradox. For example, we frequently fail to take action in an organizational setting because we fear that the actions we take may result in our separation from others, or, in the language of Mr. Porter, we are afraid of being tabbed as "disloyal" or are afraid of being ostracized as "non-team players." But therein lies a paradox within a paradox, because our very unwillingness to take such risks virtually ensures the separation and aloneness we so fear. In effect, we reverse "real existential risk" and "fantasied risk" and by doing so transform what is a probability statement into what, for all practical purposes, becomes a certainty.

Take the R&D organization described earlier. When the project fails, some people will get fired, demoted, or sentenced to the purgatory of a make-work job in an out-of-the-way office. For those who remain, the atmosphere of blame, distrust, suspicion, and backbiting that accompanies such failure will serve only to further alienate and separate those who remain.

The Watergate situation is similar. The principals evidently feared being ostracized as disloyal non-team players. When the illegality of the act surfaced, however, it was nearly inevitable that blaming, self-protective actions, and scapegoating would result in the very emotional separation from both the President and one another that the principals feared. Thus, by reversing real and fantasied risk, they had taken effective action to ensure the outcome they least desired.

One final question remains: Why do we make this peculiar reversal? I support the general thesis of Alvin Toffler and Philip Slater, who contend that our cultural emphasis on technology, competition, individualism, temporariness, and mobility has resulted in a population that has frequently experienced the terror of loneliness and seldom the satisfaction of engagement. Consequently, though we have learned of the reality of separation, we have not had the opportunity to learn the reciprocal skills of connection, with the result that, like the ancient dinosaurs, we are breeding organizations with self-destructive decision-making proclivities.

A Possible Abilene Bypass

Existential risk is inherent in living, so it is impossible to provide a map that meets the no-risk criterion, but it may be possible to describe the route in terms that make the landmarks understandable and that will clarify the risks involved. In order to do that, however, some commonly used terms such as victim, victimizer, collusion, responsibility, conflict, conformity, courage, confrontation, reality, and knowledge have to be redefined. In addition, we need to explore the relevance of the redefined concepts for bypassing or getting out of Abilene.

• *Victim and victimizer.* Blaming and fault-finding behavior is one of the basic symptoms of organizations that have found their way to Abilene, and the target of blame generally doesn't include the one who criticizes. Stated in different terms, executives begin to assign one another to roles of victims and victimizers. Ironic as it may seem, however, this assignment of roles is both irrelevant and dysfunctional, because once a business or a government fails to manage its agreement and arrives in Abilene, all its members are victims. Thus, arguments and accusations that identify victims and victimizers at best become symptoms of the paradox, and, at worst, drain energy from the problem-solving efforts required to redirect the organization along the route it really wants to take.

• *Collusion.* A basic implication of the Abilene Paradox is that human problems of organization are reciprocal in nature. As Robert Tannenbaum has pointed out, you can't have an autocratic boss unless subordinates are willing to collude with his autocracy, and you can't have obsequious subordinates unless the boss is willing to collude with their obsequiousness.

Thus, in plain terms, each person in a self-defeating, Abilene-bound organization *colludes* with others, including peers, superiors, and subordinates, sometimes consciously and sometimes subconsciously, to create the dilemma in which the organization finds itself. To adopt a cliche of modern organization, "It takes a real team effort to go to Abilene." In that sense each person, in his own collusive manner, shares responsibility for the trip, so searching for a locus of blame outside oneself serves no useful purpose for either the organization or the individual. It neither helps the organization handle its dilemma of unrecognized agreement nor does it provide psychological relief for the individual, because focusing on conflict when agreement is the issue is devoid of reality. In fact, it does just the opposite, for it causes the organization to focus on managing conflict when it should be focusing on managing agreement.

• *Responsibility for problem-solving action.* A second question is, Who is responsible for getting us out of this place? To that question is frequently appended a third one, generally rhetorical in nature, with "should" overtones, such as, Isn't it the boss (or the ranking government official) who is responsible for doing something about the situation?

The answer to that question is no.

The key to understanding the functionality of the no answer is the knowledge that, when the dynamics of the paradox are in operation, the authority figure—and others—are in unknowing agreement with one another concerning the organization's problems and the steps necessary to solve them. Consequently, the power to destroy the paradox's pernicious influence comes from confronting and speaking to the underlying reality of the situation, and not from one's hierarchical position within the organization. Therefore, any organization member who chooses to risk confronting that reality possesses the necessary leverage to release the organization from the paradox's grip.

In one situation, it may be a research director's saying, "I don't think this project can succeed." In another, it may be Jeb Magruder's response to this question of Senator Baker:

> If you were concerned because the action was known to you to be illegal, because you thought it improper or unethical, you thought the prospects for success were very meager, and you doubted the reliability of Mr. Liddy, what on earth would it have taken to decide against the plan?

Magruder's reply was brief and to the point:

> Not very much, sir. I am sure that if I had fought vigorously against it, I think any of us could have had the plan cancelled. (*Time*, June 25, 1973, p. 12.)

• *Reality, knowledge, confrontation.* Accepting the paradox as a model describing certain kinds of organizational dilemmas also requires rethinking the nature of reality and knowledge, as they are generally described in organizations. In brief, the underlying dynamics of the paradox clearly indicate that organization members generally know more about issues confronting the organization than they don't know. The various principals attending the research budget meeting, for example, knew the research project was doomed to failure. And Jeb Magruder spoke as a true Abilener when he said, "We knew it was illegal, probably, inappropriate." (*The Washington Post*, June 15, 1973, p. A16.)

Given this concept of reality and its relationship to knowledge, confrontation becomes the process of facing issues squarely, openly, and directly in an effort to discover whether the nature of the underlying collective reality is agreement or conflict. Accepting such a definition of confrontation has an important implication for change agents interested in making organizations more effective. That is, organization change and effectiveness may be facilitated as much by confronting the organization with what it knows and agrees upon as by confronting it with what it doesn't know or disagrees about.

Real Conflict and Phony Conflict

Conflict is a part of any organization. Couples, R&D divisions, and White House staffs all engage in it. However, analysis of the Abilene paradox opens up the possibility of two kinds of conflict—real and phony. On the surface, they look alike. But, like headaches, they have different causes and therefore require different treatment.

Real conflict occurs when people have real differences ("My reading of the research printouts says that we can make the project profitable." "I come to the opposite conclusion.") ("I suggest we 'bug' the Watergate." "I'm not in favor of it.")

Phony conflict, on the other hand, occurs when people agree on the actions they want to take, and then do the opposite. The resulting anger, frustration, and blaming behavior generally termed "conflict" are not based on real differences. Rather, they stem from the protective reactions that occur when a decision that no one believed in or was committed to in the first place goes sour. In fact, as a paradox within a paradox, such conflict is symptomatic of agreement!

Group Tyranny and Conformity

Understanding the dynamics of the Abilene Paradox also requires a "reorientation" in thinking about concepts such as "group tyranny"—the loss of the individual's distinctiveness in a group, and the impact of conformity pressures on individual behavior in organizations. Group tyranny and its result, individual conformity, generally refer to the coercive effect of group pressures on individual behavior. Sometimes referred to as Groupthink, it has been damned as the cause for everything from the lack of creativity in organizations ("A camel is a horse designed by a committee") to antisocial behavior in juveniles ("My Johnny is a good boy. He was just pressured into shoplifting by the kids he runs around with").

However, analysis of the dynamics underlying the Abilene Paradox opens up the possibility that individuals frequently perceive and feel as if they are experiencing the coercive organization conformity pressures when, in actuality, they are responding to the dynamics of mismanaged agreement. Conceptualizing, experiencing, and responding to such experiences as reflecting the tyrannical pressures of a group again serves as an important psychological use for the individual: As was previously said, it releases him from the responsibility of taking action and thus becomes a defense against action. Thus, much behavior within an organization that heretofore has been conceptualized as reflecting the tyranny of conformity pressures is really an expression of collective anxiety and therefore must be reconceptualized as a defense against acting.

A well-known example of such faulty conceptualization comes to mind. It involves the heroic sheriff in the classic Western movies who stands alone in the jailhouse door and singlehandedly protects a suspected (and usually innocent) horse thief or murderer from the irrational, tyrannical forces of group behavior—that is, an armed lynch mob. Generally, as a part of the ritual, he threatens to blow off the head of anyone who takes a step toward the door. Few ever take the challenge, and the reason is not the sheriff's six-shooter. What good would one pistol be against an armed mob of several hundred people who *really* want to hang somebody? Thus, the gun in fact serves as a face-saving measure for people who don't wish to participate in a hanging anyway. ("We had to back off. The sheriff threatened to blow our heads off.")

The situation is one involving agreement management, for a careful investigator canvassing the crowd under conditions in which the anonymity of the interviewees' responses could be guaranteed would probably find: (1) that few of the individuals in the crowd really wanted to take part in the hanging; (2) that each person's participation came about because he perceived, falsely, that others wanted to do so; and (3) that each person was afraid that others in the crowd would ostracize or in some other way punish him if he did not go along.

Diagnosing the Paradox

Most individuals like quick solutions, "clean" solutions, "no risk" solutions to organization problems. Furthermore, they tend to prefer solutions based on mechanics and technology, rather than on attitudes of "being." Unfortunately, the underlying reality of the paradox makes it impossible to provide either no-risk solutions or action technologies divorced from existential attitudes and realities. I do, however, have two sets of suggestions for dealing with these situations. One set of suggestions relates to diagnosing the situation, the other to confronting it.

When faced with the possibility that the paradox is operating, one must first make a diagnosis of the situation, and the key to diagnosis is an answer to the question, Is the organization involved in a conflict-management or an agreement-management situation? As an organization member, I have found it relatively easy to make a preliminary diagnosis as to whether an organization is on the way to Abilene or is involved in legitimate, substantive conflict by responding to the Diagnostic Survey shown in the accompanying figure. If the answer to the first question is "not characteristic," the organization is probably not in Abilene or conflict. If the answer is "characteristic," the organization has a problem of either real or phony conflict, and the answers to the succeeding questions help to determine which it is.

In brief, for reasons that should be apparent from the theory discussed here, the more times "characteristic" is checked, the more likely the organization is on its way to Abilene. In practical terms, a process for managing agreement is called for. And finally, if the answer to the first question falls into the "characteristic" category and most of the other answers fall into the category "not characteristic," one may be relatively sure the organization is in a real conflict situation and some sort of conflict management intervention is in order.

Coping with the Paradox

Assuming a preliminary diagnosis leads one to believe he and/or his organization is on the way to Abilene, the individual may choose to actively confront the situation to determine directly whether the underlying reality is one of agreement or conflict. Although there are, perhaps, a number of ways to do it, I have found one way in particular to be effective—confrontation in a group setting. The basic approach involves gathering organization members who are key figures in the problem and its solution into a group setting. Working within the context of a group is important because the dynamics of the Abilene Paradox involve collusion among group members; therefore, to try to solve the dilemma by working with individuals and small subgroups would involve further collusion with the dynamics leading up to the paradox.

The first step in the meeting is for the individual who "calls" it (that is, the confronter) to own up to his position first and be open to the feedback he gets. The owning up process lets the others know that he is concerned lest the organization may be making a decision contrary to the desires of any of its members. A statement like this demonstrates the beginning of such an approach:

> I want to talk with you about the research project. Although I have previously said things to the contrary, I frankly don't think it will work, and I am very anxious about it. I suspect others may feel the same, but I don't know. Anyway, I am concerned that I may end up misleading you and that we may end up misleading one another, and if we aren't careful, we may continue to work on a problem that none of us wants and that might even bankrupt us. That's why I need to know where the rest of you stand. I would appreciate any of your thoughts about the project. Do you think it can succeed?

What kinds of results can one expect if he decides to undertake the process of confrontation? I have found that the results can be divided into *two* categories, at the technical level and at the level of existential experience. Of the two, I have found that for the person who undertakes to initiate the process of confrontation, the existential experience takes precedence in his ultimate evaluation of the outcome of the action he takes.

• *The technical level.* If one is correct in diagnosing the presence of the paradox, I have found the solution to the technical problem may be almost absurdly quick and simple, nearly on the order of this:

"Do you mean that you and I and the rest of us have been dragging along with a research project that none of

ORGANIZATION DIAGNOSTIC SURVEY

Instructions: For each of the following statements please indicate whether it is or is not characteristic of your organization.

1. There is conflict in the organization.
2. Organization members feel frustrated, impotent, and unhappy when trying to deal with it. Many are looking for ways to escape. They may avoid meetings at which the conflict is discussed, they may be looking for other jobs, or they may spend as much time away from the office as possible by taking unneeded trips or vacation or sick leave.
3. Organization members place much of the blame for the dilemma on the boss or other groups. In "back room" conversations among friends the boss is termed incompetent, ineffective, "out of touch," or a candidate for early retirement. To his face, nothing is said, or at best, only oblique references are made concerning his role in the organization's problems. If the boss isn't blamed, some other group, division, or unit is seen as the cause of the trouble: "We would do fine if it were not for the damn fools in Division X."
4. Small subgroups of trusted friends and associates meet informally over coffee, lunch, and so on to discuss organizational problems. There is a lot of agreement among the members of these subgroups as to the cause of the troubles and the solutions that would be effective in solving them. Such conversations are frequently punctuated with statements beginning with, "We should do..."
5. In meetings where those same people meet with members from other subgroups to discuss the problem they "soften their positions," state them in ambiguous language, or even reverse them to suit the apparent positions taken by others.
6. After such meetings, members complain to trusted associates that they really didn't say what they wanted to say, but also provide a list of convincing reasons why the comments, suggestions, and reactions they wanted to make would have been impossible. Trusted associates commiserate and say the same was true for them.
7. Attempts to solve the problem do not seem to work. In fact, such attempts seem to add to the problem or make it worse.
8. Outside the organization individuals seem to get along better, be happier, and operate more effectively than they do within it.

us has thought would work? It's crazy. I can't believe we would do it, but we did. Let's figure out how we can cancel it and get to doing something productive." In fact, the simplicity and quickness of the solution frequently don't seem possible to most of us, since we have been trained to believe that the solution to conflict requires a long, arduous process of debilitating problem solving.

Also, since existential risk is always present, it is possible that one's diagnosis is incorrect, and the process of confrontation lifts to the level of public examination real, substantive conflict, which may result in heated debate about technology, personalities, and/or administrative approaches. There is evidence that such debates, properly managed, can be the basis for creativity in organizational problem solving. There is also the possibility, however, that such debates cannot be managed, and substantiating the concept of existential risk, the person who initiates the risk may get fired or ostracized. But that again leads to the necessity of evaluating the results of such confrontation at the existential level.

• *Existential results.* Evaluating the outcome of confrontation from an existential framework is quite different from evaluating it from a set of technical criteria. How do I reach this conclusion? Simply from interviewing a variety of people who have chosen to confront the paradox and listening to their responses. In short, for them, psychological success and failure apparently are divorced from what is traditionally accepted in organizations as criteria for success and failure.

For instance, some examples of success are described when people are asked, "What happened when you confronted the issue?" They may answer this way:

> I was told we had enough boat rockers in the organization, and I got fired. It hurt at first, but in retrospect it was the greatest day of my life. I've got another job and I'm delighted. I'm a free man.

Another description of success might be this:

> I said I don't think the research project can succeed and the others looked shocked and quickly agreed. The upshot of the whole deal is that I got a promotion and am now known as a "rising star." It was the high point of my career.

Similarly, those who fail to confront the paradox describe failure in terms divorced from technical results. For example, one may report:

> I didn't say anything and we rocked along until the whole thing exploded and Joe got fired. There is still a lot of tension in the organization, and we are still in trouble, but I got a good performance review last time. I still feel lousy about the whole thing, though.

From a different viewpoint, an individual may describe his sense of failure in these words:

> I knew I should have said something and I didn't. When the project failed, I was a convenient whipping boy. I got demoted; I still have a job, but my future here is definitely limited. In a way I deserve what I got, but it doesn't make it any easier to accept because of that.

Most important, the act of confrontation apparently provides intrinsic psychological satisfaction, regardless of the technological outcomes for those who attempt it. The real meaning of that existential experience, and its relevance to a wide variety of organizations, may lie, therefore, not in the scientific analysis of decision making but in the plight of Sisyphus. That is something the reader will have to decide for himself.

The Abilene Paradox and the Myth of Sisyphus

In essence, this paper proposes that there is an underlying organizational reality that includes both agreement and disagreement, cooperation and conflict. However, the decision to confront the possibility of organization agreement is all too difficult and rare, and its opposite, the decision to accept the evils of the present, is all to common. Yet those two decisions may reflect the essence of both our human potential and our human imperfectability. Consequently, the choice to confront reality in the family, the church, the business, or the bureaucracy, though made only occasionally, may reflect those "peak experiences" that provide meaning to the valleys.

In many ways, they may reflect the experience of Sisyphus. As you may remember, Sisyphus was condemned by Pluto to a perpetuity of pushing a large stone to the top of a mountain, only to see it return to its original position when he released it. As Camus suggested in his revision of the myth, Sisyphus's task was absurd and totally devoid of meaning. For most of us, though, the lives we lead pushing papers or hubcaps are no less absurd, and in many ways we probably spend about as much time pushing rocks in our organizations as did Sisyphus.

Camus also points out, though, that on occasion as Sisyphus released his rock and watched it return to its resting place at the bottom of the hill, he was able to recognize the absurdity of his lot and, for brief periods of time, transcend it.

So it may be with confronting the Abilene Paradox. Confronting the absurd paradox of agreement may provide, through activity, what Sisyphus gained from his passive but conscious acceptance of his fate. Thus, through the process of active confrontation with reality, we may take respite from pushing our rocks on their endless journeys and, for brief moments, experience what C. P. Snow termed "the triumphs of life we make for ourselves" within those absurdities we call organizations.

Selected Bibliography

Chris Argyris in *Intervention Theory and Method: A Behavioral Science View* (Addison-Wesley, 1970) gives an excellent description of the process of "owning up" and being "open," both of which are major skills required if one is to assist his organization in avoiding or leaving Abilene.

Albert Camus in *The Myth of Sisyphus and Other Essays* (Vintage Books, Random House, 1955) provides an existential viewpoint for coping with absurdity, of which the Abilene Paradox is a clear example.

Jerry B. Harvey and R. Albertson in "Neurotic Organizations: Symptoms, Causes and Treatment," Parts I and II, *Personnel Journal* (September and October 1971) provide a detailed example of a third-party intervention into an organization caught in a variety of agreement-management dilemmas.

Irving Janis in *Victims of Groupthink* (Houghton-Mifflin Co., 1972) offers an alternative viewpoint for understanding and dealing with many of the dilemmas described in "The Abilene Paradox." Specifically, many of the events that Janis describes as examples of conformity pressures (that is, group tyranny) I would conceptualize as mismanaged agreement.

In his *The Pursuit of Loneliness* (Beacon Press, 1970), Philip Slater contributes an in-depth description of the impact of the role of alienation, separation, and loneliness (a major contribution to the Abilene Paradox) in our culture.

Richard Walton in *Interpersonal Peacemaking: Confrontation and Third Party Consultation* (Addison-Wesley, 1969) describes a variety of approaches for dealing with conflict when it is real, rather than phony.

What Leadership Crisis?

BY JOHN NIRENBERG

Durk Jager of Procter & Gamble. Jill Barad of Mattel. Rick Thoman of Xerox. Doug Ivester of Coca-Cola. Dale Morrison of Campbell. Richard McGinn of Lucent. Michael Hawley of Gillette. All household names in the business press, all CEOs who recently stepped down.

And with each CEO out of a job, the cry goes up: "We are in a leadership crisis!" After all, look at the numbers: Outplacement firm Challenger, Gray & Christmas recorded 473 CEO departures in the first five months of 2001. If that isn't a crisis, what is?

Not everybody is unhappy about this state of affairs. For executive recruiters, it's meant great business—the industry has been growing at a double-digit rate since 1992. Not surprisingly, perhaps, recruiters are among the foremost proponents of the crisis idea. Joel Koblentz, senior partner at the Atlanta office of placement firm Egon Zehnder International, calls the leadership crisis "more acute now than ever. The stakes are so much greater and the tenure so much shorter today—down to less than four years. And finding the right mix of competencies in a candidate who can deliver under enormous pressure to add shareholder value is quite difficult."

Leadership gurus, of course, also have a vested interest in leadership. Agreeing that there's a shortage of leaders, Warren Bennis, professor of leadership at the University of Southern California, comments: "The task of leadership is significantly more complex today and harder than ever." He also suggests that some first-rate people do not have the drive to become CEOs today because they can find satisfaction in other ways.

Not everybody agrees that there's a shortage—Graef "Bud" Crystal, for one. Crystal, perhaps America's chief critic of CEO compensation, scoffs: "Bull. There's no shortage. Mergers are putting many capable CEOs on the market, and there are many successful division heads that could be moved up, not to mention 30 years of MBAs."

And, says Jeffrey Sonnenfeld, CEO of Atlanta-based Chief Executive Leadership Institute, "There is a ready bounty of CEO material currently available, but there is an unholy alliance between risk-averse boards and executive recruiters promoting marquee candidates that gives the appearance of a shortage. That very small group can't possibly perform at the messianic level expected of them, and the list gets shorter and shorter over time as the unrealistic expectations become apparent."

The False Yardstick

While one may argue whether there's a shortage, it's hardly arguable that a superstar phenomenon exists for CEOs, especially in the winner-take-all market of America's largest companies. "The value of what gets produced in [this market] often depends on the efforts of only a small number of top performers, who are paid accordingly," write Robert Frank and Philip Cook in *The Winner-Take-All Society*. They point out that the same kind of market exists in professional sports, movies, broadcast news, publishing, and consulting.

The fact is that there are truly a finite number of really top jobs (500, if you go by *Fortune*'s definition). And these positions are the focus of superheated media attention, so we shouldn't be surprised that these CEOs become celebrities in their own right, subject to a system revolving around headhunters, public-relations hype, and an ethos of competitive distinction founded in large part on "the compensation package." Indeed, these packages are part of the mechanism that reinforces the idea of the superstar CEO. Money, whether expressed in salary, stock options, or any other means, becomes the yardstick.

A false yardstick, says Crystal. "Nobody has clean hands here. Sixty percent of company directors are CEOs themselves, and they won't object to higher pay. They even encourage it, which creates the Lake Wobegon effect: The average CEO is perceived as above average and compensated accordingly."

Deserved or not, the pay package is part of the mythology that separates the CEO from the "others"—even senior executives immediately below him. Unduly? Well, Jack Welch delayed his retirement from GE in order to broker the merger—eventually stymied—between GE and Honeywell. Was this truly necessary? Or is his delayed retirement, like the lifelong tenure of a tribal shaman, merely a comfort to the boards, the investment community, and the analysts who believe in the myth that Welch can do no wrong or who simply don't feel it wise at this time to "rock the boat?" Is the second tier now occupied by his anointed successor Jeffrey Immelt and colleagues really incapable of the task? If so, why?

For every successful strategic shift, there is a slew of failures.

One responsibility of a CEO is to ensure the orderly succession of all managers and executives, according to University of Michigan professor Noel Tichy, who served as director of GE's renowned Management Development Institute at Crotonville, N.Y. Just what unique characteristics, talents, and purposes—unavailable in Immelt and his team—will Welch continue to bring to the success of the transition?

The answer might simply be that Jack Welch is Jack Welch: a nonpareil, the top dog of top dogs, an icon. But as the Leadership Institute's Sonnenfeld points out: "We forget that while GE's Welch has become an icon of great management, his selection by Reginald Jones was a risk. Jones skipped over 14 candidates and dropped down two levels to pick Welch. Most boards don't have the courage to do this. While they may have a good handle on the industry, they lack an intimate understanding of the specific technological and market complexities that drive the company and the abilities that internal candidates may possess. This is in part due to the board's lack of exposure to up-and-coming managers just a few levels down."

All this brings us to the largest question: Given the enormous compensation packages paid to CEOs and the celebrity status they have achieved, is this evidence of a real leadership shortage or just evidence of a belief system that claims, as the thinking goes: If he isn't worth it, he wouldn't be paid it, and if he's paid it, he must be worth it?

Higher, Ever Higher

To know if there is a shortage, we need to know exactly what we mean by *leadership*. Every stakeholder in the corporate arena holds a different definition of it, and there are at least four perspectives that demand attention. First is the perspective of shareholders and the board, which has been especially visible over the last eight years. To them, leadership is determined by financial success—specifically represented in shareholder value.

We have seen the giddy heights of a bullish stock market. And it was good. Not only did the boards benefit—everyone's retirement plan seemed to benefit as well. Given the low unemployment and low inflation rates, good times seemed like they'd roll on forever. The power of this view of leadership was endorsed by many in the daily push for ever-higher returns as first one, then another CEO superstar would set the pace for the pack. From this perspective, it was simple: The higher the stock price, the better the leadership.

Simple, yes, but incessantly demanding. Columbia University Graduate School of Business professor Don Hambrick points out that the current demand is for revolutionary change and "away from the status quo and incremental change. The investment community is basically saying, 'Do something extraordinary with our assets' and is impatient with less of a return than is possible." Until very recently, the limits to what is possible reached one unimagined level after another. This mentality creates the kind of pressure that leads CEOs into extreme risk-taking and a major strategic shift. But for every successful strategic shift, there is a slew of failures, and employees by the thousands suffer. How many strategies did AT&T churn through, shedding more than 30,000 people, to manage its current stock-price collapse and its third planned breakup?

From employees' perspective, there is a real and grave leadership shortage.

Does Father Know Best?

And this leads us to another powerful definition of leadership: From the employees' perspective, it means setting a vision, encouraging their performance, and yet inspiring their commitment to the organization's goals. Yet according to Gordon Miller, founder of Denver-based Delta Road, the largest consortium of career coaches, 81 percent of surveyed employees say their "boss/company had no clue how to manage them, and 37 percent said they intend to leave their companies in 2001." This unfortunate state of the world of work, captured so poignantly in the *Dilbert* comic strip, aptly categorizes life at work for an unforgivably large audience. So from employees' perspective, there appears to be a real and grave leadership shortage—not just CEOs but management generally. From this perspective, the company's leadership (that is, the CEO) is a prescient—even charismatic—father figure who will take care of them unconditionally.

He is supposed to assure not only their present but also their future, by providing continuity—a management-succession plan. By this measure, many CEOs are not up to snuff. But even if a plan is in place, there are no guarantees. The recent "textbook case" at Coca-Cola provides an egregious example. Roberto Goizueta, an enormously successful and popular CEO, was dealing with a terminal illness that worried investors and employees alike. But he had a succession plan that won accolades,

The Top Gun

Think about leadership, think about CEOs. Think about CEOs, think about the boards of directors that hire—and, increasingly, fire them. This newly aggressive role is the focus of *Corporate Boards: New Strategies for Adding Value at the Top* by Jay A. Conger, Edward E. Lawler III, and David L. Finegold. "Rare today are boardroom meetings that look like Soviet May Day parades, with a string of well-orchestrated, 'good news' presentations," they write, as they predict greater experimentation in further empowering boards.

One of the book's authors, Edward Lawler, spoke about the leadership role of boards with A.J. Vogl, editor of *Across the Board*. Lawler is director of the Center for Effective Organizations at USC and professor of management and organization at the USC Marshall School of Business.

As of May 31, there have been 473 CEO departures this year, 22 percent more than a similar period last year. Given this tremendous turnover in CEOs, I have to ask: Are boards hiring the wrong people?

The hiring process is sometimes at fault, but a lot of other things have converged to account for the turnover: the pressure of the investment community for short-term results, the lack of patience that boards show for their CEOs, and partly a supply problem. There may really be a shortage, because the demands of the job are so different than they were 15 or 30 years ago, when most CEOs started their management careers. They're not really trained or prepared for the CEO's job.

Then why do so many boards choose a well-known warhorse instead of a younger person?

Because the warhorse is a known quantity. Look at Lucent and Xerox, both of which brought in their old CEOs—both, I suppose, considered somewhat of a lower-risk proposition than bringing in somebody from inside who's never been CEO or somebody from outside who doesn't know the company. You can be critical of both these decisions, because both those guys made many of the decisions that caused Xerox and Lucent their troubles today. In some sense, they're being brought back to clean up the mess that they created.

You write that in your interviews with board members, most said that picking the CEO was their most important decision. But wouldn't you say they were overly cautious in this decision?

They wouldn't say that. I would. They are very influenced by what the sitting CEO wants, and there are all sorts of options in place to influence the process. There's the tournament model, which was recently played out at GE. There's the early-designation-of-successor model, played out at United Technologies. And then there's the toughest spot for a board: when the CEO doesn't really want a successor to appear. If the CEO shields the board from seeing internal talent, the board is forced to go outside or retain headhunters, which usually bring forth safe candidates. But that doesn't ensure CEO longevity. When push comes to shove, it's easier to shove, and boards are much more willing to shove than they were 10 years ago.

In looking for a CEO, do corporate boards consciously look for leadership?

That's not as important as I hoped it would be, or as it will be in the future. Members of boards look for people like themselves—CEOs or people with a grasp of specific functional areas—financial types who can talk numbers, for instance, or people who can talk technology if it's a technology company. CEO candidates are screened not for leadership but on nuts-and-bolts operational skills and their track record. If you look at CEOs today, very few are articulate on the issue of leadership and management as a behavior. Jack Welch, of course, is the poster boy, but after him you don't find very many.

If boards are, indeed, tougher in evaluating how the CEO leads the company, are they also tougher in evaluating themselves?

It's a muddy situation. Yes, boards evaluate the CEO, but they are also dependent to some degree on the CEO for them to be reappointed. As for board evaluation by peers and the CEO, we find that board members take criticism pretty well. But do they change? The evidence is not overwhelmingly positive.

The real test of board evaluation will come in a bear market. If CEO compensation doesn't move in parallel with shareholder value, it will be a strong indictment of the way boards manage executive compensation.

---

and when he died and Douglas Ivester became CEO, there was hardly a hiccup on Wall Street. Yet though handpicked and mentored through the transition, this veteran Coke executive ran into a string of misfortunes that eventually forced him to step down. Was a flawed succession plan at fault, or was it simply a case of bad judgment about his leadership abilities? According to James O'Toole and Warren Bennis, writing in the *Harvard Business Review*, "Ivester was emotionally inept ... and he couldn't empathize with the personal concerns of others.... [H]e was a one-man band who seldom involved others in big decisions." If this was, indeed, the case, then somebody should have noticed it before his ascension to the top job. After all, Ivester had spent 20 years with the company.

Think Different

***The Deep Blue Sea* might be a paperback mystery or a movie thriller—certainly not a leadership treatise—but Wilfred Drath does not use the image idly as the title of his new book: "Too often in thinking about leadership," he writes, "we are like persons standing on the shore, captivated by the dancing, sparkling whitecaps on the ocean and entirely missing the deep blue sea. The whitecaps are real enough, but their source lies within the action of the ocean itself." The whitecaps, he argues, represent the idea that leaders create leadership.**

Drath is group director and senior fellow at the Center for Creative Leadership in Greensboro, N.C. He spoke about his ideas to *Across the Board* editor A.J. Vogl.

Is there a leadership crisis?

Yes, but I believe it's really an epistemological crisis—a crisis in our way of knowing. Why do we feel there's not enough leadership for the challenges we face? Because we have a model that says that leadership has to be provided only by individuals. We can create leadership by the way we interact with each other to face adaptive challenges, the kind of difficult challenges an organization must face without pre-existing resources or solutions.

In looking for CEOs, are boards of directors paying too much attention to the whitecaps rather than what's underneath?

Yes. Boards are trained to think in terms of problems and people who can solve them, to think of leadership in terms of who's the person with the experience to do the job. I'm not calling into question CEO experience but, rather, the idea of the CEO as the fount of leadership—well, that day is past.

I've met a number of CEOs, and they are remarkable people in many ways, but to think they can personally encompass the adaptive challenges their organizations must face—that's a big stretch, and I think any CEO would tell you this. They would say they had to create the context for the organization to do it.

In your book, you have one of the main characters say, "I always thought there were only two ways to become a leader. Either you were born a leader or you learned how to be a leader.... I never realized that you could become a leader by thinking differently about leadership itself." Explain.

To be born a leader or trained to be one assumes that leadership is a quality the person has or can acquire. If you take that as the truth, then the question becomes: Did they get that thing by birth, or by education, training, or development? The third alternative is this: If people could change the way they think about leadership—from being a quality or possession of an individual to being something that arises when people interact with each other—when they solve a problem together, when they share an inside joke, it would give them a whole new way to think about "becoming a leader." Because then they would become participants in the process of creating leadership.

I don't think there's anything wrong with leadership as an attainment or the quality of a person, but we're sort of stuck in that box. My hope is that my book will redirect attention from the person in authority to the whole sphere of interactions in organizations—the vertical interactions between bosses and subordinates, as well as laterally, the horizontal communications that really bypass those in authority.

Have you ever explained your concept of leadership to a CEO and had him respond, "By George, that's a terrific idea. I'm going to meet with my people next week and start implementing it."

No, that's the day I still have to look forward to.

The third definition of leadership seems to be simply having the skills to get the job done. Nothing fancy here. Leadership is merely a more hip word for having the ability to manage—to set strategic direction, to organize resources, and to effectively mobilize employees to ensure quality results. There appears to be an abundance of this management talent, though it's frequently ignored, stifled, or allowed to atrophy. Hambrick, who isn't inclined to see a leadership shortage, remarks, "The challenge is to find [the leadership] talent in mid-career and to look in the unlikely places both outside the company as well as in it. The problem is that proper placement and grooming in the ranks have been insufficient."

It is a self-inflicted crisis derived from a myth.

The fourth definition of leadership is promoted by the dream weavers—consultants who see a leadership position as the embodiment of all that is good. According to them, leaders not only possess the enviable ability to make enormous returns for the organization—they are the "most knowledgeable, skilled, innovative, experienced, entrepreneurial, creative, risk-taking, super talent." This profile is drawn without jest or irony by Bruce Tulgan, founder of RainmakerThinking Inc., a New

Mixed Messages?

A soon-to-be-released Conference Board survey reveals some of senior management's thinking about leadership and how it's being transmitted into practice. While the overall message is clear, there are also some dissonances.

On the one hand, it's clear that senior management sees that the *scope* of leadership is becoming wider and more complex—indeed, now they speak of "super leaders"—and today's leaders see the need for identifying high-potential people early on, giving them experiences that offer the opportunity to develop leadership potential, offering multiple career paths to the top, and giving honest feedback along the way.

However, according to survey respondents—some 150 executives of major U.S. and foreign corporations—there may be problems as to how this thinking is being translated "on the ground":

- Almost as many respondents consider their leadership capacity to be poor as consider it to be good.
- Less than half agree that their senior leaders view leadership development as a major priority.
- Forty-four percent report a low focus on developing global leaders, compared to 30 percent reporting a high focus.
- Almost a third of respondents do not favor telling employees the results of their leadership-potential status.
- While most respondents could identify their companies' core competencies, only one-quarter of them said these competencies are understood well by most employees.
- According to respondents, the most difficult competencies for a company to develop relate to change and conceptual ability, while some of the easiest are a results orientation, customer focus, and business/technical/functional/knowledge skills.

—A.J. Vogl

Haven, Conn.-based firm that studies changes in the workplace.

Without a doubt, given the unrealistic—and sometimes conflicting—demands of boards of directors, employees, leadership gurus, recruiters, consultants, and the business press, there will forever be a leadership shortage, and it will get worse each year. And each year that passes without increasing rates of profit and share price, higher employee-satisfaction ratings, and all-around omniscience, the leader shortage will most certainly increase. Clearly, the shortage is as real as the oil crisis of the 1970s. The self-serving interests of the gurus, consultants, and journalists have overlooked the blindingly obvious. It is a self-inflicted crisis derived from a myth and perpetuated by the confusion created by wildly divergent interests.

The "Glass Floor"

"Part of the so-called leadership shortage is a socially constructed reality by the boards of directors themselves," according to professor Rakesh Khurana of Harvard Business School. Given the difficulties of the CEO job and the fear of failing in selecting a CEO, "the first mistake boards frequently make is to narrow the selection process to choose conservatively from among a small pool of successful corporate CEO survivors, while at the same time seeking dramatic and swift change!"

The same CEO names come up over and over again.

"The second error boards make is to attribute the success of a firm to a CEO alone," Khurana adds. "Using the success of the firm as a proxy for CEO success is a fallacious miscalculation. The third self-imposed limitation created by many boards is seeking only those CEO candidates most like themselves." Of course, this also leads to thinking that only a small and homogeneous pool of candidates exists. "Just as Harvard wouldn't look to community colleges for its next president, *Fortune* 500 companies are not likely to seek CEO candidates from companies outside the inner circle of the largest companies." This behavior mirrors the mentality of European royalty, and elitists everywhere, whose succession always depends on royal progeny and drawing successors from other royal houses. The recent succession of Jeffrey Immelt to CEO of GE left his two rivals with superb opportunities, having been given Jack Welch's blessing, for top jobs elsewhere. Robert Nardelli became CEO of Home Depot; James McNerney became CEO of 3M.

Because the pool for big-company CEOs is perceived as so small, even those deemed ill-suited for current needs—and sometimes even those who fail at a particular job—remain in the pool. Khurana dubs this "the glass-floor effect." Once you're in the pool, you stay in until retirement or a golden parachute eases you out. The same names come up over and over again. So the anxiety around the uncertainty of the selection outcome and the fear of failure encourages boards to select from what looks like a pool of tried-and-true candidates. Then, their choices are justified to observers regardless of the outcome. A success confirms the process. A failure is understood as undesirable but often acceptable, according to the rules defined by the conventional wisdom imbedded in the limited search process.

Sometimes, for whatever reason, boards enamored with an individual candidate get so fixated on their choice that they encourage the candidate to behave in negotiations as a virtual monopoly. If a board wants the equivalent of a Michael Jordan, and can afford him, it may find itself willing to pay anything to get him. Even attention on a lesser performer but a sole candidate proffered by a search firm drives up the board's willingness to

Ten Ways for Boards to Avoid a Leadership Crisis

- Have the courage to admit you are enamored with the appeal of the superstars, but leave their employment to Hollywood.
- Know what you need and why you need it.
- Know what will constitute a sensible compensation package; it need not be the most generous, the biggest, or without performance requirements.
- Always have at least three suitable candidates able to meet your needs; don't fish in small pools.
- Prepare for the CEO's successor as soon as that individual is hired.
- Create an internal executive-development program to prepare leaders at all levels and groom potential successors to the CEO.
- Consciously seek talented individuals whose skills fit with the specific strategy driving the organization.
- Require performance before the payoff.
- Develop the courage to be patient; give time so the new or the incumbent CEO can make real change happen without being forced into the realm of needing monumental returns instantly. It takes years for a person to settle into the position and for the organizational immune system to be readied for and coaxed through dramatic change.
- Help faltering CEOs increase their capacity for personal development and change. Long before the ax falls, indicators are present that remediation is needed. Supply it before the point of no return.

—J.N.

pay well beyond what makes sense if it is committed to its choice.

Carly Fiorina, now CEO of Hewlett-Packard, is a good example. In 1998, she secured a package worth about $85 million, including $66 million in restricted stock, before putting in a day's work. A more recent case that best exemplifies the hypnotic spell of one-and-only thinking is the recent signing of Alex Rodriguez to the Texas Rangers for a record $252 million contract spanning 10 years. As James Surowiecki noted in *The New Yorker*, even if Rodriguez continues his terrific performance and "attracts five thousand new fans every night, that's just eight million dollars more in annual revenue." And that would amount to only $80 million over the life of his contract. This is the eBay auction frenzy at its best and what tends to happen when a sole individual is perceived as a must-have. Apparently, if you want something badly enough and have the means to pay for it, intrinsic, even fair market value becomes irrelevant.

Such a choice also demonstrates to the world the financial clout of the buying organization and whatever bragging rights and heightened expectations of the candidate that might also accrue.

Many agree with Khurana that "the board is abdicating its responsibility and fails to see the complexity of the context in which a CEO works and erroneously makes the superstar, alone, a hero or villain when the performance results finally come in." Addressing the Foreign Policy Association's World Leadership Forum 2000, Russell S. Reynolds, a prominent executive recruiter and chairman of the Directorship Search Group, said, "I am appalled at the compensation being paid CEOs and other senior corporate officers by boards of directors that ought to know better." However, solutions to the propensity to throw money at leading lights are elusive. For the moment, we seem determined to perpetuate the very excesses we abhor, despite the obvious problems with this scenario, including the loss of control by the board of directors, the dependence on a person who must singlehandedly play a heroic role, the squandering of the shareholders' resources, and the discouragement of promising talent within the organization.

All for One and One for All

Ultimately, then, it would seem to come to this: Leadership is dependent on one of two fundamental approaches. The first is to see the role as the expression of a CEO's personality and idiosyncratic management style that utilizes the organization as a mere instrument made totally reliant on the CEO's personal heroics. Al Dunlap, the discredited former CEO of Sunbeam, represents the darkest side of this approach. Or, the CEO becomes the catalyst for stimulating initiative and leadership behavior throughout the ranks. This is the approach of a Percy Barnevik, for example, whose international electrical-engineering group Asea Brown Boveri is considered an exemplar of a leadership engine. ABB has created a system that imbues leadership in many people throughout the ranks and expects to draw on them to meet the leadership needs of the organization indefinitely.

This approach recognizes the importance of the artist in the CEO but liberates the organization from the wizardry of highly compensated individuals and the myth that they alone, singlehandedly, can save us—if we can only afford the price. Richard Teerlink, the CEO credited with the turnaround of Harley-Davidson, seems to understand this approach when he tells us, "People are our only long-term competitive advantage. Therefore, a leader is responsible for creating an operating environment where people can do great things. That environment includes investing in capital and processes to support the efforts of the people."

Following Teerlink's advice would build strong organizations more able to realize their strategies due to the contributions of everyone in the system. It would also make it unnecessary to hire an Al Dunlap when the organization is on its last legs, or an outsider like Lou Gerstner, who forced IBM to do what it should have been doing all along.

Filling In the "Shortage"

Large companies are neglecting the development of internal executive candidates since the old paternalistic, career-oriented employment contract was destroyed with the downsizings of the 1990s. That change effectively removed an entire tier of candidates for senior management positions and sent the message to remaining talent that they should develop general, marketable skills rather than firm-specific skills. Similarly, companies invested less in career and executive development because of the new transience and heightened career mobility. This vicious circle is obviously self-defeating.

So organizations aren't doing what they need to do to develop executive talent, yet they decry a shortage. Then they poach from other organizations, such as GE, that do prepare leaders. It seems they would rather pay a premium for their irresponsibility in executive development by hiring costly superstars rather than spend the money internally to develop their own. A small fraction of the millions initially paid to attract Carly Fiorina, for example, could, at the very least, fund a conscious executive-development effort to supply a virtually limitless stream of talent to meet Hewlett-Packard's needs indefinitely. H-P could have hired the 210 faculty members of the Harvard Business School, paid the entire living expenses (including tuition) of the 858 students of the class of 2000, and still have had almost $15 million left over for a tidy bonus system for engineering a successful culture change such as undertaken by Fiorina!

The irony is that while everyone admires Jack Welch and GE, they don't seem to emulate GE's passion for growing talent within. So, boards, in seeking peace of mind with the tried-and-true—by outsourcing the task of choosing a successor to a search firm and paying for a superstar—actually may be doing more harm to their organization than good by de-motivating their own up-and-comers.

What to do about it? Once a company believes it must compete for the superstars or be drawn into an astronomical bidding war by headhunters profiting from a money-slinging frenzy, boards talk themselves into the idea that there is really no alternative.

There is. In *The Leadership Engine: How Winning Companies Build Leaders at Every Level*, Noel Tichy outlines a plan for meeting the leadership needs of any company willing to take its "shortage" head-on. It is an obvious idea whose time has come, built upon the principle that has been recognized since ancient times when armies tested their newer soldiers in battle with the idea of promoting the courageous and victorious to increasing responsibilities. The U.S. Military Academy at West Point has been doing this for nearly two centuries. And for 30 years, the nonprofit Center for Creative Leadership, headquartered in Greensboro, N.C., has been following a similar track on a company level by providing disciplined leadership training to the corporate community. For such training to work, however, there has to be a change in thinking on the part of current CEOs and then boards. They must stop looking outside for wizards to cure company ills and instead prepare their own followers to become leaders.

Sonnenfeld of the Chief Executive Leadership Institute says boards should play a more active role: "I'd recommend that boards spend time with at least second-tier managers to get a deeper appreciation of internal talent. Some companies do this well. UPS, for example. It is felt that chairman Jim Kelly will be replaced by an internal candidate, vice chairman Michael Eskew, who is being groomed for the position through coaching and being party to the current decision-making process, Compaq was another example of a large company that found a successor from within. Second- and third-tier managers should be able to present ideas and projects to the board. Managers, then, too, should conduct peer reviews that are sent to the executive committee of the board or the compensation or HR committees. In this way, the board can become familiar with internal talent. If nothing else, there should at least be social occasions that bring potential managers and the board together."

That in turn, says Reynolds of the Directorship Search Group, might lead board members to see: "There have never been as many capable, talented people as there are now to lead our organizations, but we have to dig a little deeper to find them."

Perhaps a first step toward finding them is to demythologize the CEO—not only in the popular and business press but in academic research. Every time researchers study the effect of the CEO on firm performance, they contribute to the idea that the big boss has a make-or-break effect, even though research usually finds that he doesn't. Most people—including CEOs—would agree they can't save a company on their own, so why do corporate boards persist in looking for a savior in a shrinking (and somewhat discredited) pool of saviors?

JOHN NIRENBERG *is author of* Power Tools: A Leader's Guide to the Latest Management Thinking *(Pearson) and speaks widely on leadership issues. He can be reached at john.nirenberg@att.net.*

Effective Performance Counseling

Supervisor Cam Arnold turned the page of his monthly planner. *It's that time of the year again,* he thought. *Performance evaluations—not my favorite thing. I wish I felt more comfortable with the whole process. I wish I felt that I was doing something positive for my people. There has to be a better way...*

All supervisors and managers need to assess employees periodically in order to explain to them just how they're doing and what action is required for progress. Whether you do this at specified times under a formal evaluation system or on a continuing basis under a less formal system, you'll be more effective if you concentrate on...

The Things That Count

The key to fair appraisal and effective counseling is carefully choosing the factors that you take into consideration when evaluating employees. Some supervisors make the mistake of considering too many factors. For example, when the HR director in one workplace asked a group of supervisors what specific characteristics should be considered on a new evaluation form, she ended up with a total of 73 factors!

The key to fair appraisal and effective counseling is carefully choosing the factors that you take into consideration.

The HR director pointed out that even if there were enough time to rate employees on that many factors, the result would include a lot of unnecessary details. She suggested keeping on the list only those characteristics that could actually be observed in a worker's performance and were obviously important for effective work. The group distilled the list to six: dependability, quality, quantity, attitude, knowledge, and skills.

Remember Your Fellow Supervisors

When you evaluate your people, remember these two factors. Either of them could adversely affect an appraisal.

1. **Avoid being influenced by occurrences that are not typical** of employees or their work. Consider one factor at a time, and don't let your reaction to any one incident affect your ratings. Consider an employee's actions over the *entire* review period, not just his or her most recent ones.

2. **Always think of your fellow supervisors when you do your evaluating.** Nothing can upset morale more quickly than ratings that are either too liberal or too rigid in comparison with those of other departments.

Performance Counseling Success

Because a counseling interview is not part of the day-to-day work pattern, it takes on great importance in the minds of employees. You may be affected, too. Because you are in an unusual position, you may act and speak in a stilted manner, quite different from your normal conversational tone.

Paying attention to what employees are saying, in addition to listening to the words, is a must for effective counseling.

Here are some guidelines to help you make the chore of conducting counseling interviews easier for both you and your employees:

• **Keep the interview balanced.** A successful counseling interview remains faithful to the appraisal. Let's suppose you're talking to an employee who is rated above average in everything but job skills. He's competent enough in the work he does, but he has no interest in increasing his skills or learning different jobs.

The great temptation is to spend a minute or so commending him for his above-average rating in five categories and half an hour lecturing about the one where he's only average. While it isn't necessary to divide time equally between praise and criticism, overemphasis on the critical side produces resentment rather than the extra effort you are trying to bring forth.

• **Don't expect too much.** You can't expect to remake employees in one short counseling session. It's much more practical to set modest, attainable objectives. Asking employees to improve their performance in several areas simultaneously will only discourage them. Short-term goals that can be maintained after they've been achieved are more realistic.

• **Pay attention and listen.** Paying attention to what employees are saying, in addition to listening to the words, is a must for effective counseling. Unfortunately, it's not an easy thing to do. For one thing, while the other person is talking, you may be thinking about your own views on the subject; consequently, you'll respond to your own thoughts rather than to the thoughts being expressed.

Another reason listening is difficult is that you may have already decided what the other person is going to say. After all, you probably know the person well and have heard him or her talk about a lot of things. The result is that you hear only what you expect to hear.

The obvious result of not listening is that you don't understand what the employee is trying to tell you. You'll never be able to guide workers toward improving their performance or attitudes if you don't know what might motivate them to do it.

When workers know that they're being evaluated fairly and are being given an attainable target to shoot for, they'll change their performance to try to meet that standard.

From *Leadership for the Front Lines,* February 15, 2002, pp. 3-4.

THE Myth OF Synergy

IT'S A SLIPPERY CONCEPT, SYNERGY. FEW REALLY UNDERSTAND IT. YET THE WORD IS THROWN AROUND TO JUSTIFY ALL BIG MERGERS TODAY. TOO BAD IT'S A BASELESS IDEA.

BY JAMES SUROWIECKI

Eight months ago, when Carly Fiorina unveiled Hewlett-Packard's proposed multi-billion-dollar acquisition of Compaq, she offered a dizzying array of reasons the deal made sense. The new company, she indicated, would be able to satisfy customers' demands for "solutions capability on a truly global basis." It would have product leadership "from top to bottom, from low end to high end." It would be able to compete in services and storage. Fiorina saved her most important point for last. The new company would flourish, she said, because it would enjoy—you guessed it—"synergies that are compelling."

Synergy: It is the business buzzword that will not die. For almost 40 years now, CEOs have been justifying high-priced acquisitions by trumpeting the benefits of synergy, and even though after 40 years those benefits remain remarkably elusive, the faith in synergy has not dimmed. In the 1960s, for instance, conglomerates such as LTV—which ran businesses in electronics, aerospace, steel, sporting goods, meatpacking, and pharmaceuticals—argued that by acquiring lots of different companies and then running them all out of one headquarters, they would be able to save on overhead and wring out inefficiencies. They weren't able to. In the late '70s and early '80s, synergy was called on to justify a host of mergers in banking and financial services. Customers, companies argued, wanted a financial supermarket that offered one-stop shopping. Checking, lending, insurance, real estate, stocks: They could all fit under the same umbrella. Sears took the idea to its logical extreme, trying to combine all those financial services with its traditional department-store business. Sears would be, the argument went, the everything store. Instead, customers shied from the idea of the financial supermarket—which has since returned at places like E*Trade and Citigroup—and Sears ended up treading water for more than a decade.

Today, synergy is used most often to justify media mergers. Synergy provided the impetus for Tina Brown's failed *Talk* magazine venture, which was co-owned by Miramax and Hearst. It was the reason behind the Viacom-CBS merger, and it helped explain the AOL–Time Warner deal too. Media moguls like nothing better than to envision all of their different properties cross-fertilizing each other: CNN.com, an AOL–Time Warner company, pushing Time Inc. magazines to its users, for example, or Simon & Schuster, a Viacom property, publishing books about MTV, also a Viacom property. Still, as the HP–Compaq deal (pending at press time) suggests, the media moguls don't have a monopoly on the idea. Just the other day I came across a press release from the Zamboni Company touting its "long history of synergy with the NHL."

MOST FIRMS JUMP IN AT THE **DEEP END** WITHOUT A **LIFE JACKET**.

So what, really, is synergy? In the crudest sense, a merger creates synergy if it allows you to add one and one and get three. In economic terms, the profits that the new company earns post-merger have to be bigger than the cumulative profits the two merged companies made pre-deal. For HP's acquisition of Compaq to make sense, the new HP will have to be better—more efficient, more profitable, more productive—on its own than HP and Compaq were apart.

Given how often CEOs promise billions of dollars in savings from synergy, you'd think that wouldn't be too hard to achieve. But in fact it's almost impossible. Synergy is, for the most part, a myth. The vast majority of companies that merge in order to reap the benefits of synergy fail. According to a study by Mark Sirower of the Boston Consulting Group, about two thirds of all acquisitions actually destroy value for the acquiring company. Another study found that three quarters of all acquisitions fail to live up to their financial and strategic objectives. Part of this, to be sure, is simply because companies hurry deals and don't do enough homework before shelling out their money. When NationsBank bought BankAmerica in 1998, for instance, NationsBank reportedly spent only a few days on due diligence. Indeed, Sirower says that 8 out of 10 companies that make deals do "little pre-acquisition planning." They just jump in at the deep end without a life jacket on.

The more serious problem, though, is that companies—and, for that matter, analysts and the press—have a misguided idea of what synergy means. My favorite example of this is the cable executive who, after the AOL–Time Warner deal, was reported to have said, "MovieFone is now part of AOL. So you can call MovieFone and book your seat for the latest Warner release." This is exactly the kind of cross-promotion and cross-selling that companies like AOL Time Warner call synergy. But it isn't synergistic at all.

Why not? Well, just slapping two companies together doesn't give you synergy. You only get it when putting two companies together allows them to make goods or sell services more efficiently—or to sell more of them—than they were able to before. In the case of MovieFone and Warner Bros., even before the AOL–Time Warner merger, you could call MovieFone and buy tickets to a Warner Bros. movie. MovieFone would take its cut, Warner Bros. would get your business, and everyone would be happy. The merger changed nothing about that. All the revenue and all the profits from your transaction may now go to one company instead of two, but the total revenue and the total profit are exactly the same. The synergy here is an illusion.

Similarly, take the case of *The Rugrats Movie*. Nickelodeon owned the TV show it was based on. Paramount produced the film. Viacom owned both. A classic case of synergy, right? Not really. If Paramount had been owned by a different company, Viacom could still have sold the rights to *Rugrats* to Paramount and made a certain amount of money, and Paramount would have made the movie and made a certain amount of money, and together the two companies would have made as much as Viacom did. Nor is Paramount, as some might think, going to work especially hard to market a movie just because Viacom owns it. Paramount wants every movie it releases to succeed, and putting special emphasis on one film over others would hurt the studio, not help it.

A similar dynamic helps explain why most high-profile mergers, including Daimler-Chrysler, Vivendi–Seagram–Canal Plus, even Disney–Capital Cities/ABC, don't create any real value. In all these cases, tremendous synergies were promised, but when you look at the numbers, the mergers seem to have accomplished very little. That doesn't mean the new companies are bad companies. It just means they are not good enough to justify all the money that was spent on the deals.

Think of it this way. When you buy a company, you generally pay a premium to its current stock price. Now, the stock price reflects all the profits investors think that company will produce in the foreseeable future. So if you're going to pay more than the going rate, you have to be able to increase those profits beyond investors' expectations. If you're Viacom, you can't just have CBS grow as fast as investors thought it was going to grow. You need it to grow faster (much faster, in fact, since you spent more than $39 billion to buy CBS).

That is a very hard thing to do. This is a ferociously competitive economy. There are not too many CEOs out there who aren't keeping costs down or trying to sell their products and services in as many ways as possible. That makes it difficult to buy a company and add value. Again, take Viacom and CBS. It's hard to believe that Mel Karmazin ran CBS worse when he was by himself than he does now that he has to deal with Sumner Redstone. And if you accept that, then it's hard to see what value Viacom has added to CBS. Viacom plus CBS is certainly one plus one. But it adds up to two, not three. Of course, if cross-selling and cross-promotion were really corporate panaceas, then the merger would have been a match made in heaven. But they're not.

Synergy isn't always an illusion. Companies in similar businesses can save money by combining operations when they merge, though the savings can easily be overestimated. There are cases where customers really do prefer one-stop shopping, and if a company is able to offer a full product line, then it has profit opportunities that otherwise wouldn't have existed. And, occasionally, companies have been better off doing things in-house instead of outsourcing them. One of the greatest examples of synergy in business history—though it's not usually called that—was General Motors' acquisition of Fisher Body in 1926. Fisher made the bodies for GM cars, but when GM's needs increased, management decided it made the most sense to acquire Fisher, thereby getting the best results for the lowest possible cost. By acquiring Fisher, GM was able to make its assembly lines run the way it wanted them to, enhancing productivity and saving all the time and energy that had been wasted on bargaining.

The truth, though, is that what made sense in 1926 makes less sense today. In fact, even as companies like AOL Time Warner and HP are arguing that mergers are the only way to real efficiency, other companies have demonstrated that well-organized networks and alliances allow you to reap the benefits of partnership without any of the hassle or expense of buying another company. Dell Computer, for instance, works very closely with its suppliers, who are integral to Dell's just-in-time system (Dell builds computers to order, so it keeps almost no inventory on hand, counting on its suppliers to deliver parts as soon as it needs them). But Dell does not own its suppliers and would probably be worse off if it did. And Microsoft makes operating systems for every PC maker on the planet. But it's never felt any need to buy a PC company.

Even so, most CEOs still prefer acquisitions despite their terrible track record, which raises the obvious question: Why does the dream of synergy remain so alluring? In part, it is synergy's very ephemerality that makes it attractive. As Thomas Wilson of PricewaterhouseCoopers put it, synergies are "easy to understand... but hard to forecast accurately." It's precisely because estimates of the value of real synergies are hard to calculate, though, that it's easy to make them excessively optimistic. Or as Warren Buffett famously said, "While deals often fail in practice, they never fail in projections."

There also appears to be something deeper at work, too, which researchers Mathew Hayward and Donald Hambrick call "CEO hubris." In their 1997 study Hayward and Hambrick researched 106 major acquisitions and found that companies that were run by high-profile, overly self-confident CEOs paid the heftiest premiums when they made acquisitions. Having read their own press clippings, these CEOs believed that they could see value where the market couldn't and that they could create synergies that no one else could. But they couldn't. On average, those companies lost money for their shareholders in the end. Anticipating imaginary synergies, they spent more than they should have and set up expectations they could not fulfill. And if CEO hubris is the disease, then the perpetual quest for synergy is its most important symptom.

IN THE LEAD

When You Disagree With the Boss's Order, Do You Tell Your Staff?

BY CAROL HYMOWITZ

LAST WEEK I wrote about how managers who are excluded from decision making that affects their work can try to get included and make their views known to senior executives. But what should they do when their bosses insist that they implement decisions the managers disagree with?

Should they present a united front with senior executives and stay tight-lipped in front of subordinates in an effort to rally their staff's support? Or should they make their views known to those who report to them, while acknowledging that they have to go along with their boss's decision?

Traditionally managers have been expected to follow the former course. They have been told that they should serve as mouthpieces for their bosses and avoid voicing any dissent about a corporate decision they have been asked to implement. And they have been warned that following that approach may stir discontent and opposition among subordinates.

But a new breed of executives, many of whom have weathered mergers and other upheavals that have required them to carry out difficult directives, believe frankness is the best policy.

"No manager is ever going to agree with every decision senior management makes,"says Douglas Emond, senior vice president and chief technology officer of Eastern Bank, Lynn, Mass. And employees can usually discern when their bosses disagree with their bosses, and they will respect managers more if the managers acknowledge their opinions while still motivating their staffs to implement the decision, Mr. Emond believes.

"The key is to know why senior management wants you to do what it asks, to understand its thought process, and to be able to convey that to subordinates," he adds.

MR. Emond has held management posts in the U.S. and overseas at a half dozen financial service and other companies. With each move, he has taken on new challenges and learned to trust his own thinking, he says. "As a manager, you're not paid to agree with everything your bosses decide, but to perform tasks."

Four years ago he was chief operating officer and chief technology officer at BankBoston when Fleet Financial acquired it. While many BankBoston senior executives quickly headed for the door, he stayed on and became a member of the merger integration team. His responsibility was to integrate eight businesses at the two companies, helping to decide strategy and a new management team while also cutting staff.

When he disagreed with a decision about which senior executive would oversee one particular business and what the business's future strategy would be, Mr. Emond decided that he wasn't going to hide his views. "I told them I was given orders, and this is the way it's going to go," he says. His frankness, he believes, "better prepared people to handle what was coming" and also won him the trust and support of his management staff, which was involved in the tough task of cutting about 50% of the staff.

Mr. Emond ties his willingness to be frank with employees to a leadership lesson he learned from his father, also a banker. When his father learned that a hard-working subordinate had lied on his job application about graduating from college, "instead of firing him, he took the employee aside and asked him, 'what is it going to take for you to get that degree,'" Mr. Emond says. "My father believed in doing the right thing, and he taught me that being a leader means being true to yourself and to your people."

LAURIE SPOON, vice president of corporate communications and investor relations at software-maker Selectica Inc. in San Jose, Calif., says that when she is handed a decision she doesn't agree with, she always asks the company's chief executive and chief financial officer, "what's the reason for this? Sometimes they tell me something I didn't know, so I can explain the issues behind the decision to my staff," she says.

She also asks her bosses for help when they ask her to implement a tough task. Recently, when she and her staff were asked to put together the company's annual report in 10 days, she told the CEO and chief financial officer that they would have to be available to help her plan content. "We sat together in a room and wrote the open letter to stakeholders, whereas if we had more time we would have gone back and forth with drafts," she says.

Meanwhile, a designer on her staff suggested that adding a pocket to the back of the report for business cards would allow it to be used by the company's sales team, serving two purposes. "I encourage my staff to make adjustments to decisions they're handed, in order to make them better," she says.

Case: *Cub Scout Pack 81*

Things certainly have changed over the past six years for Cub Scout Pack 81. Six years ago, the pack was on the verge of disbanding. There were barely enough boys for an effective den, and they had been losing membership for as long as anyone could remember. The cub master was trying to pass his job onto any parent foolish enough to take the helm of a sinking ship, and the volunteer fire department that sponsored the pack was openly considering dropping it.

But that was six years ago. Today the pack has one of the largest memberships of any in the Lancaster/Lebanon Council. It has started its own Boy Scout troop, into which the Webelos can graduate, and it has received a presidential citation for its antidrug program. The pack consistently wins competitions with other packs in the Council, and the fire department is very happy about its sponsorship. Membership in the pack is now around 60 cubs at all levels, and they have a new cub master.

"Parents want their boys to be in a successful program," says Cub Master Mike Murphy. "Look, I can't do everything. We depend on the parents and the boys to get things done. Everybody understands that we want to have a successful program, and that means that we all have to participate to achieve that success. I can't do it all, but if we can unleash the energy these boys have, there isn't anything in the Cub Scout Program we can't do!"

It was not always like that. "About five years ago we placed fourth for our booth in the Scout Expo at the mall," says Mike. "Everybody was surprised! Who was Pack 81? We were all elated! It was one of the best things to happen to this pack in years. Now, if we don't win at least something, we're disappointed. Our kids expect to win, and so do their parents."

Fourth place at the Scout Expo eventually led to several first places. Success leads to success, and the community around pack 81 knows it.

"Last year, we made our annual presentation to the boys and their parents at the elementary school. We were with several other packs, each one trying to drum up interest in their program. When everyone was finished, the boys and their parents went over to the table of the pack that most interested them. We must have had well over half of the people at our table. I was embarrassed! They were standing six or seven deep in front of our table, and there was virtually nobody in front of the others."

Using the Case on *Cub Scout Pack 81*

This case shows what can happen to any organization when the people in the organization are motivated and have goals. Success builds upon success, and pack 81 is now successful. The role of the leader is to ensure the success of the organization by creating an environment in which the participants (the Cubs and their families) can continue to be winners.

Questions for Discussion

1. What do you think was the major change in pack 81's situation?
2. How does the cub master "spread the wealth"? That is, the credit and the work associated with operating the pack?
3. How do you think the success of pack 81 has affected the other Cub Scout packs in the area? Why?
4. If you were a potential Cub Scout, or a parent of a potential Cub Scout, why would you be interested in pack 81?
5. Part of leadership has been defined as getting others to accept your goals as their own. Do you think that Cub Master Mike Murphy has been successful in doing that? Why or why not?

Exercise: *Listening*

Procedure

The instructor should:

1. Instruct the students to write down the numbers 1 through 10 on a sheet of paper.
2. Advise the student that the questions will be read to them twice, and their task is to record an answer to each question on the sheet of paper.
3. Emphasize to the students that they will not be allowed to ask for any clarification. Likewise, they may not discuss the question or answer with any other student.
4. Read each of the following questions (twice) aloud to the class.

Questions

1. Does England have a fourth of July?
2. Why can't a man living in Winston-Salem, North Carolina, be buried west of the Mississippi River?

3. If you had only one match and entered a room in which there was a kerosene lamp, an oil burner, and a woodburning stove, which would you light first?
4. Some months have 30 days, some have 31; how many have 28?
5. If a doctor gave you three pills and told you to take one every half hour, how long would they last?
6. I have in my hand three U.S. coins totalling 55 cents in value. One is not a nickel. What are the coins?
7. Is it legal in Louisiana for a man to marry his widow's sister?
8. How many two-cent stamps are there in a dozen?
9. How many animals of each species did Moses take aboard the Ark with him?
10. An archaeologist claimed to have discovered some gold coins dated 46 B.C. Do you believe that she did? Why, or why not?

Alternate Question A: An aircraft flying south crashes so that the wreckage is half in the United States and half in Mexico. In which country would you bury the survivors?

Alternate Question B: How many birthdates does the average woman have?

Alternate Question C: A farmer had seventeen sheep. All but nine died. How many did he have left?

Alternate Question D: How far can a dog run into the woods?

Questions for Discussion

1. Think about the barriers to effective communication. Which, if any, of these barriers affected the communication process in this exercise (perceptual differences, language and meaning, noise, etc.)?
2. How did the medium of communication affect the communication process? Do you think you could have done better if the questions had been presented in written form rather than vocal form?
3. What effect did the time constraint have on your interpretation of the message?

Answers:

1. Yes, it follows July 3rd; 2. The man is not dead so he cannot be buried; 3. Light the match first; 4. All months have 28 days; 5. One hour. Take one immediately, followed by a second a half-hour later, and the third one hour after the first; 6. Two quarters and a nickel (the question says one is not a nickel); 7. No, the man is dead; 8. Twelve; 9. None—Noah was aboard the Ark, not Moses; 10. No, since at the time the coin was made, there was no way for someone to know it was 46 years before Christ was born; Alternate Question A: You don't bury survivors; Alternate Question B: One birthdate; Alternate Question C: Nine; Alternate Question D: Half way (because then it is on the way out).

Case: Cub Scout Pack 81; Exercise: Listening, Fred Maidment, McGraw-Hill/Dushkin, 2000.

UNIT 6

Controlling

Unit Selections

Key Points to Consider

- Control in any organization takes a variety of forms. Which one do you think is the most important for a profit-making organization? A not-for-profit-making organization?
- What impact do you think technology will have on the way that organizations control their operations in the future?
- How should organizations respond to violence in the workplace? What can be done to prevent it? What can be done once it has happened?

DUSHKIN ONLINE **Links: www.dushkin.com/online/**
These sites are annotated in the World Wide Web pages.

Bill Lindsay's Home Page
http://www.nku.edu/~lindsay/

Computer and Network Security
http://www.vtcif.telstra.com.au/info/security.html

Internal Auditing World Wide Web
http://www.bitwise.net/iawww/

Office of Financial Management
http://www.doi.gov/

The Potential Downside of the National Information Infrastructure
http://www.annenberg.nwu.edu/pubs/downside/

Total Quality Leadership (TQL) vs. Management by Results
http://deming.eng.clemson.edu/pub/den/files/tql.txt

Workplace Violence
http://www.osha-slc.gov/SLTC/workplaceviolence/

Managers must plan, organize, and direct the organization, but how do they know if they are doing a good job? Controlling is the function of management that evaluates their efforts. Is the plan a good one? Is the firm adequately organized to implement the plan effectively? Is the plan being implemented so as to maximize the desired results? What changes need to be made in the plan, or the organization, or the implementation, or any combination thereof to help the firm better achieve its goals?

It is necessary to evaluate the firm's results against some sort of criteria. For most firms, those criteria are often financial, defined in terms of profits. However, it is necessary to define and understand control, and to engage actively in procedures that will lead to effective management, as Douglas McGregor wrote in the classic article, "An Uneasy Look at Performance Appraisal."

Profitability is not the only measure of effectiveness. In fact, the entire not-for-profit sector of the economy refuses to use profitability as a measure of success. Measures come in other forms for not-for-profits as exemplified by the unqualified success of the March of Dimes in winning the battle against the deadly, crippling disease of polio. The March of Dimes was a success by any standard, but profitability would not be an appropriate criterion for it or other similar ventures. The key is whether the organization has achieved its goals, which may or may not include profitability.

When managers talk about control in the modern corporate sense, they really are talking about two different levels of control. The first is the traditional approach to controlling the firm's operation. This control is centered around the flow of information to determine what is going on in the organization as a whole. New technologies are making this easier. In this era of hostile takeovers, mergers, and acquisitions, managers are seeking to maintain control of their firms and not lose them to someone else in some new financial arrangement.

Shareholders are also awakening to this realization in terms of profitability and other issues with which management has to deal. Management is discovering that decisions concerning the firm can no longer be made solely on the basis of a good financial return. Decision makers must consider what is socially and politically acceptable to the stockholders. The decision of many firms to leave South Africa to protest apartheid was just one manifestation of the new awareness of nonfinancial goals and objectives. With the new government in place in South Africa, many firms have decided to return.

But financial control is important. It is obviously a chief concern of many firms, especially small ones, because it is usually the area where they run into trouble. Financial control is the basis of all the other types of control in the organization, because the people who own the company have the final say in what the firm does. Such control makes it possible for management to protect itself from corporate raiders, as well as giving it the ability to direct the organization in a successful manner.

Security has also taken on new importance. With the advent of the computer and the World Wide Web, most information that was once the sole possession of the organization may become public knowledge. "How Safe Is Your Job?" is a question of greater concern than it was in the past, as firms need to know

what they can do to prevent workplace violence. But traditional concerns of employee theft must also be addressed.

Production control is probably the area in which the Japanese have made the most strides in recent years. U.S. and European firms have imported many of the ideas and techniques used in Japan over the past 20 years, and the Japanese themselves have set up their own plants in the United States, demonstrating that their techniques are transferable. Many changes have taken place in the area of production, including the introduction of computers and robots. Developments do not just involve machines, they include standards, policies, and, most especially, people. As organizations strive to become more effective and efficient, it will become necessary to redesign the processes that a company uses.

"Cost vs. Quality" and customer service are now two of the hottest areas in the business world. Supply chain management is bringing all the pieces together, from raw material to the final customer, in the most efficient and economical manner, and customer service has always been an important aspect of every organization's efforts.

Are managers more responsive to human values than personnel people? If so, we had better join them in taking...

An Uneasy Look at Performance Appraisal

By Douglas McGregor

Performance appraisal within management ranks has become standard practice in many companies during the past twenty years, and is currently being adopted by many others, often as an important feature of management development programs. The more the method is used, the more uneasy I grow over the unstated assumptions which lie behind it. Moreover, with some searching, I find that a number of people both in education and in industry share my misgivings. This article, therefore, has two purposes:

- To examine the conventional performance appraisal plan which requires the manager to pass judgment on the personal worth of subordinates.
- To describe an alternative which places on the subordinate the primary responsibility for establishing performance goals and appraising progress toward them.

Current Programs

Formal performance appraisal plans are designed to meet three needs, one for the organization and two for the individual:

1. They provide systematic judgments to back up salary increases, promotions, transfers, and sometimes demotions or terminations.
2. They are a means of telling a subordinate how he is doing, and suggesting needed changes in his behavior, attitudes, skills, or job knowledge; they let him know "where he stands" with the boss.
3. They also are being increasingly used as a basis for the coaching and counseling of the individual by the superior.

Problem of Resistance

Personnel administrators are aware that appraisal programs tend to run into resistance from the managers who are expected to administer them. Even managers who admit the necessity of such programs frequently balk at the process—especially the interview part. As a result, some companies do not communicate appraisal results to the individual, despite the general conviction that the subordinate has a right to know his superior's opinion so he can correct his weaknesses.

The boss's resistance is usually attributed to the following causes:

- A normal dislike of criticizing a subordinate (and perhaps having to argue about it).
- Lack of skill needed to handle the interviews.
- Dislike of a new procedure with its accompanying changes in ways of operating.
- Mistrust of the validity of the appraisal instrument.

To meet this problem, formal controls—scheduling, reminders, and so on—are often instituted. It is common experience that without them fewer than half the appraisal interviews are actually held. But even controls do not necessarily work. Thus:

> In one company with a well-planned and carefully administered appraisal program, an opinion poll included two questions regarding appraisals. More than 90% of those answering the questionnaire approved the idea of appraisals. They wanted to know how they stood. Some 40% went on to say that they had never had the experience of being told—yet the files showed that over four-fifths of them had signed a form testify-

> ing that they had been through an appraisal interview, some of them several times!
>
> The respondents had no reason to lie, nor was there the slightest supposition that their superiors had committed forgery. The probable explanation is that the superiors, being basically resistant to the plan, had conducted the interviews in such a perfunctory manner that many subordinates did not recognize what was going on.

Training programs designed to teach the skills of appraising and interviewing do help, but they seldom eliminate managerial resistance entirely. The difficulties connected with "negative appraisals" remain a source of genuine concern. There is always some discomfort involved in telling a subordinate he is not doing well. The individual who is "coasting" during the few years prior to retirement after servicing his company competently for many years presents a special dilemma to the boss who is preparing to interview him.

Nor does a shift to a form of group appraisal solve the problem. Though the group method tends to have greater validity and, properly administered, can equalize varying standards of judgment, it does not ease the difficulty inherent in the interview. In fact, the superior's discomfort is often intensified when he must base his interview on the results of a *group* discussion of the subordinate's worth. Even if the final judgments have been his, he is not free to discuss the things said by others which may have influenced him.

The Underlying Cause

What should we think about a method—however valuable for meeting organizational needs—which produces such results in a wide range of companies with a variety of appraisal plans? The problem is one that cannot be dismissed lightly.

Perhaps this intuitive managerial reaction to conventional performance appraisal plans shows a deep but unrecognized wisdom. In my view, it does not reflect anything so simple as resistance to change, or dislike for personnel technique, or lack of skill, or mistrust for rating scales. Rather, managers seem to be expressing very real misgivings, which they find difficult to put into words. This could be the underlying cause:

> The conventional approach, unless handled with consummate skill and delicacy, constitutes something dangerously close to a violation of the integrity of the personality. Managers are uncomfortable when they are put in the position of "playing God." The respect we hold for the inherent value of the individual leaves us distressed when we must take responsibility for judging the personal worth of a fellow man. Yet the conventional approach to performance appraisal forces us, not only to make such judgments and to see them acted upon, but also to communicate them to those we have judged. Small wonder we resist!

The modern emphasis upon the manager as a leader who strives to *help* his subordinates achieve both their own and the company's objectives is hardly consistent with the judicial role demanded by most appraisal plans. If the manager must put on his judicial hat occasionally, he does it reluctantly and with understandable qualms. Under such conditions it is unlikely that the subordinate will be any happier with the results than will the boss. It will not be surprising, either, if he fails to recognize that he has been told where he stands.

Of course, managers cannot escape making judgments about subordinates. Without such evaluations, salary and promotion policies cannot be administered sensibly. But are subordinates like products on an assembly line, to be accepted or rejected as a result of an inspection process? The inspection process may be made more objective or more accurate through research on the appraisal instrument, through training of the "inspectors," or through introducing group appraisal; the subordinate may be "reworked" by coaching or counseling before the final decision to accept or reject him; but as far as the assumptions of the conventional appraisal process are concerned, we still have what is practically identical with a program for product inspection.

On this interpretation, then, resistance to conventional appraisal programs is eminently sound. It reflect an unwillingness to treat human beings like physical objects. The needs of the organization are obviously important, but when they come into conflict with our convictions about the worth and the dignity of the human personality, one or the other must give.

Indeed, by the fact of their resistance managers are saying that the organization must yield in the face of this fundamental human value. And they are thus being more sensitive than are personnel administrators and social scientists whose business it is to be concerned with the human problems of industry!

A New Approach

If this analysis is correct, the task before us is clear. We must find a new plan—not a compromise to hide the dilemma, but a bold move to resolve the issue.

A number of writers are beginning to approach the whole subject of management from the point of view of basic social values. Peter Drucker's concept of "management by objectives"[1] offers an unusually promising framework within which we can seek a solution. Several companies, notably General Mills, Incorporated, and General Electric Company, have been exploring different methods of appraisal which rest upon assumptions consistent with Drucker's philosophy.

Responsibility on Subordinate

This approach calls on the subordinate to establish short-term performance goals for *himself*. The superior enters the process actively only *after* the subordinate has (a) done a good deal of thinking about his job, (b) made a careful assessment of his own strengths and weaknesses, and (c) formulated some specific plans to accomplish his goals. The superior's role is to help the man relate his self-appraisal, his "targets," and his plans for the ensuing period to the realities of the organization.

The first step in this process is to arrive at a clear statement of the major features of the job. Rather than a formal job description, this is a document drawn up *by the subordinate* after studying the company-approved statement. It defines the broad areas of his responsibility as they actually work out in practice. The boss and employee discuss the draft jointly and modify it as may be necessary until both of them agree that it is adequate.

Working from this statement of responsibilities, the subordinate then establishes his goals on "targets" for a period of, say, six months. These targets are *specific* actions which the man proposes to take, i.e., setting up regular staff meetings to improve communication, reorganizing the office, completing or undertaking a certain study. Thus, they are explicitly stated and accompanied by a detailed account of the actions he proposes to take to reach them. This document is, in turn, discussed with the superior and modified until both are satisfied with it.

At the conclusion of the six-month period, the subordinate makes *his own* appraisal of what he has accomplished relative to the targets he had set earlier. He substantiates it with factual data wherever possible. The "interview" is an examination by superior and subordinate together of the subordinate's self-appraisal, and it culminates in a resetting of targets for the next six months.

Of course, the superior has veto power at each step of this process; in an organizational hierarchy anything else would be unacceptable. However, in practice he rarely needs to exercise it. Most subordinates tend to underestimate both their potentialities and their achievements. Moreover, subordinates normally have an understandable wish to satisfy their boss, and are quite willing to adjust their targets or appraisals if the superior feels they are unrealistic. Actually, a much more common problem is to resist the subordinates' tendency to want the boss to tell them what to write down.

Analysis vs. Appraisal

This approach to performance appraisal differs profoundly from the conventional one, for it shifts the emphasis from *appraisal* to *analysis*. This implies a more positive approach. No longer is the subordinate being examined by the superior so that his weaknesses may be determined; rather, he is examining himself, in order to define not only his weaknesses but also his strengths and potentials. The importance of this shift of emphasis should not be underestimated. It is basic to each of the specific differences which distinguish this approach from the conventional one.

The first of these differences arises from the subordinate's new role in the process. He becomes an active agent, not a passive "object." He is no longer a pawn in a chess game called management development.

Effective development of managers does not include coercing them (no matter how benevolently) into acceptance of the goals of the enterprise, nor does it mean manipulating their behavior to suit organizational needs. Rather, it calls for creating a relationship within which a man can take responsibility for developing his own potentialities, plan for himself, and learn from putting his plans into action. In the process he can gain a genuine sense of satisfaction, for he is utilizing his own capabilities to achieve simultaneously both his objectives and those of the organization. Unless this is the nature of the relationship, "development" becomes a euphemism.

Who Knows Best?

One of the main differences of this approach is that it rests on the assumption that the individual knows—or can learn—more than anyone else about his own capabilities, needs, strengths and weaknesses, and goals. In the end, only he can determine what is best for his development. The conventional approach, on the other hand, makes the assumption that the superior can know enough about the subordinate to decide what is best for him.

No available methods can provide the superior with the knowledge he needs to make such decisions. Ratings, aptitude and personality tests, and the superior's necessarily limited knowledge of the man's performance yield at best an imperfect picture. Even the most extensive psychological counseling (assuming the superior possess the competence for it) would not solve the problem because the product of counseling is self-insight on the part of the *counselee*.

(Psychological tests are not being condemned by this statement. On the contrary, they have genuine value in competent hands. Their use by professionals as part of the process of screening applicants for employment does not raise the same questions as their use to "diagnose" the personal worth of accepted members of a management team. Even in the latter instance the problem we are discussing would not arise if test results and interpretations were given *to the individual himself*, to be shared with superiors at his discretion.)

The proper role for the superior, then, is the one that falls naturally to him under the suggested plan: helping the subordinate relate his career planning to the needs and realities of the organization. In the discussions the boss can use his knowledge of the organization to help the subordinate establish targets and methods for achieving them which will (a) lead to increased knowledge and skill, (b) contribute to organizational objectives, and (c) test the subordinate's appraisal of himself.

This is help which the subordinate wants. He knows well that the rewards and satisfactions he seeks from his career as a manager depend on his contribution to organizational objectives. He is also aware that the superior knows more completely than he what is required for success in this organization and *under this boss*. The superior, then, is the person who can help him test the soundness of his goals and his plans for achieving them. Quite clearly the knowledge and active participation of *both* superior and subordinate are necessary components of this approach.

If the superior accepts this role, he need not become a judge of the subordinate's personal worth. He is not telling, deciding, criticizing, or praising—not "playing God." He finds himself listening, using his own knowledge of the organization as a basis for advising, guiding, encouraging his subordinates to develop their own potentialities. Incidentally, this often leads the superior to important insights about himself and his impact on others.

Looking to the Future

Another significant difference is that the emphasis is on the future rather than the past. The purpose of the plan is to establish realistic targets and to seek the most effective ways of reaching them. Appraisal thus becomes a means to a *constructive* end. The 60-year-old "coaster" can be encouraged to set performance goals for himself and to make a fair appraisal of his progress toward them. Even the subordinate who has failed can be helped to consider what moves will be best for himself. The superior rarely finds himself facing the uncomfortable prospect of denying a subordinate's personal worth. A transfer or even a demotion can be worked out without the connotation of a "sentence by the judge."

Performance vs. Personality

Finally, the accent is on *performance*, on actions relative to goals. There is less tendency for the personality of the subordinate to become an issue. The superior, instead of finding himself in the position of a psychologist or a therapist, can become a coach helping the subordinate to reach his own decisions on the specific steps that will enable him to reach his targets. Such counseling as may be required demands no deep analysis of the personal motivations or basic adjustment of the subordinate. To illustrate:

Consider a subordinate who is hostile, short-tempered, uncooperative, insecure. The superior need not make any psychological diagnosis. The "target setting" approach naturally directs the subordinate's attention to ways and means of obtaining better interdepartmental collaboration, reducing complaints, winning the confidence of the men under him. Rather than facing the troublesome prospect of forcing his own psychological diagnosis on the subordinate, the superior can, for example, help the individual plan ways of getting "feedback" concerning his impact on his associates and subordinates as a basis for self-appraisal and self-improvement.

There is little chance that a man who is involved in a process like this will be in the dark about where he stands, or that he will forget he is the principal participant in his own development and responsible for it.

A New Attitude

As a consequence of these differences we may expect the growth of a different attitude toward appraisal on the part of superior and subordinate alike.

The superior will gain real satisfaction as he learns to help his subordinates integrate their personal goals with the needs of the organization so that both are served. Once the subordinate has worked out a mutually satisfactory plan of action, the superior can delegate to him the responsibility for putting it into effect. He will see himself in a consistent managerial role rather than being forced to adopt the basically incompatible role of either the judge or the psychologist.

Unless there is a basic personal antagonism between the two men (in which case the relationship should be terminated), the superior can conduct these interviews so that both are actively involved in seeking the right basis for constructive action. The organization, the boss, and the subordinate all stand to gain. Under such circumstances the opportunities for learning and for genuine development of both parties are maximal.

The particular mechanics are of secondary importance. The needs of the organization in the administration of salary and promotion policies can easily be met within the framework of the analysis process. The machinery of the program can be adjusted to the situation. No universal list of rating categories is required. The complications of subjective or prejudiced judgment, of varying standards, of attempts to quantify qualitative data, all can be minimized. In fact, *no* formal machinery is required.

Problems of Judgment

I have deliberately slighted the many problems of judgment involved in administering promotions and salaries. These are by no means minor, and this approach will not automatically solve them. However, I believe that if we are prepared to recognize the fundamental problem inherent in the conventional approach, ways can be found to temper our present administrative methods.

And if this approach is accepted, the traditional ingenuity of management will lead to the invention of a variety of methods for its implementation. The mechanics of some conventional plans can be adjusted to be consistent with this point of view. Obviously, a program utilizing ratings of the personal characteristics of subordinates would not be suitable, but one which emphasizes *behavior* might be.

Of course, managerial skill is required. No method will eliminate that. This method can fail as readily as any other in the clumsy hands of insensitive or indifferent or power-seeking managers. But even the limited experience of a few companies with this approach indicates that managerial *resistance* is substantially reduced. As a consequence, it is easier to gain the collaboration of managers in developing the necessary skills.

Cost in Time

There is one unavoidable cost: the manager must spend considerably more time in implementing a program of this kind. It is not unusual to take a couple of days to work through the initial establishment of responsibilities and goals with each individual. And a periodic appraisal may require several hours rather than the typical 20 minutes.

Reaction to this cost will undoubtedly vary. The management that considers the development of its human resources to be the primary means of achieving the economic objectives of the organization will not be disturbed. It will regard the necessary guidance and coaching as among the most important functions of every superior.

Conclusion

I have sought to show that the conventional approach to performance appraisal stands condemned as a personnel method. It places the manager in the untenable position of judging the personal worth of his subordinates, and of acting on these judgments. No manager possesses, nor could he acquire, the skill necessary to carry out this responsibility effectively. Few would even be willing to accept it if they were fully aware of the implications involved.

It is this unrecognized aspect of conventional appraisal programs which produces the widespread uneasiness and even open resistance of management to appraisals and especially to the appraisal interview.

A sounder approach, which places the major responsibility on the subordinate for establishing performance goals and appraising progress toward them, avoids the major weaknesses of the old plan and benefits the organization by stimulating the development of the subordinate. It is true that more managerial skill and the investment of a considerable amount of time are required, but the greater motivation and the more effective development of subordinates can justify these added costs.

Note

1. See Peter Drucker, *The Practice of Management* (New York, Harper & Brothers, 1954).

INTERNATIONAL ACCOUNTING

TRANSFER PRICING: A Truly Global Concern

By Steven D. Felgran and Mito Yamada

As businesses continue globalization efforts and fiscal authorities become increasingly concerned with claiming their fair share of tax revenues, transfer pricing has evolved from primarily a United States' concern to a truly global one.

Numerous tax authorities have followed the lead of the Internal Revenue Service (IRS), enforcing the "arm's length standard" for transfer pricing by means of documentation requirements with penalties for noncompliance.

This heightened scrutiny has caused multinational corporations to face increased risk of transfer pricing audits and income adjustments, particularly in the U.S., Canada, the United Kingdom, Germany, France and Japan. The introduction of the euro has further increased exposure, due to the greater pricing transparency caused by a single European currency.

Global transfer pricing documentation has become increasingly important as multinational corporations need to document that their multiple transfer prices are consistent with the arm's length standard. Taxpayers perform detailed documentation studies in order to show compliance with rules and to avoid penalties in numerous jurisdictions. As the arm's length principle underlies the transfer pricing regulations of most tax jurisdictions, global documentation provides a consistent and effective solution that can be efficiently prepared.

Taxpayers now have the option of using state-of-the-art software programs as a management tool to manage transfer pricing systems and possibly reduce their company's effective tax rate. Software can be used to analyze complex transfer prices quickly and generate country-specific or global documentation.

U.S. and OECD Requirements

The U.S. government was the first to enforce the arm's length standard as the overarching principle in setting transfer prices when, in 1994, the IRS issued final regulations accompanying section 482 of the Internal Revenue Code requiring that related party transactions meet the standard. A transaction meets the standard if its results are consistent with the results that would have been realized if uncontrolled taxpayers had engaged in a comparable transaction under comparable circumstances.

The final penalty regulations accompanying section 6662 became effective in 1995 and provide that valuation misstatement penalties can be imposed for failure to comply with the section 482 regulations. The IRS has authority, in certain circumstances, to reallocate income among related parties if it determines that such reallocation is necessary to clearly reflect income. Such penalties may be up to 40 percent of the additional taxes that result from income adjustments. Taxpayers can avoid penalties for transfer pricing adjustments by complying with the standard, reporting arm's length results on their income tax returns, contemporaneously documenting their transfer pricing using methods described in the section 482 regulations and providing that documentation to the IRS upon request.

Similar to the section 482 regulations, the Organization for Economic Cooperation and Development (OECD) Transfer Pricing Guidelines for Multinational Enterprises and Tax Administrators ("OECD guidelines") endorse the arm's length principle as the international standard for the evaluation of intragroup pricing.

A transaction is considered to be compliant with the arm's length principle when conditions imposed and prices paid in related-party transactions are comparable to those imposed and paid by independent enterprises in comparable circumstances. Most transfer pricing regimes outside of the U.S. have adopted the OECD guidelines, thus subscribing to the arm's length principle.

Enforcement Spreading

In recent years, some of the leading industrialized countries have enacted new regulations that enforce strict transfer pricing requirements. A summary of current practices follows:

United Kingdom: The U.K. recently revised its rules, including them within its self-assessment regime, the Corporation Tax Self Assessment (CTSA). Under the new rules, which fully adopt the OECD guidelines and apply to accounting periods ending on or after July 1, 1999, taxpayers are required to apply the arm's length principle in computing profits for tax purposes. Taxpayers must also prepare and maintain sufficient transfer pricing documentation as part of routine tax preparation to have a complete return.

Also, the Inland Revenue may impose penalties if it determines that the tax return was not prepared in compliance with the arm's length principle or that the return was submitted fraudulently or negligently. In such cases, penalties of up to 100 percent of any additional tax can be imposed, and penalties of up to £3,000 can be charged for failure to keep proper records documenting transfer prices.

Canada: Major legislative changes, made in 1997, have resulted in more stringent requirements that broadly follow the OECD guidelines. Taxpayers are required to disclose all non–arm's length transactions with foreign affiliates and to confirm that they have "prepared or obtained" all the relevant documentation to support their transfer prices. Penalties will be charged if an adjustment is made and the tax authorities conclude that the taxpayer did not make "reasonable efforts" to prepare the appropriate supporting documentation by the tax return due date. These penalties equal 10 percent of the full amount of the adjustments made in a tax year beginning after 1998, but only when the adjustments exceed the lesser of 10 percent of the taxpayer's gross revenue for the year and Cdn $5 million.

Germany: The proposed regulations—in draft form since August 2000—require that transfer pricing documentation following the OECD guidelines be provided at the request of the tax authorities at the time of audit. Although no specific penalties exist under the current legislation, severe penalties, including imprisonment, can be applied in case of fraud.

> Powerful software programs enable using a single application for analysis of multi-country related-party flows of tangibles, intangibles, services and loans.

It is expected that the regulations will remain in draft form for some time, as the highest tax court has ruled that no legal basis exists in Germany for field tax auditors to demand special transfer pricing documentation. However, the German Ministry of Finance plans to create a legal basis for the documentation requirement.

France: The importance of transfer pricing documentation has increased due to recent legislative changes. As French tax authorities have heightened their interest, taxpayers are advised to prepare documentation showing that transfer prices are in line with the regulations, which closely follow the OECD guidelines. Penalties of 40 to 80 percent of additional tax may be imposed if a taxpayer is considered to have acted fraudulently or negligently. In addition, the taxpayer may be disqualified from seeking relief from double taxation that occurs as a result of the adjustment. Fixed fines of Fr 50,000 may also be charged for not complying with the tax regulations.

Japan: The National Tax Administration (NTA) has adhered generally to the spirit of the OECD guidelines in creating its regulations. Although Japanese taxpayers are not required to maintain documentation, a penalty of 10 percent of the additional tax due may be imposed if an adjustment is made, and the penalty is increased to 15 percent if the additional tax due is more than 500,000 yen or more than the amount of tax paid on the original return—whichever is greater. Also, in cases of fraud, a 35 percent penalty may be charged separately. It's expected that the regulations will become stricter in the next few years as the government reviews current regulations to possibly make Japanese transfer pricing taxation more compatible with other countries' systems.

The Euro and Globalization

Taxpayers with European operations should reconsider the transfer pricing systems currently in place in light of the transition to a single European currency. The euro affects inter-company pricing structures in three ways.

- *More competitive pricing.* Customers will be better able to make price comparisons without having to consider exchange rates. This will give the euro the effect of pushing prices for the same goods—that may differ by country—toward a common value. This more competitive pricing will mean that suppliers will need to readjust pricing and margins at all levels, thus placing strains on existing inter-company pricing structures and profits.
- *Price and market changes affect the benchmarks that companies may have used for setting or validating inter-company transactions in Europe.* Changes in prices and profits driven by the common currency will mean that arm's length roy-

alty rates, comparable uncontrolled prices, resale margins and operating profit standards (e.g., returns on operating assets) may differ greatly pre- and post-euro.

- *The clarity that a single currency brings to transfer pricing will enable tax authorities to more easily challenge intra-group pricing assumptions.* Pre-euro, a multiple-country transfer pricing study might have involved a complex, exchange rate-driven justification of profit and loss allocations. The euro changes currency risk profiles and brings a transparency that necessitates revisiting intragroup pricing to ensure an accurate reflection of risks beyond exchange rate exposure.

To avoid the challenges listed above, taxpayers can update their policies to reflect current conditions and ensure that the new policies are well documented. While European tax authorities may not yet approach transfer pricing consistently, multinationals do, and with the euro in view, the timing is good time for an inter-company policy and documentation review.

Global Documentation and Planning

Fortunately, from the standpoint of efficiency in generating transfer pricing documentation, the arm's length standard is the firmly established principle underlying inter-company pricing rules. Combining this common principle with the increasing desire by tax authorities to see contemporaneous evidence of compliance, it's clear that transfer pricing documentation is most efficiently done once for global use and distributed as needed.

A point of debate is whether in the course of a single project, the taxpayer produces a single document or multiple documents that are somewhat customized, either for better application in multiple taxing jurisdictions or for additional detail regarding some local complexity that may be irrelevant to other taxing jurisdictions. Indeed, global transfer pricing documentation projects may provide substantial advantages to a multinational, including:

- Centralized control of worldwide transfer pricing and documentation at group headquarters.
- Current compendium of information by legal entity readily available to headquarters personnel.
- Appreciation by affiliates of actions that affect group tax rates, through participation in an organized fact gathering process designed to understand functions and arm's length benchmarks.
- Significant leveraging of project information and cost-effective preparation of documentation.
- Consistent presentation of the multinational's transfer pricing posture across jurisdictions.
- Greater consideration of the global business environment faced by the multinational than individual country studies.

Technology and Transfer Pricing

As global planning and documentation becomes increasingly important, tax directors now have the option of using software programs to manage and document their processes. Powerful software programs enable using a single application for analysis of multi-country related-party flows of tangibles, intangibles, services and loans.

With software programs, tax professionals can use the financial information of publicly traded companies provided by outside databases to determine whether their transfer prices meet the arm's length standard. Software programs also allow tax professionals to collect and organize information and to generate documentation studies to help meet tax authority requirements.

The software will become considerably more powerful when it becomes available in a Web-enabled version, allowing a multinational's tax professionals in all locations to maintain transfer pricing-related information on one single platform. The software can also be used as a management tool, to possibly reduce a company's effective tax rate by testing different scenarios of a company's functions and risks in various locations.

One such product, KPMG's Interpreter™ software, is currently being upgraded to a fully functional Web-enabled version that can be made available on a company's server or through access to KPMG's server. The software offers transfer pricing guidance in over 30 countries and can be used to document inter-company transactions for each of these and other countries that generally follow the OECD guidelines.

As globalization continues, transfer pricing is becoming one of the most challenging issues multinationals face. As scrutiny becomes more prevalent, and a single European currency makes transfer pricing more transparent, multinationals are well-advised to prepare global transfer pricing documentation. A global approach helps to protect taxpayers from potential penalties and can support coordinating, planning and documenting transfer prices worldwide.

Steven D. Felgran, Ph.D., is KPMG LLP's National Partner in Charge—Transfer Pricing, based in New York City, and Mito Yamada is a Senior Consultant with KPMG Fidal, based in Paris. The authors state that this information is of a general nature and is not intended to address the circumstances of any individual or entity. They suggest seeking professional advice before taking action.

How Safe Is *Your* Job?: The Threat of WORKPLACE VIOLENCE

"Changes in the American workplace have created fertile ground for breeding discontent and potential violence."

BY LAURENCE MILLER

"A DISGRUNTLED [pick one: postal worker, law client, insurance claimant, store customer, hospital patient, factory worker] stormed into a place of business yesterday, killing six people before turning the gun on himself. Film at 11." You've heard this one before. Often, the lead story is followed by interviews with coworkers or associates whose comments almost invariably follow one of two main themes:

"He was always a little strange, you know, quiet. Kept to himself a lot, didn't get along with too many people, but came in, did his job, and never caused any real trouble. Certainly, nobody figured him for the violent type. Man, we didn't see this one coming." Or: "Damnit, I knew it was just a matter of time till something like this happened. This guy was bad news, a ticking bomb, and we all knew it. But there were no precautions or any real kind of discipline at all. We tried to tell management, but they just got annoyed, said there was nothing they could do, and told us not to stir up trouble. When he finally snapped, we were sitting ducks."

Most traumas I deal with in my clinical and forensic psychology practice strike suddenly and without warning or control. In those cases, the emphasis is on treating the victims, survivors, and their families after the fact. However, in virtually no other high-risk area is education, training, planning, and prevention so vital as in the case of workplace violence. In many cases, you *can* see this one coming and you *can* do something about it.

The National Institute of Occupational Safety and Health reports that homicide is the second-leading cause of death in the workplace. Murder is the number-one workplace killer of women and the third-leading cause of death for men, after motor vehicle accidents and machine-related fatalities. The majority of workplace homicides are committed by firearms. For every actual killing, there are anywhere from 10 to 100 sublethal acts of violence committed at work.

According to Michael Mantell and Steve Albrecht in *Ticking Bombs: Defusing Violence in the Workplace*, the cost of workplace violence for American businesses runs more than $4,000,000,000 annually, including lost work time, employee medical benefits, and legal expenses. Additional costs of workplace violence include replacing lost employees and retraining new ones, decreased productivity, higher insurance premiums, raised security costs, bad publicity, lost business, and expensive litigation.

While demographics suggest that the majority of workplace violence is committed by strangers—robbers, disaffected clients and/or customers, etc.—the news media tend to focus attention on acts of lethal aggression committed by coworkers. That is because there is an almost visceral fear we all have of someone we see and talk with every day—someone *we thought we knew*—suddenly turning into a demon of destruction.

Joseph Kinney, executive director of the National Safe Workplace Institute, warns in *Violence at Work: How to Make Your Company Safer for Employees and Customers* that current and future generations of workers will continue to have less emotional maturity, greater feelings of unearned entitlement, poorer social skills, little experience in nonviolent conflict resolution, less respect for older generations, a lower attention span, poorer self-discipline, and higher rates of violence. The newly emerging young workforce is ill-equipped for the world of work, work culture, and work ethic. High turnover encouraged by low wages and poor management reinforces the impression that everyday work is for "chumps," and further denigrates loyalty and authority.

Kinney points out that, for the past 20 years, people have been bombarded by the egocentric message that all personal problems are caused by "society." Individuals are not responsible for their actions, and all blame is externalized. At the same time, there has been a breakdown in traditionally stabilizing institutions such as family, home, church, school, and community. Some workplace violence perpetrators have been quite up front in stating that they want to "strike back" and hurt as many people as they can, no matter who those people are, because of the supposed wrongs committed against them.

In practice, I've found that reported workplace threats actually vary widely in terms of their explicitness. A few threats are direct and unambiguous ("I'm gonna blow that SOB away"), while a far-greater number are nonspecific, falling into a gray zone ("You'll be sorry" or "He deserves whatever's coming to him") that makes it difficult for managers to take action against. Some threats may occur in the form of commiseration with violent news events ("Too bad about all those people, but I know how that restaurant shooter felt").

Indeed, glamorized violence is a staple of the entertainment media, and they have naturally taken an enormous interest in workplace violence, though they often misinterpret and misrepresent those events and the reasons behind them. The common conclusion of this sound-bite journalism is that the lethal perpetrator is either a "nut case" or else engaged in a crusade of "righteous" retribution against an unfair or even darkly conspiratorial employer. This may lead marginally disturbed viewers to "justify" their own future acts of violence.

Changes in the American workplace have created fertile ground for breeding discontent and potential violence. Levels of stress accumulate in many work settings as survivors of downsized corporations are made to take on extra work and fill multiple jobs. For the terminated, anger and hopelessness mount at the inability to replace lost jobs, compounded by the accompanying financial and family stresses. The sense of long-term common corporate purpose that once may have existed between managers and the rank and file has largely disappeared. The changed culture of resentment and entitlement in the workplace says that "This company *owes* me something, and if they don't give it to me, I'm gonna take it the hard way."

Managers and supervisors are increasingly unable or unwilling to use effective discipline or promote fair and effective management practices. Like dysfunctional families, dysfunctional workplaces share common characteristics, such as chronic labor-management disputes, frequent grievances filed by employees, excessive numbers of stress disability claims, persistent pilfering and/or tampering, understaffing and overwork, and a rigidly authoritarian and/or inconsistent management style.

According to forensic psychiatrist Robert Simon in *Bad Men Do What Good Men Dream*, satisfying work affords more than just an income. For most people, it provides stability, direction, security, a sense of achievement, self-worth, camaraderie, and a feeling of belonging. Most workers would regard losing a job as a traumatic event, but one they eventually come to resolve by picking up the pieces, going forward, and searching for new opportunities. However, for a small minority of vulnerable personalities, job loss—especially if perceived as "unfair"—is a devastating blow to the psyche, a mortal narcissistic wound. If the situation is further compounded by financial difficulties, health problems, family friction, and lack of personal support, the person may feel bereft of options.

For such individuals, job stress or job loss can trigger overwhelming rage. Blame is externalized, and vengeance brews as the worker begins to think, "Who do they think they are? I'll show them they can't do this to me and get away with ruining my life." For some, the intolerability of the job loss leads to hopelessness and suicidal intentions with a retaliatory sting: "If they wanna screw me, I can screw them back—big time. Why should other people go on living their happy lives, having what they want, when I can't? I may be going out, but I'm not going out alone." The idea percolates in the perpetrator's mind that, after he's gone, his Ramboesque exploits will be reported to millions around the world and his name will become a household word. Far from meekly slinking away, defeated and unnoticed, he will leave this world in a blaze of horror and glory—just like in the movies.

Preventing violence

While there will always be a few unstable, psychopathologically violence-prone individuals in any large organization, the current emphasis on "offender profiling" obscures a greater contributor to workplace violence and general worker malaise, a set of factors that many companies might find far more difficult to address. These involve the twin evils of generally unfair management practices and lack of a specific workplace violence prevention and response plan.

While not every situation can be planned for, the absence of even the most rudimentary security measures and contingency plans in many organizations is appalling. The steps a firm takes to make its employees feel secure say a lot about corporate culture and workplace morale, and while no organization desires to operate under a fortress mentality, a few important measures can go a long way toward demonstrating concern for worker safety.

As deceptively simple as it sounds, the best way to avoid workplace violence is not to hire violent workers. Efforts in this regard include thorough application reviews and background checks, careful interviewing of prospective employees, and administering appropriate psychological screening measures.

Companies should have clear, strong, fair, and consistent written policies against violence and harassment, along with effective grievance procedures, efficient security programs, a reasonably supportive work environment, open channels of communication, and training in resolving conflicts through team building and negotiation skills. Plans should be in place that specify how threats are reported and to whom, as well as a protocol for investigating them.

The ideal goal of any disciplinary program is to strike a balance between an overly rigid and heavy-handed approach that presents management as hard and unreasonable, and a too-lax one that gives employees the impression of poor control in the organization. By identifying areas of agreement and disagreement, looking for alternatives, thinking creatively, and eventually finding solutions that have the support and commitment of all parties, a human resources manager is more likely to defuse the tension and resentment that may spark workplace violence. Discipline should occur in stages, with a clear policy and rationale, and with written documentation.

If it comes down to having no choice but to fire a worker, this should be done in a firm, but humane, manner. It should be made as clear as possible to the employee that the termination is for a specific reason, rather than for general "attitude" problems or personal reasons. The worker should understand that the termination action is final, and should be informed of any counseling or other services offered by the company for the transition period.

An example of this approach that has been successfully applied to violence occurring in health care facilities is Robert Flannery's Assaulted Staff Action Program (ASAP). It provides a range of services, including individual critical incident debriefings of assaulted staff members and entire wards, a staff victims' support group, employee victim family debriefing and counseling, and referrals for follow-up psychotherapy as needed. The ASAP team structure is comprised of 15 direct-care staff volunteers, three supervisors, and the team director, who is responsible for administering the entire program and for ensuring that the quality of the services is maintained.

The program's developers claim that ASAP has proven useful in reducing the traumatic impact of patient assaults on employee victims and in significantly lowering the overall level of violence in facilities where it has been applied. More germane to the bottom line, ASAP saves the previously mentioned costs of workplace violence.

When violence happens

Sometimes, despite the best efforts at prevention, a dangerous situation begins to brew and a violent incident becomes a distinct possibility, or an incident just erupts explosively and personnel have to respond immediately. The nature of the response will depend on how thorough the pre-incident planning and training have been.

Warning signs may be observed hours, days, or weeks prior to a violent incident, and may be preceded by a history of work-related problems. In all too many cases, the sparks of a potentially violent reaction have been fanned into flames by abusive discipline, clumsily executed termination, or failure of management to address employee–employee grievances, causing the worker to "take matters into his own hands."

Plans and training for defusing violent episodes must be developed, put in place, and reviewed periodically. These include initial actions to take when a violent episode appears to be threatening, codes and signals for summoning help, a chain of command for handling emergencies, appropriate use of verbal control tactics and body language, scene control and bystander containment, measures for dealing with weapons, and procedures for resolving hostage situations.

The crisis is not over when the police and TV crews leave. People may have been killed, others wounded, some held hostage, and many psychologically traumatized. Plans and policies for dealing with the aftermath of workplace violence are just as important as planning for the incident itself, and both may come under sharp scrutiny in later investigations, litigation, and corporate public relations. Companies should proactively set up policies and procedures for responding to the aftermath of a workplace violence incident. They should include mobilization of mental health services, media and public relations responses, family interventions, collaboration with law enforcement, physical security and cleanup, legal measures, postincident investigations, and plans for getting back to business. During the crisis and in its aftermath, the overriding question that will be asked by employees, their families, stakeholders and customers, the media, and the general public is: "What is this company doing to help its workers get through this?"

In this regard, commitment from the top of the management organization—"executive buy-in"—is crucial to determining how effectively such interventions will operate. In the worst case I can remember, a bank branch grudgingly arranged for a staff stress debriefing after a holdup, only because the service was mandated by their managed care contract. The branch managers clearly regarded the intervention as a waste of time that cut into employees' work hours. An uncomfortable backroom lunch and storage area was designated for the debriefing, which was frequently interrupted by people coming in and out to use the kitchen and bathroom. Some of those coworkers could be heard to make cracks about "free time." As a result, the participants wanted the whole thing over with as quickly as possible, and little therapeutic work was accomplished.

The best case I can remember (in terms of company support) involved a hostage and shooting crisis perpetrated by a disturbed customer of a medium-sized investment firm, resulting in two deaths and several injuries. The CEO immediately suspended business as usual, arranged for temps to cover the basic needs of the company, offered his home to be used for almost round-the-clock debriefings, and provided food, beverages, and, in a few cases, bed and board to employees who were too upset to drive home. He and the senior management staff offered help to survivors and their families, personally checked on proper funeral arrangements for the slain workers, frequently visited injured employees in the hospital, and generally shared in the grief and recovery of the members of their staff. Far more than any specific clinical services I could provide, this sincere and unselfish human response by senior management to tragedy within their ranks—a true expression of leadership—helped this firm to heal quickly and move on, always holding a place of respect for their slain comrades, but honoring their memories by productively continuing their work.

This brings us back to an earlier point: Bad things *do* happen to good companies—but they happen a lot less often than to bad ones. There will always be a few dangerously unstable people scattered among the workforce. However, businesses that treat their employees honorably, take the time and concern to implement safety measures, use firm but fair disciplinary procedures, and make it clear that harassment of its employees—by coworkers or management—will not be tolerated tend to have fewer violent incidents than less-well-run companies. Some workers may indeed have a short fuse, but fairly run and well-managed firms seem to know how to keep those fuses from being lit. This isn't just a safety issue—it's good business.

***Laurence Miller**, a psychologist in Boca Raton, Fla., specializing in neuropsychology, business psychology, and corporate counseling, is the author of* Shocks to the System: Psychotherapy of Traumatic Disability Syndromes.

LEAN MANUFACTURING

CO$T VS QUALITY

MUST QUALITY TAKE A HAIRCUT WHEN MANUFACTURERS AGGRESSIVELY TRIM COSTS?

DOUG BARTHOLOMEW

WHAT IS THE COST OF QUALITY? TO FORD MOTOR CO. AND Bridgestone/Firestone Inc., one of the costs of quality is the inestimable damage to both companies' reputations as wary consumers think twice about purchasing Ford Explorers or Bridgestone/Firestone tires.

> **"I've never walked into a plant where anybody knew the cost of quality."**
>
> Kevin Smith, president, Productivity Group, Div. Productivity Inc..

What is the cost of quality? DaimlerChrysler AG may find out when results are in from its decision earlier this year to require suppliers to reduce costs by a fixed percentage. "Whether DaimlerChrysler's decision will have a quality impact is uncertain, but it may affect the quality of what they demand from suppliers," observes Joe Ivers, partner and executive director of quality and customer satisfaction research at J.D. Power & Associates, Agoura Hills, Calif.

Cost reductions alone need not translate to a lower-quality product. According to INDUSTRYWEEK'S 2000 Census of Manufacturers, which surveyed some 3,000 companies, manufacturers that were able to cut their costs by reducing scrap and waste tended to show more improvement in quality than those whose costs increased.

Manufacturers over the last 20 years have invested billions of dollars in various quality-improvement efforts. Among the most popular today are the principles of lean manufacturing as pioneered by Toyota Motor Corp. and the Six Sigma standards that help companies refine their quality efforts to achieve still greater improvements. In most cases, investments in these programs have been more than recovered by lower production costs, less scrap, fewer defects, and reduced warranty expense.

Even with these gains, the costs associated with badly designed, poorly made products continue to haunt the manufacturing community. "The cost of poor quality in terms of rework, scrap, and warranty expense is still a big number," says Bonnie Smith, director of the LeanSigma program at TBM Institute, a training and consulting firm in Durham, N.C. But most companies haven't got a clue as to what that cost is. "I've never walked into a plant where anybody knew the cost of quality," says Kevin Smith, president, Productivity Group, Div. Productivity Inc., Portland, Oreg. "It's amazing what design engineers don't know about manufacturing," says Jane Algee, producibility manager for the Comanche helicopter electro-optical sensor system program at Lockheed Martin Missiles and Fire Control in Orlando. Currently on a leave of absence in Tokyo, Algee, immediate past president of the Institute of Industrial Engineers, agrees that most product designers have little or no idea of the impact a poor design can have on both quality and cost.

"It's eye-opening that a lot of these designers have been in industry over 30 years, yet they don't understand the cost of quality—how pinching a penny now can cost you a hundred times over in the future," Algee says. "It's kind of the American mistake."

Complicating matters, the rampant cost-cutting over the last two decades has caused manufacturers to take a hard look at just what level of durability and material quality they are willing to design into their products. Toyota, for instance, may have gone overboard with quality, some observers believe. "Toyota looked at their products and discovered their quality was too good," says Jeffrey Liker, professor of industrial and operations engineering at the University of Michigan, Ann Arbor. "They didn't need stainless steel parts in the engine area. They saved $100 billion by commonizing parts—using less expensive materials that perform the same function," says Liker, who wrote the book *Becoming Lean* (1998, Productivity Press).

While it's common for manufacturers to pay lip service to quality, it's clear to anyone who has ever bought a screwdriver that broke the first time it was used, discovered the rear-door lock on a brand-new SUV was defective, or had the transmission on a new car fail after less than 10,000 miles, that there is quality, and then there is *quality*. In sum, all products are not created equal.

Take the Bridgestone/Firestone-Ford controversy. Ford president and CEO Jacques Nasser has stated that Ford's research into its former supplier's tires indicates that "customer safety would be at risk" if Ford customers were to continue to ride on Bridgestone/Firestone tires. Likewise, John Lampe, chairman, president, and CEO of Firestone, says an expert hired by his firm concluded that the Ford Explorer could be unusually prone to skidding out of control in the event of a sudden tire failure, and that the vehicle's design, not the tires, put its occupants at risk. Despite the charges, both companies continue to claim their own products are safe.

The unusual public brouhaha raises serious concerns about the quality of two of America's foremost brands. During a recent Congressional investigation, Deputy Transportation Secretary Michael Jackson said the National Highway Traffic Safety Administration may investigate the Explorer's tendency to roll over. And U.S. Rep. John Dingell (D, Mich.) questioned whether Firestone had shaved the quality of its tires as part of cost-trimming efforts in the mid-1990s.

In what was perceived by some observers as an admission of poor quality in manufacturing at one of its plants, Bridgestone/Firestone in June announced plans to close its Decatur, Ill., tire facility, the main source of tires prone to suffer tread separations that led to more than 200 rollover fatalities, most of them involving Explorers. Executives said the decision to close the plant and idle close to 1,500 workers was not related to quality problems but rather to the need to reduce capacity.

That may be, but Ford's analysis of the tires that failed on its Explorers showed that an inordinate number that suffered tread separations were made at the Decatur plant, calling into question the quality procedures at the 59-year-old facility. The plant would have required substantial capital investment to upgrade. By closing it down, Bridgestone/Firestone will save more than $100 million a year. Sales of Bridgestone/Firestone replacement tires were down 50% in the first half of this year, compared with sales for the first six months of 2000, as wary consumers, concerned about quality, avoided the brand in droves.

"Every auto executive in Detroit knows they're hurting because of quality."

Martin Piszczalski, president, of Sextant Research

Industry-wide, automotive manufacturers are notorious for cutting corners on their products to save a buck. For example, many motorists remember the days when all new cars came with a full-size spare tire. Today, most new cars come with a skinnier, cheaper wheel and tire combination that looks as if it belongs on a bicycle, not an automobile. These "donut" spares typically come stamped with a warning that they are not intended to be driven over 50 mph nor for more than 50 miles. By instituting this subtle change, auto manufacturers reaped huge savings on tens of millions of vehicles, because the smaller units cost less to make. Unfortunately, the switch—of which buyers were never informed—resulted in reduced quality for the consumer.

Clearly, careful attention to the design of a product—in terms of its manufacturability as well as its functionality and durability in the field—is critical. The flip side is poor design and engineering that, in the auto industry, leads to recalls and higher warranty costs for automakers.

"Warranty costs are huge in this industry," says Ivers of J.D. Power. "When not enough attention is paid to design in terms of manufacturability and engineering, you wind up with vehicles that need a lot of fixing." He cites the spate of problems owners had a few years ago with automobiles equipped with "T-tops"—sunroofs that leaked as a result of poor design that caused a lack of adequate weatherproofing.

Too Many Recalls

RECALLS ARE COMMON. EVERY MONTH, AUTO-MAKERS announce recalls to replace products or parts that fail. These include such things as fuel lines that rupture, components that melt due to proximity to a hot manifold, or electronic failures that may cause the vehicle to stop dead in traffic for no apparent reason. "Every auto executive in Detroit knows they're hurting because of quality," observes Martin Piszczalski, president of Sextant Research, an Ann Arbor, Mich., IT consulting firm.

DaimlerChrysler recently announced that 16,000 owners of its 2000 Mercedes-Benz M-Class vehicles should replace their rear-middle-seat belt anchor plate because it does not meet specifications. In the same week, Isuzu recalled 3,100 of its 2001 Rodeo Sport vehicles to replace fuel return hoses that crack and leak.

Last April, an Alameda County, Calif., judge ordered Ford to replace defective ignition devices on an estimated two million 1983-1995 vehicles prone to stalling. A class-action suit charged that Ford had placed its thick-film-ignition module, which regulates electric current to the spark plugs, too close to the engine block where it was exposed to high temperatures, thus causing the module to fail.

Documents introduced in court showed that Ford confirmed the problem in its internal studies and could have moved the module to a cooler location at an added cost of $4 per vehicle. Ford denied the devices are defective, but the automaker has settled numerous other suits related to allegations of vehicles stalling. In August Ford reached a tentative settlement, agreeing to double the warranty protection to 100,000 miles on 5 million vehicles to cover the estimated $1 billion cost of fixing them.

In the last year or so, Ford has been plagued with quality problems, and CEO Nasser has publicly admitted the company's quality is "about average." Its Escape mini-SUV has suffered five product recalls. Overall, the automaker came in last among the top seven auto manufacturers in J.D. Power's latest ranking. Through its lean initiative, Ford this year plans to cut 4% out of the cost of making its vehicles, for about $800 million in savings.

Perhaps most embarrassing for Ford was a pair of recalls the automaker announced earlier this year on its redesigned 2002 Explorer. The first was for over 50,000 vehicles built at the company's Louisville, Ky., plant, where a jagged edge along a section of the assembly line may have sliced tires. The second was for 56,000 new Explorers, built at both Louisville and at a St. Louis plant, that may have loose rear-hatch windows that can shatter when shut.

Despite all these well-publicized slip-ups in quality, J.D. Power says overall quality of cars is improving. One reason for the apparent disparity may be that J.D. Power's annual survey of automobile owners focuses on their experience during the first three months of ownership of a new vehicle. It does not address durability or any problems that may arise when a vehicle has been owned for six months, a year, or five years.

In just the last three years the number of problems reported by new owners dropped from 176 per 100 vehicles in 1998 to 147 in 2001. "Things gone wrong, what we call TGWs, are evidence of a lack of quality," Ivers says.

Toyota and its Lexus luxury brand dominated the J.D. Power quality rankings for 2001, grabbing the top spots in seven of 16 different vehicle market segments. The Toyota Corolla ranked as the compact with the fewest complaints in the first three months of ownership. Similarly, the Toyota Avalon took first among premium midsize cars. Likewise, the Lexus ES 300 was the number-one-ranked entry luxury vehicle, while its big sister, the Lexus LS 430, rolled off with gold honors among premium luxury cars.

It comes as no surprise that the chief reason Ford, GM, and Chrysler continue to lose market share to Japanese and German automakers, analysts say, is the public's perception of the quality of American vehicles.

Quality Payback

TO BE SURE, QUALITY-IMPROVEMENT EFFORTS ARE BIG IN manufacturing today. For instance, Caterpillar Inc. is investing $20 million this year to train 2,700 employees in Six Sigma theory and practice. "It's a massive investment, and our goal this year is to at least break even on documented savings as a result," says Jim Owens, group president and executive office member.

Employees at Caterpillar Inc.'s Lafayette, Ind., plant use high-tech assembly processes to ensure quality products.

"We see it as an investment in quality that will yield a return in terms of reduced reliability problems and improved warranty performance," Owens says. He is quick to point out that "the back-end cost of poor quality is only the tip of the iceberg. Quality affects the customer's buying decision in the future."

While some companies, such as DaimlerChrysler and Toyota, have ordered their suppliers to trim a fixed percentage of cost out of their operations, Owens says Caterpillar doesn't take that route. "I flinch when I hear blanket demands for cost reductions, as if those suppliers are going to take that out of their margins. We are cognizant that our suppliers are our partners who are committed to working with us to manage the cost of parts down." The bottom line, though, as Owens puts it, is, "Our quality is only as good as our supplier quality."

Caterpillar keeps close tabs on its certified suppliers in order to maintain quality. For instance, suppliers are prohibited from making changes in materials or processes without its concurrence. "The reason is that we have been burned a couple times when that happened," Owens says.

It's no secret that many manufacturers have succeeded in linking cost-cutting with quality improvement. Toyota, for instance, expects a 3% reduction in costs each year from its supplier firms, says Dan Cavanagh, plant manager at Dana Corp.'s automotive frame plant in Stockton, Calif. Producing 150,000 frames annually, the sprawling facility is a captive supplier to its sole customer, the General Motors-Toyota joint venture New United Motor Manufacturing Inc. (NUMMI) plant 60-plus miles away in Fremont, Calif.

Workers at the plant, which performs 115 ft of welds on each 300-lb frame, are constantly looking for ways to improve quality and reduce costs. Each worker is expected to come up with three ideas per month, and in a recent month the average was 3.8, Cavanagh says.

In one work area, cycle time was reduced by 10 to 18 seconds by adding another welder, thereby reducing defects and eliminating a buildup of parts in that area. That one change led to both reduced costs and improved quality.

Unfortunately, it's a lot easier for managers under the gun to trim costs by exchanging one supplier's part for another's lower-priced one. After all, who's going to notice or care that a set of seals on a pump or valve came from a different manufacturer, or that substandard steel was used to make a part that otherwise would cost half again as much?

"We analyze our returns, which are really low, and attack those issues."

Brad Miller, senior manufacturing engineer, Medeco High Security Lock Co.

Toyota notices. "You shouldn't compromise quality for other issues, including cost-saving initiatives," says Ed Mantey, former chief engineer for the 2000 Avalon who is based at the Toyota Technical Center in Ann Arbor, Mich. "It's not a tradeoff—we want quality to increase and cost to come down. Toyota's reputation for quality differentiates our product from our competitors'."

Mantey says that when he ran the 2000 Avalon project, the company analyzed what buyers perceived were the strengths and weaknesses of the car's predecessor. "One thing people wanted us to improve was the front-door wind noise," he says.

In response, Toyota engineers completely redesigned the way the door was manufactured. Instead of what is known in the industry as a press-type door, they switched to a frame-type door. The first type of door is made from a one-piece stamping, while the latter requires that the steel section that forms the channel to hold the window glass be welded to the door's sheet metal.

The new type of door has a stiffer upper section that offers a better sealing surface for the weather stripping that seals out wind and noise. Despite the need for welding, which is done both robotically and with hand-finishing, the frame-type door costs less to make. One reason is that with the press-type door, sections of metal have to be cut away for the guts of the door mechanism, and this metal becomes waste. The end result, says Mantey, is that "the customer gets better quality at lower cost."

Toyota also saved money without sacrificing quality by using local U.S.-made materials over those made in Japan. "We saved millions of dollars this way, and the part performance we found was at least equal or better to the original part but at a lower cost," Mantey adds.

Those within the auto industry are well aware of the tradeoffs that often occur between quality and cost, Mantey confides. "At one point a competitor said to me, 'It's less expensive to pay warranty claims than to over design the part.' All too often we have suppliers say to us, 'It's good enough for the Big Three, why isn't it good enough for you?'"

Mantey confirms that Toyota requires its suppliers to cut costs 2% to 3% each year. Even so, he says Toyota works with them to help them achieve these reductions while improving quality, as opposed to sacrificing it. He says one of the benefits of forcing suppliers to make such efforts is that "they don't keep cranking out the same parts year after year—they must continually improve them.

Mantey notes he just approved a supplier's request to use a new formula for electrodeposition coating on metal. "It's lower cost and gives better protection than the previous coating," he says. Toyota prohibits suppliers from arbitrarily changing processes or parts suppliers without seeking and obtaining approval from Toyota. "We do not allow them to compromise the quality of our vehicles for cost reductions," he says.

Supply-Chain Partnerships

OTHER INDUSTRIES ARE USING SIMILAR APPROACHES TO improve quality while reining in costs. "We work with our supply chain, forming partnerships with the producers of component parts," says Brad Miller, senior manufacturing engineer at Medeco High Security Lock Co. in

Salem, Va. Medeco's locks are sold only through locksmiths, primarily for commercial buildings such as government offices, banks, and convenience stores.

Medeco locks cost more than other brands. A typical deadbolt set alone costs $120, five or six times an average set. Because they come with antipick technology and security keys that cannot be duplicated at a hardware store, buyers feel the extra level of security is worth the price.

"If we are having trouble with a part, either dimensionally or functionally, instead of trying to accommodate a sloppy part, we'll visit the vendor to help them get back on track to provide a better part for us," says Miller. For instance, he recently had to visit a supplier to help the company redesign its process to correct a structural-integrity problem with its parts. Also, "We analyze our returns, which are really low, and attack those issues," he says.

Not all manufacturers analyze their failures. "It's tricky to do that kind of analysis, and often what caused the failure is difficult to determine and it takes a lot of time," says Alice E. Smith, professor of industrial and systems engineering at Auburn University, Auburn, Ala. "And manufacturers often don't want to know."

But Miller believes even one product return a year should be cause for concern. "The biggest cost of poor quality is the image of the product and the company," he says. "Poor quality costs the company hugely in lost revenues."

That's the cost of quality.

DBARTHOLOMEW@INDUSTRYWEEK.COM

From *Industry Week*, September 2001, pp. 34-41. © 2001 by Reprint Management Service.

Case: *Evaluation of Organizational Effectiveness*

The American Corporation, a $2.4 billion diversified conglomerate, acquired the $130 million Cordle Manufacturing Company. At a private luncheon with Sam Priest, American's chief executive officer, Carla Judson, a strategic planner with American's Division of Strategic Planning, learned that she was one of several persons being considered to replace, on an acting basis, Cordle Manufacturing Company's president, whose resignation was part of the acquisition agreement. Priest informed Judson that if the acting president could function effectively, the position would be permanent. He indicated, however, that one troublesome problem would have to be eliminated within six months. The problem had been revealed through a confidential survey conducted among 25 members of Cordle's middle management group. Judson was told that the survey results would be available to her and that a meeting of all officers would be held in two weeks to select the acting president. At that time, all candidates would be required to make a presentation outlining how problems revealed by the survey could best be handled.

In studying the survey results, Judson learned that each of the middle managers had been asked to evaluate other departments. The survey was designed to determine, if possible, the respect, cooperation, and goodwill generated between departments. Of the departments evaluated, all were rated satisfactory in efficiency, organization, work relationships, and cooperativeness, except for the sales department. From the 25 questionnaires returned, 18 participants said the sales department needed reorganizing. They said department members were difficult to work with and rarely cooperated with other departments.

As a strategic planner, Judson knew there were a number of feasible strategies she could present to American's officers. She knew that the survey results might be challenged as unreliable and invalid. On the other hand, she was aware that the distinct nature of the objectives, activities, and responsibilities associated with various departments often led to conflict between individuals in various areas. If she acknowledged the survey's validity, she would have to outline a plan for achieving efficient integration and coordination among departments and functional areas. Judson realized her future at American would be decided in the next few days by how her strategies would be perceived by American's officers and then by how effectively she could implement her strategies. What to decide on was her major task.

Using the Case on *Evaluation of Organizational Effectiveness*

Carla Judson is faced with the problem of trying to propose an organization for the new Cordle Manufacturing division of the American Corporation based upon the results of a study that was recently completed at the newly acquired business. The study indicates that most of the departments work well together with one major exception—sales. Ms. Judson's task is to develop a strategy to address and rectify this condition.

Discussion Questions

1. Should Ms. Judson challenge the validity and reliability of the study?
2. If Ms. Judson accepts the study, what are some of the possible strategies she could use to address this situation?

Exercise: *Win as Much as You Can!*

1. Divide the group into groups of eight and have each group (cluster) divide into teams of two (dyads).
2. The goal of this exercise is to win as much money as you can.
3. Using the chart at the top of the tally sheet, each dyad is to decide whether it will choose an "X" or a "Y" (with the hope of winning money). The dyads then write their choices on their tally sheets for round 1 while not letting any other dyads see their choices. No conversation among dyads should occur, except when provided for in rounds 5, 8, and 10.
4. After the allotted time for round 1 (2 minutes) has passed, each dyad will show its choice to the other dyads in the cluster. Using the chart on the tally sheet, each dyad should determine how much money it won or lost in round 1, and record this amount on the tally sheet. No comments among dyads are allowed. Proceed immediately to round 2, then 3, and so forth, as outlined on the tally sheet. Note that in rounds 5, 8, and 10, dyads can confer with each other at the beginning of the round. Note also that theamounts won or lost in these rounds are multiplied by three, five, and ten.

5. At the end of the exercise, determine which dyad won the most and which ended up furthest behind. Then compare clusters.

4 X's:	Lose $1.00 each
3 X's: 1 Y:	Win $1.00 each Lose $3.00
2 X's: 2 Y's:	Win $2.00 each Lose $2.00 each
1 X: 3 Y's:	Win $3.00 Lose $1.00 each
4 Y's:	Win $1.00 each

Strategy: You are to confer with your partner(s) on each round and make a joint decision. Before rounds 5, 8, and 10, you confer with the others in your cluster.

Questions for Discussion

1. How was the goal defined? What conflict did it create? (Do I win for my dyad or my cluster?)
2. Do people react differently in games than they do in real life? Do goals in life create conflict?
3. How does trust relate to influence? How many times can one person betray another and still retain his/her confidence? Did anyone stick to her/his word throughout?
4. What effect did communication have on the influence process?
5. What strategies were used to win? What conflict did these strategies create? What strategies were used to manage the conflict?

- The win/lose approach = self-oriented. (I win at your expense.)
- The lose/win approach = martyrdom. (You win at my expense.)
- The lose/lose approach = pride and revenge. (I may lose, but you do, too.)
- The win/win approach = trust. (We both win.)

6. Why is the win/win approach the most effective strategy in life?

Round	Time Allowed	Confer With	Your Choice Circle	Clusters Patterns of Choices	Payoff	Balance	
1	2 mins.	partner					
2	1 min.	partner					
3	1 min.	partner					
4	1 min.	partner					
5	3 mins. 1 min.	cluster partner					Bonus round payoff × 3
6	1 min.	partner					
7	1 min.	partner					
8	3 mins. 1 min.	cluster partner					Bonus round payoff × 5
9	1 min.	partner					
10	3 mins. 1 min.	cluster partner					Bonus round payoff × 10

Case: Evaluation of Organizational Effectiveness; Exercise: Win as Much as You Can!, Fred Maidment, McGraw-Hill/Dushkin, 2000.

UNIT 7

Staffing and Human Resources

Unit Selections

Key Points to Consider

- What do you think of the idea of a "Mommy Track"? What do you think of the idea of a "Daddy Track"? What do you think this does to people's careers in highly competitive organizations?
- For years women have talked about the networks that men have when developing their careers. Do you think women should develop their own? Does this exclude men? Is this fair? Why or why not?
- What are some of the workplace trends for this century? How do you think organizations can find and keep good employees?
- What are some of the ways that companies can reward their employees that are different from what was done in the past? Do you think it is more effective?

DUSHKIN ONLINE **Links: www.dushkin.com/online/**
These sites are annotated in the World Wide Web pages.

Electronic Frontier Foundation "Privacy" Archive
http://www.eff.org

School of Labor and Industrial Relations Hot Links
http://www.lir.msu.edu/hotlinks

U.S. Equal Employment Opportunity Commission
http://www.eeoc.gov

Managers of organizations get things done through people. Managers can plan, organize, direct, and control, but the central focus of all their efforts is people. People determine whether an organization is going to succeed, and the way that people perceive their treatment by management is often the key to that success. In today's world, it is necessary to recognize that people have different needs, wants, and desires. Women have different needs than men, which the organization is going to have to address if it wants to hold onto top performers. Some of these differences are discussed by Felecia Schwartz in "Management Women and the New Facts of Life," the article that started the talk about the "Mommy Track," which soon led to talk about the "Daddy Track."

Since human resources are a key to the success of any organization, firms need to hire the very best people they can find, because it is people who make the plans, organize the operation, direct the processes to accomplish the organizational goals, and evaluate the results. But while people contribute directly to a firm's success, they also represent a significant cost to the organization. Not only salaries but also the costs of benefits are rising at an alarming rate. Benefits cost more today than just a few years ago, and workers not only want to keep the benefits they have but seek to add others. Some of their demands include dental and eye care plans, child care, and senior care for their relatives. The Americans With Disabilities Act has established new criteria for employees with disabilities. Technology is changing the way people work, and management is going to have to deal with that, as seen in "Secrets of Finding and Keeping Good Employees."

The workforce is changing. It includes more minorities, women, and other groups with different needs, and if a corporation wants to hire these people, many of whom are outstanding, they are going to have to meet their needs. Otherwise, these potential employees will go elsewhere, frequently to the competition. No organization can afford to turn its back on such a large pool of potential talent.

Human resources often involve labor unions. While unions in North America have suffered in recent years from declining membership and plant closings, they have nevertheless served an important historical role as well as providing a balance for the potential excesses of management. American labor unions need to redefine their roles in industry, and their leaders must implement these changes. Unions will have to change the way they conduct business if they plan to survive.

Because of the increasing demand for qualified employees, organizations will have to do everything possible to retain good workers. Firms are responding to changes in the workforce in a variety of ways. To meet the needs of the future, management must recognize that people, organizations, and the environment will continue to evolve, and that what motivates workers will change in the future.

Management Women and the New Facts of Life

Felice N. Schwartz

The cost of employing women in management is greater than the cost of employing men. This is a jarring statement, partly because it is true, but mostly because it is something people are reluctant to talk about. A new study by one multinational corporation shows that the rate of turnover in management positions is 2 ½ times higher among top-performing women than it is among men. A large producer of consumer goods reports that one half of the women who take maternity leave return to their jobs late or not at all. And we know that women also have a greater tendency to plateau or to interrupt their careers in ways that limit their growth and development. But we have become so sensitive to charges of sexism and so afraid of confrontation, even litigation, that we rarely say what we know to be true. Unfortunately, our bottled-up awareness leaks out in misleading metaphors ("glass ceiling" is one notable example), veiled hostility, lowered expectations, distrust and reluctant adherence to Equal Employment Opportunity requirements.

Career interruptions, plateauing, and turnover are expensive. The money corporations invest in recruitment, training, and development is less likely to produce top executives among women than among men, and the invaluable company experience that developing executives acquire at every level as they move up through management ranks is more often lost.

The studies just mentioned are only the first of many, I'm quite sure. Demographic realities are going to force corporations all across the country to analyze the cost of employing women in managerial positions, and what they will discover is that women cost more.

But here is another startling truth: The greater cost of employing women is not a function of inescapable gender differences. Women *are* different from men, but what increases their cost to the corporation is principally the clash of their perceptions, attitudes, and behavior with those of men, which is to say, with the policies and practices of male-led corporations.

It is terribly important that employers draw the right conclusions from the studies now being done. The studies will be useless—or worse, harmful—if all they teach us is that women are expensive to employ. What we need to learn is how to reduce that expense, how to stop throwing away the investments we make in talented women, how to become more responsive to the needs of the women that corporations *must* employ if they are to have the best and the brightest of all those now entering the work force.

Two facts matter to business: only women have babies and only men make rules.

The gender differences relevant to business fall into two categories: those related to maternity and those related to the differing traditions and expectations of the sexes. Maternity is biological rather than cultural. We can't alter it but we can dramatically reduce its impact on the workplace and in many cases eliminate its negative effect on employee development. We can accomplish this by addressing the second set of differences, those between male and female socialization. Today, these differences exaggerate the real costs of maternity and can turn a relatively slight disruption in work schedule into a serious business problem and a career derailment for individual women. If we are to overcome the cost differential between male and female employees, we need to address the issues that arise when female socialization meets the male corporate culture and masculine rules of career development—issues of behavior and style, of expectation, of stereotypes and preconceptions, of sexual tension and harassment, of female mentoring, lateral mobility relocation, compensation, and early identification of top performers.

The one immutable, enduring difference between men and women is maternity. Maternity is not simply childbirth but a continuum that begins with an awareness of the ticking of the biological clock, proceeds to the anticipation of motherhood, includes pregnancy, childbirth, physical recuperation, psychological adjustment, and continues on to nursing, bonding, and child rearing. Not all women choose to become mothers, of course, and among those who do, the process varies from case to case depending on the health of the mother and baby, the values of the parents, and the availability, cost, and quality of child care.

In past centuries, the biological fact of maternity shaped the traditional roles of the sexes. Women performed the home-centered functions that related to the bearing and nurturing of children. Men did the work that required great physical strength. Over time, however, family size contracted, the community assumed greater responsibility for the care and education of children, packaged foods and household technology reduced the work load in the home, and technology eliminated much of the need for muscle power at the workplace. Today, in the developed world, the only role still uniquely gender related is childbearing. Yet men and women are still socialized to perform their traditional roles.

Men and women may or may not have some innate psychological disposition toward these traditional roles—men to be aggressive, competitive, self-reliant, risk taking; women to be supportive, nurturing, intuitive, sensitive, communicative—but certainly both men and women are capable of the full range of behavior. Indeed, the male and female roles have already begun to expand and merge. In the decades ahead, as the socialization of boys and girls and the experience and expectations of young men and women grow steadily more androgynous, the differences in workplace behavior will continue to fade. At the moment, however, we are still plagued by disparities in perception and behavior that make the integration of men and women in the workplace unnecessarily difficult and expensive.

Let me illustrate with a few broadbrush generalizations. Of course, these are only stereotypes, but I think they help to exemplify the kinds of preconceptions that muddy the corporate waters.

Women who compete like men are considered unfeminine. Women who emphasize family are considered uncommitted.

Men continue to perceive women as the rearers of their children, so they find it understandable, indeed appropriate, that women should renounce their careers to raise families. Edmund Pratt, CEO of Pfizer, once asked me in all sincerity, "Why would any woman choose to be a chief financial officer rather than a full-time mother?" By condoning and taking pleasure in women's traditional behavior, men reinforce it. Not only do they see parenting as fundamentally female, they see a career as fundamentally male—either an unbroken series of promotions and advancements toward CEOdom or stagnation and disappointment. This attitude serves to legitimize a woman's choice to extend maternity leave and even, for those who can afford it, to leave employment altogether for several years. By the same token, men who might want to take a leave after the birth of a child know that management will see such behavior as a lack of career commitment, even when company policy permits parental leave for men.

Women also bring counterproductive expectations and perceptions to the workplace. Ironically, although the feminist movement was an expression of women's quest for freedom from their home-based lives, most women were remarkably free already. They had many responsibilities, but they were autonomous and could be entrepreneurial in how and when they carried them out. And once their children grew up and left home, they were essentially free to do what they wanted with their lives. Women's traditional role also included freedom from responsibility for the financial support of their families. Many of us were socialized from girlhood to expect our husbands to take care of us, while our brothers were socialized from an equally early age to complete their educations, pursue careers, climb the ladder of success, and provide dependable financial support for their families. To the extent that this tradition of freedom lingers subliminally, women tend to bring to their employment a sense that they can choose to change jobs or careers at will, take time off, or reduce their hours.

Finally, women's traditional role encouraged particular attention to the quality and substance of what they did, specifically to the physical, psychological, and intellectual development of their children. This traditional focus may explain women's continuing tendency to search for more than monetary reward—intrinsic significance, social importance, meaning—in what they do. This too makes them more likely than men to leave the corporation in search of other values.

The misleading metaphor of the glass ceiling suggests an invisible barrier constructed by corporate leaders to impede the upward mobility of women beyond the middle levels. A more appropriate metaphor, I believe, is the kind of cross-sectional diagram used in geology. The barriers to women's leadership occur when potentially counterproductive layers of influence on women—maternity, tradition, socialization—meet management strata pervaded by the largely unconscious preconceptions, stereotypes, and expectations of men. Such interfaces do not exist for men and tend to be impermeable for women.

One result of these gender differences has been to convince some executives that women are simply not suited to top management. Other executives feel helpless. If they see even a few of their valued female employees fail to return to work from maternity leave on schedule or see one of their most promising women plateau in her career after the birth of a child, they begin to fear there is nothing they can do to infuse women with new energy and enthusiasm and persuade them to stay. At the same time, they know there is nothing they can do to stem the tide of women into management ranks.

Another result is to place every working woman on a continuum that runs from total dedication to career at one end to a balance between career and family at the other. What women discover is that the male corporate culture sees both extremes as unacceptable. Women who want the flexibility to balance their families and their careers are not adequately committed to the organization. Women who perform as aggressively and competitively as men are abrasive and unfeminine. But the fact is, business needs all the talented women it can get. Moreover, as I will explain, the women I call career-primary and those I call career-and-family each have particular value to the corporation.

With too few men to go around, women have moved from a buyer's to a seller's market.

Women in the corporation are about to move from a buyer's to a seller's market. The sudden, startling recognition that 80% of new entrants in the work force over the next decade will be women, minorities, and immigrants has stimulated a mushrooming incentive to "value diversity."

Women are no longer simply an enticing pool of occasional creative talent, a thorn in the side of the EEO officer, or a source of frustration to corporate leaders truly puzzled by the slowness of their upward trickle into executive positions. A real demographic change is taking place. The era of sudden population growth of the 1950s and 1960s is over. The birth rate has dropped about 40%, from a high of 25.3 live births per 1,000 population in 1957, at the peak of the baby boom, to a stable low of a little more than 15 per 1,000 over the last 16 years, and there is no indication of a return to a higher rate. The tidal wave of baby boomers that swelled the recruitment pool to overflowing seems to have been a one-time phenomenon. For 20 years, employers had the pick of a very large crop and were able to choose males almost exclusively for the executive track. But if future population remains fairly stable while the economy continues to expand, and if the new information society simultaneously creates a greater need for creative, educated managers, then the gap between supply and demand will grow dramatically and, with it, the competition for managerial talent.

The decrease in numbers has even greater implications if we look at the traditional source of corporate recruitment for leadership positions—white males from the top 10% of the country's best universities. Over the past decade, the increase in the number of women graduating from leading universities has been much greater than the increase in the total number of graduates, and these women are well represented in the top 10% of their classes.

The trend extends into business and professional programs as well. In the old days, virtually all MBAs were male. I remember addressing a meeting at the Harvard Business School as recently as the mid-1970s and looking out at a sea of exclusively male faces. Today, about 25% of that audience would be women. The pool of male MBAs from which corporations have traditionally drawn their leaders has shrunk significantly.

Of course, this reduction does not have to mean a shortage of talent. The top 10% is at least as smart as it always was—smarter, probably, since it's now drawn from a broader segment of the population. But it now consists increasingly of women. Companies that are determined to recruit the same number of men as before will have to dig much deeper into the male pool, while their competitors will have the opportunity to pick the best people from both the male and female graduates.

Under these circumstances, there is no question that the management ranks of business will include increasing numbers of women. There remains, however, the question of how these women will succeed—how long they will stay, how high they will climb, how completely they will fulfill their promise and potential, and what kind of return the corporation will realize on its investment in their training and development.

There is ample business reason for finding ways to make sure that as many of these women as possible will succeed. The first step in this process is to recognize that women are not all alike. Like men, they are individuals with differing talents, priorities, and motivations. For the sake of simplicity, let me focus on the two women I referred to earlier, on what I call the career-primary woman and the career-and-family woman.

It is absurd to put woman down for having the very qualities that would send a man to the top.

Like many men, some women put their careers first. They are ready to make the same trade-offs traditionally made by the men who seek leadership positions. They make a career decision to put in extra hours, to make sacrifices in their personal lives, to make the most of every opportunity for professional development. For women, of course, this decision also requires that they remain single or at least childless or, if they do have children, that they be satisfied to have others raise them. Some 90% of executive men but only 35% of executive women have children by the age of 40. The *automatic* association of all women with babies is clearly unjustified.

The secret to dealing with such women is to recognize them early, accept them, and clear artificial barriers from their path to the top. After all, the best of these women are among the best managerial talent you will ever see. And career-primary women have another important value to the company that men and other women lack. They can act as role models and mentors to younger women who put their careers first. Since upwardly mobile career-primary women still have few role models to motivate and inspire them, a company with women in its top echelon has a significant advantage in the competition for executive talent.

Men at the top of the organization—most of them over 55, with wives who tend to be traditional—often find career women "masculine" and difficult to accept as colleagues. Such men miss the point, which is not that these women are just like men but that they are just like the *best* men in the organization. And there is such a shortage of the best people that gender cannot be allowed to matter. It is clearly counterproductive to disparage in a woman with executive talent the very qualities that are most critical to the business and that might carry a man to the CEO's office.

Clearing a path to the top for career-primary women has four requirements:

1. Identify them early.
2. Give them the same opportunity you give to talented men to grow and develop and contribute to company profitability. Give them client and customer responsibility. Expect them to travel and relocate, to make the same commitment to the company as men aspiring to leadership positions.
3. Accept them as valued members of your management team. Include them in every kind of communication. Listen to them.
4. Recognize that the business environment is more difficult and stressful for them than for their male peers. They are always a minority, often the only woman. The male perception of talented, ambitious women is at best ambivalent, a mixture of admiration, resentment, confusion, competitiveness, attraction, skepticism, anxiety, pride, and animosity. Women can never feel secure about how they should dress and act, whether they should speak out or grin and bear it when they encounter discrimination, stereotyping, sexual harassment, and paternalism. Social interaction and travel with male colleagues and with male clients can be charged. As they move up, the normal increase in pressure and responsibility is compounded for women because they are women.

Stereotypical language and sexist day-to-day behavior do take their toll on women's career development. Few male executives realize how common it is to call women by their first names while men in the same group are greeted with surnames, how frequently female executives are assumed by men to be secretaries, how often women are excluded from all-male social events where business is being transacted. With notable exceptions, men are still generally more comfortable with other men, and as a result women miss many of the career and business opportunities that arise over lunch, on the golf course, or in the locker room.

The majority of women, however, are what I call career-and-family women, women who want to pursue serious careers while participating actively in the rearing of children. These women are a precious resource that has yet to be mined. Many of them are talented and creative. Most of them are willing to trade some career growth and compensation for freedom from the constant pressure to work long hours and weekends.

A policy that forces women to choose between family and career cuts hugely into profits and competitive advantage.

Most companies today are ambivalent at best about the career-and-family women in their management ranks. They would prefer that all employees were willing to give their all to the company. They believe it is in their best interests for all managers to compete for the top positions so the company will have the largest possible pool from which to draw its leaders.

"If you have both talent and motivation," many employers seem to say "we want to move you up. If you haven't got that motivation, if you want less pressure and greater flexibility, then you can leave and make room for a new generation." These companies lose on two counts. First, they fail to amortize the investment made in the early training and experience of management women who find themselves committed to family as well as to career. Second, they fail to recognize what these women could do for their middle management.

The ranks of middle managers are filled with people on their way up and people who have stalled. Many of them have simply reached their limits, achieved career growth commensurate with or exceeding their capabilities, and they cause problems because their performance is mediocre but they still want to move ahead. The career-and-family woman is willing to trade off the pressures and demands that go with promotion for the freedom to spend more time with her children. She's very smart, she's talented, she's committed to her career, and she's satisfied to stay at the middle level, at least during the early child-rearing years. Compare her with some of the people you have there now.

Consider a typical example, a woman who decides in college on a business career and enters management at age 22. For nine years, the company invests in her career as she gains experience and skills and steadily improves her performance. But at 31, just as the investment begins pay off in earnest, she decides to have a baby. Can the company afford to let her go home, take another job, or go into business for herself? The common perception now is yes, the corporation can afford to lose her unless, after six or eight weeks or even three months of disability and maternity leave, she returns to work on a full-time schedule with the same vigor, commitment, and ambition that she showed before.

But what if she doesn't? What if she wants or needs to go on leave for six months or a year or, heaven forbid, five years? In this worst-case scenario, she works full-time from age 22 to 31 and from 36 to 65—a total of 38 years as opposed to the typical male's 43 years. That's not a huge difference. Moreover, my typical example is willing to work part-time while her children are young, if only her employer will give her the opportunity. There are two rewards for companies responsive to this need: higher retention of their best people and greatly improved performance and satisfaction in their middle management.

The high-performing career-and-family woman can be a major player in your company. She can give you a significant business advantage as the competition for able people escalates. Sometimes too, if you can hold on to her, she will switch gears in mid-life and reenter the competition for the top. The price you must pay to retain these women is threefold: you must plea for and manage maternity, you must provide the flexibility that will allow them to be maximally productive, and you must take an active role in helping to make family supports and high-quality affordable child care available to all women.

The key to managing maternity is to recognize the value of high-performing women and the urgent need to retain them and keep them productive. The first step must be a genuine partnership between the woman and her boss. I know this partnership can seem difficult to forge. One of my own senior executives came to me recently to discuss plans for her maternity leave and subsequent return to work. She knew she wanted to come back. I wanted to make certain that she would. Still, we had a somewhat awkward conversation, because I knew that no woman can predict with certainty when she will be able to return to work or under what conditions. Physical problems can lengthen her leave. So can a demanding infant, a difficult family or personal adjustment, or problems with child care.

I still don't know when this valuable executive will be back on the job full-time, and her absence creates some genuine problems for our organization. But I do know that I can't simply replace her years of experience with a new recruit. Since our conversation, I also know that she wants to come back, and that she *will* come back—part-time at first—unless I make it impossible for her by, for example, setting an arbitrary date for her full-time return or resignation. In turn, she knows that the organization wants and needs her and, more to the point, that it will be responsive to her needs in terms of working hours and child-care arrangements.

In having this kind of conversation it's important to ask concrete questions that will help to move the discussion from uncertainty and anxiety to some level of predictability. Questions can touch on everything from family income and energy level to child care arrangements and career commitment. Of course you want your star manager to return to work as soon as possible but you want her to return permanently and productively. Her downtime on the job is a drain on her energies and a waste of your money.

For all the women who want to combine career and family—the women who want to participate actively in the rearing of their children and who also want to pursue their careers seriously—the key to retention is to provide the flexibility and family supports they need in order to function effectively.

Time spent in the office increases productivity if it is time well spent, but the fact that most women continue to take the primary responsibility for child care is a cause of distraction, diversion, anxiety, and absenteeism—to say nothing of the persistent guilt experienced by all working mothers. A great many women, perhaps most of all women who have always performed at the highest levels, are also frustrated by a sense that while their children are babies they cannot function at their best either at home or at work.

In its simplest form, flexibility is the freedom to take time off—a couple of hours, a day, a week—or to do some work at home and some at the office, an arrangement that communication technology makes increasingly feasible. At the complex end of the spectrum are alternative work schedules that permit the woman to work less than full-time and her employer to reap the benefits of her experience and, with careful planning, the top level of her abilities.

> Incredibly, very few companies have ever studied the costs and statistics of maternity leave.

Part-time employment is the single greatest inducement to getting women back on the job expeditiously and the provision women themselves most desire. A part-time return to work enables them to maintain responsibility for critical aspects of their jobs, keeps them in touch with the changes constantly occurring at the workplace and in the job itself, reduces stress and fatigue, often eliminates the need for paid maternity leave by permitting a return to the office as soon as disability leave is over, and, not least, can greatly enhance company loyalty. The part-time solution works particularly well when a work load can be reduced for one individual in a department or when a full-time job can be broken down by skill levels and apportioned to two individuals at different levels of skill and pay.

I believe, however, that shared employment is the most promising and will be the most widespread form of flexible scheduling in the future. It is feasible at every level of the corporation except at the pinnacle, for both the short and the long term. It involves two people taking responsibility for one job.

Two red lights flash on as soon as most executives hear the words "job sharing": continuity and client-customer contact. The answer to the continuity question is to place responsibility entirely on the two individuals sharing the job to discuss everything that transpires—thoroughly, daily, and on their own time. The answer to the problem of client-customer contact is yes, job sharing requires re-education and a period of adjustment. But as both client and supervisor will quickly come to appreciate, two contacts means that the customer has continuous access to the company's representative, without interruptions for vacation, travel, or sick leave. The two people holding the job can simply cover for each other, and the uninterrupted, full-time coverage they provide together can be a stipulation of their arrangement.

Flexibility is costly in numerous ways. It requires more supervisory time to coordinate and manage, more office space, and somewhat greater benefits costs (though these can be contained with flexible benefits plans, prorated benefits, and, in two-paycheck families, elimination of duplicate benefits). But the advantages of reduced turnover and the greater productivity that results from higher energy levels and greater focus can outweigh the costs.

A few hints:

- Provide flexibility selectively. I'm not suggesting private arrangements subject to the suspicion of favoritism but rather a policy that makes flexible work schedules available only to high performers.
- Make it clear that in most instances (but not all) the rates of advancement and pay will be appropriately lower for those who take time off or who work part-time than for those who work full-time. Most career-and-family women are entirely willing to make that trade-off.
- Discuss costs as well as benefits. Be willing to risk accusations of bias. Insist, for example, that half time is half of whatever time it takes to do the job, not merely half of 35 or 40 hours.

The woman who is eager to get home to her child has a powerful incentive to use her time effectively at the office and to carry with her reading and other work that can be done at home. The talented professional who wants to have it all can be a high performer by carefully ordering her priorities and by focusing on objectives rather than on the legendary 15-hour day. By the time professional women have their first babies—at an average age of 32—they have already had nine years to work long hours at a desk, to travel and to relocate. In the case of high performers, the need for flexibility coincides with what has gradually become the goal-oriented nature of responsibility.

Family supports—in addition to maternity leave and flexibility—include the provision of parental leave for men, support for two-career and single-parent families during relocation, and flexible benefits. But the primary ingredient is child care. The capacity of working mothers to function effectively and without interruption depends on the availability of good, affordable child care. Now that women make up almost half the work force and the growing percentage of managers, the decision to become involved in the personal lives of employees is no longer a philosophical question but a practical one. To make matters worse, the quality of child care has almost no relation to technology, inventiveness, or profitability but is more or less a pure function of the quality of child care personnel and the ratio of adults to children. These costs are irreducible. Only by joining hands with government and the public sector can corporations hope to create the vast quantity and variety of child care that their employees need.

Until quite recently, the response of corporations to women has been largely symbolic and cosmetic, motivated in large part by the will to avoid litigation and legal penalties. In some cases, companies were also moved by a genuine sense of fairness and a vague discomfort and frustration at the absence of women above the middle of the corporate pyramid. The actions they took were mostly quick, easy, and highly visible—child care information services, a three-month parental leave available to men as well as women, a woman appointed to the board of directors.

When I first began to discuss these issues 26 years ago, I was sometimes able to get an appointment with the assistant to the assistant in personnel, but it was only a courtesy. Over the past decade, I have met with the CEOs of many large corporations and I've watched them become involved with ideas they had never previously thought much about. Until recently, however, the shelf life of that enhanced awareness was always short. Given pressing, short-term concerns, women were not a front-burner issue. In the past few months, I have seen yet another change. Some CEOs and top management groups now take the initiative. They call and ask us to show them how to shift gears from a responsive to a proactive approach to recruiting, developing, and retaining women.

I think this change is more probably a response to business needs—to concern for the quality of future profits and managerial talent—than to uneasiness about legal requirements, sympathy with the demands of women and minorities, or the desire to do what is right and fair. The nature of such business motivation varies. Some companies want to move women to their positions as role models for those below them and as beacons for talented young recruits. Some want to achieve a favorable image with employees, customers, clients, and stockholders. These are all legitimate motives. But I think the companies that stand to gain most are motivated as well by a desire to capture competitive advantage in an era when talent and competence will be in increasingly short supply. These companies are now ready to stop being defensive about their experience with women and to ask incisive questions without preconceptions.

Even so, incredibly, I don't know of more than one or two companies that have looked into their own records to study the absolutely critical issue of maternity leave—how many women took it, when and whether they returned, and how this behavior correlated with their rank, tenure, age, and performance. The unique drawback to the employment of women is the physical reality of maternity and the particular socializing influence maternity has had. Yet to make women equal to men in the workplace we have chosen on the whole not to discuss this single most significant difference between them. Unless we do, we cannot evaluate the cost of recruiting, developing, and moving women up.

Now that interest is replacing indifference, there are four steps every company can take to examine its own experience with women:

1. Gather quantitative data on the company's experience with management-level women regarding turnover rates, occurrence of and return from maternity leave, and organizational level attained in relation to tenure and performance.
2. Correlate this data with factors such as age, marital status, and presence and age of children, and attempt to identify and analyze why women respond the way they do.
3. Gather qualitative data on the experience of women in your company and on how women are perceived by both sexes.
4. Conduct a cost-benefit analysis of the return on your investment in high-performing women. Factor in the cost to the company of women's negative reactions to negative experience, as well as the probable cost of corrective measures and policies. If women's value to your company is greater than the cost to recruit, train, and develop them—and of course I believe it will be—then you will want to do everything you can to retain them.

We have come a tremendous distance since the days when the prevailing male wisdom saw women as lacking the kind of intelligence that would allow them to succeed in business. For decades, even women themselves have harbored an unspoken belief that they couldn't make it because they couldn't be just like men, and nothing else would do. But now that woman have shown themselves the equal of men in every area of organizational activity, now that they have demonstrated that they can be stars in every field of endeavor, now we can all venture to examine the fact that women and men are different.

On balance, employing women is more costly than employing men. Women can acknowledge this fact today because they know that their value to employers exceeds the additional cost and because they know that changing attitudes can reduce the additional cost dramatically. Women in management are no longer an idiosyncrasy of the arts and education. They have always matched men in natural ability. Within a very few years, they will equal men in numbers as well in every area of economic activity.

The demographic motivation to recruit and develop women is compelling. But an older question remains: Is society better for the change? Women's exit from the home and entry into the work force has certainty created problems—an urgent need for good, affordable child care; troubling questions about the kind of parenting children need; the costs and difficulties of diversity in the workplace; the stress and fatigue of combining work and family responsibilities. Wouldn't we all be happier if we could turn back the clock to an age when men were in the workplace and women in the home, when male and female roles were clearly differentiated and complementary?

Nostalgia, anxiety, and discouragement will urge many to say yes, but my answer is emphatically no. Two fundamental benefits that were unattainable in the past are now within our reach. For the individual, freedom of choice—in this case the freedom to choose career, family, or a combination of the two. For the corporation, access to the most gifted individuals in the country. These benefits are neither self-indulgent nor insubstantial. Freedom of choice and self-realization are too deeply American to be cast aside for some wistful vision of the past. And access to our most talented human resources is not a luxury in this age of explosive international competition but rather the barest minimum that prudence and national self-preservation require.

Felice N. Schwartz is president and founder of Catalyst, a not-for-profit research and advisory organization that works with corporations to foster the career and leadership development of women.

GIRL GANGS

They got it goin' on.

By Ann C. Logue

Networking is a powerful way to meet people and get things done. Unfortunately, it's one of those important but not urgent things that don't always get the attention they deserve. For women in particular—who may also be running households and raising children (and who almost always shoulder most of the responsibility for those things, according to recent reality checks)—there isn't enough time to attend a formal networking meeting. And the more informal contacts one makes could be more helpful by being more specific and less guarded about giving advice and sharing information. It's easier to ask a friend about salary negotiation than to ask someone sitting across from you at a luncheon meeting.

Many women have risen to the challenge by forming their own small groups—Girl Gangs—that get together regularly in person, by phone, or via email to talk about life and career. These buddies share ideas and contacts, celebrate personal and professional successes, and help their members get more done. The power they represent is as awesome as that of any the Powerpuff Girls on Saturday morning TV.

No less a personage than Oprah Winfrey says she relies on informal networks. In the July/August 2000 issue of her magazine, *O,* she writes about her "Spa Girls," a group of friends who get together to encourage each other in their diet, exercise, and personal growth programs. Because the members are all media executives, there's at least some professional networking going on during their workouts.

In this era of multitasking, Oprah isn't the only woman who is mingling her personal and professional lives with the help of an informal network of like-minded people. Given the demands faced by the average American woman juggling work, family, and life in general, an informal group offers a great way to harness the energy of different people dealing with similar situations.

Let's look at a few groups that have formed informally and that are helping their members advance professionally while providing friendship and personal support. Perhaps we'll inspire you to draw on this power for yourself or for your organization.

True stories

The Corporate Manager. In a big company, one needs to network just to navigate efficiently. In fact, it's as important to network within a company as it is to network outside of it.

Daimler-Chrysler has 13,000 people working in its Auburn Hills, Michigan headquarters. Kathryn Lee, staff labor programs administrator, is proud that her company supports a Women's Network Group and provides a number of opportunities for after-hours networking, including guest speakers and presentations. But as a working mother of two young children, formal networking is a low priority for her right now.

"Being perfectly candid, I would rather spend my evening with my family and pass on the optional business gatherings," she says. Intentionally or not, her company has provided a networking opportunity for women in the exact same circumstance.

Main Points

- Many women have risen to the time-crunch challenge by forming small groups called Girl Gangs that get together regularly in person, by phone, or via email to talk about life and career.
- Given the demands faced by the average American woman juggling work and family, an informal group offers a great way to harness the energy of different people in similar situations.
- Typically, exchanging ideas informally leads to better formal work and getting tapped for larger, more visible projects in the organization.

After her second child was born, Lee started spending her lunches and breaks in Daimler-Chrysler's lactation room, where she met a lot of other women.

"You could spot us a mile away," she says, "with the sweater or suit jacket to cover up leaks and the oversized Pump-

The Girl Gangs in Your Company

Here are some suggestions for institutionalizing several aspects of informal networking. There are many great ideas and good work being done within informal networks in your organization. Just be aware of the risks as well as the opportunities. After all, some of these groups are forming because people don't feel comfortable where they work.

Kirshenbaum Bond & Partners, a New York-based advertising agency, has a working mothers group that meets regularly to discuss various relevant issues. Angela Renfroe, the human resources manager who runs the group, has a few tips. The first is, once again, use technology.

"Here, the culture is that we communicate through email," says Renfroe. "I've set up an email address book for the working mothers, and they us it for referrals, tips, and support."

Renfroe also found that the members preferred holding meetings onsite rather than offsite, in part because they didn't have time for long lunches.The support of senior management in setting up the group and listening to its suggestions has made the group powerful. Besides such relatively simple matters as getting a lactation room set up, the group asked for flextime.

"We were able to do it in accounting," says Renfroe.

You would think that any organization might want to use informal networks to create positive change.

Nina Adams, a consultant who helps organizations use technology to improve performance, is a big believer in the use of informal networking to grow organizations. One of the things she does is help companies use their intranets to create peer-networking opportunities. She points to a large bank as an example.

"The kinds of problems a teller supervisor in Chicago has might be the same as those of a teller supervisor in Los Angeles. If a bank were to set up an [informal network] of teller supervisors, they could use email or Web meetings to share information and learn new skills."

"That," Adam believes, "could lead to increased power within the organization. Maybe the network develops a list of FAQs for supervisors that gets on the company's intranet. Then, the network members are affecting policy and could be asked to work on larger assignments, such as best practices."

You would think that any organization might want to use informal networks to create positive change from within rather than have people pooling resources to get new jobs elsewhere. But that isn't always the case. One interviewee, who asked that neither she nor her company be identified, told this story:

When she was working for a large consulting firm, women within each department tended to meet regularly for lunch to talk about work and to share ideas. One year, the annual promotion list came out and no women in the firm were on it. When people started asking around, it turned out that many women throughout the firm had similar issues that had been discussed informally. Several decided to form a formal group to write a letter to senior management in the hope of making changes.

"Once it became formal, it was viewed as a bad thing politically to be involved in," she says. Instead of becoming agents for positive change, the women involved were considered to be whiners and complainers, and almost all of them left the firm within two years.

N-Style bag. Since we were all on a schedule, we got to know each other pretty well. It felt like we were in a secret club."

In part because they didn't work together, these women would use their pumping sessions to share ideas for work as well as to talk about kids. Lee credits the group for helping her stick to nursing for a year, which isn't easy. She says she's also grateful for the opportunity to meet others in her company without taking extra time to attend meetings after work.

"I learned which areas in the company have great bosses, which departments have a lot of international travel, and other information that I can use on my job," she says. And her companion nursing mothers formed a cross-departmental network as strong as any within the company.

The Academic. Universities are hardly free from the political and career-management demands of corporate life. Marita Golden is a writer and professor in the M.F.A. Graduate Creative Writing Program at Virginia Commonwealth University in Richmond. She often meets with a group of other African American women teaching at colleges in the Washington, D.C. area.

"The group has helped us feel that we are supported in the trenches, even though we're not all at the same university," she says. "It's very good to know that you're not alone and that your experiences are valid."

Golden believes these groups are vitally important. "Even in a university, there are very few situations where we get together to talk about what we are doing creatively," she says.

In Golden's experience, an informal group gives members a better chance to talk about their research or their articles in progress than in an organized faculty forum, which often degenerates into discussions about students, grading, and university policies. Her group finds that exchanging ideas informally leads to better formal academic work in the long run. They also enjoy discussing their lives in general with colleagues who have become friends.

"One woman in the group was a grandmother who provided greater wisdom about life that we came to rely on," says Golden.

That powerful combination of the personal and the professional is one reason that members come to rely on their girl gangs.

The Entrepreneur. Betsy Beaumon is an electrical engineer by training who worked for Lam Research and Cisco Systems before starting an Internet company, selling it, and then joining another startup as a vice president. In fact, if she weren't a woman, she'd be the very stereotype of the young Silicon Valley executive.

Beaumon is part of a girl gang that has been a source of great camaraderie and professional support as she has moved up in her career. The group formed years ago, when she linked up with five other women who were going to the same trade shows "even though we lived only 10 miles apart. We were just too busy."

The group gets together regularly to help each other navigate the ever-turbulent waters of high technology. The members communicate almost daily by email. "It's the same kind of things guys do," Beaumon says. "We even get together and slam down a goodly number of cosmopolitans when the opportunity arises."

Though their meetings are generally social, their discussions are not. Among other things, Beaumon says the group has exchanged leads on office space and phone systems as well as shared advice on cultural issues within startups and technology companies.

"It's an interesting dynamic when the group is together," she says, "and it's helpful to have someone you can bounce ideas off of and explain how things work. With my current job at a startup, it was great to have friends who knew how to negotiate stock options and salaries for a high-level position."

Although the economy is changing quickly, the shared strengths of Beaumon's girl gang let the members view the change as a fabulous opportunity.

How to Form Your Own Girl Gang

Chances are, you know people with whom you can share ideas and insight. But how can you harness that energy? Here are a few ideas to get you started.

First, there is no substitute for taking charge, whether your group ultimately becomes structured or informal. That's how Marita Golden launched her group. While she was teaching at George Mason University, other African American women who were teaching there kept telling her that they should get together for lunch someday.

"Finally, I just put my foot down and said, 'Hey, we're having a potluck at my house this Sunday.' "

If you have friends and colleagues with similar good intentions, maybe it's time to pick a date and invite everyone over. To make it easier, you can use an online invitation service like Yahoo! Invites (invites.yahoo.com) or evite(www.evite.com).

You can use technology other ways. Liz Ryan turned to Topica, an email list-management service (www.topica.com), when she started ChicWit. Topica lets people organize and operate their own email lists. It's one way to build informal contacts over a wide group of people, such as alums from your school, former coworkers, and people who work in the same profession in your town. Who knows? Someone may have already set up a list that's appropriate for you. To find out, check Topica.

Last, if you have a specific goal, such as changing your job or starting a fitness program, you may want to look at the ground rules that Oprah Winfrey established with her Spa Girls. She recommends creating a routine for meetings and keeping a record of members' progress, which may be what you need to do to reach your goal. Her Website has some information on how to get organized (www.oprah.com/spagirl/spagirl_landing.html).

The email list

It's relatively easy to form a girl gang if you're running into like-minded people in the course of your day. But what if you aren't?

That was one of the problems facing Liz Ryan, co-founder and vice president of Ucentric Systems. She needed to hire a lot of technical people for her company and hoped for a good gender balance among the new employees.

"I thought, I want to meet these women. Where are they?"

Last July, Ryan started the Chicago Women in Technology—aptly shortened to ChicWit—email list as a virtual version of a traditional networking group. It also quickly took on characteristics of an informal group as many subscribers use the list for help with nonprofessional aspects of their life. Along with job listings and announcements for business events, there are also frequent requests for recommendations for nannies, financial planners, and even hairdressers. Some subscribers have even used it to form their own version of Oprah's Spa Girls.

"People trust the members to help them," says Ryan. By getting help with some of the personal aspects of their lives, the list members can put more energy into their careers.

ChicWit spread quickly. "I told a couple of friends, and they told a few more," says Ryan, until there were more than 1,600 subscribers. They, including Ryan, almost immediately saw a need for similar lists in other cities.

"I started MassWit when Ucentric moved to Boston and I had to hire people there," Ryan says. When that list also took off, she took the list global. There are currently 29 local lists in the United States, Canada, and Australia, with more being added wherever there are women in technology looking to meet others.

The email girl gang now has a formal name, WorldWit (www.worldwit.org).

The power of the Girl Gang

Networks don't have to involve monthly dress-up luncheon meetings at downtown hotels. There are people you know—or can find—who may have ideas for helping you run your business and your life better. By forming your own girl gang, you can draw on possibilities to make all of the members more powerful.

How do I know these networks exist? When I got the story assignment, I sent out two emails—one to my own girl gang of friends, relatives, and acquaintances and one to the ChicWit email list, which I subscribe to because I write a lot of Web content. Every anecdote, every expert, every person mentioned in this article came from those two messages. If my gang is that good, yours can be, too.

Ann C. Logue *is principal of Freelance Communications, based in Chicago; annl@bignet.net.*

From *Training & Development*, January 2001, pp. 24-28.

Secrets of Finding and Keeping GOOD EMPLOYEES

"To do the best job possible, it is important for America's hiring professionals to challenge their interview processes."

BY JIM SIRBASKU

EVERY JOB IN A COMPANY is important, or it wouldn't exist. In other words, there is a good job for everyone—one where each individual makes a valuable contribution, regardless of where that job is in a company's structure. Finding that person, though, requires a scientific process. That conviction comes from over 35 years experience recruiting, interviewing, and selecting nearly 10,000 salespeople.

Many people believe gut instinct works like magic in selecting key personnel. This is especially true when the person doing the hiring is also successful at doing the job. For example, a top sales producer may think that he or she is the best person to pick other people who will be able to sell successfully. In reality, that likelihood results in less than a 50% success ratio. With stats like that, a toss of the coin could save recruiters a lot of time, energy, and money.

In most job searches, those responsible for doing the hiring sell the job before they select a candidate. This approach is backwards. Why sell the job to someone who isn't a candidate? After all, a savvy applicant may be a good "interview"—well-groomed, friendly, professional, enthusiastic, interested, a good listener, etc. What happens in this case is the recruiter starts doing the talking, telling about the job requirements before the interview starts. It's the candidate who's doing the listening, learning how to appeal to the recruiter. The result is that,

HOW NOT TO KEEP GOOD EMPLOYEES

"Teamwork means that each of you do exactly what I tell you to do."

since most individuals can mask their true tendencies for at least 45 minutes, the interviewer rarely gets an accurate picture of the job candidate. Alternatively, why not learn profiles of interviewees before taking the time to sell the job? Then, it may not be necessary to disclose job specifics once this information is gathered if the candidate doesn't represent a good fit.

By selling the job before selecting a candidate, the individuals responsible for hiring often fall prey to pre- and postselection variables. It's a sink-or-swim philosophy that says, "Recruit them in masses; train them in classes; and roll them out on their hockey skates." *That* is postselection. This method is not effective, so some people camouflage it to make it look different. Preselection is when one tries to learn about the candidates and gather information *before* putting them on the job. For instance, accountants typically have personalities that are relatively high-energy, usually indicate a good learning pace, and show an interest in working with numbers and data in general. Yet, these traits cannot be assumed simply because a person is interviewing for an accountant position. The only way to really determine, at the end of an interview, if a job candidate is a potential match is to take the time *up front* to learn about an interviewee.

The art of interviewing is and always has been highly underrated. Many people can ask good questions, but those aren't always as specific to the position as they could be. For example, if you are hiring an accountant, there are questions designed specifically for determining whether a person is capable of offering what an employer needs. By knowing the position requires conscientious behavior and discourages spontaneity, interviewers can design and ask more-targeted and appropriate lines of inquiry, such as: Describe what you've done in the past to make your job easier, or Explain the types of circumstances in which you have felt it necessary to overlook some policies or procedures because they got in the way of reaching a goal. The responses to such inquiries can help uncover whether a person believes that rules can be interpreted loosely.

Similarly, if the position requires an organized individual vs. a reactive one, questions should be asked to zero in on those behaviors, such as: What system do you use to ensure nothing is lost or overlooked?, or Typically, how much time do you spend on planning and handling the small details at your work? The answers here help clarify whether the person will react to situations as they develop instead of creating proactive, detailed plans. Moreover, they show whether the person would have to go against his or her nature to do well in a structured organization with many rules, tight deadlines, and strict codes of behavior.

To do the best job possible, it is important for America's hiring professionals to challenge their interview processes. This includes looking closely at steps that lead up to final hiring decisions and estimating the degree to which hiring decisions are riddled with personal biases. The more scientific the interview is, the less likely emotional decisions will direct the ensuing course of events.

Let's face it; the right job is the only one you have. It may not be the best job, but it's the right job. Recruiting and hiring the wrong person into the right job set[s] in motion a chain of events that can prove disastrous.

Imagine the interviews where emotional hiring decisions are made. The wrong people begin the right jobs and, after trying to perform them, the new hires begin to feel uncomfortable with their obvious lack of progress. Their inability to move forward within a reasonable amount of time naturally brings on stress. The ongoing stress that now burdens these new employees regularly begins to manifest itself negatively. For example, they start to focus on contrary, pessimistic points of view. This should come as no surprise, considering the overwhelming insecurity they feel at this stage.

It is something of an imposter phenomenon. Employees know that, if the hiring process had been based on scientific data alone, they wouldn't have been considered past the first interview. Employees feel out of their league, assume that they are unable to meet expectations, and, thus, a continually defeatist attitude is born.

Heightened feelings of stress become part of the mismatched employee's every workday. Although stress is a psychosomatic illness, it manifests itself in physiological problems, one of which is fatigue. Watch these victims, and notice they tend to speak with a breathy tone once they have reached this stage of stress. Whether aware of it or not, this depressed tone is primarily due to their oppressive sense of fatigue. The next symptom is an increase in absenteeism or increasing difficulty to make it through a full day of work.

Most managers want to reduce and eliminate poor performers by just firing them on the spot. However, that drastic step is far different than what actually should be done. Consider the fact that business moves at the speed of thought, yet relationships aren't given the time or attention necessary to develop. So what typically happens is managers get frustrated and angry with their people and choose to employ the KITA (kick-in-the-ankle) motivation technique.

Often, the boss feels better by going in and turning up the heat. While the big boss walks out like a magician exiting the stage from an applauding audience, the already stressed-out employee enters the meltdown stage. This is when the search for self-preservation begins. They seek out partners-in-crime, meaning others whom dislike the boss, and begin the conflict stage.

After recruiting the coworkers who share their same defeatist attitude toward the company, they spend (waste) time discussing how unjustified the boss' actions are.

Once the word gets around, he is compelled to find a solution before the wrongly hired employee recruits even more malcontents, which could spiral the war between employer and employee out of control. Hiring the wrong person for the right job can set off a chain of events that often does irreparable damage.

Barring some unforeseen miracle, a person's personality doesn't change significantly. People cannot be what they are not meant to be for very long, and that is a painful realization for individuals who run companies. Hiring professionals, trainers, and managers cannot perform magic. Simply telling employees what you want them to become doesn't mean they can internalize those requests and strive to match the profile they were given. The result is that so much time and money are spent on hiring and training the wrong people for the right jobs.

The mistake to avoid goes beyond just having hired the wrong type of person. The real error comes from not realizing that, by simply moving that individual into a more-appropriate position within the company, the problem could easily be fixed. Otherwise, it's very difficult to move the wrong people out of the right jobs—especially if they are putting forth great effort in an ongoing attempt to succeed at what they are not meant to be doing anyway.

This can become a vicious circle that inevitably results in a lose-lose situation for all parties involved. If at all possible, the sensible solution is to relocate a mismatched employee elsewhere in the company. As the saying goes, "For every pot, there's a cover." For every job, there's a person who will perform it with excellence.

What works, what doesn't

Group interviews don't work. They are superficial and more like a game of tag. Selections based on first impressions are flawed. Recruiters' personal biases get in the way. What does work is testing. To understand why, consider a brief chronology of the industry's progress with identifiable components of the hiring process:

Interviews. For far too long, the most important factor in deciding whom to hire was the interview. Experience has shown only a coincidental correlation between the ability to deliver well in an interview and to do so on the job. Studies have pegged this correlation at 14%, or one good employee out of every seven hires. This number increases to 26% if the candidate can pass a background check.

Personality characteristics assessments. The first assessments used to improve the selection process measured personality characteristics. They helped raise the hiring success percentage to 38%.

Abilities assessments. When applicants were assessed for abilities as well as personality, employers found they were hiring the right people approximately 54% of the time.

Interests assessments. Becoming more sophisticated, interests assessment was added to the mix, improving results to 66%.

Integrated assessments. Most impressive to date, these measure a combination of factors, as well as introduce the component of "job match." Cutting-edge technology coupled with empirical data evaluate "The Total Person" in such a way as to measure how much candidates are like the employees who are exemplary in performing their duties. These assessments have increased an employer's ability to identify potentially excellent employees better than 75% of the time.

Assessment vehicles dramatically facilitate the hiring process. The job-match function is the most valuable feature of this process. It refers to the assessment's approach to analyzing a person's job-related attributes and compares them to the qualities required to perform successfully in a given job. By measuring thinking styles, occupational interests, and behavioral traits, the combination allows for a visualization of "The Total Person."

In an interview capacity, people only let you see what they want you to see. Therefore, it's true that individuals can be compared to icebergs in that what you don't see is more significant than what you do. In typical interviews, employers see/scan resumes for work history and education. They observe the way prospects dress, accessorize, and how they carry and conduct themselves. On the other hand, there are significant blind spots for interviewers who choose to ignore assessment testing.

Take, for instance, thinking styles. Evaluating how quickly people can solve problems or absorb information and how capable they are at dealing with simple numbers or comprehending written language are examples of these thinking styles. Occupational interests, as they relate to a particular job or position, are a significant factor in the results and productivity achieved by an individual. Essentially, this part of assessing means learning what will stimulate excitement and commitment from workers. Finally, the assessment of behavior tendencies, as they relate to a particular position, is a significant factor in the results and productivity achieved by an individual:

- *Accommodating* measures a person's general tendency to be friendly, helpful, and agreeable, to be a team person.
- *Assertiveness* measures a tendency to take charge, to be a leader.
- *Attitude* measures a tendency to have a positive attitude.
- *Energy level* measures a tendency to be self-motivated, energetic, to show a high sense of urgency and a capacity for a fast pace.
- *Independence* measures a tendency to make decisions, be self-

reliant, and take independent action.

- *Objective judgment* measures a tendency to be objective in decisionmaking.
- *Sociability* measures a tendency to be people-oriented, to be socially active and outgoing.
- *Manageability* measures the tendency to follow policies, accept external controls and supervision, and work within the rules.
- *Decisiveness* measures the tendency to utilize available information to make decisions quickly.

For a general indication of what happens "behind the scenes" with assessment testing, consider a firm that needs to hire salespeople. A tool is created that matches current top producers from a pattern of their behavioral traits, occupational interests, and learning styles. The combined pattern created is called a Job Match Pattern.

Dig further into the job's requirements by interviewing the people who will be managing the new hires. Ask these managers questions that will uncover their true expectations of the position that needs to be filled. A Job Profile Survey is then filled out and the results are combined with the Job Match Pattern, which ultimately produces a profile of the characteristics required to do the task successfully. In cases where there isn't an incumbent, those who know the job best determine the traits required by the position.

A war for talent is currently under way. This includes a price war, which CEOs need to avoid at all costs. One positive alternative to salary hikes is to offer opportunities for personal growth. In addition, companies should create a culture where employee recognition and appreciation are built into it. These steps will keep worker retention rates high. Here are some effective tools for accomplishing these goals:

- Use a newsletter to recognize an employee-of-the-month. This motivates everyone to get involved. Whether a person is hoping to be nominated or doing the nominating, the process is exciting and meaningful. Consider giving each month's winner a monetary bonus.
- Create an ambience where staff is comfortable. If offices have large windows, plants, outdoor patios, a pleasant dining area, etc., people can take a break and relax.
- Give employees the day off on their birthdays, and celebrate those birthdays at the office with a cake and/or other refreshments.
- Conduct a weekly training session, one night per week. At these meetings, allow each company executive the opportunity to lead a 30-to-60-minute discussion on whatever subject he or she chooses. In some cases, these might be emotional/personal stories. They can be serious or fun. At other times, an executive might want to discuss a recently read book, an industry event, or leadership and management topics. In addition to the presentations, set aside time for exchanging ideas and always include a segment for bringing employees up to date and up to speed, which is when all important company information is announced.
- For computer programmers, consider giving them keys to the building so they can have control over their specific areas. Allow them to work any hours they select and dress however they choose. It works for them. Many like staying up all night and working in little conclaves.

Remember, though, that the value and success of these opportunities are dependent on selecting the right person for the position and creating the right corporate culture.

"The importance of hiring the right people for the job cannot be overstated. That's why CEOs and managers can't become lazy in the hiring process."

As a company grows, CEOs have to be cautious about their span of control. It is very hard to know 100 people very well, but not so difficult to know 10 very well. This means knowing that group's spouses, children, birthdays, what makes them happy, and what discourages them. Most importantly, it means understanding the three key characteristics—occupational interests, thinking styles, and behavioral traits.

When these characteristics are known, it helps managers to learn how certain workers will respond to stress, frustration, and conflict very differently than others. Some react by leaping into action, while others fold like a cheap suitcase. Therefore, the answer to learning what rewards and incentives work best is getting to know employees. Some are motivated by time off, others by freedom to come and go as they please. There is no alternative to and no advantage like getting to know what makes employees tick.

The importance of hiring the right people for the job cannot be overstated. That's why CEOs and managers can't become lazy in the hiring process. As the saying goes, "there's fish in every pond," so a constant stream of applicants coming through the door should be maintained. Doing this requires using nontraditional avenues to find them. The reality is that the classified section isn't the prevailing starting point for hiring anyone. Getting the message out means advertising on radio, television, including local cable, and the Internet. Since it is estimated that well over 50% of people aren't happy with their current jobs, it is likely that they are looking at these media for a stab at self-improvement or upward mobility.

Once the likely candidates are gathered, the importance of using assessments in the hiring process is critical. Be sure that all the assessments utilized have job-match concepts and that any tool used has been tested for validity and reliability. Don't be afraid to ask applicants to take a test that runs as long as an hour. It's their time, and you are not paying them for it.

In the end, this process creates a win-win situation for everyone. People are happier, produce more, and experience less stress. Every company needs more individuals who are able to get up in the morning, go to work, and enjoy what they do all day long. People need to think of ways they can do things instead of reasons they cannot. They have to look to their strengths over their weaknesses and their power over their problems. When companies focus on a good job match, by finding the best human capital available for the job, the real benefit goes to the employees. Employers owe it to society to match the right people to the right jobs.

Jim Sirbasku *is CEO, Profiles International, a Waco, Tex.-based employment evaluation firm.*

From *USA Today* magazine (Society for the Advancement of Education), January 2002.

CIPD REWARD CONFERENCE

Pay it forward

Sophisticated reward systems are based on performance: not only by individuals but at company, business unit and team level too. If your organisation has not yet managed this, these tactics will show you how

PATRICIA ZINGHEIM AND JAY SCHUSTER

BRANDING TOTAL REWARD SCHEMES has become globally popular. But there is a problem. Too often, when companies talk about "total reward" they simply mean providing generous benefits and a positive place to work. This makes a company attractive to the workforce in general but perhaps not to those who will make your enterprise prosper. We believe companies need to fashion their workplace to be attractive to people who are dedicated to adding value to the business. This is a critical priority, especially during these competitive business times.

It is true that the best people work for more than pay. But our experience shows that there are four essential components which create an atmosphere in which the best people will want to work (*see panel, "Total Reward Components"*). Offer employees an opportunity to grow from a career perspective and a chance to commit to a future they can help make a reality. Make the workplace positive and supportive of high performance. And provide total pay comprised of base pay, variable pay (incentives and equity), benefits, and recognition. While companies' packages vary in emphasis, this combination—our model of total reward—is key to making a company attractive to those who are essential to its success.

Companies have always given lip service to " paying for performance". But if you can capture the hearts, minds and performance of your workforce through a total reward model, instead of merely "sloganising", your company will perform better. It brands your company as an enterprise that wants those who are willing to perform and add value to the business.

Changing rewards is a "hot" change, meaning one that quickly gets everybody's attention. Other tools, such as training and employment policies, are "cold"—they are slow to act and may not even affect current members of staff. Cold changes are much easier but far less effective at boosting performance.

We encourage HR to focus during competitive times on more action-oriented change tools and a total reward solution is the most powerful. But this requires courage and patience. It isn't a quick-fix solution. Even if the effects are fast, it can take time to put in place and may mean following best effective practice rather than just prevailing practice and sometimes breaking new ground in your industry or country.

We propose that your package aims to reward performance at a variety of levels including the company, business unit, small team and individual. Companies wanting to provide attractive total rewards must justify any extra cost in terms of both organisational and workforce outcomes. The workforce must also understand that providing total rewards is reliant upon a sustained level of measured outcomes for organisation growth. Growth is essential—the top organisations seldom shrink to greatness.

Guaranteeing jobs, supporting an attractive work-life balance, adding pay and incentives, encouraging personal development and making the workplace appealing all make poor business sense without an understanding of the need for high performance. Yet we feel most existing solutions ignore performance and encourage entitlement.

Creating such a performance culture requires a relationship between business results and rewards. This means developing an effective performance measurement system that allows the company to credibly reward performance. This isn't an easy job under any circumstances, and not one that can be undertaken without sponsorship from the organisation's leaders and workforce involvement. It needs close attention to the design of the systems and tools that will be needed and effective communication. It isn't as simple as just matching what other companies have done and hoping for the best relative to workforce performance.

Total Reward Components	
Individual Growth	Compelling Future
Total Pay	Positive Workplace

Getting serious about total rewards in the context of value added to the business is the only logical reason to change reward design and communicate a new cultural direction. Here are some tactics to gain lasting value from reward change:

1. **Build the business case and strategy.** Decide why you are changing rewards, what the company will get from it and how this relates to making the enterprise more effective. Set down a meaningful strategy and tactical plan and build a logical business case that justifies why doing this is a priority.
2. **Design measurement metrics and tools.** If you decide to focus total rewards on performance improvement (and we hope you do!), determine what, how, and where performance will be objectively and credibly measured. Then measure it. Do a cost/benefit analysis so you know whether total rewards are adding value to your business.
3. **Target workforce groups.** Focus on the people who are most important to your enterprise. Make total rewards highly attractive to employee groups who have skills and competencies closest to those your company needs and the essential short-supply talent necessary for your business model. Target workforce members who are willing to go the extra mile to get the rewards.
4. **Develop total reward components.** Using our four components of total rewards as a guide, develop your company's total reward solution, keeping the first three tactical suggestions above, in mind. Build a business logic for what you are offering, describe your expectations and identify which employee groups will be attracted to work in a company with this total reward structure.
5. **Solidify champions for longer haul.** Make sure leaders are willing to sponsor the initiative. Help them appreciate that changing rewards may be a " noisy" process and that they will need to get the company through this to make a new reward model work. Be certain they understand that this new reward model applies to them as well as everyone else. Reward role models are very important to making lasting cultural change.
6. **Get people involved.** Involve employees through focus groups or participation in the design process. People more readily accept change they help to create, so getting those to whom the total reward solution is directed into the design process, is critical. An involved workforce can make acceptance much easier.
7. **Address technical design.** Make the total reward design technically sound. Give details the attention they deserve. But remember that a reward solution that is technically excellent but has a poorly conceived strategy is unlikely to add value.
8. **Communicate, follow up and fine-tune.** Strong and consistent communication and follow-up are essential even when you would like to congratulate yourself for a job well done. Constant tuning will be needed to fill any gaps. While cultural change can get a boost from a reward change, this remains a long-term commitment of time and resources.

There's no going back to reward designs that make either the employee the only customer for the reward change or the company the only beneficiary of the reward design. We will increasingly see reward formulas that have something nearly all current pay and reward designs miss: meaningful performance solutions and reward solutions.

Patricia K Zingheim and Jay R Schuster are speaking at the CIPD's Annual Reward Conference on 12 February at the Novotel London West Hotel, Hammersmith. For further details, call 020 8263 3434 or visit www.cipd.co.uk/RewardConference. They are partners in Schuster-Zingheim and Associates, Inc., a Los Angeles-based international pay and rewards consultancy founded in 1985. They were selected as pay and motivation gurus in *The Guru Guide* and wrote *Pay People Right! Breakthrough Reward Strategies to Create Great Companies,* (Jossey-Bass, 2000), along with the all-time best selling book on workforce pay, *The New Pay: Linking Employee and Organizational Performance,* (Jossey-Bass, 1996). They are international speakers and authors of over 100 articles.

Case: *The "Homes" Is Where the Union Is*

Recently 700 employees of a city nursing home and the city home for the aged (two facilities located on the same plot of land) voted overwhelmingly to be represented by a union. The bargaining unit includes a great variety of employees, from custodial and maintenance to social workers and professional nurses. When interviewed after the union had won bargaining rights, the employees claimed that arbitrary and inconsistent treatment by management, and the supervisors in particular, comprised the main reasons for their voting for the union. They charged discriminatory treatment and flagrant favoritism. They also charged that the supervisors made it a practice to discharge employees for trivial reasons or without adequate prior warnings. Employees were subjected to frequent criticism by their supervisors with regard to their job performance. Although many of the supervisors had been promoted from the "ranks," many of them seemed to abuse their authority in dealing with their subordinates.

Top managers in both locations were genuinely surprised when they first learned during negotiations about this serious and widespread employee discontent.

Using the Case on The *"Homes" Is Where the Union Is*

For this case you should consider yourself an arbitrator who has been presented with this case. After reading the case, what decision would you give, knowing that other people had had time off and that memos were only requested at varying intervals?

Go over the review questions at the end. How does the class feel about this as a group? Why?

Exercise: *Assumptions About People at Work*

Instructions

The purpose of this exercise is to help you better understand the assumptions you make about people and their work behaviors. On the following questionnaire, you will find 10 sets of questions. Assign a rank from 0 to 10 to each item in each pair. (0 indicates that you completely disagree with the statement, and 10 means that you completely agree with the statement.) Answer each question as honestly as you can. There are no correct answers, so don't give a response to a question that will sound good to others or that you think is the way you are supposed to answer.

Questions

1. It's only human nature for people to do as little work as they can get away with. ____ (a) When people avoid work, it's usually because their work has been deprived of its meaning. (b)
2. If employees have access to any information they want, they tend to have better attitudes and behave more responsibly. ,____(c) If employees have access to more information than they need to do their immediate tasks, they will usually misuse it. ____ (d)
3. One problem in asking for the ideas of employees is that their perspective is too limited for their suggestions to be of much practical value. ____ (e) Asking employees for their ideas broadens their perspective and results in the development of useful suggestions. ____ (f)
4. If people don't use much imagination and ingenuity on the job, it's probably because relatively few people have much of either. ____ (g) Most people are imaginative and creative but may not show it because of limitations imposed by supervision and the job. ____ (h)
5. People tend to raise their standards if they are accountable for their own behavior and for correcting their own mistakes. ____ (i) People tend to lower their standards if they are not punished for their misbehavior and mistakes. ____ (j)
6. It's better to give people both good and bad news because most employees want the whole story, no matter how painful. ____ (k) It's better to withhold unfavorable news about business because most employees really want to hear only the good news. ____(l)
7. Because supervisors are entitled to more respect than those below them in the organization, it weakens their prestige to admit that a subordinate was right and they were wrong. ____ (m) Because people at all levels are entitled to equal respect, a supervisor's prestige is increased when s/he supports this principle by admitting that a subordinate was right and s/he was wrong. ____ (n)
8. If you give people enough money, they are less likely to be concerned with such intangibles as responsibility and recognition. ____ (0) If you give people interesting and chal-

lenging work, they are less likely to complain about such things as pay and supplemental benefits. ____ (p)

9. If people are allowed to set their own goals and standards of performance, they tend to set them higher than the boss would. ____ (q) If people are allowed to set their own goals and standards of performance, they tend to set them lower than the boss would. ____ (r)
10. The more knowledge and freedom a person has regarding his job, the more controls are needed to keep him/her in line. ____ (s) The more knowledge and freedom a person has regarding his/her job, the fewer controls are needed to ensure satisfactory job performance. ____ (t)

After Completing the Questionnaire

When you have completed all of the questions, you may score the questionnaire in the following manner. Add together the scores of items: (a), (d), (e), (g), (j), (I), (in), (o), (r), and (s). The sum of these scores will provide you with your 'Theory X" score. Then add together the remaining scores: (b), (C), (f), (h), (i), (k), (n), (p), (q), and (t). The sum of these scores will give you your Theory Y" score.

In a group, discuss the relative strength of each of your scores. Is there a significant difference in the two scores? What might this mean? How do you believe your assumptions might affect your actions as a manager? Do your past experiences support the self-profile that has emerged from your discussion? Discuss with other members of your group how your scores may be related to the concepts of "espoused theory" and "theory-in-use."

Case: The "Homes" Is Where the Union Is; Exercise: Assumptions About People at Work, Fred Maidment, McGraw-Hill/Dushkin, 2000.

UNIT 8

Perspectives and Trends

Unit Selections

Key Points to Consider

- In the future, organizations are going to have to take a more proactive role in the affairs of the communities around them. How do you see them being involved in those activities?
- Multinational corporations are growing in power and in influence. How do you see this affecting the economy both in the United States and abroad?
- Corporate culture is one of the most powerful forces in any organization. How do you see this as determining the type of course organizations are likely to take in the future?
- Ethics are a primary concern of any organization. Is it OK to take home a pen, a pencil, or make personal copies on the office copier? Where do you draw the line? When do people cross it?
- Enron is the largest bankruptcy in history. What do you see coming out of the scandal? How do you think it is going to affect other organizations?

DUSHKIN ONLINE **Links: www.dushkin.com/online/**

These sites are annotated in the World Wide Web pages.

Institute for International Economics
http://www.iie.com

Small Business Management
http://management.tqn.com/msubs.htm

World Trade Organization (WTO) Web Site
http://www.wto.org/index.htm

Managers are facing new challenges. While it is never possible to determine exactly what the future will hold, there are certain trends and movements that can be perceived by an aware and thoughtful manager. Derek Bok, former president of Harvard University, offered some interesting insights into possible future trends for prospective managers in his June 1982 baccalaureate address, which has been adapted in the reading "Social Responsibility in Future Worlds." Bok speaks from two perspectives here, for not only was he an academic trying to look into the future but he was also the manager of a very old and reasonably large and diverse organization, Harvard University.

The multinational corporation is changing the way people do business. These corporate giants are coming to dominate the global economy in ways that have not been foreseen. Most of these companies started in the United States, but there are also organizations with European and Japanese roots that would fall into this category. These organizations are very powerful, and there is concern that they may come to dominate, not only in the economic and commercial arena but in other ways as well, as shown by Lawrence E. Mitchell in "American Corporations: The New Sovereigns."

Corporate culture is an aspect of organizations that many people know about but few truly understand. Every organization has a culture, which to a certain degree is a reflection of the values and ethics of senior management, as well as the values and ethics of the society of which the organization is a part. Paying attention to the culture is a key element in developing the organization and achieving success. Organizations that have strong cultures tend to be more successful than organizations that do not, and ensuring the strength of the organizational culture is a primary concern of management because it is from the culture that so many other aspects of the organization flow, as seen in "Helping Organizations Building Community."

Managers and their organizations have been criticized over the past several years for a lack of ethics and morality. A small and, when they are caught, highly publicized minority has indeed played fast and loose with the law and with ethics. Some continue to do so, especially in the global arena, as seen in "The Short Arm of the Law," where it has sometimes been difficult to enforce the rules of the corporations themselves concerning illegal acts. This has caused all managers to look more closely at their own behavior, and the courts are starting to take a dimmer view of white-collar crime, to the point of sending some executives, such as Charles Keating and Michael Milkin, to prison. Ethical and principled behavior on the part of executives in organizations will lead to greater competitive strength and profitability, as shown in "The Workplace Ethic—Is It a Crime?" Unprincipled behavior, on the other hand, will lead to legal difficulties and government investigations, as may be seen in "Corporate Probes: A Scorecard."

Enron is a special case when it comes to corporate malfeasance. It has already led to the demise of Arthur Andersen, the accounting firm. Enron is the largest bankruptcy in history, dwarfing other bankruptcies such as Global Crossing, which would have been the largest bankruptcy had it not been for Enron. The executives at Enron were obviously in business to make money for themselves. Their stockholders, customers, and employees were of little concern to them. Enron, along with other examples of executive malfeasance, as seen in "Enron: The Studebaker of the 21st Century?" and "The Fallout From Enron," is bound to generate a host of reforms that have only begun.

Finally, managers are starting to examine their careers in light of the new developments in the marketplace. In earlier generations, managers would work for the same firm for their entire working lives. That is no longer the case. Managers in today's environment must be flexible. They have to be responsible for their own careers, because the firms they join could go out of business or be purchased, and they could be left without employment. Managers must look after themselves and make career moves independently if they hope to succeed.

Social Responsibility in Future Worlds

Derek C. Bok

Derek C. Bok, President, Harvard University, Cambridge, Mass.

PROFESSIONAL STUDY

If the past is any guide, more than 90 percent of you will eventually find yourselves studying law, business, or medicine or enrolling in some other kind of graduate or professional school. The training you receive will open the door to a vocation of your choice. But what sort of experience will you find there? What will it do for you? And what kinds of dangers should you be on guard to avoid?

Many people have a slightly distorted view of what a good professional training can achieve. Some feel that it stocks the mind with a vast supply of specialized knowledge—about legal rules and procedures, about corporate organization and behavior, or about the human body and how it functions. Others think that professional training gives students a set of special tools and advanced techniques with which to pry open problems impervious to the lay mind. Both these notions are partly true, but both are incomplete. A good professional education does convey a lot of special knowledge and a grasp of sophisticated technique but it incorporates them into something greater and more important—an instinctive ability to recognize the characteristic problems of the profession and to break them down into manageable parts that can be thought through systematically. The normal way to develop this ability is to subject students to a period of total immersion in which almost all their time is spent in studying, going to class and living and talking and arguing about the problems of the profession with other students like themselves.

Such training brings great benefits to those who pursue it diligently. Not only can you receive the proper credentials of your calling; you gain a power of analysis not available to people outside your profession. That power in turn opens up opportunities to render great service to others, to achieve the satisfactions of good craftsmanship, to find an identity to define your role in life, not to mention gaining your economic security and material rewards.

Along with all these benefits, however, come certain dangers. As Richard Wilbur once remarked, the genie is powerful because we have pressed him into a bottle. The pressures imposed by a good professional education can be a transforming experience. But few transformations occur without the risk of losing something of value along the way. In graduate education, the risk you run is of acquiring a somewhat distorted perspective, a set of values that seem slightly askew, a cast of mind that evidences what the French describe as "deformation professionelle."

THE DEFORMATION OF PROFESSIONALISM

And what, precisely, are these deformations? One of them surely is a tendency to grow less concerned about society's problems and more preoccupied with the special predicament of your client. It is the client, after all, to whom you will owe your loyalty and it is the client who pays the fee. Most of all, it is the client's problem that has immediacy and concreteness. What are the distant issues of national health insurance or neighborhood clinics compared with the urgent details of a swelling tumor, a baby's cleft palate, or a damaged heart? How long can you be distracted by the injustices of our penal system or the wasteful delays of our trial courts in the presence of a corporate client facing a union election, a company take-over, or an antitrust decree?

TENDENCY TO WITHDRAW FROM SUFFERING

As you address the problems of your clients, it is also tempting to conceive of their predicament in terms that are more and more intellectual and less and less human. All professional schools tend to turn human situations into problems that can be picked apart and analyzed rationally. Professional life often supports this view of the world. Most of you who enter law or business will offer your services to banks, manufacturing companies, or retail stores—and it is easy to perceive these organizations as hollow abstractions rather than communities of living people. In medicine, the process of abstraction is even more understandable and compelling. As every study of medical education reveals, few students have feelings tough enough to cope with the terrifying immediacy of death and disease. Many tend to withdraw from the suffering and abnormalities of their patients and begin to conceive of them less as frightened, vulnerable human beings and more as a puzzling deficiency in red blood cells, an unusual kidney malfunction, an odd lesion in the lower intestine. Reinforcing these pressures is the image of success that society has imposed on all of our professions, the image of the emotionless practitioner—cool, detached, objective, and totally in control.

Still another tendency in graduate or professional school is to become so steeped in its special methods of analysis that one ignores other ways of apprehending human experience. Each of these schools arouses an immediate insecurity in its students and a corresponding desire to prove themselves by mastering the technical apparatus of the profession. As you grow more and more adept in these techniques, it is only natural that you be tempted to press these methods on problems where they do not fit. Business school students may cease to wonder about how to work with other human beings and begin to think about the efficient management of human resources. Law students may seize their yellow pads and jot down all the arguments for and against marrying their high school sweethearts. Psychiatrists often see every conceivable human situation as a product of repressed sexual desires.

The quirks I have described may strike you as quaint, but they can have serious effects, not only on your personal and family life, but on your careers as well.

HUMAN DIMENSIONS

I mentioned that most professional schools tend to emphasize the intellectual aspects of practice and to set aside the personal, the emotional, the deeply human dimensions of their calling. The bias is understandable, since formal learning is much more suited to dealing with intellectual and analytic problems than with the more intuitive and psychological aspects of experience. And yet, if you begin to accept this view of the world, you may lose many of the greatest rewards of professional life by failing to perceive much of the human interest and drama that arise in every professional practice. Not only can your work grow colorless and dull; you may accomplish less as well. After all, solutions to most legal disputes and most corporate problems cannot be found through analysis alone but depend on being aware of the feelings, the motives, the needs and aspirations of all the human beings involved. The same is even true in more technical fields such as medicine. How can anyone expect to cope effectively with human health by scientific methods alone when one-third of all patients fail to take the drugs their doctors have prescribed, when half of all illness results from drinking, smoking, and other personal habits; when one-third to a half of all cases in general medicine practice have a strong psychosomatic base.

GREAT SOCIAL CONTRIBUTIONS

Apart from the effects on your careers, the deformations I have described can also have consequences for the professions themselves. For example, if you come to regard the problems of your clients as an intellectual challenge and not as an intensely human predicament, you are likely to move toward certain kinds of careers where the intellectual demands seem greatest—toward the sophisticated specialties in medicine; toward corporate legal practice; toward finance, planning, or consulting in business. While there is nothing inherently wrong with these lines of work, they are not necessarily the fields in which the greatest social contributions lie. For the next generation at least, our health care system will probably need able practitioners in primary care and family medicine more than specialists in cardiology or neurosurgery. As attorneys, you may serve society better as public interest lawyers and neighborhood practitioners, or dare I say it—by not becoming lawyers at all, than you will by being fresh recruits for corporate tax, securities regulation, and antitrust litigation. The economy, with its lagging productivity, may benefit more from production managers than from investment analysts, corporate planners, or roving consultants.

ETHICAL DILEMMAS

Another byproduct of professional training is that the constant emphasis on solving problems through conventional modes of analysis may cause young professionals to ignore the ethical dilemmas of their practice. Alas, you are not likely to detect much serious attention to ethics in the professional school you enter. And that is a serious deficiency at a time when every profession bristles with moral dilemmas and the public trust in professionals has everywhere declined. As a "New York Times" article recently concluded: "If medical education does not come to grips with the ethical as well as the technical problems of the field, society may soon discover that modern medicine has given a relatively small number of men and women enormous power—which they have not been adequately trained to wield." Exactly the same could be said of all the other major professions as well.

There is a final danger to consider that may be even more important. I have already observed that students in professional schools grow more and more preoccupied with the needs and problems of the clients they serve and less and less concerned with the impact of their profession on the larger society. That would be a problem in any era. It is a particularly serious problem today.

SOCIETY'S CONCERNS

I cannot remember a time when society's concerns about the professions have seemed more distant from the daily preoccupations of our professional schools and the body of practitioners they serve. In medicine, for example, the public is not greatly troubled by the technical quality of ser vice that doctors offer their patients. What does concern the public is how medical services can be organized to extend adequate care to all segments of society; how to contain medical costs so that they cease to rise at much faster rates than those of other goods and services; and how to address the great moral dilemmas of euthanasia, abortion, and artificial insemination. What troubles thinking people most about our legal system is not that lawyers are poorly trained but that we rely too much on law and litigation in most of our institutions while failing to insure that poor people have proper access to basic legal services at prices they can afford. In business, our principal concern is how our corporations can work more effectively with government to increase productivity and address social problems and how business can be kept accountable to the public interest in an age when markets do not provide a perfect discipline and government regulation is often inefficient and ineffective.

FAILURE OF GOVERNMENT REGULATION

These are not problems that receive much attention in our professional schools today despite their high priority in the public mind. And that is a serious matter, for there is one thing that we have surely learned from the failures of government regulation over the years. If we wish our professions to serve the public better, we must enlist the active cooperation of professionals themselves. Without their help, little of lasting value can occur.

The problems I have described are not your problems now, but they will be your problems very soon. I hope that you will address them boldly and never regard yourselves as human clay to be molded and shaped by your professional school experience. There was a time when I could not have brought myself to utter this last remark: it would have seemed too obvious and banal. But I was startled to find in my last years as a faculty member that many students had managed to persuade themselves that the Law School was "programming them" for lucrative corporate practice and co-opting them from careers fighting for noble causes or serving the needy. Such attitudes are not merely far-fetched; they are extremely dangerous, for they offer easy rationalizations to avoid responsibility for what you make of your lives. Professional schools graduate every kind of practitioner serving every conceivable segment of society. They give you tools with which to work. But the ends and values to which you direct your talents are yours and yours alone to decide, and professional maturity begins with that realization.

FRESH FIELDS AND PASTURES NEW

In making these decisions, you begin with a strong defense against narrowing tendencies of professional training, for you would not have been admitted to Harvard College had you not been interested in a broad range of human and social questions, and four years here should have helped to cement that foundation. In one respect, however, I fear that your Harvard experience may not have served you well. By gaining admission here you prevailed in a remarkably stiff competition. By working hard to win acceptance by a professional school, you have continued to run in a demanding race. Fresh opportunities lie before you to compete for the best residencies, the best law firms, the best positions in the best corporations. These competitions are excellent motivation devices that call on powerful human instincts.

A LIFE THAT ENGAGES ALL OF YOUR INTERESTS

But it is a characteristic that one must play by other people's rules and compete for prizes that other people have chosen. And that is a poor preparation for life, especially if you mean to live an independent existence and resist the deformations I have tried to describe.

To guard against these dangers, I hope that you will pause now and then to free your minds from your immediate problems and ambitions and imagine how your lives will seem to you at the end of your careers. If you can somehow manage the feat of looking back upon your future lives, I suspect that you will begin to feel less concerned with whether you succeed by narrow professional standards. Instead, I suspect that you will hope more and more for a life that continuously engages all of your interests and absorbs all of your energies. And as you think further, I suspect you will come to realize that no life can engage you fully unless it is open to the feelings of everyone around you and that no career can absorb your energies for very long unless it allows you to contribute generously to the welfare of others. If these be your sentiments, I hope that you will guard them well so that you can make a life that is worthy of your talents and equal to this brave beginning. Congratulations to you all. You deserve the very best. I feel sure that you will find it.

From *Readings in Management,* 1986, pp. 45-50. Published by South-Western Publishing Company. Originally from *Computers and People,* September/October 1982.

American Corporations: the New Sovereigns

By Lawrence E. Mitchell

ONE of the most striking yet overlooked aspects of the current globalization debate is the quiet retreat of sovereign power—including that of the United States—in the face of imperial conquests by modern American corporations. At least until the recent downturns in the stock market—both the general one in 2000 and the sharper one following the attacks of September 11—a number of these companies, including Wal-Mart, Microsoft, Intel, General Electric, and Hewlett-Packard, have had market capitalizations larger than the gross national products of a number of developed and developing countries, including Spain, Kuwait, Argentina, Greece, Poland, and Thailand. The statistics overwhelmingly demonstrate that such corporations and American capital are increasingly dominant throughout the world. At last count, American institutional assets constituted an aggregate 66.8 percent of the total in five major foreign economies, including those of France and Germany.

Modern democracies are built to ensure the restraint of power and the pursuit of public will by forgoing efficiency for patience and consensus. In contrast, the modern American corporation, with its centralized control and absolute power in the board, is brilliantly and devastatingly built for economic efficiency—the ability to amass huge resources and deploy them instantly. No socialist economy has ever had the command-and-control capacities of the American corporation.

The scary thing is that we have come to see these corporations as built for a single purpose, to maximize stockholder wealth, and we have created them in a manner that exempts them from any of the normal moral constraints we expect from governments or individuals.

It has not always been so. Several factors led to the development of this new ethic over the last couple of decades. Among them were deregulation beginning during the Reagan era, together with an increased emphasis on wealth maximization as a social goal; the expectations created in stockholders by the quick money made in hostile takeovers, especially during the 1980s; and the charging bull market of the 1990s. Those phenomena have instilled stockholder expectations of large and immediate returns.

AMERICAN CORPORATIONS and their managers are thus increasingly driven by the faceless, soulless capital markets—markets composed of individuals with consciences but creating a collective that lacks one. Moreover, pressure on corporations to show higher stock prices fast has been increased by the enormous growth in institutional investors, which now own about half of the equity market in the United States.

They also dominate institutional investing in foreign markets like those of Western Europe. Institutional investors compensate their managers on the basis of their ability to raise the values of their portfolios immediately, so those managers have every incentive to push for short-term stock-price maximization over long-term gain and corporate stability.

In addition to the pressure of institutional investors, American investment banks, and consulting companies, markets are driven by nongovernmental organizations like the World Bank and the International Monetary Fund. Those players have implicitly, and sometimes explicitly, conditioned the supply of American capital (and in the case of the nongovernmental organizations, largely Western capital) to overseas markets on those markets' adoption of American-style, stockholder-centered, corporate capitalism.

To be sure, American corporations have brought the world great benefits: increased travel, communication, health, nutrition, and production capabilities. They have also brought Americans a higher material standard of living. But it is, in large part, the stockholder-centered nature of the corporation that leads it to behave in ways that no thoughtful person really wants, ways that most of us would consider to be irresponsible.

Although no legal doctrine requires it, American capitalist culture has adopted the view that maximizing stock price is the purpose of the corporation, its reason for being. Capital markets demand that maximization, and punish those corporations that fail to meet short-term expectations—just look at the stock price of any corporation that reports disappointing quarterly earnings. Corporate structure implies stock-price maximization: Only stockholders vote for directors, only stockholders have the right to sue, and only stockholders have the ability to sell the company out from under the directors.

Coupled with the maximization goal is the limited liability that shields the corporation. While corporations can be sued for causing harm, and sometimes even criminally prosecuted, the extent of their risk is finite. When a chemical plant in Bhopal, India, explodes because corners were cut, or Love Canal is poisoned because it is cheaper to pollute, or asbestos sickens thousands because the product is unsafe, the injured can recover only from the assets of the corporation. Directors and stockholders generally are not liable for its debts, and so many of the costs of maximizing stock price can be externalized onto all of those people and things, other than the stockholders, whom the corporation's behavior affects—workers, consumers, entire communities, the environment.

Layoffs are a fast way to cut costs and raise stock price. Saving a few dollars by placing a gas tank in not necessarily the safest spot, or by paying insufficient attention to tire safety, increases profit margins. Polluting entails limited risk of being caught and penalized, and the benefits, in terms of savings, sometimes exceed that risk. It's cheaper to shut down plants in areas of high labor cost and move them to other regions, no matter how dependent the community may be on the corporation.

Freed from the responsibilities of ownership, with surrogates directed to manage their corporations to maximize their wealth, American stockholders can, and for the most part do, wash their hands of responsibility for their corporations' behavior. Add to this the fact that most Americans tend to invest in corporations through intermediary institutions—mutual funds, pension funds, and the like—and yet another layer is placed between the stockholder and any feeling of responsibility.

WITH THESE CONDITIONS in place, American corporations have exported the dislocations they often cause at home through devices such as the leveraged, hostile takeover, and norms like stock-price maximization. *BusinessWeek* predicted (again, before the current recession) at least a $1-trillion mergers-and-acquisitions business in Europe, a region that has long celebrated its corporate stability. The profits drawn from such disruptions abroad go directly into the pockets of American stockholders, who demonstrate no concern with the effect of corporate behavior on anyone else. Arguments that transnational business helps the world's disadvantaged by raising their standard of living are disproved by the numbers. A recent United Nations report showed that American-style economic dominance has accelerated the widening gap between rich and poor throughout the world.

According to the UN's *Human Development Report 1999*, "the top fifth of the world's people in the richest countries enjoy 82 percent of the expanding export trade and 68 percent of foreign direct investment—the bottom fifth, barely more than 1 percent." That same wealthy population has 86 percent of the world's gross domestic product, and the income of that group was 74 times that of the bottom fifth in 1997, up from 60 times in 1990. And such data reflect only material wealth—not quality of life, leisure, education, or happiness.

Because the goal of the corporation is to maximize stock price, managers use corporations narrowly and amorally as tools to achieve that end.

At least as dangerous as increasing inequality is the standard of behavior American corporate practices create for companies' managers. Because the goal of the corporation is to maximize stock price, managers use corporations narrowly and amorally as tools to achieve that end. When an ordinary human being with ordinary moral constraints walks into a board room or executive suite, he assumes those tunnel-visioned behaviors. That is, after all, his job. His own sensibilities can be left at the door—and even if they need not be, even if there is latitude (as there surely is) for good corporate behavior, he knows that the market will punish him unless his morality is reflected on the bottom line.

Like many social roles (that of a lawyer comes to mind), this one comes with a socially sanctioned set of expectations. But unlike most other roles, which exist and must interact in a wider social system, we so narrowly define the role of corporate actors as to give them a moral anonymity and a moral out. The corporate managerial role not only leads us to exculpate corporations for simply doing what we've created them to do, but it allows managers themselves to avoid feeling responsible, and being accountable, for their behavior. They have no personal contact with the people their decisions affect—those people are only numbers. The managers don't carry out the decisions themselves and witness the consequences, so they avoid the experiences that might help ensure empathy and restraint.

THE PROGRESS of the American corporation has been toward ever greater world dominance, not only in the products it sells and the services it provides, which export American culture throughout the world, but also in its exportation of American-style, stockholder-take-all capitalist practices. Given corporations' efficiency and speed in contrast to those of governments, corporations can establish strongholds and affect entire cultures long before those cultures have time to react. And once in place, corporate wealth and economic dominance allows them to remain firmly entrenched.

The problem is not only one of America against the developing world. American corporations, aided by the investment community, have also largely colonized the various forms of capitalism that used to distinguish Western European business from ours. Corporate behavior in Germany, France, Scandinavia, and Italy, for instance, was designed to provide for full employment, social stability, and social welfare. American companies, and American practices, have eroded those core values.

The European anger directed against President George W. Bush on his first visit there in June (somewhat abated since September 11 by a different anger, sympathy, and fear) is symptomatic of even the developed world's feelings of helplessness in the face of the continued onslaught by American-style corporate capitalism.

The recent terrorist attacks have been directed against sovereign governments. But to the extent that much of the unsettled state of the world derives from the increasing divide between haves and have-nots, to the extent that culture wars in America and abroad are driven at least in part by rear-guard actions against disappearing ways of life, the cause lies less in the behavior of sovereign governments such as our own than it does in the collective behavior of corporate America and the American investment community.

Only government has the power, the resources, and the right to restrain corporate conduct and to demand corporate accountability. For far too long we've taken the attitude that business is business, as if that very mantra exempted corporations from the normal moral and responsible conduct that we expect from individual citizens. At the same time, we have granted our corporations almost all of the rights and freedoms of individual citizens. But unless we control our corporate goals and practices, unless our government regulates markets in a way that restrains our voracious drive for wealth, international strife and discord will only worsen.

Lawrence E. Mitchell, a law professor at George Washington University, is the author of Corporate Irresponsibility: America's Newest Export, *published recently by Yale University Press.*

Offshore Sourcing: An Optimal Operational Strategy?

Robert H. Lowson

Many retailers are making use of lower-priced goods offered by foreign vendors. The vendors, taking advantage of low wages in their countries, are able to undercut competitors operating in domestic markets. However, the characteristics of these consumer goods—clothing, footwear, food, drink, toys, furniture, appliances, electronics, household goods, and so on—are dynamic and complex, usually being sold in discrete seasons. Low cost, though important, is not the only purchasing criterion for either end consumers or retail buyers.

What exactly are the advantages and disadvantages of foreign imports as opposed to their domestic counterparts? What trade-offs are involved? What are the true costs? And what are the best sourcing strategies for the retail community?

STRATEGIC PURCHASING, PROCUREMENT, AND SOURCING

Purchasing and supply management has evolved from the adversarial, clerical transaction between supplier and customer into a strategic, cooperative, buyer–seller relationship. Subsequently, this evolution has led to a rise in supply base reduction strategies—a restructuring in the way companies do business with "key" suppliers in order to gain competitive advantage.

Typically, low cost seems to be the primary purchasing requirement for many businesses, with the strategic objective of a supplier relationship being cost reduction. Stuart and McCutcheon (2000) identify four primary mechanisms for achieving this objective:

1. lower production costs of suppliers;
2. improved conformance quality (consistently meeting specifications);
3. material/location substitution; and,
4. lower transaction costs, including those of incoming material inspections, vendor searches and evaluations, corrected supplier problems, and communication with suppliers.

But what other strategic objective might a firm strive for? Are these strategic supply decisions really made in full knowledge of all the cost/ benefit trade-offs involved?

Sourcing Locations and Discounts

The respondents in the study conducted for this research were divided between North American (44 percent) and U.K. (56 percent) retailers. First they were asked to confirm their sourcing locations over the previous 12 months (it should be remembered that for most firms in a consumer goods environment, sourcing is a dynamic activity that changes from season to season). The retailers also provided an indication of the average discount (percent lower unit cost) achieved from "offshore" sourcing. **Table 1** details the findings.

Clearly, the cost implications of offshore sourcing are evident. For both North America and the U.K., retailer discounts of between 20 and 30 percent are attainable in Central America and Asia. This demonstrates the importance that retailers attach to low cost. But what other factors might a firm take into account when making sourcing decisions?

Sourcing Objectives

Table 2 details the main sourcing objectives for both North American and U.K. respondents. The participants ranked these objectives, which were divided between domestic and foreign (to include the advantages in each case).

For both sets of retailers, low cost is again a prime advantage in foreign sourcing. Offshore, quality ranks second for both North American and U.K. retailers. Domestic sourcing decisions are less clear. Quality, response time, design, and flexibility all have high scores. Cost, then, may not be the only sourcing aspiration; other objectives can be seen, although these clearly change from season to season.

Given that there are a number of purchasing goals, this study sought to establish what cost/ benefit trade-offs or measures might be used when assessing the advantages of foreign versus domestic supply and when making strategic purchasing decisions. To do this, two

Table 1

Sourcing Location, Percent of Goods Purchased Over Previous Year, and Discount Available

	Sourcing Locations and % of Goods Purchased Over Last 12 Months						
	USA	*U.K.*	*Europe*	*Central America*	*Asia*	*Africa*	*Other*
North American Retailers	52	0	1	24	20	3	0
Average Discount Available (% lower cost)	–	0	5–10	20–25	20–30	10–15	–
U.K. Retailers	3	34	24	0	36	2	1
Average Discount Available (% lower cost)	1–5	–	10–15	–	25–35	15–20	5–10

Table 2

Sourcing Objectives and Advantages of Domestic and Foreign Suppliers

	Domestic Sourcing Objectives & Advantages	*Offshore Sourcing Objectives & Advantages*
North American Retailers	Quality (41%) Response Time (30%) Design (15%) Flexibility (8%) Innovation (3%) Cost (3%)	Lower Cost (53%) Quality (27%) Innovation (13%) Design (5%) Response Time (2%)
U.K. Retailers	Response Time (25%) Flexibility (22%) Design (20%) Innovation (18%) Quality (15%)	Lower Cost (66%) Quality (32%) Design (2%)

pertinent factors were analyzed: (a) the levels and types of responsiveness and flexibility available from both foreign and domestic vendors; and (b) the hidden costs associated with foreign supply and any subsequent inflexibility.

Sourcing Responsiveness and Flexibility

First, to deal with the responsiveness and flexibility retailers achieved from their suppliers in various geographic regions, the respondents supplied data for the average lead times or advance ordering times necessary for the supply of finished goods. The data were assessed by examining the "open to buy" periods involved. As can be seen from **Figure 1**, there is a direct relationship between this lead time (the advance ordering point) and major sales forecast error ahead of a sales season.

Figure 2 addresses responsiveness by examining the advance lead time retailers had to provide when finalizing orders with vendors in different locations. It is apparent that the longer lead times or advance ordering times required for products sourced from Asia, Africa, and Central America may prove problematic to all in the supply system.

The next two tables investigate flexibility issues. In **Table 3**, the respondents commented on the latitude that suppliers (in various regions) offered for volume and mix change once an order had been placed both *before* and, more crucially, *during* a sales season. Here is powerful evidence of the wider strategic sourcing debate. There are, it seems, many important issues beyond just unit item cost. The flexibility of suppliers after initial orders have been placed—in other words, once demand trends become clear—may be sought in both the volumes needed as well as the product mix. The flexibility required by a retailer will apply at both the pre- and post-season opening, though it is harder to adjust to the latter despite better-known demand trends. With domestic suppliers (suppliers to retailers in North America and the U.K.), there is generally substantial latitude for volume and mix change *before* the start of the sales season, whereas in Asia, Central America, and Africa vendors have little flexibility then. Similarly, *during* a sales season, domestic vendors offer much more

Table 3
Vendors' Latitude For Volume and Mix Change Both *Before* and *During* Sales Season (by Geographic Region)

		Once order is placed, what is the vendors' latitude for change?					
		Order Volume Change (% respondents)			*Order Mix Change (% respondents)*		
	Sourcing Regions	*None*	*Some*	*Substantial*	*None*	*Some*	*Substantial*
Before the start of the sale season	North America	16	49	35	21	49	30
	U.K.	9	52	39	21	46	33
	Europe	29	43	28	37	38	25
	Central Am.erica	41	38	21	46	34	20
	Asia	66	22	12	70	19	11
	Africa	58	19	23	62	20	18
	Other	34	40	26	30	37	33
After the start of the sale season	North America	39	33	28	47	29	24
	U.K.	19	46	35	28	39	33
	Europe	35	38	27	41	35	24
	Central America	52	33	15	63	30	7
	Asia	70	21	9	86	12	2
	Africa	66	16	18	73	8	19
	Other	32	42	26	39	37	24

flexibility than their foreign counterparts. It appears, then, that flexibility is an important objective in strategic procurement.

Table 4 shows the flexibility of vendors by region *after* the sales season has been completed. In other words, it shows their adaptability to deal with surpluses by way of returns, discounts and markdowns. A pattern similar to Table 3 emerges. At the end of the season, domestic suppliers seem to be more flexible than foreign ones when it comes to such negotiations.

To summarize, there seems to be something of a paradox. Table 1 shows that greater cost discounts are obviously available from foreign vendors, particularly in Asia, Central America, and Africa. However, Table 2 demonstrates that lower cost is not the only objective; quality, response time, flexibility, and design also have a strong role to play. Yet we see from Tables 3 and 4 that many offshore sources of supply fail to offer any of these advantages. Moreover, Table 1 tells us that North American retailers source 47 percent of their goods over a 12-month period from such offshore regions, and U.K. retailers 38 percent. From these findings, we are left to assume that the strategic purchasing objectives of these firms are clearly suboptimal in nearly half the North American cases and 40 percent of the U.K. cases.

Given the various advantages and disadvantages of domestic versus foreign purchasing, the next consideration must be whether they can be quantified and the various trade-offs properly assessed. We know that the unit cost of goods—the main attraction—is often lower offshore, but what are the costs of inflexibility and lack of responsiveness? What is the result when these costs are compared? Is offshore supply such an attractive option in those circumstances?

The Hidden and Inflexibility Costs of Offshore Sourcing

Many of the costs of sourcing offshore can be classified as *hidden costs*. The retailers in this study were asked to suggest the cost categories associated with purchasing abroad, apart from the cost of the goods themselves (see **Table 5**).

It would seem that the impact of these hidden costs is not insubstantial. However, it is unclear whether the respondents in fact quantify these costs or compare them with the advantages of offshore sourcing (an area for future research). In justification of the reason to import, the retailers cite the fact that low offshore prices allow sales at below traditional price points, while still giving attractive margins. Yet those margins may be substantially eroded when the hidden costs are quantified. In addition to the hidden costs, we also need to recognize the costs of using suppliers that are inflexible and unresponsive—the *inflexibility costs*.

The costs of importing may well be closely linked to the type of sourcing strategy used. This research indicates

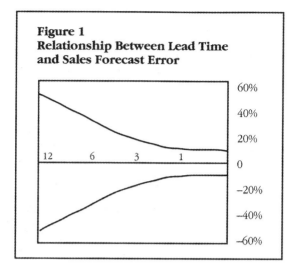

Figure 1
Relationship Between Lead Time and Sales Forecast Error

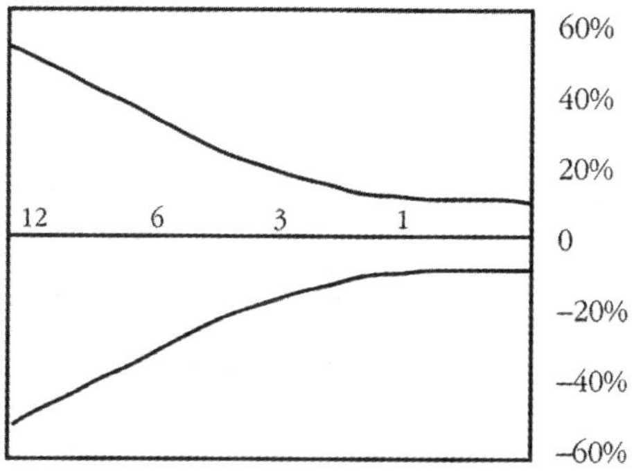

Figure 2
Advanced Finalization and Lead Time for Orders (by Vendor Geographic Region)

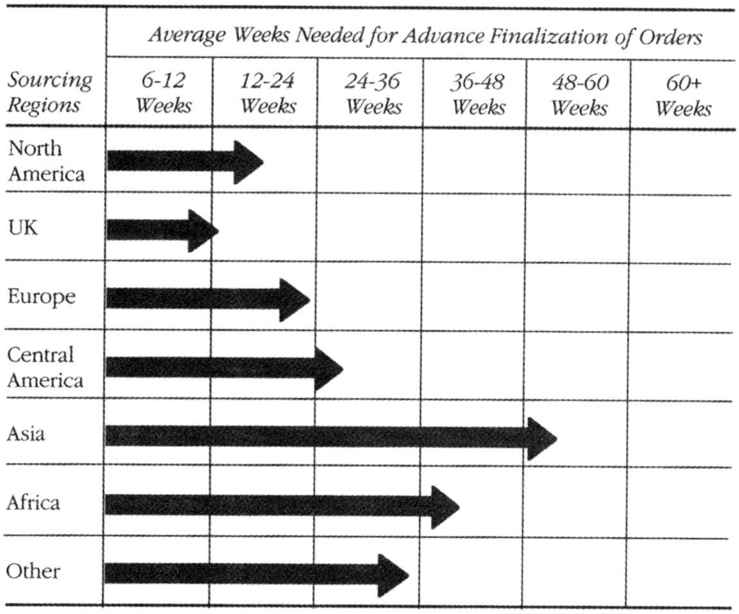

that retailers' use strategies that can be classified into three generic types:

1. *Offshore, low-cost.* A foreign manufacturer produces and ships 100 percent of the goods needed for a sales season prior to the start of the season. Purchasing decisions are made considerably in advance of the season, before any demand indication is known.

2. *Combined.* A foreign manufacturer ships a large proportion of the goods needed prior to the start of the season. The retailer then makes weekly replenishment orders from a domestic supplier. However, point of sale (PoS) information is often not shared with this domestic vendor, so supply is often shipped from its stock holding built as a buffer against uncertainty. This approach is similar to Vendor Managed Inventory (VMI), although it is suboptimal as far as the supplier—and ultimately the retailer—are concerned.

3. *Domestic, responsive, and flexible.* A domestic manufacturer ships a proportion (say, 40 percent) of the goods needed before the start of the sales season. Thereafter, in-season manufacturing is based on a reestimation of actual demand using PoS data provided by the retailer and a reorder using Electronic Data Interchange (EDI) to provide for a quick turnaround in manufacturing and shipping products in demand. For the retailer, this strategy results in more accurate stocking that reflects demand preferences, reduces inventory, and enhances customer service metrics.

Again, there are advantages and disadvantages associated with each of these strategies. Low unit cost is available offshore, but domestic suppliers are more flexible and responsive and are operating according to actual demand requirements. The latter, it is argued, is actually cheaper for the retailer in the long term. If the inflexibility costs could be measured properly, offshore sourcing may not be the most cost-effective strategy. Further research is needed to quantify the costs of these various sourcing scenarios.

In an initial attempt to analyze the implications of the three sourcing strategies described, three retailers of apparel goods provided details of performance measurements for sourcing the same clothing item (men's denim jeans) during a single apparel season in 1999–2000. As shown in **Table 6**, Retailer A sourced jeans mainly from Hong Kong during the season; Retailer B used two

Table 4
Suppliers' Latitude for Dealing with Surpluses *After* a Sales Season (by Geographic Region)

	At the end of a sales season, vendor flexibility for agreeing to returns and discounts, etc., for surplus goods (% respondents)		
Sourcing Regions	*None*	*Some*	*Substantial*
North America	24%	54%	22%
U.K.	11%	70%	19%
Europe	33%	49%	18%
Central America	50%	41%	9%
Asia	73%	23%	4%
Africa	66%	34%	0%
Other	40%	53%	7%

Table 5
The Hidden Costs of Importing

Cost Categories	*Degree of Importance (% of respondents)*
Irrevocable letters of credit charges	15%
Delays at the port of entry	7%
Last minute use of air freight	5%
Expensive administrative travel and quality problems	11%
The requirement of an early commitment to manufacturing before sales trends are clear	25%
Limited ability to change mix or volume of orders shortly before or during the sales season	37%

suppliers in the season, bulk orders from Thailand, then reorders from the U.K.; and Retailer C used entirely domestic vendors with flexible and responsive operations.

The performance measurements supplied were for orders of similar size and were adjusted for exchange rates and so on. At this level we are not trying to establish any direct relationship between sourcing performance and a particular supplier and/or supplier location. We do, however, suggest that there are strong reasons for using a range of performance measures (over and above price alone) when analyzing the performance of different sourcing strategies. These different measures demonstrate the advantages and disadvantages of each source of supply and should be used in a combination, not in isolation. This is also an example of how future research might establish different types of cost measurement (including hidden and inflexibility costs) that should be a part of any sourcing calculation.

From Table 6 we can see that for the three retailers involved, the use of domestic, responsive, and flexible vendors emerged as the best sourcing strategy in all performance measures, apart from gross margin/sales. We can speculate that the underlying reason for the superior retail performance of goods sourced using such strategies is the realization that no forecasts are perfect—it is only during the sales season, when customer demand is revealed, that intelligent supply decisions can be made.

This research, then, does suggest one important finding: In nearly all performance measures, domestic, responsive, and flexible sourcing can be far more efficient and optimal than offshore supply, despite the lower unit cost of the latter. Moreover, it can be demonstrated that these domestic manufacturers can charge nearly 25 percent more per item and still prove a cheaper option for their retail customers. This is due to their flexibility and responsiveness and the savings they offer by avoiding the hidden and inflexibility costs associated with importing. The advantages associated with speed of response and flexibility will also allow a retailer (using offshore supply) to reduce price points by as much as 30 percent below that of a competitor, and still earn the same returns as the competitor.

The operational strategy of purchasing, procurement, and sourcing has assumed a great deal of importance for many companies. But those seeking low unit cost of goods from offshore sources as their principal goal could be in for a big disappointment if they fail to consider flexibility, responsiveness, and other advantages available from local suppliers.

Further research is needed to establish the exact costs of importing and to assess whether or not these are actually computed by retailers when making sourcing decisions. But this study is a first step toward an axiomatic framework, widely accepted across a number of consumer industries, that demonstrates the full implications of domestic versus offshore purchasing. Research is currently under way to develop a Total Acquisition Cost Model (TACM) that will allow the full implications of these strategic sourcing decisions to be properly analyzed and assessed using all the relevant information available. Such a model will also help domestic vendors demonstrate to their retail customers the advantages of using their flexible and responsive services, rather than continuing the current practice of relying on the somewhat inefficient use of cheap offshore sourcing.

References and Selected Bibliography

T.L. Gilreath, J.M. Reeve, and G.E. Whalen, Jr., "Time Is Money," *Bobbin*, March 1995, Pp. 50–55.

N.A. Hunter, R.E. King, and R.H. Lowson, *The Textile/Clothing Pipeline and Quick Response Management* (Manchester, UK: The Textile Institute, 2001).

R.E. King and N.A. Hunter, "Demand Re-estimation and Inventory Replenishment of Basic Apparel in a Specialty Retail Chain," *The Journal of the Textile Institute, 87*, 1 (1996): 31–41.

R.H. Lowson, "The Impact of Quick Response in the Textile and Clothing Industry: Analysis and Application," unpublished Ph.D. dissertation, Cardiff University, UK, 1999.

R.H. Lowson, R.E. King, and N.A. Hunter, *Quick Response: Managing the Supply Chain to Meet Consumer Demand* (Chichester, West Sussex, UK: Wiley, 1999).

R.H. Lowson, "Customised Operational Strategies for Retailers in Fast Moving Consumer Industries," *International Journal of Retail, Distribution and Consumer Research*, April 2001, pp. 201–224.

M.E. Porter, "What Is Strategy?" *Harvard Business Review*, November–December 1996, pp. 61–78.

F.I. Stuart and D.M. McCutcheon, "The Manager's Guide to Supply Chain Management," *Business Horizons*, March–April 2000, pp. 35–44.

Robert H. Lowson is the director of the Strategic Operations Management Centre, a lecturer in operations strategy, and the Leverhulme Trust Research Fellow at the University of East Anglia, Norwich, U.K.

Table 6
Retail Sourcing Performance Measurements

Measure	**RETAILER C** **Domestic, Responsive, and Flexible Strategy** *Retailer with mfg. operation. Large European and North American operation. Sources from contract mfrs. in U.K., N. America, Asia, Europe, and C. America*	**RETAILER B** **Combined Strategy—using foreign & domestic sources in same season** *Independent U.K. retailer. "Private" label goods, increasingly provided from Asia but reorders from U.K.*	**RETAILER A** **Offshore, Low-Cost Strategy** *U.S.-based specialty clothing store. European & North American outlets. No mfg. capability. Sources mostly offshore (Asia & Central America)*
Gross Margin to Sales Revenue	0.47	0.46	0.59
Gross Margin ROI	5.30	4.40	2.50
Inventory Turns per Sales Season	6.20	5.40	1.80
Average Inventory Carried During Sales Season[1]	1.00	1.70	3.43
Sales Revenue During Sales Season[1]	1.00	0.74	0.59
Service Level (% of times customer finds first choice of SKU)	94.00	83.00	72.00
Lost Sales (% of times customer finds none of first choice)	6.00	11.70	18.00
Sell Through (proportion of season's merchandise selling at initial set price)	90.40	81.90	72.90
Sold Off (% of unwanted units remaining after season)	0.90	6.80	16.00

[1]*Scaled to domestic supply = 1*

Research Profile

This article marks an initial milestone in a four-year empirical research study begun in 1999 of the retail consumer goods sector. It is an international initiative, covering retailers and suppliers/vendors in both North America and Europe. The overall objective of the project is a better understanding of operational strategies. It applies a working hypothesis that many of the firms involved are having to adopt new and radically different methods of operation in the face of increasingly volatile and dynamic demand patterns that mark this particular commercial setting.

In this part of the project, senior managers from 167 different retailers were identified in a number of industries forming the retail consumer goods sector, the qualifying feature being that each organization had a retailing function of some kind. The sample, though not totally random, was intended to be representative of the sectors that provide such goods normally available in a shopping mall or department store. Of the 167 mailed surveys delivered, 5 were returned as no longer operating as a retail function, and 78 were completed. This gave an adjusted return of 48% (adequate for analysis and discussion). Each of the respondents was subsequently interviewed (many more than once) in order to seek clarification and some expansion of a number of issues.

From *Business Horizons*, November/December 2001, pp. 61-66.

Helping Organizations Build Community

A sense of community at work can make all the difference

September 11 changed how many employees view their jobs and workplace. People may find it difficult to focus on learning. Building a sense of community in organizations can help refocus people on shared values and create an environment of support in which employees are fully engaged.

by Tracy Mauro

I was introducing a group of managers to the concepts in James Autry's book *Love and Profit* when I heard about the World Trade Center and Pentagon attacks. The class had started at 8:30 a.m., just before the first plane hit. Managers who came to the session late shared fragmented updates of the situation they'd heard on television. People began talking and asking questions, none of which pertained to Autry's book. As our small, suburban Chicago office was evacuated, a senior manager canceled the session. I realized in that moment that everything would change—not just the onset of war or tightened security but the way people view their workplace, their co-workers, and even the meaning of their work.

Training professionals have a difficult job right now. We're trying to impart knowledge to employees who are at best distracted or apathetic and at worst scared and disillusioned. Abraham Maslow's hierarchy of needs proposes that people are motivated by unsatisfied needs and that "lower needs" such as safety and security have to be satisfied before attending to "higher needs" such as personal growth and development. How can learning professionals do their jobs and help organizations become successful when employees are wondering whether their mail is laced with anthrax? The answer may lie in helping to create an environment of support and belonging, in which employees have the opportunity to do their best. Economic downturn and massive layoffs make that a challenge, but not impossible. In fact, people might be especially receptive now to opportunities to shape and have more control over their surroundings. One way to encourage that is by building a sense of community.

Powering community in the workplace isn't new. The quality movement in the late 1970s touched on the idea of participative management as a way to bring [illegible]s of employees together around comm[illegible] principles, such as quality. In the early 1990s, Peter Senge and James Autry talked about the necessary elements of a productive community to produce learning organizations and caring leaders. Autry writes: "Community is the new metaphor for organizations," saying that before the industrial age, all values entered society through the church and stare.

People witness healthy and destructive values played out in the workplace. A community teaches values, and those values have the power to strengthen its members or divide them. Like it or not, the pillars of commerce have become a central place where people learn values. Organizations that want to survive cultivate healthy values that bring success to staff and shareholders.

The need to belong and feel supported in the workplace becomes more important as our world becomes more uncertain. Many people spend at least half of their waking hours during the week at work, making the workplace a home away from home. Think for a moment about the home where you live and the reasons you chose to live there. The community and people were probably major factors in your decision. It's no different in the workplace. In community-building exercises I lead, I ask participants to remember a time when they experienced a positive community and to list the characteristics that made it special. Later in the exercise, they usually discover that the characteristics they listed are the same attributes they seek in their workplace now.

Clifton Taulbert, in his book *Eight Habits of the Heart: The Timeless Values That Build Community Within Our Homes and Our Lives,* writes: "From the classroom to the... office cubicle, there are people who wait to hear someone say, 'Welcome.' No one really enjoys eating alone or having no one to talk with."

The profound effect of the events of September 11 and since offer organizations a new opportunity to create places of support and acceptance. Organizational leaders can stabilize their workforces by recognizing what Autry calls "the sudden, compulsive search for connection and a sense of community," in which the workplace is the neighborhood and co-workers are extended family.

A home by any other name

Training professionals must first have a clear definition of what community is before they can begin the process of helping an organization build one. Although there is no commonly accepted definition of community, most definitions include similar characteristics. Community seems to be categorized by either sharing a common space or common interests. The definitions in *Merriam-Webster's* combine both of those aspects: "an interacting population of various kinds of individuals in a common location" or "a body of persons of common and especially professional interests scattered through a larger society." Community researcher Carl Moore provides a simple definition appropriate for the workplace: "[where people] work together to bring the greatest good for the greatest number of people."

Many management experts think that shared values and goals are an important part of the definition of community within organizations. James Kouzes and Barry Posner, in their book *Credibility: How Leaders Gain and Lose It, Why People Demand It*, say that in order for people to perceive themselves as part of a community, they need to believe that their goals are cooperative and that they share a common purpose. Only then will people make their co-workers' problems their own and solve them together.

Regardless of how learning and workplace performance professionals define *community*, the word evokes unique images in the minds of participants. Many think of a physical place where they experienced a sense of *community*, such as the neighborhood where they grew up. Taulbert recalls the small town in the Mississippi Delta where he grew up amidst segregation in the years before Martin Luther King Jr.: "But I realize now that the place was just a set.... In other words, the real community I knew as a child was not held captive by geography, nor was it defined by the physical stuff that was part of our place." Rather, he says, community was defined by the actions and behavior of the members. Taulbert underscores that definition: "Community is an intangible that is so real that you miss it when it can't be found."

In May 1999, the National League of Cities held a conference to help representatives foster inclusion and belonging in their hometowns. When asked to finish the sentence "Community is...," participants mentioned working together and caring, having a sense of collective responsibility and ownership, and providing a safe environment for citizens to participate in. As any trainer knows, those are essential elements in fostering an environment for learning to take place.

The value of creating a sense of community in the workplace might be obvious to people in the learning and performance profession, but some powers-that-be will want an explanation of how that's useful to the company. Some executives may view community building as another soft-skills program that takes employees off the floor but doesn't produce immediate results. Taulbert, who teaches community building to executives, says he generates buy-in from his high-level audiences by showing that community makes a clear connection between employees' hearts and minds and improved job performance.

"You have to bring leaders back to the point of realizing that nothing can be built without people. People are still the key to building the business," says Taulbert. Most of the time, people aren't fully engaged and working at 100 percent capacity, especially when distracted by crises. Employees choose every day when and how much extra effort they will expend after meeting the minimum performance standards, which Kouzes and Posner refer to as discretionary effort. When companies create an environment in which employees want to be fully engaged, they "touch the soul," as Taulbert describes it, and people are more likely to expend their discretionary effort.

Once employees are fully engaged in their work, extraordinary things start to happen. The presence of positive community leads to tangible results. The advisory council for the NLC has found several benefits of building a sense of community in cities, which are readily applicable in organizations. Employees can be involved in every step of a community-building process, which when combined with the values a supportive community espouses, creates a sense of responsibility people feel towards other community members and their organizations. People are more likely to fulfill obligations and perform at their best when they feel committed to the organization and its members. An environment of mutual support also empowers teams themselves to solve their problems and leads to shared ownership of work results. In addition, problems are identified early when employees anticipate that they'll receive help from others and can openly discuss the issues.

Last, employees who perceive themselves as community members can be expected to interact more frequently than employees in other groups. The process of learning about each other can break down stereotypes. Though community can't be measured quantitatively, that doesn't take away from its real and powerful importance.

Getting started

The good news about beginning the process of building community in the workplace is that most organizations don't need to start from scratch. Elements of positive community are probably already apparent. Supportive and caring connections between people have been forming spontaneously in organizations as long as they've been around. Such relationships are often formed without the support—and, in some cases, the efforts—of management.

Says Autry, "In the new workplace, the bonds of family and neighborhood have emerged so strongly that managers, running to catch up, may arrive to find an environment the employees have already created." In other words, employees will create some form of community on their own. Workplace communities are like gardens that may grow wild when unattended or flourish when guided. Organizations can build on the best qualities of the community employees have already formed to help it develop in a positive direction.

An NLC 1998 report, "Building a Nation of Communities," recommends starting a conversation at all organizational levels about the need to create community. The focus should depend on the audience. Training professionals working with a group of executives will want to drive home the potential effect on productivity and give examples of other organizations that have reaped rewards from community building. Managers will want to know how strengthening community will make their jobs easier regarding their teams. Individual contributors will be interested in hearing how community building will benefit them and what the organization will do to support them in that endeavor.

Community building is an unstoppable process once it gets started.

One question to anticipate from management is how to deal with employees who don't buy into the community-building effort. Taulbert suggests asking managers to think of creating community in the same way as implementing any standard work process. "Suppose you had a process in place for how work was going to get done," he says "You would forge ahead."

As with any major organizational initiative, leaders should champion the effort to foster a healthy community and work with people who want to take part. That will drive momentum around the community, have a positive effect on relationships and the organization, and win over stragglers. "Community building is an unstoppable process once it gets started," says Taulbert.

Building and sustaining a community requires strong leadership. Taulbert cautions that "it isn't for the faint of heart and requires tough leadership in the presence of community. " Leaders must be fully committed and must maintain commitment from others even in difficult times. Although employees form positive communities in spite of unsupportive leadership, that's not the usual or best case.

Positive values

Two important components of a discussion around community are allowing people to explore what community means to them and educating employees about elements that might be found in a positive community. Participants can uncover their personal meaning of community by finishing the statement "Community is…." Unfortunately, some people have never experienced a healthy community, either at home or in the workplace, and will lack a model. Organizations need to make sure employees have a clear idea of what positive community values are so that the community can grow in a productive direction.

One way to educate employees about what a positive community looks like is to provide examples of how other organizations have successfully built communities or values found in productive communities. In his book, Taulbert describes these important values of any healthy community:

A nurturing attitude. Members care about each other and believe that the organization cares about them. For example, a manager might call a sick employee at home to see how that person is feeling. Autry talks about a group of employees at a municipal water plant who donated part of their vacation time so that a co-worker with cancer could extend his medical leave.

Dependability. Employees need to be able to rely on their co-workers, especially in times when they can't depend on the organization for support. Members of strong communities don't want to let co-workers down and will often fulfill their commitments despite challenging circumstances.

Responsibility. Employees who are part of a community care about their workplace and feel individually responsible for maintaining a productive environment. They realize that every act, no matter how small, has the power to build or break community.

Friendship. "When friendship is absent, people often live in envy and fear. " Taulbert's words highlight the importance of the often-overlooked element of friendship. People don't leap out of bed in the morning to be with co-workers they don't like and who don't care about them. Friendships at work help people get through the day and make them want to contribute to the team.

Brotherhood and sisterhood. A strong community is needed to bring together people with differing agendas so that they can work side-by-side as equals. Organizational boundaries can blur as technology enables global influences to permeate physical barriers. Taulbert alludes to the challenge of diversity by saying we've "entered a global community where we're challenged to reach beyond the comfort of our closest relationships to welcome others different from ourselves. " Leaders can model diversity acceptance by holding themselves accountable to the same expectations they have for their staff and by pitching in to help when needed.

High expectations. Expectations have power because people will rise to the level of high expectations or live down to low ones. Leaders who make a daily practice of telling employees that they're valuable and competent build a community in which people are encouraged to maximize their talents.

Courage. Creating a positive community will test the character of everyone involved. Says Taulbert,"It takes courage to keep your gaze on what's right when all around you, people are padding their expense accounts… or cheating customers…. " He adds, courage is "speaking out on behalf of others, and making a commitment to excellence in the face of adversity or the absence of support."

Employees need to see their leaders model ethical behavior at all costs to know what the organization values and expects.

Hope. Hope sustains people during the worst of times, and communities that pull together for the common good create an abundance of hope.

Once commitment to the process is secured and employees understand the concept of community, the next step is to engage employees by creating and encouraging activities that promote community. If community is defined partly by the behavior of its members, then it makes sense to establish a set of shared values and goals; that's where many experts suggest starting. Unless people know what they have in common and realize that their individual goals can be met only by cooperating with others, there's little reason for them to commit to building a community. It's important that the values upon which a community is based be shared among its members and leaders, because people won't support values, individually or as a group, if they can't identify with them. Shared values also strengthen commitment to the organization when employees find that their personal values match the values that their work community practices.

Identifying shared community values as a group can flow naturally from the initial discussion about what community means to each person. Team members will often mention similar aspects of community that can translate into defined team values. The leader of the community is responsible for structuring processes that reinforce the shared values and that create shared goals. Managers can give team members projects that require them to make recommendations or solve problems as a group. Kouzes and Posner say that most people are genuinely interested in helping others, as long it doesn't mean they'll lose if the other team wins. Leaders who reward team success as opposed to individual efforts will avoid power struggles.

If you build it, they will come.

Employees who have identified a set of shared community values and are engaged in cooperative projects should be encouraged to take their new community and run with it. Taulbert challenges his clients to become general contractors responsible for building the community. It's crucial to encourage people to think of their community at work in the same way as their community at home. Sometimes, physical transformations can facilitate the community-building process.

Some employees choose to make their workplace resemble a small town by giving aisles street names and setting up a coffee shop in a shared space. Employees also form birthday committees and organize team potluck lunches. Such activities might seem frivolous to some people, but they can go a long way towards creating a friendly, nurturing environment that promotes trust and strengthens commitment to team members. It's why most organizations hold holiday parties and employee picnics in the summer.

Community-building efforts that affect work directly shouldn't be ignored. Community members, either as a team or through a designated committee, should be guided to identify business-related challenges held by members of their community, to develop the means to address those issues, and to set goals and priorities for their community.

The final step in building a workplace community is to sustain the effort for the long term. Trainers can be especially helpful in this phase because if employees don't have the interpersonal skills that will help them build positive relationships, they'll need training. Ideally, training should start during the formation of the community-building initiative so that employees are prepared by that stage. Of course, people don't learn trust and respect in a classroom but by doing. In those instances, trainers can serve as coaches.

An organization's leaders play an important role in sustaining communities, which is similar to maintaining a house: The physical structure demands a continual process of upkeep. In the workplace, employees can't just grow community one time; they must cultivate it for as long as they're together. Leaders can nurture the community by establishing the strong expectations that employees will develop cooperative work relationships and deal openly with problems. Leaders should back up those expectations by rewarding employees who practice the community's values and by coaching those who don't. Managers can use hiring practices that find candidates who already share at least some of the key community values, and new-employee orientation can communicate the values.

Last, it's essential to review community values periodically so that teams can renew themselves as the environment changes. For example, a critical event such as those on September 11 may cause a team to focus more on a value such as connectedness—not only within the community, but also with neighboring teams and external communities.

A strong sense of community tends to correlate with exceptional company performance.

Ultimately, the community is responsible for its survival. Like all organization initiatives, communities will go through dormant and renewal phases. Fear not when you see the spirit of community wax and wane. Scott Peck, author of *A World Waiting to Be Born,* contends that a group doesn't have to be in a genuine state of community at all times to be healthy. "It's normal for groups to fall out of this genuine state and into temporary emptiness or even chaos. Truly healthy groups are determined by how quickly its members recognize that they have lost community and by their willingness to rapidly rebuild it."

The principles of positive community can reach far beyond the physical boundaries of a single office building. Organizations with employees who are located internationally, who telecommute, or who work in a virtual community can build strong communities that reach out to distant groups. Companies with offices in other parts of the world will find that, though the languages may differ, the yearning to belong is universal.

Creating community is especially important in virtual organizations, where employees may never meet their coworkers or customers. Developing relationships with members of the community can combat feelings of isolation.

A strong sense of community tends to correlate with exceptional company performance. Two popular examples are eBay and Southwest Airlines. Chat rooms, bulletin boards, and newsletters have made eBay a 24/7 forum for people who like to trade and collect. Some eBay community members hold picnics and take trips together.

At first, eBay founder and chairman Pierre Omidyar was surprised by the response. "I thought people would simply buy and sell things, but what they really enjoyed was meeting other people," he says in the February 2001 issue of *Inc.* Executives at eBay educate new employees during orientation about shared values, and those values are reinforced. President and CEO Meg Whitman strives to foster connections between employees and customers by encouraging staff to start collections of their own.

One of the few airlines that didn't seek a federal loan after September 11 was Southwest. It's no coincidence Southwest has done well financially even in hard times. The airline reinvented air travel with low fares, exceptional service, and a strong sense of identity. It found success by being courageous enough to create an environment in which people can love and care at work.

Several months have passed since the events on September 11, and life at work has returned to a new form of normalcy. I repeatedly hear from company leaders that we should "get back to business as usual" and "move on." They may not see that many employees are still glued to Internet news sites every time a plane crashes or when another person contracts anthrax. Executives may see training sessions packed with participants, but not their eyes staring through the instructor as they worry about not receiving raises this year because business is down. Letting employees remain disengaged is unhealthy for them and financially disastrous for an organization.

Leaders should be encouraged to take advantage of this present opportunity to unite people around common values that will create a place where people feel good about the work they do. Your company's survival may depend on it.

Tracy Mauro *is a management trainer at MCI WorldCom; tracy.mauro@wcom.com.*

From *Training & Development,* February 2002, pp. 52-58. © 2002 by ASTD Magazines. Reprinted by permission.

INVESTIGATIONS

CORPORATE PROBES: A SCORECARD

With so much happening, it's getting hard to keep up

Lately, you can't open a newspaper without reading about the Securities & Exchange Commission launching a new investigation of another company or industry. From Enron to Edison Schools, from hedge funds to Wall Street analysts, the list of players under SEC scrutiny just keeps growing. Indeed, with 64 accounting and financial-reporting cases opened in the first quarter alone—more than double the year-earlier total—following all the action is a full-time job. To make things easier, here's a scorecard on the players and the issues under investigation:

ACCOUNTING

ARTHUR ANDERSEN

• Destruction of documents relating to its audits of Enron and allegations of shortcomings in its audits of Enron, Global Crossing, Qwest, and WorldCom. Criminal trial under way on obstruction of justice. Andersen denies wrongdoing.

DELOITTE & TOUCHE

• Deloitte's audits of Adelphia Communications and its failure to tell Adelphia's audit committee that the founding Rigas family used company credit lines to buy Adelphia stock. Deloitte says it met professional standards.

ERNST & YOUNG

• Marketing agreement to sell software with PeopleSoft, an auditing client, may violate auditor independence rules. The SEC wants E&Y to give back PeopleSoft audit fees paid between 1994–2000. E&Y is fighting the charge. The SEC is also scrutinizing the firm's audits of companies such as Computer Associates and PNC Financial Services.

KPMG

• KPMG's failure to catch alleged revenue-inflating maneuvers by Xerox, an audit client. KPMG denies wrongdoing. Also, the accounting firm's $25 million investment in the AIM mutual fund, an audit client, allegedly in violation of auditor independence rules. Without admitting fault, KPMG agreed to take steps to avoid future investments in audit clients.

PRICEWATERHOUSE COOPERS

• PwC's audits of MicroStrategy, which settled SEC charges of financial fraud in 2001 for overstating revenues without admitting fault, are still under investigation.

ENERGY

CMS ENERGY

• Round-trip trades with other energy wholesalers that allegedly overstated revenues by $1 billion in 2000 and $4.2 billion in 2001. The Justice Dept., Commodity Futures Trading Commission, and the Federal Energy Regulatory Commission are also investigating.

DYNEGY

• Round-trip trades that allegedly inflated revenues. Also, a natural gas transaction that allegedly made cash flow from operations appear larger than it was.

ENRON

• Widespread alleged abuses of accounting and disclosure rules to inflate profits. Ongoing probes by the SEC and a Justice Dept. task force.

HALLIBURTON

• Accounting policies that treated cost overruns on construction jobs as revenue, regardless of whether its customers agreed to pay part of the overbudget costs. Halliburton says it stands by its accounting.

RELIANT RESOURCES

• The energy trader's restatement of earnings for two quarters in 2001 after it determined that some derivative transactions accounted for as cash-flow hedges should have been valued at the market price.

SOFTWARE

COMPUTER ASSOCIATES

• Overstating revenues in 1998 that allegedly inflated its stock price just before and after the awarding of $1 billion in stock to three top managers. Ongoing SEC and Justice Dept. investigations.

NETWORK ASSOCIATES

• Alleged accounting inaccuracies that may have understated expenses or overstated revenues in 1998–2000.

TELECOM

GLOBAL CROSSING

• Capacity swaps allegedly done with other carriers for the purpose of inflating revenues. Ongoing SEC and Justice Dept. investigations.

LUCENT TECHNOLOGIES

• Booked $679 million in revenue from sales to its distributors before the distributors were able to actually sell the products.

QWEST COMMUNICATIONS

• Capacity swaps with other carriers as well as equipment sales to customers in return for Internet services, both allegedly designed to inflate revenues.

WORLDCOM

• Accounting practices, including treatment of goodwill, and company loans totaling $408.2 million to former CEO Bernard Ebbers. WorldCom defends its accounting.

WALL STREET

CREDIT SUISSE FIRST BOSTON

• CSFB's allocation, as lead underwriter, of shares of hot IPOs to customers in return for allegedly excessive commissions on other trades. Similar practices alleged at J.P. Morgan Chase, Morgan Stanley Dean Witter, Goldman Sachs, and other investment banks under investigation. CSFB agreed to pay a $100 million fine to the National Association of Securities Dealers and to change how it allocates IPO shares, without admitting fault. The others are cooperating with the probe.

HEDGE FUNDS

• Incidents of fraud, conflicts of interest at firms that manage both hedge funds and mutual funds. The SEC is considering the need for regulation.

iCAPITAL MARKETS

• Alleged illegal trades that iCapital, formerly Datek Securities, made for its own account through Nasdaq's small-order execution system from 1993–1998. Investigation settled after iCapital Markets agreed to pay a $6.3 million fine, without admitting fault.

MERRILL LYNCH

• Alleged conflicts of interest for research analysts who work alongside investment bankers. Merrill agreed to pay $100 million in a May 21 settlement with New York Attorney General Eliot Spitzer without admitting wrongdoing. SEC probe is ongoing. Other brokers, including Morgan Stanley and Goldman Sachs, are also being investigated by the SEC, as well as by state officials.

OTHER INDUSTRIES

ADELPHIA COMMUNICATIONS

• The cable-TV operator's alleged failure to adequately disclose $5.6 billion in loan guarantees to the family of founder John Rigas. SEC and two grand jury investigations are ongoing.

EDISON SCHOOLS

• For-profit operator of public schools didn't disclose that nearly half its revenues consisted of funds that school districts paid directly to teachers and vendors. Edison agreed to add a director of internal audit, without admitting fault.

KMART

• Accounting for vendor discounts and other transactions that allegedly underreported 2001 losses by at least $1.7 billion. SEC probe is ongoing; FBI and Justice are also investigating.

PNC FINANCIAL SERVICES

• Both the SEC and Federal Reserve are investigating the Pittsburgh bank's accounting treatment of three companies it set up with insurer American International Group to hold corporate loans PNC wanted off its balance sheet.

TRUMP HOTELS

• Allegedly misleading statements in a 1999 press release that suggested the company's positive results were due to operations rather than a one-time gain. Without admitting or denying guilt, Trump consented to an SEC cease-and-desist order.

WASTE MANAGEMENT

• Founder and five former top officials allegedly used fraudulent accounting to inflate profits by $1.7 billion between 1992 and 1997. The SEC filed suit in March, charging the ex-execs with falsifying and misrepresenting the company's results. They deny the charges.

XEROX

• Accelerated recognition of lease and servicing revenues in a scheme that allegedly inflated revenues by $3 billion from 1997–2000. SEC settled with the copier maker in April, imposing a record $10 million fine. Xerox agreed to restate earnings for 1997–2000 and form a panel of its outside directors to review accounting policies and practices without admitting guilt.

Data: Company reports, SEC Filings, SECA

By Amy Borrus, with Mike McNamee, in Washington, and Susan Zegel in New York

Special report Bribery and business

The short arm of the law

Plenty of laws exist to ban bribery by companies. But big multinationals continue to sidestep them with ease

NEW legislation has just come into force in Britain extending anti-bribery laws to cover British nationals and companies abroad. For the Americans it is none too soon. Anti-bribery legislation covering American citizens abroad has been in force for a quarter of a century, and the American government has been battling for some time to persuade Britain that it has been failing in its commitments under an OECD convention on bribery that it signed at the end of 1997. The convention, now signed by 35 countries, decrees that "enterprises should not, directly or indirectly, offer, promise, give, or demand a bribe or other undue advantage to obtain or retain business." Anywhere.

The Americans claim that, so long as legislation elsewhere falls short of their own Foreign Corrupt Practices Act (FCPA) of 1977, they are at a disadvantage in bidding for international contracts. The FCPA outlaws the payment of bribes by American firms to foreign officials, political parties, party officials and candidates. The Department of Justice claims that, between early 1994 and early 2001, "the US government learned of significant allegations of bribery by foreign firms in over 400 competitions for international contracts valued at $200 billion. The practice is global in scope, with firms from over 50 countries implicated in offering bribes for contracts in over 100 buyer countries during the seven-year period."

The implication is that American firms lost out as a result. That may be so. But in fact there is little to stop the subsidiaries of British or American companies from offering and accepting bribes in a host of countries that have not signed the OECD convention, and indeed in many that have. Some of the bribers referred to by the Department of Justice may actually have been subsidiaries of America's own multinationals. For there are holes in the anti-bribery laws that are big enough for a half-blind elephant to blunder through.

Mere facilitation

The FCPA applies to companies registered in America and to any foreign companies that are quoted on an American stock exchange. In 1998 the overseas coverage was extended to include bribery by foreign firms on American territory. It is also, in theory, possible (but it has scarcely ever happened in practice) that an American parent company could be held liable for the acts of foreign subsidiaries "where they authorised, directed or controlled the activity in question".

The power of American legislation to bring charges for bribery by non-nationals is, however, negligible. John Mayo, a former finance director of GEC, a British defence group later renamed Marconi, wrote with impunity in the *Financial Times* last year that "US acquisitions had to be made for cash as GEC was not compliant with the FCPA and so could not list in the US."

The law against bribery abroad is rendered still more ineffective by the acceptance of what are known as "facilitation payments". These are small payments made to expedite routine business needs—clearing customs, obtaining permits, and so on. BP and Unilever, two British multinationals that are quoted in America, admitted to a British parliamentary committee a year ago that they make facilitation payments. At the same time, BP professes that "we will never offer, solicit or accept a bribe in any form."

Britain's Department of Trade and Industry concedes that there is no clear definition of a facilitation payment or of precisely how it differs from a bribe. An amendment to the FCPA specifically exempts "facilitating payments for routine governmental action" from the American definition of a bribe. Another not-very-thin end of the wedge.

An article in the *Vanderbilt Journal of Transnational Law* of November 1999, by Christopher Corr and Judd Lawler, reports on what "appears to be the first non-resident foreign national to be indicted for violating the FCPA". The case involved the Dutch chairman of Saybolt North America Inc, an American subsidiary of a Dutch petroleum-inspection company. A $50,000 bribe had been paid in a Panama City bar to help the company secure a lease on a waterfront site adjoining the Panama Canal. The case was settled in August 1998.

Before that, all cases involving foreign payments had been brought only against American residents. And there were not too many of them, either. The application of the American legislation to quoted companies is the responsibility of the SEC. The Department of Justice oversees the rest. The SEC has brought only three cases involving bribes abroad in the first 20 years of the FCPA. The Department of Justice—armed, as the SEC puts it, "with the greater evidence-gathering tools available to criminal prosecutors"—brought all of 30 cases involving foreign bribery. That is a rate of 1.5 a year, surely a drop in the ocean.

The pace of prosecution is at least accelerating. The SEC settled three cases in 2001. One involved IBM Argentina, a wholly-owned subsidiary of the American computer giant, which paid some $4.5m in bribes to officials of Banco de la Nacion Argentina in order to win a contract to modernise the computer system of the government-owned bank.

On the surface, this looks like a breakthrough in the pursuit of subsidiaries of multinationals. But there are several things to dampen the enthusiasm of those battling against bribery. In the first place, it was IBM itself that discovered the bribes, and it was the IBM parent company that reported them to the SEC. The SEC ordered IBM to pay a civil penalty of a mere $300,000, in a year when its turnover was over $85 billion. This hardly amounts to a punishing deterrent. Moreover, had the Argentine bank been in the private sector (and not state-owned) it is not clear that IBM would have had to report the bribes to anybody, since the FCPA covers only payments made to public officials.

Present and correct

In another case, settled in September last year, the SEC also stumbled across bribes paid by Baker Hughes only because the American oil-and-gas technology company reported them. In this case, because of the "strong corrective action" taken by the company, the SEC did not impose any civil penalty at all. It is, however, pursuing Baker Hughes's Indonesian accounting firm, KPMG Siddharta Siddharta & Harsono, in its first-ever joint action with the Department of Justice. The Indonesian affiliate of KPMG is alleged to have been the conduit through which a $75,000 payment was funnelled to an Indonesian tax official in charge of a Baker Hughes tax assessment. This case could push the extraterritorial ambitions of the American authorities a bit further.

The new British law on bribery and corruption applies if "a national of the United Kingdom or a body incorporated under the law of any part of the United Kingdom does anything in a country or territory outside the United Kingdom." A Home Office spokeswoman says that the legislation will apply "if there is conspiracy between a UK parent and a foreign subsidiary". But this is nowhere spelt out in the three meagre sections of the Antiterrorism, Crime and Security Act 2001 that extend the bribery laws to non-nationals. British lawyers believe that any legal action taken over bribes paid by a foreign subsidiary of a British multinational would have to be pursued in the country of registration of that subsidiary.

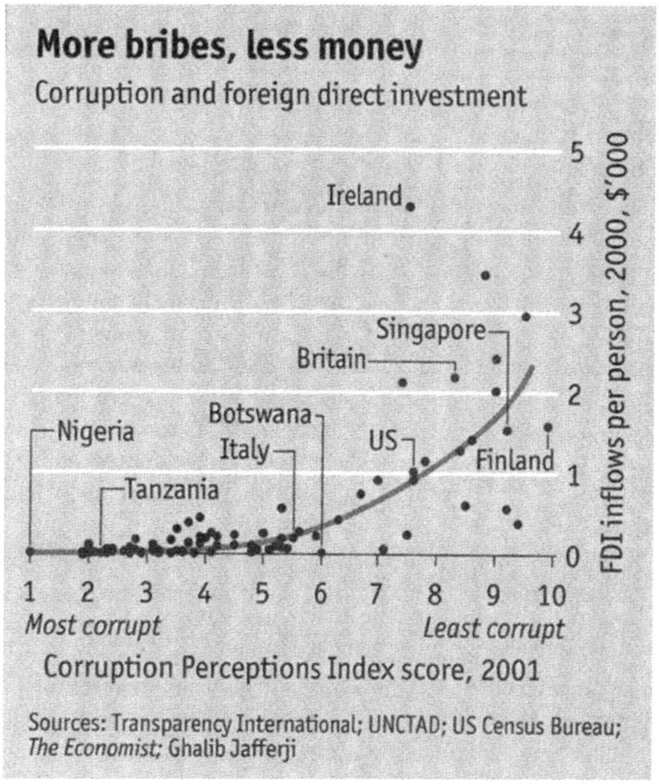

The government maintains, as it did to the aggrieved Americans before the new legislation came into force, that Britain's existing anti-bribery laws, dating back to 1889, are sufficient to deal with cases involving foreigners. But if they are, they have yet to prove it. One British lawyer says that there has been only one successful prosecution for bribery of a public official in Britain in the past century, never mind a prosecution of anybody abroad.

Despite their records, Britain and America persist in trying to appear purer than each other in their pursuit of bribery overseas. Baroness Symons, a British foreign office minister, told a recent conference that "the UK has a strong reputation for honesty and integrity... we were one of the first countries in the world to introduce an anti-corruption law."

To vindicate itself further, the British government likes to refer to the Bribe Payers Index, a measure devised by Transparency International, a Berlin-based non-governmental organisation devoted to combating corruption. The index ranks countries according to perceptions of how corrupt they and their companies are, and the British authorities eagerly point out that Britain is ranked as the second least corrupt among the G7 countries (after Canada)—ie, it comes above the United States.

In the latest ranking, Britain comes 13th, with America in 16th place. Italy (at 29th) is the lowest of the G7 countries, beaten by (among others) Botswana, Chile and Estonia (see chart). This suggests that the biggest and most prevalent bribes are not necessarily always paid by or in the poorest countries. Bottom of the heap is Nigeria, a place where, it is widely acknowledged, bribery has become endemic.

Shell game

Nigeria is also a big oil producer and home to large subsidiaries of foreign multinationals such as BP, Shell and Standard Chartered Bank. Shell is often held up as a paragon of virtue in its treatment of bribery. Baroness Symons recently cited the company as an exemplar of British cleanliness in this matter. The Shell report for 2000 proclaims that "we are a 'no bribes', fair competition business"; it also publishes a chart of the internal reported cases of bribery in recent years. This is promoted as pioneering stuff. No other large public company seems to do the same.

The Shell chart shows no reported cases in 2000 of "bribes offered and/or paid by Shell company employees directly or indirectly to third parties". In 1999 there was one case (of a bribe of $300)—exactly the same number and amount as in 1998. The company also says that in 2000 "Shell companies reported four instances in which a total of seven employees were detected soliciting/accepting bribes directly or indirectly. The total financial value was estimated to be $89,000. All seven employees were dismissed."

The reference to "Shell companies" implies that these figures cover all companies in the group, including the hundreds of subsidiaries that operate in the 135 countries in which Shell has a presence. The extraordinary low numbers in the chart have been questioned by several people who have worked with or for Shell in Nigeria. Either the company's internal investigation and reporting systems are inadequate, they allege, or the figures are being economical with the truth.

Their suggestions are reinforced by the fact that the Shell chart covers a period when the notoriously corrupt Sani Abacha was in power in Nigeria (he died in 1998). When the Nigerians appointed a former staff member of Transparency International to look into bribery during that time, he decided that only the biggest offenders should be prosecuted. Punishing everybody would have meant sacking almost the entire civil service, bringing government to a standstill. Yet despite such prevalence of bribery, in 1998 Shell's internal systems threw up only one small bribe paid by any of its thousands of staff.

How widespread is the problem of bribery? There is some evidence that the practice is growing. Friends Ivory & Sime (FIS) is a large British fund manager which, as part of its policy on corporate governance, "seeks to support and encourage companies in their efforts to manage significant risks, such as those arising from bribery and corruption." Those risks, it believes, are increasing.

FIS has just published a report on a survey of 82 large quoted companies in 12 countries, all companies in which FIS invests. The survey sought to find out what were the companies' policies towards bribery, and what systems they had in place to deal with it. FIS maintains that corruption is an issue that is all too rarely probed by investors. Like managers, investors are often equivocal about the impact on their organisation's bottom line. Many believe that in large parts of the world a company that does not pay bribes does not do business.

But it ain't necessarily so. United Technologies, an American conglomerate that makes Otis lifts, Sikorsky helicopters and Pratt & Whitney engines, once fired the president of a foreign subsidiary for making gifts to officials in violation of the FCPA. After the firing, said the head of the American parent company, "market share and profitability stayed up and even increased in one of the more notorious problem countries."

In any case, as Shell puts it, "bribery drives up prices for products and services". One World Bank report estimates that bribes in Uganda increase companies' overall costs by 8%. Some of those costs will eat into profits: even if a single company gains from paying a bribe, collectively, companies (and shareholders) will lose. Bribery is also bad for the economic health of countries. And it is their economic health that most affects the long-run ability of companies to increase profits.

The World Bank's latest *World Development Report* says that "it is now widely accepted that corruption has large costs for economic development. Across countries there is strong evidence that higher levels of corruption are associated with lower growth and lower levels of per capita income." For sound economic reasons, foreign investors and international aid agencies are increasingly taking the level of bribery and corruption into account in their investment and lending.

Walls of silence

The first disturbing finding of the FIS survey is that 33% of the respondents chose not to answer the questionnaire at all. As an investor, FIS finds their silence less than golden. Of those that did reply, FIS says "a large proportion appear to have inadequate policies and implementation mechanisms." One company, for example, does not allow its employees to accept bribes, but it does allow them to give bribes.

FIS says that poor implementation means, among other things, not having "clear lines of accountability from the board downwards". Very few companies give clear advice about the steps people should take to report suspected cases of corruption. Shell produces a 56-page management primer, "Dealing with Bribery and Corruption", written with the help of KPMG's Ethics and Integrity Consulting Unit—the same KPMG whose Indonesian affiliate is currently being pursued by the SEC and the Department of Justice for passing bribes on behalf of Baker Hughes. The Shell document is an interesting history of anti-bribery legislation and of the philosophical dilemmas behind it. But it is not bursting with telephone numbers and e-mail addresses of people to contact when a dilemma slaps a puzzled expatriate manager in the face.

When allegations of bribery come from outside, they often face a wall of silence as a company closes up to protect its own. Take the case of Jarrn Tankers & Trucking, once a supplier to BP Tanzania. Set up by Robert Satchwell, a former British Treasury official, to be a "clean" company, Jarrn's contract with BP was, in effect, terminated at short notice in 1999. Jarrn alleges that this happened because it refused to pay the bribes that were demanded by the oil company's local employees.

BP has conducted three investigations into the matter. Each one has come under the control of BP's Africa division, and each has avoided investigating Mr Satchwell's specific allegations: allegations that are, moreover, supported by sworn statements from four independent outsiders. The tenacious Mr Satchwell has persisted in demanding an independent inquiry, and in October 2001 BP at last set up an inquiry team with outsiders, including a former British fraud-squad officer. The team has visited Tanzania but has not yet presented its findings.

The BP case highlights another good reason for coming down hard on bribery. It is often a means for companies to circumvent health and safety regulations. In October 2000, a local newspaper reported finding that "80% of trucks using Tanzanian trunk roads and carrying transit cargo were overloaded, but proceeded to their destinations unchecked after money changed hands." Mr Satchwell's trucks delivered BP aviation fuel to Kilimanjaro International airport. Any suggestion that these unexploded bombs are short-circuiting safety regulations should be a matter of the very highest priority to BP. Mr Satchwell has written about this matter on five different occasions to all of the non-executive directors of BP. They have not sent him a single reply.

Pursuing cases involving bribery overseas is not easy. Even Finland, which has headed Transparency International's list for the past two years, and is also the most advanced in implementing the OECD convention, has yet to bring a single criminal case involving the bribery of a foreign public official. Mark Pieth, professor of criminal law at the University of Basel and chairman of the OECD working group on bribery in international business transactions, wrote recently that the further pursuit of corporate bribery "will require prosecutors to take a fresh look at the behaviour of their highly respected local companies when operating outside their home market. And this will involve a reappraisal of investigative techniques, in particular with regard to the collection of evidence from abroad."

In the meantime, multinationals have been left pretty much to their own devices. A few have taken serious steps to stamp out bribery—Procter & Gamble even closed a Pampers plant in Nigeria rather than pay a bribe to a customs inspector. Many more, however, have merely pretended to stamp it out. Companies that are serious about implementing a "no bribery" policy need to do a lot more than just pontificate about the evils of corruption and ask managers to fill in a form once a year.

From *The Economist*, March 2, 2002, pp. 63-65. © 2002 by The Economist, Ltd. Distributed by the New York Times Special Features. Reprinted by permission.

THE WORKPLACE ETHIC—IS IT A CRIME?

Two out of three employees say they lie to their boss. And many managers say they know this and accept it. An MT/KPMG survey puts the moral grey areas of the workplace into black and white.

Matthew Weait

Waiter, can we have two receipts, please? That's OK, driver—just leave it blank. I can't come in today—I think I've got food poisoning. And so it goes... A fiddle on expenses is technically unlawful. A little white lie to your boss is naughty. But do you see either as a crime? Sure, say some, but many find it hard to draw the line. There's no black and white, they say, merely awkward shades of grey. As Groucho Marx once said: 'Those are my principles. If you don't like them, I have others.'

WHICH SIDE OF THE LINE DO *YOU* PUT THESE ACTIVITIES?

	Acceptable
Charging personal entertainment to expenses	2%
Taking a sicky after the office party	6%
Minor fiddling of travel expenses	6%
Favouring family or friends when awarding contracts	6%
Taking software home	15%
Using company petrol for personal mileage	17%
Surfing the net for pleasure in worktime	22%
Taking pens and pencils from work	48%
Making personal phone calls from work	75%

The fact is that 'unethical behaviour'—from pilfering pens and surfing the net while at work to outright fraud—remains endemic in the British workplace. And it runs from the boardroom to the shop floor. Although most managers have a fundamentally ethical approach to business, a majority are aware of dishonest conduct in the workplace but accept it as inevitable. They simply cost it into operations and don't blow the whistle on offenders.

These are some of the key findings of a major new survey conducted recently by MT and KPMG Forensic Accounting, which took in responses from more than 800 directors, managers and partners. About half were women, who intriguingly appear to be more liberal/lax in their ethical views than men. People over 40 are more scrupulous than their younger counterparts, and public-sector workers are more disapproving of unethical behaviour than those in the private sector. More than two in three (including six out of 10 board directors) say that everyone lies to the boss on occasion, and less than half consider the people at the top of their organisations to be strong ethical role models.

To assess their attitudes, the participating managers were given a hypothetical scenario (shown below) and asked a number of questions. The results were collated and analysed, along with any comments the respondents offered. A number who took part were subsequently interviewed by telephone. Generally, respondents were disapproving of conduct that on the face of it might be considered unethical. Over 90% disapproved of taking a 'sick day' after the Christmas party, of charging personal entertainment to expenses, of favouring family and friends when awarding contracts, and of posting Christmas cards from work. More than 80% disapproved of taking home software and using company petrol for personal mileage, and more than 70% disapproved of surfing the net for pleasure on company time. Even taking pens from work was condemned by just over half. More people disagreed than agreed with the statement that there is no need to worry about a bit of petty fiddling so long as you come in on time and within budget, or that it is acceptable to artificially inflate profits so long as no money is stolen.

WHERE DO YOU DRAW THE LINE?

WHAT WOULD YOU DO?

Jim takes a taxi to a business meeting. He has plenty of time and he could have gone by public transport, which is reliable where he lives, for £1.40. At the end of the cab journey—which costs £4.50, to which Jim adds a 50p tip—the cab driver offers him a receipt for £4.50, excluding tip, or a receipt for £5.00, which covers the fare and the tip, or a blank receipt. Jim accepts the blank receipt, fills it in for £6.50 and claims it on expenses.

Just over 50% saw the tip as a legitimate expense. A more prudent 35% thought Jim should have used public transport instead. Only a tiny minority were prepared to exploit the situation and make a fraudulent claim.

However, this glowing show of ethics is not the whole story. More disturbing is the finding that a significant number of people in senior positions are prepared to condone conduct that amounts to theft, false accounting and fraud and have a 'relaxed' approach to workplace ethics. Over 20% thought it was OK to surf the net for pleasure during work time. Using company petrol for personal mileage was deemed acceptable by 16%. One in four would not say that favouring friends and family in awarding contracts was totally unacceptable. And 7% agreed that it is acceptable to artificially increase profits, so long as no money is stolen (for board directors, the proportion was just under one in seven).

Some of these figures may seem low, but they are not insignificant. They tell us that some people, many in senior positions, are comfortable with conduct that may reduce profitability and, in some cases, amount to serious crimes. Take expenses claims. Under the Theft Act 1968, dishonest falsification of any document used for accounting purposes amounts to false accounting, an offence that can carry a sentence of up to seven years' imprisonment. Yet fewer than one in five respondents were prepared to say that charging personal entertainment to expenses was totally unacceptable [among board directors it was even less at 15%). Similarly, only six out of 10 were prepared to say that minor fiddling of business expenses was totally unacceptable.

These shocking figures did not square with the almost sanctimonious responses to our hypothetical case in which an employee turns a profit on his taxi receipt. Only 1 % condone it on the basis that it was a small amount and everybody does it. Half thought it acceptable to tip 50p and claim it as a legitimate business expense, but one in 10 thought he shouldn't claim the tip and more than a third thought he should take public transport and save his employer money. Survey results varied according to the size of the organisation represented by the respondent. For example, one female board director, Jo Brown of Ojwatch Service, commented: 'We are a small company and so it's easy to see how people's conduct impacts on others. It's also easier to maintain standards. Everyone has to be responsible for their own actions. It's also important to be flexible. Take time management—it's fine to take time out from work for a personal appointment, so long as you make up that time. In large firms it is all too easy for people to think, why should I bother, who's going to notice?'

ETHICS MAN/ETHICS WOMAN

In six out of the 10 examples of unethical conduct, a higher percentage of women than men considered them to be acceptable or totally acceptable.

More women than men were comfortable with making personal phone calls from work, and although three out of four men were not prepared to give a clean reference to someone who had been involved in some sort of fraud, the proportion of women was only two-thirds.

One should, however, be careful before leaping to the conclusion that women are more dishonest than men. Perhaps women are less willing to condemn in the absence of information about the context of and reasons for 'unethical' conduct. Or it may be simply that women are more honest in their responses to the questionnaire.

The relative ethics of women and men was just one of the surprising results of the survey. Just as interesting were the findings that respondents over 40, people in financial positions and those in the public sector take a more judgmental approach to unethical conduct. We can only speculate as to why. The over-40s may have had a stronger sense of responsibility; or, with senior positions under their belt, they may now be less forgiving than their juniors; or do they believe they are more likely to be found out?

As for those in the public sector, three explanations spring to mind. First, public duty may attract those who take ethical matters more seriously. Second, it may be an awareness that they are dealing with taxpayers' money. And third, controls on resources may be tighter in the public sector. For those in financial positions, it may be a case of 'the cost buck stops here'. An accounting background is supposed to include professional ethical training, so it is unsurprising that they take a harder line than others—not that every accountant is as pure as the driven snow.

In the survey we did not ask about the behaviour of the respondents themselves. We tested ethical attitudes and people do not always practise what they preach. But how common is such misconduct? There is little statistical information on the incidence of workplace theft and fraud, but what there is paints a worrying picture. The most recent crime statistics published by the Home Office show that there were some 18,000 recorded offences of theft by employees nationally in the 1998–99 financial year, and more than 1,300 of false accounting. Employee theft accounted for 13% of all crimes against business premises in Scotland in '98.

However, the official figures provide only a partial picture of dishonesty in the workplace. Much of it never comes to light, and even if it does, many employers choose not to report it. A survey published this year by the British Retail Consortium reported 25,000 incidents of theft by staff in that sector alone in 1999—an increase of 32% on the previous year—while thefts by customers rose by only 3%. And the value of such thefts increased from £364 million in 1998 to £519 million in 1999, a rise of 43%.

Although our survey did not ask specifically about theft, half of those who responded said they were aware of dishonest or fraudulent practices at work. Of these, nearly two-thirds considered that this was unchanged from five years ago.

Some of the comments from participants reflected the view that there are two sides to the question of ethical standards. Nick Burns, a former senior manager and director of a manufacturing company, observes: 'The work relationship is reciprocal, so there is a mutual ethical obligation. Most jobs depend on a degree of goodwill and trust. If the company becomes concerned about people making personal phone calls etc, then it should adopt similar values for itself. For example, should it require extra work or time outside the terms defined by a contract of employment? Overall, it is swings and balances—but it is very easy to damage the relationship. The goodwill of the personnel is worth a lot.'

If the incidence of workplace misconduct is as commonplace as our survey indicates, there is clearly a problem. How is it best tackled? One of the most obvious ways is for people to blow the whistle on those they know to be engaged in unethical practices. This rarely occurs. Although just under a third of respondents said they had reported on colleagues, most had not—one in 10 had not even considered doing so. The main reason for restraint was a fear of being alienated from colleagues, followed closely by the attitude that 'other people's conduct is none of my business'. This indicates first that many people sense a lack of support from those to whom they might turn; second, that their own organisational culture doesn't foster a sense of collective responsibility and integrity.

If these are indeed the reasons, they are disturbing. But it is important to recognise that blowing the whistle does not address the fundamental issue of prevention. It is all very well to deal with problems after the event, but such an approach fails to address their cause. Such is the view of Alex Plavsic, fraud investigation partner in KPMG's Forensic Accounting group. 'If people are unsure about what conduct is and is not acceptable, they inevitably rely on their own—usually flawed—judgment!

WHY WOULDN'T YOU BLOW THE WHISTLE?

	MEN	WOMEN
Alienate myself from my colleagues	21%	26%
None of my business	49%	40%
Jeopardise my job	13%	18%
Everybody's doing it	30%	42%
It's fair game	5%	5%
Some people had other reasons		

KPMG, which for 10 years has published a leading trend indicator in its Fraud Barometer, reported a marked decrease in the value of fraud cases—from £500 million in the first nine months of 1999 to £174 million for the same period in 2000—but no decline in the number of offences. Jeremy Outer, KPMG Forensic Accounting partner, warned that if minor fraud goes undetected, fraudsters may become more-ambitious, and 'the cumulative effect may be just as devastating to a company's reputation'. Firms should keep their security systems under constant review.

Ethics in the workplace are a matter of considerable complexity and importance, and yet eight out of 10 respondents said their organisation provided no training on the subject. But the overwhelming majority thought such training should be provided. It is hoped that if this survey achieves anything, it will at least encourage those who have the power and authority to effect change in workplace culture to answer the call.

After studying law at Cambridge, Matthew Weait completed a masters in criminology, worked for the Centre for Socio-Legal Studies at Oxford University, and set up the law department at the University of London. He now lectures in law at the Open University's business school and is a trained barrister. This all makes him the perfect judge and juror on ethics in the workplace—our breakthrough research with an unexpected twist.

From the Editor

Enron: The Studebaker of the 21st Century?

In December 1963, following years of losses, Studebaker Corporation decided to close its manufacturing plant in South Bend, Indiana. The plant closing resulted in the dismissal of more than 5,000 workers and the termination of a pension plan covering 11,000 members of the United Automobile Workers (UAW). The assets of the plan (85 percent of which consisted of Studebaker stock) were far less than needed to provide the benefits that had vested under the plan. Ultimately, Studebaker and the UAW agreed to allocate the plan's assets in accordance with default priorities specified in the plan. Approximately 3,600 retirees and active workers who had reached age 60 received the full pension promised under the plan, and roughly 4,000 other vested employees received lump-sum distributions of roughly 15 percent of the value of their accrued benefits. The remaining employees, whose interest had not yet vested in any benefits under the plan, received nothing.

Studebaker was the most prominent example cited by ERISA's proponents for the need for greater regulation of private pensions and, 11 years after Studebaker's shutdown, ERISA was signed into law by President Ford. The recent Enron situation has been compared to Studebaker by many who would like to revamp ERISA's regulation of defined contribution pension plans, and President Bush and several members of Congress have proposed ERISA reform bills that would attempt to prevent an Enron reoccurrence. In addition, there have been a number of class action lawsuits filed on behalf of Enron 401(k) plan participants.

Background

Other than the War on Terrorism, no recent event has garnered more attention than the collapse of Enron. In particular, because close to 60 percent of the assets of Enron's 401(k) plan (which included an employee stock ownership plan ("ESOP") feature) were invested in Enron stock, its employees' retirement nest eggs took a hit in excess of $1 billion.

All the time this column is being written, the facts surrounding Enron's collapse and its effect on the 401(k) plan are still developing. Some of the most important facts include the following:

- Employees could elect among a wide variety of options for investment of their own "401(k)" deferrals. The alternatives included various mutual funds as well as Enron stock. The various lawsuits filed after Enron's collapse allege that Enron strongly encouraged its employees to invest their contributions in Enron stock.
- Enron's matching contributions were made in Enron stock and were required to remain invested in Enron stock until the employee attained age 55 with at least 10 years of service. The "55/10" diversification option was included pursuant to the Internal Revenue Code rules governing ESOPs.
- At the time many of the details regarding the alleged malfeasance and misfeasance of Enron's management were released, the 401(k) plan was in the midst of a "lockdown" due to a change of recordkeepers. The lockdown lasted for approximately two weeks, and participants were not permitted to change their investment options during the lockdown in order to permit the new recordkeeper to obtain and reconcile data from the previous recordkeeper.
- Enron had an unusual arrangement that benefits payable under its defined benefit plan were offset by the value of participants' 401(k) balances. In determining the offset, 401(k) balances as of December 31, 1999 (when Enron stock was trading at a high value), rather than the current value of Enron stock, were used. Thus, the collapse of Enron's stock did not serve to increase benefits under the defined benefit plan, because the 401(k) plan "offset" was set at an unrealistically high value. The Tax Reform Act of 1986 generally outlawed such arrangements, except that it "grandfathered" arrangements in place when TRA '86 was enacted.

- The Labor Department is in the process of attempting to take over the Enron plan and oust the current fiduciaries of the plan.

The universe of plans with potential "Enron problems" is relatively small, although those plans do cover large numbers of participants. A recent survey by the Employee Benefits Research Institute and the Investment Company Institute found that only .1 percent of plans with under 100 participants, .8 percent of plans with 100–500 participants, and 3.8 percent of plans with 501–1,000 participants allow investments in company stock. However, nearly 22 percent of plans with more than 1,000 participants allow for company stock investments. Where company stock is offered as a match and an investment alternative, about 33 percent is invested in these securities; but where employer contributions are not in company stock, but it is offered as an investment alternative, only about 22 percent of account balances are in company stock.

Rules Applicable to Defined Contribution Plan Investments in Employer Stock

ERISA and the Code are designed to encourage employers to make contributions in the form of, and employees to elect to invest in, employer stock. For example, employees may receive favorable tax treatment on "net unrealized appreciation" of employer stock included in a distribution from a defined contribution plan. And, as recently as June 2001, Congress included a provision in the Economic Growth and Tax Relief Reconciliation Act of 2001 to make it easier for corporations to deduct dividends paid on stock held by an ESOP, thereby further encouraging the spread of ESOPs.

Russell Long is the name most associated with ESOPs. He believed that they would make possible "worker capitalism." In fact, some large companies—for example, United Airlines—are owned in large part by their ESOPs. ERISA does place limits on the amount of employer stock that may be held by retirement plans, but those rules generally do not apply to 401(k) and other "individual account" plans (including ESOPs). In fact, the assets of an ESOP are required to consist "primarily" of employer stock, and ESOPs generally are exempt from ERISA's rule requiring diversification of plan investments.

Lawsuits

The lawsuits against Enron make three basic claims: first, that Enron's fiduciaries violated their duties by providing incomplete and/or incorrect information to participants who invested in Enron stock; second, that there was a fiduciary duty to sell some or all of the Enron stock held by the plan; and third that the "lockdown" period was too long (or Enron's motives in implementing the lockdown were impure).

With respect to the first claim, Enron fiduciaries likely will be liable for violating their fiduciary duties if they encouraged employees to invest in Enron stock by making misleading or false disclosures. The allegations harken to *Varity Corp. v. Howe* (1996), in which the Supreme Court held that misleading disclosures by plan fiduciaries who induced employees to transfer to an affiliated entity were fiduciary breaches. Critical in this analysis will be whether any of the Enron fiduciaries had knowledge of the upcoming collapse, and whether they were wearing fiduciary rather than settlor "hats" when encouraging investments in Enron stock.

The second claim, regarding the duty to diversify out of Enron stock, has been addressed by courts in recent years. The seminal case is *Moench v. Robertson* (3d Cir. 1995). In that case, the terms of an ESOP required the ESOP to invest solely in employer stock. The Third Circuit did not allow the plan terms as an absolute defense against claims that the shares of employer stock should have been sold when the fiduciaries became aware of the employer's dim prospects. The Third Circuit notes that while the fiduciary in *Moench* presumptively was required to invest in employer securities, "there may come a time when such investments no longer serve the purpose of the trust, or the [employer's] intent." The court concluded that the fiduciary's decision to remain invested in employer stock would be subject to judicial review under an abuse of discretion standard. Because this standard is a fairly high hurdle for plaintiffs to overcome, it may be difficult for them to recover for losses resulting from the failure to diversify out of Enron stock if the Fifth Circuit (where most of the Enron ERISA cases will be litigated) follows the Third Circuit's lead in *Moench*.

The third claim, that the "lockdown" period was too long, seems rather weak. It is common practice to have such a period when plan recordkeepers are changed; the period is necessary for the outgoing recordkeeper to reconcile its books and to transfer files to the new recordkeeper, and for the new recordkeeper to adapt the files to its format. If anything, Enron's lockdown period seemed shorter than the average. Thus, unless additional facts are shown (such as that the lockdown period was purposely designed to disallow selling of Enron stock during a period when management knew bad news would be released), this claim seems to lack substantial merit. Nevertheless, the Labor Department and the plaintiffs in the various class action lawsuits appear to be focusing on the lockdown period, so perhaps there are additional facts that have not yet been disclosed.

Even if the plaintiffs in these lawsuits prevail, it is not clear who would be able to make the plaintiffs whole. Any breaching fiduciaries will be jointly and severally liable for the losses caused by their breaches, but this will be meaningless unless at least one of the breaching fiduciaries is a "deep pocket." The fiduciaries likely have some form of fiduciary insurance, but such insurance generally includes a cap on claims ($10 million would be typical).

Where from Here?

The lawsuits probably will take years to resolve. Congress, on the other hand, is likely to act fairly quickly in enacting some changes to ERISA. Enron has engendered numerous "reform" proposals. The most limited is from the Bush Administration, which would require 401(k) and other defined contribution plans to allow participants to sell their employer-contributed company stock and diversify into other investment options after three years of participation in the plan. At the other extreme, Senators Boxer (D-CA) and Corzine (D-NJ) have introduced legislation that would (1) limit to 20 percent the investment employees may have in any one stock in their individual account plans; (2) limit to 90 days the time that an employer can force an employee to hold a matching employer stock contribution in the employee's individual account plan; (3) reduce to 50 percent (from 100 percent) the tax deduction that an employer can take on a matching contribution to an individual if that contribution is made in stock; and (4) lower to 35 years of age and five years of service the triggers that allow an employee to diversify his or her investments in an ESOP. In addition, there are a number of "middle ground" bills that would limit investments in employer stock (or increase diversification rights) in one way or another. Finally, a number of proposed bills would limit the "lockdown" period to a specified amount of time (for example, ten days).

When it debates making changes, Congress should keep in mind that the Enron debacle is rare, its benefit structure unique; the 401(k) system generally has served employers and employees quite well. Congress needs to be careful that it does not enact changes that are counterproductive. When it substantially amended the tax qualification rules in the 1980s, Congress thought it was strengthening the private pension system. Unfortunately, one result of these very complex changes has been the near death of defined benefit plans—non-governmental defined benefit plans declined from 173,000 in 1983 to only 64,000 by 1995.

Many of the proponents of "reform" obviously assume that if employers currently contribute amounts in stock, they will automatically switch to cash (or will continue making the contributions in stock) if there is an accelerated diversification requirement. This is an untested assumption. More targeted changes may be better considered. The Bush Administration's proposal to reduce the period during which ESOPs may prohibit participants from diversifying their investments strikes at a significant area of abuse without raising major uncertainties.

In this regard, Congress should carefully consider whether there is a true need for a maximum "lockdown" period before it imposes one. Such a provision may have unintended side effects, such as causing employers to remain with more costly and less efficient recordkeepers or causing errors by new recordkeepers as they rush through data to comply with the maximum period. Given the paucity of evidence that lockdown periods have harmed participants in more than a few isolated instances, changing ERISA in this regard would appear to be unwise.

Finally, Congress has long recognized the desirability of allowing employees to invest in their employer's stock through qualified retirement plans. Most of the evidence indicates that the system works fairly well. It aligns employee and employer interests and in many instances has produced significant returns for employees. Although some limitation on the holding periods for such investments bears serious consideration, aggressive limiting of the right to invest in employer securities does not.

Unlike when Studebaker collapsed in 1963, today there is an ERISA to protect employees' rights. As Congress considers various legislative proposals, it should also pay attention to a law not often acknowledged: the law of intended consequences.

William J. Kilberg
Editor-in-Chief

From *Employee Relations Law Journal*, Summer 2002, pp. 1-6. © 2002 by John Wiley & Sons, Inc.

The Fallout From Enron

LESSONS AND CONSEQUENCES

Address by HENRY KAUFMAN, *President, Henry Kaufman & Company, Inc.*
Delivered to the Boston Economic Club, Boston, Massachusetts, April 3, 2002

Today I would like to talk about an event that has rocked the financial community: the collapse of the Enron Corporation. Much has been said and written about Enron in recent weeks, but it seems to me that too little attention has been paid to either the underlying issues posed by the demise of the Enron Corporation, or to the likely consequences of this failure for financial markets.

Not very long ago, Enron was widely heralded in the business and financial community for its spectacular growth, its innovative achievements, and its future potential. All of that changed suddenly and dramatically late last year. Since then, many pundits have pointed the finger of blame at Arthur Andersen. But it would be wrong to conclude that Enron's failure stemmed chiefly from the accounting shortcomings of its outside auditors. To be sure, Andersen probably was derelict in carrying out its responsibilities. No accounting firm should have the kind of intimate and conflicting relationship that Andersen had with Enron. Auditing and concurrent consulting arrangements with clients just don't mix, for they pose very real conflicts of interest that compromise objectivity and independence.

Even so, I am not convinced that a complete dismantling of Arthur Andersen would serve the larger interests of all stakeholders. To be sure, any senior officers and managers at Andersen found to have compromised sound accounting standards should be fired. But from a social perspective the thousands of Andersen employees who were innocent of high-level misdeeds do not deserve to be displaced.

The issue here is even more complicated. On the one hand, dismantling Andersen would push forward by a giant step the concentration in the accounting business that already is quite high. On the other hand, no business organization should be considered to be too-big-to-fail. Otherwise, competition, which should be the market equalizer, will be distorted. In addition to these considerations is the fact that focusing on Andersen simply deflects the spotlight away from the misdeeds of Enron itself. It offers Enron's officials and all the others involved in the Enron relationship, from the private sector to people in government, a convenient scapegoat, and increases the likelihood that we will fail to learn important lessons from the energy trader's debacle. That would be very unfortunate.

The failure of Enron is a drama with many dimensions. It encapsulates a remarkable number of the kind of misbehaviors, shortcomings, and excesses that have plagued business and financial life in the last few decades. Even if we look back over financial crises in the half-century since World War II, it is difficult to find one with as many salient elements as the Enron failure.

Consider, for example, the volatile decade of the 1970s. The calamities began in 1970, with the staggering collapse of the Penn Central Railroad. The Pennsy was derailed by its excessive short-term borrowing, mainly in the form of commercial paper, supported by weak earnings. Later on, the Hunt brothers succeeded in cornering the silver market, but financed their manipulations with heavy short-term borrowings. Many of their lenders used silver as collateral, which led to a massive sell-off in the silver market when the Hunts exhausted their borrowing capacity. Then there were the oil crises of the 1970s, which set off a crippling round of defaults among key Latin American nations that had borrowed heavily from large money market banks. Because these banks had failed to exercise prudent credit judgment, the financial pressure of the oil shocks plunged debtors and creditors alike into serious trouble.

The 1980s had its share of financial excesses. The decade's economic boom had been fed in large measure by the liberal lending policies of banks—especially savings and loan associations—and by the massive leveraging of many corporations through junk bond financing. These financial splurges later made it initially difficult to jump-start the economic recovery in the early 1990s.

As for the 1990s: the serious financial strains in Mexico and in several Asian countries, as well as the recent debt default of Argentina—all remain fresh in our memories. Then, as the decade drew to a close, the financial world was rocked by a financial debacle that threatened the very viability of key money market institutions. I am referring here, of course, to the dramatic fall of Long Term Capital Management in late 1998. Enron's collapse, however, did not pose a systemic risk to the financial system the way LTCM's failure did, although some of Enron's senior managers and creditors have suggested as much during their negotiations with government officials. To their credit, regulators and central bankers did not step in to rescue the faltering energy giant from its own misdeeds.

Which brings us back to the lessons to be derived from the Enron case. It seems to me that Enron—by bringing together a range of issues and problems that have plagued the U.S. financial system for decades—raises a host of questions that we simply must address:

- How effectively do boards of directors discharge their responsibilities?
- What are the inadequacies of senior managers?
- Are lenders conducting effective due diligence?
- Are sell-side analysts objective in their analysis, or are they compromised?
- Should employees be permitted to invest a high portion of their pensions in the equity of the corporations that employ them?
- Is official oversight adequate?
- Can elected officials be objective in dealing with financial excesses given that they may be conflicted by contributions?
- Should a public accounting firm serve a client as both an auditor and a consultant?

These vexing issues lie at the heart of the Enron debacle. To a large extent, they point to a fundamental problem that has been festering for some time, namely, the separation of corporate ownership and control. This problem has become more acute in recent decades because of structural changes in finance and investments. But the issue hardly is new. In fact, it is a symptom of advanced industrial capitalism, in which firms become too large to be owned and managed by individuals or even wealthy families.

One of the most penetrating critiques of the concentration of corporate control appeared back in 1932, when Adolf Berle, a law professor and reformer, and economist Gardiner Means published their landmark book, The Modern Corporation and Private Property. As Berle and Means noted vividly:

It has often been said that the owner of a horse is responsible. If the horse lives he must feed it. If the horse dies he must bury it. No such responsibility attaches to a share of stock. The owner is practically powerless through his own efforts to affect the underling property. The spiritual values that formerly went with ownership have been separated from it.... [T]he responsibility and the substance which have been an integral part of ownership in the past are being transferred to a separate group in whose hands lies control.

In the financial markets of the last few decades, this problem has become more acute with the rise of hostile takeovers, leveraged buyouts, golden parachutes, green mail, and many other financial innovations that are associated with corporate control. Many corporate raiders have become instant celebrities.

At the same time, there have been some significant changes in the role that senior managers play within the corporation. In recent years, many are given incentives that encourage them to strive to achieve near-term objectives through a variety of compensation schemes. Rarely is management actually penalized for failing to achieve their objectives. Their cash bonuses may be reduced, but they still are entitled to stock options. If the price of the company's stock is down, many firms in the past lowered the exercise price of the outstanding options. More recently, many corporations simply issue more options at the lower prevailing price level. The gatekeepers for many of the compensation awards are outside consultants who rarely exercise strong control over the compensation process. Very often they merely codify what others are doing in the industry.

For their part, equity investors rarely are involved in the affairs of a corporation. Indeed, portfolio practices today have a short-term fuse. Portfolio performance is measured over very short-term horizons—monthly, quarterly, or at most yearly. Underperformance is penalized very quickly. Today, day trades and portfolio shifts based on the price momentum of the stock are commonplace. Institutional investors now hold a majority of outstanding stocks, but they rarely want to be involved in their portfolio companies. Instead, a novel but powerful alliance often exists between the highest bidder in a corporate takeover and many of its institutional shareholders. Thus, stockholders are largely temporarily holders of a certificate that legally is called "equity."

This is clearly demonstrated by the huge increase in the turnover of the stocks listed on the New York Stock Exchange. The turnover of these stocks has escalated sharply over the last forty years—from an average of 20% from 1960 to 1980, to 75% times in the 1990s, with last year's average reaching 94%. Only a few large investors, such as Warren Buffett, truly are involved as stockholders. In today's financial marketplace, they are a rare breed.

Because corporate control typically rests in the hands of senior managers, they and directors assume responsibilities that are difficult to fill in the current structure of the marketplace. Let me try to explain what I mean here by referring to the management of large financial institutions, where I spent a good part of my career. And much of what I have to say in this regard is applicable to the problems of Enron.

I first realized the enormity of the challenge of managing large financial institutions when I joined Salomon's board following our merger with Phibro in 1981. The outside members of the board brought diverse business backgrounds to the table. With the exception of Maurice "Hank" Greenberg, none had strong first-hand experience in a major financial institution. How, then, could they possibly understand, among other things: the magnitude of risk taking at Salomon, the dynamics of the matched book of securities lending, the true extent to which the firm was leveraging its capital, the credit risk in a large heterogeneous book of assets, the effectiveness of operating management in enforcing trading disciplines, or the amount of capital that was allocated to the various activities of the firm and the rates of return on this capital on a risk-adjusted basis? Compounding the problem, the formal reports prepared for the board were neither comprehensive enough nor detailed enough to educate the outside directors about the diversity and complexity of our operations.

Today, this problem is magnified as firms extend their global reach and their portfolio of activities. In recent years, quite a few major U.S. financial institutions have become truly international in scope. They underwrite, trade currencies, stocks, and bonds, and manage the portfolios and securities of industrial corporations and emerging nations. Some of the largest institutions contain in their holding company structures not only banks but also mutual funds, insurance companies, securities firms, finance companies, and real estate affiliates.

The outside directors on the boards of such firms are at a major disadvantage when trying to assess the institution's performance. They must rely heavily on the veracity and competency of senior managers, who in turn are responsible for overseeing a dazzling array of intricate risks undertaken by specialized, lower-level personnel working throughout the firm's wide-flung units. Indeed, the senior managers of large institutions are beholden to the veracity of middle managers, who themselves are highly motivated to take risks through a variety of profit compensation formulas. It is easy for gaps in management control to open up between these two groups.

Unfortunately, the accounting profession has been of little help to outside board members. Few audit reports truly reflect a firm's range of risk taking. Reports on assets and liabilities would be far more meaningful if they were shown in gross terms instead of net figures. The off-balance-sheet activities most often cited in footnotes should be integrated into reports to reveal the total flow of activities and liabilities. Unfortunately, when the FASB proposes conservative accounting rules, operating managers generally oppose them. This is because such rules tend to reduce stated profits and encourage conservative lending and investing policies, thus infringing on the stated profits. But managers should recognize that such rules, over the long run, will strengthen their institution's credit quality.

What often is missing for new directors is an intensive orientation program. Large financial institutions are very complex. As I noted earlier, they engage in a wide range of activities—traditional banking, underwriting and trading of securities, insurance, risk arbitrage, financial derivatives from the simple to the complex, and domestic and foreign transactions. The new directors should be given a detailed analysis of the institution's accounting procedures. They should be educated about exactly the kind of activities that Enron directors failed to appreciate: (1) transactions with affiliated companies, (2) transfer of assets/debts to special-purpose entities in order to achieve "off balance sheet" treatment; (3) related-party and insider transactions; (4) aggressive use of restructuring changes and acquisition reserves; and (5) aggressive derivative trading and use of exotic derivatives; and (6) aggressive revenue recognition policies.

Directors of financial institutions also should be familiarized with their institution's quantitative risk analysis techniques. Indeed, the risk analysis group should be independent of the trading and underwriting department. It should be well compensated and have reporting responsibilities to the chief executive, to the chief operating officer, and to the board of directors itself. As part of the orientation process, new directors should be required to meet with members of the official supervisory agencies such as the Federal Reserve, the Comptroller of the Currency, and the Securities and Exchange Commission, all whom should explain what these agencies require from the institution. Legal counsel should also meet with new directors to explain their responsibilities and liabilities from a legal perspective.

But this kind of orientation process alone is not enough to achieve effective board oversight. Board meetings should be allotted more time. Directors should be given more detailed information than highly sanitized and summarized financial information. Board expertise in accounting, quantitative risk analysis, and information technology will become more and more essential in our complex world of finance.

To be sure, the primary task of boards is to define strategy and set policy, to represent the interests of the shareholders and creditors, not to operate the institution. But unless boards devote enough time to handle their responsibilities, the financial industry will suffer even more upheavals, forcing government to step in to clean up messes—and, increasingly, to regulate and control.

I want to turn now to the question, "Can sell-side research be objective?" As many of you here know, when I was at Salomon I managed for many years a large research group that grew to more than 450 professionals by the time I left in 1988. In formulating my own forecasts over those many years, I was never urged to modify my views to conform with the immediate underwriting or trading activities of the firm, and I know of no researcher in my department who was coerced to change his analytical conclusion.

To be sure, there were occasional complaints from trading and underwriting desks because of one or another view I expressed publicly (usually in written form); but as head of research, I was in a unique position to fend off any criticism. I was a senior partner and a member of the firm's Executive Committee, where no member ever asked that research accommodate the underwriting or trading activity.

In recent decades, however, the objectivity of sell-side research has been compromised more and more. One obvious result is that it is hard to find negative reports these days. Few, for instance, warned of the speculative bubble in the high tech industry. Many analysts wrote glowingly about companies with no earnings, high cash burn rates, and shares selling at high prices relative to sales volume and distant profit prospects. In place of rigorous analyses of firms and industries, one usually saw reports that parroted the views of corporate management and that of historical evaluation norms.

And the scope of the problem is vast. Public attention is most focused on the role that sell-side analysts play in attracting new issues of securities. But very few, if any, seem concerned about the potential for the sell-side institution to front-run trading positions on the basis of soon-to-be-released research reports. The fact is, traders typically have many opportunities in their conversations with equity analysts to ferret out a change in the analyst's view or to learn of the timing of upcoming press releases.

I believe that these problems facing the sell-side analyst can at best be mitigated. To begin with, my experience strongly suggests that the head of research should be a member of senior management. This would establish his authority to deal with research issues at the highest level. Of course, I agree with the suggestion that the relationship of the sell-side institution with the company being analyzed should be stated in the report in bold letters. But it would also be helpful if the analyst stated the performance of the company and the price movement of the stock since the last report, and drew explicit conclusions.

The logical solution to this conflict is for sell-side institutions to provide no research reports to clients. Research would serve only an in-house function by providing analyses that would help the institution assess the merits of the securities it is underwriting and trading. Institutional investors and independent research firms would then fill the gap. This method presumably would lower the cost of research at sell-side firms, which in turn would lower trading and underwriting costs and offset a healthy portion of the increased research costs on the buy side.

Let me also comment briefly on another matter raised by the Enron debacle. Should employees be required to limit their employee retirement investments in the stock of their company? Considering the losses suffered by the Enron employees, the tendency is to respond positively. There is, however, no simple quantitative rule that will be an equitable solution for all employees. They possess vast differences in ages, compensations, personal responsibilities, health, and personal net worth. What government regulation can do justice to all of these factors? The alternative solution is for the employer to provide investment counseling where these characteristics are reviewed and discussed before the employee decides on the size of the investment to be made in the shares of the corporation.

While many of the consequences of the Enron's demise already are manifest in the market, it seems to me that the most important one is really unpredictable. This is whether more "Enrons" will surface in the near future. If they do, market participants will pull away from equity markets and high yield bonds, because new doubts will be raised about the quality of earnings and the accuracy of other reported financial information.

But already we can see other repercussions from Enron's fall quite clearly. In the securities industry, merger activity has slowed and—by the standards of recent years—will remain at a low volume for the foreseeable future. No conglomerate that is on the brink of going below a credit rating of "below investment grade" will be able to gain ready access to funds for some time to come. And while initial public offerings of stock are trickling into the market again, I think we have seen the end of the kind of huge speculative offerings that have been fairly common in recent years. Meanwhile, financial institutions, with lower near-term profit margins, will be encouraged to shed more overhead. Research analysts will be particularly vulnerable if institutions cannot use them to help market new issues and trading positions.

For business corporations, financing costs are rising. This began last year when corporations issued a huge volume of bonds and reduced short-term debt, mainly outstanding commercial paper. In doing so, they paid off lower-cost debt and increased higher-cost debt. The financial problems of Enron and of a handful of other companies late last year has inspired commercial paper investors to become more discerning, thereby forcing corporate issuers to activate bank lines or new bond issuance to pay off maturing paper. The paper market is now virtually closed to all issuers below the top credit rating.

The liquidation of outstanding commercial paper held by nonfinancial corporations has taken place on an unprecedented scale. Since 2000, it has declined by $175 billion, or a remarkable 49%. This trend has reduced commercial paper to levels that were outstanding in 1997. Moreover, this $175 billion shift in borrowing probably has boosted corporate financing costs by anywhere from $6 billion to $8 billion. Financing costs probably also will rise, as banks raise their fees for back-up lines of credit, although these lines have an uncertain value. On the one hand, they do provide liquidity for the corporate issuer of paper when paper investors want their money. On the other hand, the runoff of paper tends to accelerate when market participants become aware of the utilization of the bank line.

While creditors generally will increase their alertness to corporate credit quality as a result of Enron, credit rating agencies surely will intensify the scope of their work and the speed of their responsiveness to changing corporate credit conditions. Already, we hear of the likely issuance of corporate liquidity ratings by the ratings agencies. This closer scrutiny will occur on top of another year in which more corporate credit ratings will be lowered rather than raised.

Yet another likely outcome from the Enron episode is improved accounting standards. This will lower reported corporate profits in the short term, but the the more conservative profit data will enhance investor confidence in the long run. Let us also hope that there may be an effort to put some of the off-balance-sheet financing onto the balance sheet. If so, the corporate debt data that I spoke about earlier will look worse—but again, the long-term effect for investors will be positive.

Incidentally, two other costs not related to financing costs are likely to rise as a consequence of Enron's travails. These are audit fees and the cost of liability insurance for directors and officers.

Of course, all of these costs could be more than offset through a sharp increase in corporate profits. I suspect that this is unlikely. Business does not have pricing power. Excess capacity is high here and around the world. Unfortunately, Enron unraveled at a time when the general financial condition of nonfinancial corporations was probably the worst—for the end of a recession and the start of a new economic recovery—for the entire post-World War II period. From 1995 to 2001, the equity position (retained earnings plus new issuance or minus retirement of stock) of non-financial corporations has contracted by $423 billion, while net debt has increased by $2.3 trillion in the same period. Indeed, this exceeded the debt-leveraging binge in the 1984–90 period when net equity contracted by $457 billion and debt rose by $1.3 trillion.

The combination of the cyclically weak financial position of corporations, moderate profit recovery, and closer scrutiny of corporate activity by management, auditors, creditors, rating agencies, and officially supervisory agencies will—in the near term—inhibit corporate activity, especially capital expenditures. Thus, once the current inventory restocking ends a few months from now, the economic recovery will moderate significantly.

In short, there are likely to be some difficult adjustments in the near-term horizon, several of them a direct result of Enron's wayward ways. But all would be a modest price to pay for a return to more reasonable and responsible conduct in business and financial markets.

Case: *What to Do?*

You are the administrator, chief operating officer of a large medical school. You have been informed by your board chair that he has been able to gain major funding from a single giver, a major distiller and brewer, for a center to study and treat alcohol and drug abuse. This would enable the medical school to become far and away the leader for such issues in your geographical region.

- What do you do?
- What are your reasons for doing that?
- What values do those reasons reflect?

Using the Case of *What to Do?*

This is obviously the Faustian bargain, the chance to do good with the powers of evil. This case would be particularly interesting after a discussion of ethics and morality in industry. Try to get a discussion going on the merits of each position. It will be hard to tell where it may lead, but it could be very interesting.

Exercise: The Résumé—A Career Management Tool

By Fred Tesch

Résumés get us interviews. A good résumé prevents our being "de-selected" from the application process. Résumés represent us to the recruiters and others who screen applicants to find the few that match their position. As extensions of ourselves résumés should present us in our best, not our worst, light. How well does your résumé represent you?

In this exercise you will (a) do some research on résumé writing—formats, layouts, key information, (b) write your résumé (one or two pages), and (c) write a brief (i.e., five page maximum) paper explaining your thinking as you constructed your résumé.

Background

There is no "one true way" to write a résumé. You need to find the approach, formats, and layouts that tell your story. Résumés based on the "lowest common denominator" (often reflecting the formula presented by the overworked placement office at your school) too often hide rather than accent your unique strengths and competencies. Finding the best way to tell others who you are requires some research. You can learn a lot about what works and what doesn't by reading lots of résumés. If you do not have access to hundreds of résumés, turn to your library and the Internet.

Beatty, Richard H. (2000). The resume kit. New York: Wiley.

Farr, J. Michael. (2000). The quick resume & cover letter book: Write and use an effective resume in only one day. Indianapolis, IN: JIST Works.

Noble, David F. (2001). Gallery of best resumes: a collection of quality resumes by professional resume writers. Indianapolis. IN: JIST Works.

Parker, Yana. (1996). The dame good resume guide: A crash course in resume writing. Berkeley, CA: Ten Speed Press.

Thompson, Mary Anne. (2000). The global resume and DV guide. New York: Wiley.

Wendleton, kate. (1999). Building a great resume: For job hunters, career changers, and freelancers. Franklin Lakes, NJ: Career Press.

www.jobweb.com

www.damgood.com

www.montant.edu/~wwwcp/tips

Consult your librarian for other sources.

The Assignment

The résumé. You've done your research. You know what information you wish to include. You found formats that fit your information. You are ready to write your first draft.

Prepare a one-page résumé. Use a second page if it is justified. Be sure to have someone proofread it.

Write a second draft.

Write a third draft.

The rationale. Why did you write your résumé the way that you did? Why did you choose the functional rather than the chronological format? What does listing your hobbies convey about you. Why did you place your educational credentials after your work experience?

Write a brief papter (i.e., 5 pages maximum) explaining why you wrote your résumé the way you did.

The Payoff

Submit your résumé and paper to someone who has the ability to do a good critique of it. Perhaps a favorite professor? A previous boss? A relative? In fact, submit it to three or four qualified people.

Using their feedback, write a new draft of your résumé.

Finally, you should have a résumé that represents you rather than embarrasses you.

Good Luck!

Fred Tesch is a professor at Western Connecticut State University.

Case: What to Do? by Fred Maidment, McGraw-Hill/Dushkin; Exercise: The Résumé—A Career Management Tool by Fred Tesch., 2000.

Index

P

Q

R

S

T

U

V

W

X

Test Your Knowledge Form

We encourage you to photocopy and use this page as a tool to assess how the articles in *Annual Editions* expand on the information in your textbook. By reflecting on the articles you will gain enhanced text information. You can also access this useful form on a product's book support Web site at *http://www.dushkin.com/online/*.

NAME: DATE:

TITLE AND NUMBER OF ARTICLE:

BRIEFLY STATE THE MAIN IDEA OF THIS ARTICLE:

LIST THREE IMPORTANT FACTS THAT THE AUTHOR USES TO SUPPORT THE MAIN IDEA:

WHAT INFORMATION OR IDEAS DISCUSSED IN THIS ARTICLE ARE ALSO DISCUSSED IN YOUR TEXTBOOK OR OTHER READINGS THAT YOU HAVE DONE? LIST THE TEXTBOOK CHAPTERS AND PAGE NUMBERS:

LIST ANY EXAMPLES OF BIAS OR FAULTY REASONING THAT YOU FOUND IN THE ARTICLE:

LIST ANY NEW TERMS/CONCEPTS THAT WERE DISCUSSED IN THE ARTICLE, AND WRITE A SHORT DEFINITION:

We Want Your Advice

ANNUAL EDITIONS revisions depend on two major opinion sources: one is our Advisory Board, listed in the front of this volume, which works with us in scanning the thousands of articles published in the public press each year; the other is you—the person actually using the book. Please help us and the users of the next edition by completing the prepaid article rating form on this page and returning it to us. Thank you for your help!

ANNUAL EDITIONS: Management 03/04

ARTICLE RATING FORM

Here is an opportunity for you to have direct input into the next revision of this volume.
We would like you to rate each of the articles listed below, using the following scale:

1. **Excellent: should definitely be retained**
2. **Above average: should probably be retained**
3. **Below average: should probably be deleted**
4. **Poor: should definitely be deleted**

Your ratings will play a vital part in the next revision.
Please mail this prepaid form to us as soon as possible.
Thanks for your help!

RATING	ARTICLE
______	1. Address by George W. Bush, President of the United States
______	2. Hearts, Minds, and the War Against Terror
______	3. The Manager's Job: Folklore and Fact
______	4. Managing From A to Z
______	5. Why Companies Fail
______	6. Management Lessons From the Bust
______	7. What's Right With the U.S. Economy
______	8. Reinventing How We Do Business
______	9. A New Look at Managerial Decision Making
______	10. Management Accounting Master: Closing the Gap Between Managerial Accounting and External Reporting
______	11. Michael Porter: What Is Strategy?
______	12. New Rules of the Game
______	13. The Americanization of Toyota
______	14. Classifying the Elements of Work
______	15. Organizing for the New Economy
______	16. Creating a Learning Organization
______	17. Open Book Management—Optimizing Human Capital
______	18. The Abilene Paradox: The Management of Agreement
______	19. What Leadership Crisis?
______	20. Effective Performance Counseling
______	21. The Myth of Synergy
______	22. When You Disagree With the Boss's Order, Do You Tell Your Staff?
______	23. An Uneasy Look at Performance Appraisal
______	24. Transfer Pricing: A Truly Global Concern
______	25. How Safe Is Your Job? The Threat of Workplace Violence
______	26. COST vs. QUALITY
______	27. Management Women and the New Facts of Life
______	28. Girl Gangs
______	29. Secrets of Finding and Keeping Good Employees
______	30. Pay It Forward
______	31. Social Responsibility in Future Worlds
______	32. American Corporations: The New Sovereigns
______	33. Offshore Sourcing: An Optimal Operational Strategy?
______	34. Helping Organizations Build Community
______	35. Corporate Probes: A Scorecard
______	36. The Short Arm of the Law
______	37. The Workplace Ethic—Is It a Crime?
______	38. Enron: The Studebaker of the 21st Century?
______	39. The Fallout From Enron

(Continued on next page)

ANNUAL EDITIONS: MANAGEMENT 03/04

NO POSTAGE NECESSARY IF MAILED IN THE UNITED STATES

BUSINESS REPLY MAIL

FIRST-CLASS MAIL PERMIT NO. 84 GUILFORD CT

POSTAGE WILL BE PAID BY ADDRESSEE

McGraw-Hill/Dushkin
530 Old Whitfield Street
Guilford, Ct 06437-9989

ABOUT YOU

Name Date

Are you a teacher? ❐ A student? ❐
Your school's name

Department

Address City State Zip

School telephone #

YOUR COMMENTS ARE IMPORTANT TO US!

Please fill in the following information:
For which course did you use this book?

Did you use a text with this ANNUAL EDITION? ❐ yes ❐ no
What was the title of the text?

What are your general reactions to the *Annual Editions* concept?

Have you read any pertinent articles recently that you think should be included in the next edition? Explain.

Are there any articles that you feel should be replaced in the next edition? Why?

Are there any World Wide Web sites that you feel should be included in the next edition? Please annotate.

May we contact you for editorial input? ❐ yes ❐ no
May we quote your comments? ❐ yes ❐ no